K. B. McFarlane once proposed that an examination of the lives of the gentry would enhance our understanding of late medieval society. In response to his challenge this book examines the fifteenth-century gentry of Leicestershire under five broad headings: as landholders, as members of a social community based on the county, as participants in and leaders of the government of the shire, as members of the wider family unit and, finally, as individuals.

The book reveals that while the Leicestershire gentry were not immune from the economic problems of the age, they were sufficiently flexible and opportunistic to weather these economic squalls better than most. Economically assertive, they were also socially cohesive, this cohesion being provided by the shire community. In a county not dominated by large ecclesiastical or lay magnate estates, the shire also provided the most important political unit, controlled by an oligarchy of superior gentry families who were relatively independent of outside interference. The basic social unit was the nuclear family, but external influences, provided by concern for the wider kin, the lineage or economic and political advancement, were not major determinants of family strategy. Individualism among the gentry was already established by the fifteenth century, revealing its personnel as a self-assured and confident stratum in late medieval English society.

Cambridge Studies in Medieval Life and Thought

A GENTRY COMMUNITY

Cambridge Studies in Medieval Life and Thought
Fourth series

General Editor:
D. E. LUSCOMBE
Professor of Medieval History, University of Sheffield

Advisory Editors:
R. B. DOBSON
Professor of Medieval History, University of Cambridge, and Fellow of Christ's College

ROSAMOND MCKITTERICK
Reader in Early Medieval European History, University of Cambridge, and Fellow of Newnham College

The series Cambridge Studies in Medieval Life and Thought was inaugurated by G. G. Coulton in 1921. Professor D. E. Luscombe now acts as General Editor of the Fourth Series, with Professor R. B. Dobson and Dr Rosamond McKitterick as Advisory Editors. The series brings together outstanding work by medieval scholars over a wide range of human endeavour extending from political economy to the history of ideas.

For a list of titles in the series, see end of book.

A GENTRY COMMUNITY

Leicestershire in the Fifteenth Century, c.1422–c.1485

ERIC ACHESON

Lecturer in History,
University of New England,
Armidale,
New South Wales

CAMBRIDGE
UNIVERSITY PRESS

Published by the Press Syndicate of the University of Cambridge
The Pitt Building, Trumpington Street, Cambridge CB2 1RP
40 West 20th Street, New York, NY 10011–4211, USA
10 Stamford Road, Oakleigh, Victoria 3166, Australia

First published 1992

Printed in Great Britain at the University Press, Cambridge

A catalogue record for this book is available from the British Library

Library of Congress cataloguing in publication data
Acheson, Eric.
A gentry community: Leicestershire in the fifteenth century, *c.*1422–*c.*1485 /
Eric Acheson.
p.   cm. – (Cambridge studies in medieval life and thought; 4th ser.)
Includes bibliographical references and index.
ISBN 0 521 40533 5
1. Leicestershire (England) – History. 2. Gentry – England – Leicestershire – History.
3. Great Britain – History – Henry VI, 1422–1461. 4. Great Britain – History – Edward IV,
1461–1483.
I. Title. II. Series.
DA670.L5A24 1992
942.5′4043′0862 dc20 91 29063 CIP

ISBN 0 521 40533 5 hardback

To
P. D. Withers
in memoriam

CONTENTS

MAPS

ACKNOWLEDGEMENTS

This study of the Leicestershire gentry would not have been possible without the generous assistance of many others. A profound debt of gratitude is owing to the late Sr Maureen Purcell, OP, who first kindled my interest in medieval history. Thanks are due to the staff of various record offices and libraries I visited both in England and Australia, especially the ever-helpful staff at Leicestershire Record Office, the Public Record Office, Lincolnshire Archives Office, Northamptonshire Record Office and the British Library; to the staff at the rare books department of the National Library in Canberra, the inter-library loans department of the Dixson Library at the University of New England and, in particular, to Mrs L. Wissman, who laboured unstintingly on my behalf to overcome 'the tyranny of distance'. My thanks are also due to colleagues and other scholars who read and commented upon earlier drafts of the work, to Dr K. Walsh who supervised the original thesis upon which this book is based, Miss N. Townsend, Associate Professor G. Quaife, Dr M. Bennett and Professor R. A. Griffiths, all of whom provided helpful suggestions. I am deeply indebted to Professor R. B. Dobson, Professor D. E. Luscombe and to Mr W. Davies of the Cambridge University Press for their guidance and expressions of support during the preparation of the text for publication; to Miss M. Hyson who prepared the typescript and to Mr M. Roach of the cartographic unit at UNE who produced the maps. The greatest debt of all, however, I owe to my wife, Sue, whose constant help and encouragement deserve greater acknowledgement than mere words can convey.

ERIC ACHESON

ABBREVIATIONS

B.I.H.R.	*Bulletin of the Institute of Historical Research*
B.J.R.L.	*Bulletin of the John Rylands Library*
B.L.	British Library
Bateson	*Records of the Borough of Leicester*, ed. M. Bateson, revised by W. H. Stevenson and J. E. Stocks, 3 vols., London and Cambridge, 1899–1905
Bodl.Lib.	Bodleian Library
C	Public Record Office, Chancery
C.A.D.	*A Descriptive Catalogue of Ancient Deeds in the Public Record Office*, 6 vols., London, 1890–1915
C.C.R.	*Calendar of the Close Rolls Preserved in the Public Record Office*, 1422–85, 9 vols., London, 1933–54
C.Ch.R.	*Calendar of Charter Rolls*, VI, 5 Hen. VI–8 Hen. VIII, 1427–1516, London, 1927
C.F.R.	*Calendar of the Fine Rolls Preserved in the Public Record Office*, 1422–85, XV–XXI, London, 1935–61
C.I.P.M.	*Calendar of Inquisitions Post Mortem Preserved in the Public Record Office, Henry VII*, 3 vols., London, 1898–1955
C.P.R.	*Calendar of the Patent Rolls Preserved in the Public Record Office*, 1399–1485, 15 vols., London, 1900–11
Common Lawyers	E. W. Ives, *The Common Lawyers of*

xiii

	Pre-Reformation England: Thomas Kebell, A Case Study, Cambridge, 1983
Croyland	*Ingulph's Chronicle of the Abbey of Croyland with the Continuations by Peter of Blois and Anonymous Writers*, trans. H. T. Riley, London, 1854
D.K.R.	*Reports of the Deputy Keeper of the Public Records*
D.N.B.	*Dictionary of National Biography*, ed. Sir L. Stephen and Sir S. Lee, 21 vols., London, 1937–8
Dugdale	Sir William Dugdale, *The Antiquities of Warwickshire*, 2 vols., London, 1730
E	Public Record Office, Exchequer
E.H.D.	*English Historical Documents*
E.H.R.	*English Historical Review*
Econ. Hist. Rev.	*Economic History Review*
Eg.Roll	British Library, Egerton Roll
An English Chronicle	*An English Chronicle of the Reigns of Richard II, Henry IV, Henry V, and Henry VI. Written before the Year 1471*, ed. J. S. Davies, Camden o.s. 64, London, 1856, Johnson repr., New York, 1968
Epis. Reg.	Lincolnshire Archives Office, Episcopal Register
Feudal Aids	*Inquisitions and Assessments Relating to Feudal Aids . . . 1284–1431*, 6 vols., London, 1899–1920, Kraus repr. Nendeln, Liechtenstein, 1973
G.E.C.	G. E. Cokayne, *The Complete Peerage*, rev. V. Gibbs, 2nd edn, 12 vols., London, 1910–59
Gregory's Chronicle	*The Historical Collections of a Citizen of London in the Fifteenth Century*, ed. J. Gairdner, Camden n.s. 17, London, 1876, Johnson repr., New York, 1965

H.M.C.	Historical Manuscripts Commission
Harl.	British Library, Harley Manuscripts
Italian Relation	*A Relation, or Rather a True Account, of the Island of England*, ed. C. A. Sneyd, Camden o.s. 37, London, 1847
JUST	Public Record Office, Justices Itinerant
KB	Public Record Office, King's Bench
L.A.O.	Lincolnshire Archives Office
L.R.O.	Leicestershire Record Office
Lincoln's Inn, Admissions	*The Records of the Honorable Society of Lincoln's Inn. Admissions, 1420–1790*, London, 1896
Lincoln's Inn, Black Books	*The Records of the Honorable Society of Lincoln's Inn. The Black Books*, I, 1422–1586, London, 1897
Lists and Indexes, IX	*List of Sheriffs for England and Wales*, P.R.O., Lists and Indexes, no. IX, London, 1898
'Medbourne Deeds'	S. D. Thomson, 'Some Medbourne Deeds from the Peake (Neville of Holt) Manuscripts (Third Deposit)', unpublished University of London Diploma in Archives Administration, 1955
Nichols	J. Nichols, *The History and Antiquities of the County of Leicester*, 4 vols. in 8, London, 1795–1815, S. R. Publications repr., Wakefield, 1971
P.P.C.	*Proceedings and Ordinances of the Privy Council of England*, ed. N. H. Nicolas, 7 vols., London, 1834–7
P.R.O.	Public Record Office
Paston Letters	*Paston Letters and Papers of the Fifteenth Century*, ed. N. Davis, parts I and II, Oxford, 1971–6
Paston Letters 1422–1509	*The Paston Letters 1422–1509*, ed. J.

	Gairdner, 6 vols., London, 1904, Ams Press repr., New York, 1965
Pedigrees	G. Farnham, *Medieval Pedigrees*, Leicester, 1925
PROB	Public Record Office, Prerogative Court of Canterbury Wills
Proc. Brit. Acad.	*Proceedings of the British Academy*
Quorndon Records	*Quorndon Records*, ed. G. Farnham, London, 1912
Readings and Moots	*Readings and Moots at the Inns of Court in the Fifteenth Century*, I, ed. S. E. Thorne, London, 1954 for 1952
Return	*Return of Every Member, Part I, Parliaments of England, 1213–1702*, London, 1878
Rock. C	Rockingham Castle
Rot. Parl.	*Rotuli Parliamentorum; ut et Petitiones et Placita in Parliamento*, II–VI, London, 1767–77
Somerville	R. Somerville, *History of the Duchy of Lancaster*, I, 1265–1603, London, 1953
Stat. Realm	*The Statutes of the Realm*, 11 vols., London, 1810–28
Stemmata Shirleiana	E. P. Shirley, *Stemmata Shirleiana*, 2nd edn, London, 1873
T.L.A.H.S.	*Transactions of the Leicestershire Archaeological and Historical Society*
T.L.A.S.	*Transactions of the Leicestershire Archaeological Society*
T.R.H.S.	*Transactions of the Royal Historical Society*
V.C.H.	*Victoria County History*
Village Notes	G. Farnham, *Leicestershire Medieval Village Notes*, 6 vols., Leicester, 1929–33
Visitation	*Visitation of the County of Leicester in the*

	Year 1619 taken by William Camden, ed. J. Fetherson, London, 1870
W.H.R.	*A Calendar of Charters and Other Documents Belonging to the Hospital of William Wyggeston at Leicester*, ed. A. H. Thompson, Leicester, 1933
Warrants for Issues, 1399–1485	*List and Index of Warrants for Issues, 1399–1485*, P.R.O., Lists and Indexes, Supplementary series no. IX, vol. 2, London and New York, 1964
Wedgwood, *Biographies*	J. C. Wedgwood, *History of Parliament: Biographies of the Members of the Commons House 1439–1509*, London, 1936
Wedgwood, *Register*	J. C. Wedgwood, *History of Parliament: Register of the Ministers and of the Members of both Houses 1439–1509*, London, 1938

INTRODUCTION

The heated and often vitriolic debate, the 'Storm over the Gentry', which attempted to explain the origins of the English Civil War, produced much sound and fury.[1] Like any storm, it eventually abated, leaving in its wake, if not tattered reputations, certainly bruised egos and, no doubt, the belated recognition by some British historians that the age of chivalry is indeed dead. But it would be unfair to suggest that the sound and fury signified nothing beyond the obvious or that, after all, the debate had been little more than a storm in a tea-cup. On the positive side, the controversy soon revealed that theory had overrun the available evidence and that more research was required. A new generation of historians readily accepted the implied challenge, producing county and regional studies which shed light on, as opposed to generating heat about, the economic and political concerns of the sixteenth- and seventeenth-century gentry.[2]

Interest in the English gentry, however, has not been confined to historians of the sixteenth and seventeenth centuries. K. B. McFarlane, in his 1945 lecture on bastard feudalism, proposed that late medieval society would 'only yield its secrets to the investigator who can base his conclusions upon the study of hundreds of fragmentary biographies'.[3] A year earlier, McFarlane had

---

[1] R. H. Tawney, 'The rise of the gentry, 1558–1640', *Econ. Hist. Rev.*, 11, 1941, pp. 1–38; L. Stone, 'The anatomy of the Elizabethan aristocracy', *Econ. Hist. Rev.*, 18, 1948, pp. 1–53; H. R. Trevor-Roper, 'The Elizabethan aristocracy: an anatomy anatomized', *Econ. Hist. Rev.*, 2nd ser., 3, 1951, pp. 279–98; L. Stone, 'The English aristocracy – a restatement', *Econ. Hist. Rev.*, 2nd ser., 4, 1952, pp. 302–21; H. R. Trevor-Roper, *The Gentry 1540–1640*, Economic History Review Supplement 1, London, 1953; R. H. Tawney, 'The rise of the gentry: a postscript', *Econ. Hist. Rev.*, 2nd ser., 7, 1954, pp. 91–7. See, too, J. H. Hexter, 'Storm over the gentry', *Encounter*, 10, 5, 1958, pp. 22–34. A fuller version of the same article and a more complete bibliography appear in his *Reappraisals in History*, London, 1961, pp. 117–52.
[2] See R. C. Richardson, *The Debate on the English Revolution*, London, 1977, pp. 113–25, 173–6, for an extensive bibliography.
[3] K. B. McFarlane, 'Bastard feudalism', *B.I.H.R.*, 20, 1943–5, p. 173.

attempted to counteract notions of the knights of the shire in parliament as the political pawns of the lords. 'If there is any tendency to underrate the capacity of these early M.P.s', he wrote, 'it can be corrected by a study of their lives ... As we make ourselves familiar with the lives and achievements of the country gentry, and especially of those who sat in the commons, the main outlines of local and central politics may be expected to emerge.'[4] McFarlane was asking for nothing less than the application of Sir Lewis Namier's method to studies of the fifteenth-century gentry.

'Namierization' of the fifteenth-century gentry had, in fact, already begun some years earlier, in 1937, when J. S. Roskell published his work on the knights of the shire in the palatinate of Lancaster.[5] Nevertheless, it was about thirty years before students answered McFarlane's specific call. Over the past ten to fifteen years, the 'slow and tedious work'[6] of providing biographies of the late medieval gentry has steadily progressed.[7] Most of these studies have concentrated on the gentry as economic and political entities but rarely, if ever, do we see them as fully rounded human beings. This failure cannot be attributed to any lack of sensitivity on the part of historians or to their refusal to follow the poet's injunction to 'listen to the voice'. The fact of the matter is that apart from a mere handful of families, the Pastons,

---

[4] K. B. McFarlane, 'Parliament and "bastard feudalism"', first published *T.R.H.S.*, 4th ser., 26, 1944, pp. 53–79. Reprinted in K. B. McFarlane, *England in the Fifteenth Century*, ed. G. L. Harriss, London, 1981, pp. 12, 20–1.

[5] J. S. Roskell, *The Knights of the Shire for the County Palatine of Lancaster (1377–1460)*, Manchester, 1937, pp. 29–201.

[6] G. L. Harriss's introduction to McFarlane, *England in the Fifteenth Century*, p. xxvii.

[7] G. G. Astill, 'The medieval gentry: a study in Leicestershire society, 1350–1399', unpublished PhD thesis, University of Birmingham, 1977; M. J. Bennett, *Community, Class and Careerism: Cheshire and Lancashire Society in the Age of 'Sir Gawain and the Green Knight'*, Cambridge, 1983; C. Carpenter, 'Political society in Warwickshire c. 1401–72', unpublished PhD thesis, University of Cambridge, 1976; I. D. Rowney, 'The Staffordshire political community 1440–1500', unpublished PhD thesis, University of Keele, 1981; N. Saul, *Knights and Esquires: The Gloucestershire Gentry in the Fourteenth Century*, Oxford, 1981; S. M. Wright, *The Derbyshire Gentry in the Fifteenth Century*, Chesterfield, 1983. Shorter works include: P. W. Fleming, 'Charity, faith, and the gentry of Kent 1422–1529', in *Property and Politics: Essays in Later Medieval English History*, ed. A. J. Pollard, Gloucester, 1984; A. J. Pollard, 'The Richmondshire community of gentry during the Wars of the Roses', in *Patronage Pedigree and Power in Later Medieval England*, ed. C. Ross, Gloucester, 1979; M. G. A. Vale, *Piety, Charity and Literacy among the Yorkshire Gentry, 1370–1480*, Borthwick Papers no. 50, York, 1976. More extensive biographies appear in C. Richmond, *John Hopton: A Fifteenth Century Suffolk Gentleman*, Cambridge, 1981; *Common Lawyers*.

the Plumptons, the Stonors and the Celys, the gentry have been silent about themselves and their concerns; there have been too few voices to hear.

Although historians have recognized the constraints imposed by the nature of the evidence and its scarcity, there has been recent concern that our view of the gentry is becoming too deterministic, too mechanistic.[8] We are in danger, it seems, of reducing the gentry's rôle to that of automatons whose reactions have been predetermined by economic, political or social forces outside their own control. The present study, therefore, is not merely an attempt to add to the pool of 'fragmentary biographies' called for by McFarlane but to do so in a way which will take these justifiable concerns into account. Naturally, the gentry's economic, political and social activities must remain central to any enquiry but our major concern has been to minimize the dragooning influence of predeterminism and to accentuate the essentially humanizing element of free will.[9]

While the late medieval gentry continue to warrant historians' attention, the specifically Leicestershire gentry are worthy of scrutiny. During the fifteenth century, the county witnessed and occasionally played host to events of national importance. Historians have noted that at times of political crisis Henry VI invariably forsook his capital and retreated, or intended to retreat, to what he increasingly regarded as the safety of the Midlands.[10] In fact it is a barometer of the troubled state of the realm that during the years 1456–61 the court's establishment at Kenilworth, Coventry and Leicester had become a semi-permanent arrangement.[11]

The reasons for these withdrawals to the Midlands are, of course, not difficult to fathom. The area was well placed to provide access to any corner of the kingdom, a consideration which was important not only for dealing with trouble but also for increasing the number of available options if further flight from danger were necessary. Also, contact with the south, and particularly London, could be maintained without jeopardizing

[8] C. Richmond, 'After McFarlane', *History*, 68, 1983, pp. 57–8.
[9] See Louis MacNeice's, 'Prayer before birth' which, in very general terms, anticipates Richmond's concerns.
[10] B. Wolffe, *Henry VI*, London, 1981, pp. 230, 252, 290–1; R. A. Griffiths, *The Reign of King Henry VI*, London, 1981, pp. 253, 740–1, 777–8; see, for example, *An English Chronicle*, pp. 71, 198.
[11] Wolffe, *Henry VI*, pp. 302–5.

access to the important military recruiting grounds of Cheshire and Lancashire whose archers had provided such invaluable service as royal body-guards to Henry's predecessors.[12]

Just as important as these strategic reasons was the fact that within the counties of Staffordshire, Warwickshire, Northamptonshire, Derbyshire and Leicestershire were centred those lands which formed the bulk of the honors of Tutbury and Leicester and the castle of Kenilworth, all appurtenances of the king's personal holding, the duchy of Lancaster.[13] Admittedly, the honors and castle in question had formed part of the queen's dower since 1445,[14] but her tenure seemed to have no adverse effect on the region's loyalty to the king. It is possible that Margaret's interest in, and concern for, her tenants even served to enhance that loyalty.[15] Strategic reasons apart, Henry's recourse to the Midlands in times of crisis indicates that the region's support for his cause was expected and suggests, too, that those expectations were largely fulfilled. The area bounded by Kenilworth, Coventry and Leicester, at least till 1461, was the king's territory. Furthermore, there is some indication that its Lancastrian sympathies could still manifest themselves as late as 1464 when a strong commission of oyer and terminer, headed by the earls of Warwick, Arundel and Worcester, was despatched to the county to quell disturbances there.[16]

Moving to the troubled year of 1471, we find a remarkable swing in the region's loyalties, but particularly in those of Leicestershire. It may be recalled that Edward IV arrived in Yorkshire from Flanders in March 1471 and here he doubtless supposed that his substantial estates in the county would provide him with a personal following. However, Hull refused him entry altogether; the city of York's welcome was less than enthusiastic and, even at Wakefield, near Edward's own Yorkshire estates, he

---

[12] J. F. Willard et al., eds., *The English Government at Work 1327–1336*, 3 vols., Cambridge, Mass., 1940, I, p. 341; John Capgrave, *The Chronicle of England*, ed. F. C. Hingeston, Rerum Britannicorum Medii Aevi Scriptores, Rolls Series, 1, London, 1858, p. 264; J. L. Gillespie, 'Richard II's Cheshire archers', *Transactions of the Historic Society of Lancashire and Cheshire*, 125, 1974, p. 11.

[13] Somerville, I, pp. 2–3, 7, 8.

[14] A. R. Myers, 'The household of Queen Margaret of Anjou, 1452–3', *B.J.R.L.*, 40, 1957–8, p. 82.

[15] *Letters of Queen Margaret of Anjou*, ed. C. Monro, Camden o.s. 86, London, 1863, Johnson repr., London, 1968, pp. 98–9, 126–7, 146–7, 150–1, 154.

[16] *C.P.R.*, 1461–7, p. 303; C. Ross, *Edward IV*, London, 1974, p. 57.

gathered fewer supporters than he would have wished.[17] Surprisingly, it was not until Edward's march brought him to Leicester that there 'came to the Kynge ryght-a-fayre felawshipe of folks to the nombar of iij[m] men, well habyled for the wers'.[18] The anonymous chronicler goes on to suggest that these followers were not attracted to Leicester from Yorkist territories in Wales or the Welsh Marches but were well-wishers of the chamberlain of Edward's household, the lord Hastings, and may have come from within Leicestershire itself.[19]

Leicestershire also played host to the final struggle between the houses of Lancaster and York, the battle of Bosworth being fought a few miles west of the county borough. Leicester was, indeed, the last sizeable English town to say farewell to Richard III on Sunday 21 August 1485 and the first to welcome the victorious Henry VII the following day.[20] However, to suggest that the worthies of the county played any significant part in this particular fray would be to strain the evidence, for Leicestershire nobility and gentry do not feature largely in the lists of casualties provided by Polydore Vergil and the Croyland continuator, and the latter's assertion that on Richard's arrival in Leicester, 'here was found a number of warriors ready to fight on the king's side',[21] is appropriately ambiguous. Nevertheless, it is fair to conclude that Leicestershire both witnessed and may have participated in some of the momentous events of the fifteenth century which facts make it an area worthy of study.

But our catalogue of momentous events merely tells us of the county's rôle in the calculations of kings, their fears and ambitions. It tells us nothing of the attitudes, fears and ambitions of the local aristocracy, the nobility and gentry, and especially the gentry who would have constituted the bulk of the politically active and aware. Indeed, it only raises a series of important questions. Who were the gentry and what were their concerns? How did they cope with the problems attendant on teetering and toppling crowns? If their horizons were hardly confined to cabbages, did they resent the intrusion into their community of the

---

[17] *Historie of the Arrivall of Edward IV in England and the Finall Recouerye of his Kingdomes from Henry VI AD 1471*, ed. John Bruce, Camden o.s. 1, London, 1838, pp. 4, 5, 7.
[18] *Ibid.*, p. 8.   [19] *Ibid.*, p. 9.
[20] This and what follows is based on accounts of the battle found in *Croyland*, pp. 500–5, and *Three Books of Polydore Vergil's English History, Comprising the Reigns of Henry VI, Edward IV and Richard III*, ed. Sir Henry Ellis, Camden o.s. 29, London, 1844, pp. 216–17.   [21] *Croyland*, p. 502.

affairs of kings? Or did they relish the opportunity to play a part on the national stage? Answers to such questions can be forthcoming only by providing a detailed study of the local aristocratic community and the relationships formed not only amongst its members but also between them and the central government, either directly or through noble intermediaries. As a further response to McFarlane's challenge, it is these questions which the current study attempts to address.

1

LEICESTERSHIRE: THE COUNTY, THE CHURCH, THE CROWN AND THE NOBILITY

Lying almost in the centre of England, Leicestershire has assumed a strategic importance from at least Roman times. The Fosse Way, which connected the Roman camps at York and Lincoln with the recreational hot springs at Bath, bisects the county and passes through the then sizeable Roman settlement of what is now called Leicester.[1] Watling Street, too, which provided contact between London and Chester, marks the south-western border of the present-day county.[2]

The ninth-century Danes, like the Romans before them, also recognized the area's military significance. Leicester, along with Derby, Nottingham, Lincoln and Stamford, was one of the famous Five Boroughs, control of which was seen as so important to the consolidation of the Danelaw and its possible extension over what remained of Anglo-Saxon England.[3] Danish insight did not escape the notice of Edward the Elder who realized that his success in reasserting Anglo-Saxon dominion over the Danelaw depended upon the capture of these towns.[4] The line of fortresses built by king Edward and his sister, Æthelflæd, lady of the Mercians, suggests that both sides understood that the midland area held the key to the domination of England.[5] Æthelflæd, in particular, used her fortified boroughs at Tamworth, Stafford and Warwick as bases to threaten, and eventually capture, Danish-held Derby and Leicester.[6]

In the post-Conquest period, Leicestershire's importance was

---

[1] R. G. Collingwood, *Roman Britain*, new edn, London, 1953, p. 19; F. Haverfield, *The Roman Occupation of Britain*, London, 1924, p. 199.

[2] I. D. Margary, *Roman Roads in Britain*, 2 vols., London, 1957, II, p. 23.

[3] H. R. Loyn, *Anglo-Saxon England and the Norman Conquest*, Harlow, 1981, pp. 56–7.

[4] F. M. Stenton, 'The Danes in England', *Proc. Brit. Acad.*, 13, 1927, p. 206.

[5] F. T. Wainwright, 'Æthelflæd lady of the Mercians', in *The Anglo-Saxons*, ed. P. Clemoes, London, 1959, pp. 58–9.

[6] Æthelflæd's military exploits may be followed in the 'Mercian Register', *E.H.D., c. 500–1042*, pp. 208–18.

no less marked. It seems that William the Conqueror may have laid waste to the county in 1068,[7] no doubt an indication that here, as in the north, the 'Norman yoke' was not altogether welcomed, but also confirmation that the shire's subjugation was seen as necessary for the safety of the regime. The latter consideration may also have prompted Henry III's march through Leicester in 1264.[8]

In the seventeenth century the county failed to play host to any of the major campaigns of the Civil War, though the battle of Naseby was fought a mere 5 miles or so beyond its southern border. But it should not be taken that the protagonists in this conflict ignored Leicestershire's significance, for the king's forces occupied Leicester before the battle of Naseby, and Fairfax reasserted parliamentary control of the town after the engagement.[9] It appears, then, that Leicestershire's importance to the control of England was not merely a fifteenth-century aberration.

This view of the shire's strategic value is not to suggest, however, that it was possessed of topographical attributes which made it more attractive to the tramp of marching feet or the clash of arms than any number of other English counties. Throughout the middle ages, and beyond, the cockpit of England was very much a movable arena. In Leicestershire's case, the prime consideration on that count seems to have been its central geographical location. Nevertheless, topography can not be ignored, for the nature of the land has a direct bearing on land tenure which in turn will affect the economy and the internal politics of the shire.

Most of Leicestershire consists of undulating plain covered with boulder clay and varying in height from 200 to 500 feet above sea level.[10] This conjunction of low hills and a veneer of boulder clay has made the county eminently suitable for agriculture. The perceptive eye of the seventeenth-century traveller, Celia Fiennes, certainly noticed its richness in corn and grassland,[11] and William Camden judged the soil to be 'rich and fertile'.[12] Nevertheless, to

---

7 F. M. Stenton, 'Introduction to the Leicestershire Domesday', in *V. C. H. Leics.*, I, pp. 283–4.
8 F. M. Powicke, *King Henry III and the Lord Edward. The Community of the Realm in the Thirteenth Century*, 2 vols., London, 1947, II, p. 462.
9 M. Ashley, *The English Civil War*, London, 1974, pp. 119–25.
10 *V. C. H. Leics.*, I, pp. 1–2; D. Holly, 'Leicestershire', in *The Domesday Geography of Midland England*, ed. H. C. Darby and I. B. Terret, 2nd edn, Cambridge, 1971, p. 353. See map 1.
11 *The Illustrated Journeys of Celia Fiennes 1685–c. 1712*, ed. C. Morris, London, 1982, p. 145.
12 William Camden, *Britannia*, trans. Richard Gough, 2nd edn, 4 vols., London 1806, Georg Olms Verlag repr., Hildesheim and New York, 1974, II, p. 301.

the west, in the Charnwood Forest region, elevations reach as high as 900 feet above sea level;[13] but such modest crags failed to impress one nineteenth-century topographer who dismissed them as 'too insignificant to form striking subjects for the pencil, or to excite the higher emotions of sublimity'.[14] Aesthetic considerations apart, the Charnwood area's topography determined its economic development and did have significance for medieval land tenure.[15]

Not only is the county devoid of spectacular mountain ranges but it also lacks major rivers. The upper reaches of the Avon and the Welland form most of its southern border with Northamptonshire, and the Trent similarly traces part of the boundary between Leicestershire and Derbyshire to the north. But the only rivers of any note within the county are the Soar, which rises in the south-west and flows northward through Leicester to the Trent, and the Soar's tributary, the Wreake, which rises in the east near Wymondham and flows westward to join the Soar east of Rothley.[16] Alluvial deposits along the banks of these rivers and of their many tributary brooks and streams provided the meadow land which was so highly prized by medieval landholders.[17]

The Soar valley conveniently divides the county into two distinct areas. Today, the western part occasionally reveals the smears of two centuries of industrial toil, whereas the east is still oriented towards agriculture. However, a twofold division can be seen as early as Anglo-Saxon times when the western portion is said to have been virtually uninhabited.[18] In the light of more recent investigations which point to the very scattered nature of many

[13] G. H. Dury, *The East Midlands and the Peak*, London, 1963, p. 28.
[14] J. Curtis, *A Topographical History of the County of Leicester*, Ashby de la Zouch, 1831, p. xxxv.
[15] For Charnwood's economic significance see below pp. 11, 13, 61, 67. The wastes of the manors of Barrow, Groby, Whitwick and Shepshed and about 780 acres of the waste of Loughborough manor converged on the Charnwood Forest area. Shortly after the Conquest these manors were held by the earls of Chester and Leicester. By the fifteenth century part of the waste had been cleared by religious beneficiaries of twelfth- and thirteenth-century grants of land there and the manors in question had passed, mainly by a process of female descent, to lord Ferrers of Groby, lord Beaumont of Beaumont, lord la Zouche of Ashby and lord Lovel, and by grant to the Erdyngtons. The fact that Charnwood Forest had never been a royal forest in post-Conquest times may have helped to ensure that the area never fell under the sway of a single landlord. (*T.L.A.S.*, 15, 1927–8, pp. 2–32.)
[16] *Ordnance Survey Maps*, 1:50,000, 129, 130, 140, 141. See map 1.
[17] Holly, 'Leicestershire', p. 346.
[18] *V. C. H. Leics.*, I, p. 221.

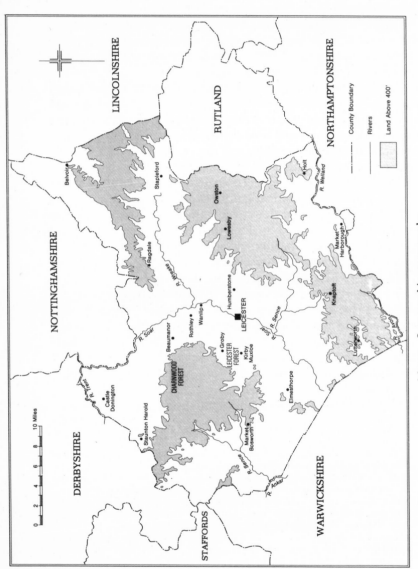

Map 1 Leicestershire topography

Anglo-Saxon settlements in isolated farmsteads and small hamlets, we must allow for a degree of exaggeration in such statements.[19] Nevertheless, the Domesday survey certainly reveals that the less fertile soils and the paucity of meadow in the west made the area unattractive to early settlers and ensured it would remain the poorer half of the county until the eighteenth century.[20] The Domesday evidence is further supported by the lay subsidy returns for 1524–5 which show that western Leicestershire was paying less than 20s. per square mile while parts of the eastern region were paying 40s. and more per square mile.[21] We can assume on the basis of this evidence that the general picture of a more depressed west will hold for the fifteenth century as well.

The difference between the east and west also extends to the distribution of woodland. By the fifteenth century the east was almost devoid of wood except for limited stands near the Rutland border around Owston.[22] The west, in contrast, boasted two large woodland areas, the Leicester Forest, just west of Leicester, and Charnwood Forest which lay to the north-west of the town. Surprisingly, these wooded areas escaped the notice of William Camden who claimed that the county was mostly without wood.[23] Wood-clearing was, of course, an ongoing process, but John Leland noted the well-wooded land between Bradgate and Leicester in the early sixteenth century, and in the early eighteenth century Daniel Defoe could still comment on the 'fine forest' between Market Bosworth and the Soar valley.[24] The fact that the towns of both Leicester and Loughborough were built mainly of wood until the end of the seventeenth century indicates that timber was in plentiful local supply even at this late date.[25] Although the sale of timber and of pannage and pasture rights may

[19] See C. Taylor, *Village and Farmstead. A History of Rural Settlement in England*, London, 1984, pp. 109–24.

[20] W. G. Hoskins, *Leicestershire. An Illustrated Essay on the History of the Landscape*, London, 1957, pp. 3, 18; Holly, 'Leicestershire', pp. 321, 353, 357.

[21] A. H. R. Baker, 'Changes in the later middle ages', *A New Historical Geography of England before 1600*, ed. H. C. Darby, Cambridge, 1976, p. 196.

[22] Holly, 'Leicestershire', pp. 344, 355, 357. This area had formed part of the Royal Forest of Leicester and Rutland but the Leicestershire section had been disafforested in 1235. R. A. McKinley, 'The forests of Leicestershire', in *V. C. H. Leics.*, II, p. 266. See below, chapter 3.

[23] Camden, *Britannia*, II, p. 297.

[24] *The Itinerary of John Leland*, ed. L. T. Smith, 5 vols., London, 1906, Centaur Press, repr., London, 1964, I, p. 17; Daniel Defoe, *A Tour through England and Wales*, 2 vols., London, 1928, II, p. 88.

[25] *The Illustrated Journeys of Celia Fiennes*, p. 145; *The Itinerary of John Leland*, I, p. 14.

have given the western woodland areas some economic significance, when compared to incomes from rents, the returns would
have been relatively modest, thereby reinforcing the general
economic backwardness of the western region.

Despite the west's comparative poverty, Leicestershire was still,
overall, one of the most populous midland counties and one of the
wealthiest. With a conservatively estimated population of about
51,000 people (based on the poll tax returns of 1377), Leicestershire outstripped its midland neighbours to the north and west.
Warwickshire and Nottinghamshire, with about 45,000 and
43,000 people respectively, were marginally less populous than
Leicestershire, but Derbyshire and Staffordshire lagged even
further behind with about 36,500 and fewer than 34,000 people
respectively.[26] With over forty persons per square mile, population density was also greater in Leicestershire than in its northern
and western neighbours. In Warwickshire and Nottinghamshire
there were between thirty and forty persons per square mile; in
Derbyshire between twenty and thirty; and in Staffordshire
between ten and twenty.[27]

In wealth, Leicestershire fell within the median range of English
counties, being neither as poor as Derbyshire to the north nor
quite as rich as Northamptonshire to the south. R. S. Schofield,
using the tax assessment of 1334, has calculated on the basis of lay
wealth that Leicestershire ranked twenty-first out of thirty-eight
counties, Derbyshire thirty-third and Northamptonshire
twelfth.[28] He further discovered that by the early sixteenth
century, these relativities had not altered markedly. Given that
Schofield's calculations are based upon figures for the whole
county and would therefore include the more backward west,
eastern Leicestershire must have been a very wealthy area indeed.

These comfortable economic circumstances were not the
consequence of mineral resources. Coal deposits in the north-west
of the county were being mined as early as the fourteenth century,

---

[26] J. C. Russell, *British Medieval Population*, Albuquerque, 1948, p. 132–3. Russell's use of a
multiplier of 3.5 has been criticized as being too low. See J. Krause, 'The medieval
household: large or small?', *Econ. Hist. Rev.*, 2nd ser., 9, 1957, p. 432; M. McKisack, *The
Fourteenth Century, 1307–1399*, Oxford, 1959, p. 313.

[27] R. A. Pelham, 'Fourteenth-century England', in *An Historical Geography of England
before A.D. 1800*, ed. H. C. Darby, Cambridge, 1936, p. 232.

[28] R. S. Schofield, 'The geographical distribution of wealth in England, 1334–1649', *Econ.
Hist. Rev.*, 2nd ser., 18, 1965, p. 504.

but their full potential was not to be realized till a later age.[29]
Slate was quarried at Swithland and high-quality mortar-lime was
extracted from extensive pits at Barrow-on-Soar. Both were used
in the building industry.[30] However, there is nothing to suggest
that the medieval extractive industry was on anything but a small
scale, no doubt important to the very local or parish economy and
to the income of individual landholders, but of lesser significance
to the economy of the shire as a whole. Furthermore, Leicestershire in the fifteenth century had not as yet developed its
reputation as a manufacturing county, though hosiers were
already present in the borough of Leicester then.[31]

As one would expect in a pre-industrial economy, the shire's
economic activity was confined almost exclusively to agriculture.
R. H. Hilton stresses the subsistence level of medieval agriculture
there, with only a small proportion of the produce of tillage,
namely barley, peas and beans, some wheat and negligible quantities of rye and oats, reaching the market.[32] However, Leicestershire was also a wool producing area, noted for the quality, and
therefore the value, of its staple which was taken to the fairs of the
east coast. While some of this wool was manufactured locally into
cloth, for the medieval period this industrial output was not of
great economic consequence.[33] Although sheep were grazed
throughout the county, the most significant areas were the higher
ground or wolds in the north-east, and to the west of the Soar
valley in the Charnwood Forest. Since the latter area had been
colonized by the monastic orders in the twelfth century, wool
production became economically important to religious houses, at
least until the end of the fourteenth century.[34]

Despite this ecclesiastical involvement in the county's economy, few monasteries in Leicestershire aspired to great wealth and
influence. As with the rest of the Danelaw, Leicestershire was not
burdened with the vast estates of a large Benedictine house such as

[29] *V. C. H. Leics.*, III, pp. 30–2.
[30] Curtis, *Topographical History*, pp. xxxiii–xxxiv; *V. C. H. Leics.*, III, p. 43.
[31] *W.H.R.*, no. 613.
[32] R. H. Hilton, *The Economic Development of Some Leicestershire Estates in the 14th and 15th Centuries*, London, 1947, p. 64; R. H. Hilton, 'Medieval agrarian history', in *V. C. H. Leics.*, II, pp. 174–5. For a contrary view see E. Power, *The Wool Trade in English Medieval History*, London, 1941, pp. 1, 39 n. 1.
[33] Hilton, *The Economic Development of Some Leicestershire Estates*, pp. 31–2; Pelham, 'Fourteenth-century England', p. 250; R. A. McKinley, 'Medieval political history', in *V. C. H. Leics.*, II, pp. 93–6.
[34] Hilton, 'Medieval agrarian history', p. 190; *V. C. H. Leics.*, III, p. 132 n. 14.

the very wealthy Glastonbury Abbey in Somerset or St Albans in Hertfordshire or the plethora of prosperous houses of the west-midland counties of Gloucestershire and Worcestershire.[35] One must assume that any pre-Conquest monastic foundations which may have existed in the area, were, along with the diocese of Leicester, swept away by the Danish invasions and settlement of the ninth and tenth centuries.[36] Whatever the reason, the fact remains that all fifteenth-century religious houses in the county were founded after the Norman Conquest and mainly in the twelfth and thirteenth centuries when the scale of their endowment was modest.[37] The only Benedictine foundation was the small alien cell at Hinkley. That this was granted to Mount Grace Priory, the Carthusian foundation in Yorkshire, in 1415, is, perhaps, as much an indication that its marginal income could no longer sustain continued independent existence as it is of Henry V's wartime chauvinistic fervour.[38] Nor was Hinkley alone in being a poorly endowed house. By the middle of the fifteenth century, Aldermanshaw, another alien cell belonging to the Cluniac order, was in ruins, and Charley Priory, a house of Augustinian canons, was similarly described in 1444.[39] One must admit that these are abnormal cases. In fact, most of Leicester-shire's assortment of priories and abbeys managed to survive well enough until the Dissolution on incomes ranging from as low as £20 per year at Bradley Priory to about £400 at Launde Priory and Croxton Abbey.[40] Nevertheless, such relatively limited resources were insufficient to permit these houses an overweening influence on the economy or the politics of the shire as a whole.

The single possible exception to this might have been the Augustinian abbey of St Mary-in-the-Fields at Leicester. At the

---

[35] *Documents Illustrative of the Social and Economic History of the Danelaw*, ed. F. M. Stenton, Records of the Social and Economic History of England and Wales, v, London, 1920, pp. liii–liv; R. H. Hilton, *A Medieval Society. The West Midlands at the End of the Thirteenth Century*, London, 1967, pp. 25–8.

[36] F. M. Stenton, *Anglo-Saxon England*, 3rd edn, London, 1971, pp. 437–8, 445. For a revisionist view see P. Sawyer, *The Age of the Vikings*, 2nd edn, London, 1971, pp. 144–5.

[37] See n. 34 above. R. A. McKinley, 'The religious houses of Leicestershire', in *V. C. H. Leics.*, II, pp. 1–30.

[38] Sir William Dugdale, *Monasticon Anglicanum*, ed. J. Caley, H. Ellis and B. Bandinel, 6 vols., London, 1817–30, VI, p. 1030; D. Knowles and R. N. Hadcock, *Medieval Religious Houses: England and Wales*, London, 1971, pp. 52–8, 83, 88.

[39] Knowles and Hadcock, *Medieval Religious Houses*, pp. 96, 98, 139, 153.

[40] *Ibid.*, pp. 138, 141, 149, 163, 184, 187.

Dissolution, St Mary's had a net income of £951 and held more manors within Leicestershire than any other landholder, whether ecclesiastical or lay.[41] Leaving aside the obvious dangers inherent in counting manors,[42] one must bear in mind that over £163, or about 17 per cent of this income, derived from holdings outside the county and that a further £327, or 34 per cent of net income, was acquired from spiritualities.[43] It would be unwarranted, therefore, to consider £951 as entirely indicative of the abbey's economic or political influence based on land held within the county. Furthermore, during the fifteenth century the abbey suffered an economic decline. By the end of the century it had ceased to be a wool producer and, like most owners of large estates, had come to rely on income from rents.[44] In fact, only £41 of the gross £570 derived from temporalities within Leicestershire was the product of direct cultivation.[45] The extent of the abbey's decline can be further gauged by its debt of £410 at the Dissolution.[46] Whatever the reasons, Leicester Abbey does not appear to have been a major force in the county, either socially or politically.

After 1399, the greatest lay, as opposed to ecclesiastical, estate in Leicestershire belonged to the king by right of his duchy of Lancaster. The duchy's honor of Leicester was not, of course, coterminous with its county namesake. With parts of the bailiwick of Sileby lying in Nottinghamshire and Rutland, and the entire bailiwicks of Warwick and Northampton lying within those counties, 78 (that is, half) of the honor's 156 midland vills were outside the county altogether.[47] Also, the duchy, like the abbey of St Mary at Leicester, witnessed a movement away from direct involvement in agriculture and, by the fifteenth century, had rented out its properties.[48] Any influence which the

---

[41] Hilton, *The Economic Development of Some Leicestershire Estates*, p. 6.

[42] See J. P. Cooper, 'The counting of manors', *Econ. Hist. Rev.*, 2nd ser., 8, 1956, pp. 377–89.

[43] *Valor Ecclesiasticus*, 6 vols., London, 1810–34, IV, pp. 145–8.

[44] Hilton, *The Economic Development of Some Leicestershire Estates*, pp. 79–91; A. Savine, *English Monasteries on the Eve of the Dissolution*, ed. P. Vinogradoff, Oxford Studies in Social and Legal History, I, Oxford, 1909, pp. 55, 149, 154. This was a trend of the times (Power, *The Wool Trade in English Medieval History*, pp. 37–8).

[45] *Valor Ecclesiasticus*, IV, pp. 146–7.

[46] Dugdale, *Monasticon Anglicanum*, I, p. 462.

[47] L. Fox, *The Administration of the Honor of Leicester in the Fourteenth Century*, Leicester, 1940, pp. 11, 20, and map between pp. 74–5.

[48] Somerville, I, pp. 93–4.

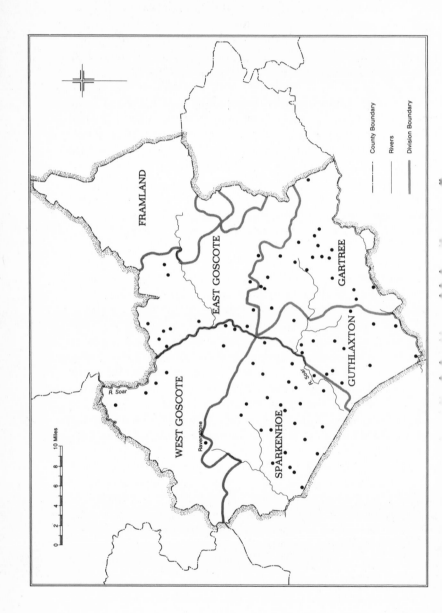

FRAMLAND

EAST GOSCOTE

GARTREE

GUTHLAXTON

WEST GOSCOTE

R. Soar

Ravenstone

R. Soar

SPARKENHOE

County Boundary
Rivers
Division Boundary

0 2 4 6 8 10 Miles

king wielded in the county in right of the duchy of Lancaster came from the profusion of honorial offices such as steward-ships, receiverships and the various posts of forester, bailiff and castle-constable which lay within the royal gift.[49] These offices were sought after not only for their salaries but also for the prestige and power they could bestow. Therefore, although the king's holdings in Leicestershire were slightly more modest than those of the abbey of St Mary, and although he too was a 'rentier' with the added disadvantage of being far removed from local affairs, he was, nonetheless, potentially well placed to assert his influence because of the patronage at his disposal. This patronage was not confined to the honor of Leicester either, but flowed from the wider duchy and from the crown itself.[50]

If we apply the already established economic division of the county into distinct eastern and western zones to the way in which the duchy of Lancaster possessions were distributed, there appears to be little correlation between the two. Thirty-three of the seventy-eight Leicestershire vills, or about 42 per cent, lay west of the river Soar, but an analysis on a hundred basis proves more revealing. In the south-east, in the hundreds of Gartree and Guthlaxton, there were altogether thirty-three vills; in Sparken-hoe in the south-west, twenty-five; in West Goscote to the north-west, eight; in East Goscote, east of the lower Soar, twelve; and in Framland to the extreme north-east of the county there were no duchy vills.[51] In West Goscote most of the duchy's eight vills were to be found either along the Soar valley or close to it in the valleys of the Soar's eastward-flowing tributaries. Only Raven-stone fails to comply with this generalization, being situated in the west of the hundred beyond the Charnwood Forest. In Sparken-hoe, nineteen duchy vills (76 per cent) were in the more prosperous west of the hundred, skirting the less attractive Leicester Forest, or Chase, area. Although one may reasonably conclude, on the basis of this brief analysis, that the distribution of Lancastrian vills is indeed a reflection of topographical and, therefore, economic realities, the aim here has been to draw attention to the fact that in Framland, East and West Goscote and in the east of Sparkenhoe, duchy of Lancaster possessions were

---

[49] *Ibid.*, pp. 563–75.   [50] But see below, chapter 4.
[51] For distribution of vills see n. 47 above. Hundredal divisions are to be found in Nichols. See map 2.

relatively sparse. As it happens, these are the areas where one finds the bulk of the estates of the upper aristocracy, the nobility.

Those nobles with major holdings in Leicestershire in the period under consideration were the lords Roos, Thomas and Edmund;[52] the lords, later viscounts, Beaumont, John and William;[53] the lords Ferrers of Groby, William Ferrers, Edward Grey and Thomas Grey;[54] the lords Lovel, William, John and Francis;[55] the dukes of Norfolk, John Mowbray I and his son, John II;[56] the lords Zouche of Harringworth, William I, William II and John;[57] and, after 1461, William lord Hastings.[58] Other nobles such as James Butler, earl of Wiltshire,[59] the Greys of Codnor,[60] the Greys of Ruthin,[61] the Scropes of Masham,[62] the Scropes of Bolton,[63] and the Beauchamp and Neville earls of Warwick[64] were seised of lands and rights too inconsequential to involve them in the politics of the shire.

Although Thomas, lord Roos, took an interest in the local politics of Lincolnshire and, to a lesser extent, Norfolk, Yorkshire and Northamptonshire,[65] he displayed an almost total lack of concern for the internal affairs of Leicestershire. In part, this neglect may be explained by the geographical isolation of those manors he held in demesne which were closely confined to the north-eastern corner of the hundred of Framland in the Vale of Belvoir, and in part to the fact that he possessed very few overlordships elsewhere in the county.[66] In addition to these constraints, in the first half of the fifteenth century the Roos estates were burdened by a series of minorities, culminating when

---

[52] Thomas died 1464. Edmund died 1508 (G.E.C., xi, pp. 105–7).
[53] John died 1460. William died 1507 (*ibid.*, ii, pp. 62–3).
[54] William Ferrers died 1445. The title passed to Edward Grey (died 1457) in right of his wife, Elizabeth, William Ferrers' granddaughter and heir. Thomas Grey (died 1501) was Elizabeth and Edward's grandson (*ibid.*, v, pp. 354–62).
[55] William died 1455. John died 1465 and Francis died probably in 1487 (*ibid.*, viii, pp. 221–5).
[56] John I died 1461. John II died 1476 (*ibid.*, ix, pp. 607–9).
[57] William I died 1462. William II died 1468. John died 1526 (*ibid.*, xii, pp. 944–6).
[58] Died 1483 (*ibid.*, vi, pp. 370–1).   [59] Died 1461 (*ibid.*, x, pp. 126–8).
[60] *Ibid.*, vi, pp. 130–3; Nichols, ii, p. 557.
[61] G.E.C., vi, pp. 155–60; Nichols, ii, p. 869.
[62] G.E.C., xi, pp. 567–70; Nichols, ii, pp. 18, 19.
[63] G.E.C., xi, pp. 543–6; Nichols, ii, pp. 446, 509.
[64] G.E.C., xii, pp. 378–97; Nichols, ii, p. 635.
[65] *C.P.R.*, 1452–61, p. 603; G.E.C., xi, p. 105; *Paston Letters*, ii, p. 185.
[66] Nichols, ii, pp. 18, 38, 296, 300, 713. For distribution of manors held in demesne by the nobility, see map 3.

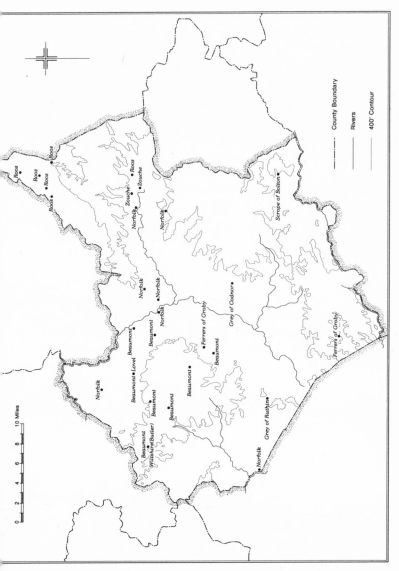

Map 3 Manors held in demesne by the nobility before 1461

Legend:
- — · — · — County Boundary
- ——— Rivers
- ——— 400' Contour

Scale: 0 2 4 6 8 10 Miles

Labels on map: Roos, Roos, Roos, Roos, Zouche, Roos, Zouche, Norfolk, Norfolk, Norfolk, Norfolk, Scrope of Bolton, Norfolk, Beaumont, Lovel, Beaumont, Norfolk, Ferrers of Groby, Grey of Codnor, Beaumont, Ferrers of Groby, Norfolk, Beaumont, Beaumont, Beaumont, Beaumont (Wiltshire/Butler), Beaumont, Norfolk, Grey of Ruthin

Thomas came of age in 1446.[67] While the Roos males tended to be comparatively short-lived, their women-folk clung tenaciously to life with a pertinacity rivalling that of Margaret of Brotherton in the fourteenth century.[68] Thomas's grandmother, Margaret lady Roos, lived until 1430; his aunt Margery, wife of John lord Roos, survived her husband by almost sixty years, eventually dying at a ripe age in 1478; and his mother, Eleanor, outlived her son by three years.[69] A widow's jointure was a heavy burden on the patrimony and for most of the fifteenth century each succeeding lord Roos failed to have full possession of his estate.

Onerous as these tricks of fate undoubtedly were, they alone need not have proved permanently prejudicial to the family fortunes. However, Thomas's political miscalculations and his son Edmund's insanity had more enduring adverse consequences. Thomas's unswerving loyalty to the Lancastrian cause, even after the change of regime in 1461, led to the forfeiture of his estates and his subsequent execution in 1464.[70] Following the swing of the political pendulum in 1485, Edmund regained his lands and titles only to lose his wits shortly afterwards. Found to be 'not of sufficient discretion', he was placed under the guardianship of his brother-in-law, Sir Thomas Lovel, under whose roof he passed his days until his death, without issue, in 1508.[71]

As with the lords Roos, the lords Beaumont had interests outside Leicestershire, again notably in Lincolnshire where they had received grants of land when the barony was created early in the fourteenth century.[72] However, unlike the Rooses, they played an active part in Leicestershire affairs.[73] This was surely a reflection of the more central location of the manors they held in demesne, for although these were largely concentrated in the poorer and less densely populated western part of the county

[67] *C.P.R.*, 1441–6, p. 445.
[68] Margaret outlived her brother, two husbands, her children and her eldest grandson. R. E. Archer, 'Rich old ladies: the problem of late medieval dowagers', *Property and Politics: Essays in Later Medieval English History*, ed. A. J. Pollard, Gloucester, 1984, pp 28–9; K. B. McFarlane, *The Nobility of Later Medieval England*, Oxford, 1973, p. 66; G.E.C., IX, pp. 600–1.
[69] G.E.C., XI, pp. 102–4.   [70] *Ibid.*, XI, p. 105.
[71] *Ibid.*, XI, p. 106.   [72] *Ibid.*, II, p. 59.
[73] *C.P.R.*, 1429–31, p. 619; *ibid.*, 1436–41, p. 584; *ibid.*, 1441–6, p. 473; *ibid.*, 1446–52, p 590.

where the process of subinfeudation had been relatively slow, they at least were not confined to an isolated corner of the shire.[74]

The Beaumont manors were grouped in the north and east of Sparkenhoe and in West Goscote on the edge of Charnwood Forest. In addition to these, in 1447 and 1453 John, viscount Beaumont, inherited two manors from his maternal grandmother and her sister, one at Hallaton and one at Thorpe Langton, and these holdings provided the family with further interests in Gartree hundred in the south-east.[75] Also, unlike the Rooses, the Beaumonts held a number of overlordships in each of the county's six hundreds.[76] Given the extent of their Leicestershire estate it would be surprising had the Beaumonts not played a significant part in local affairs.

Nevertheless, the fate of the Beaumonts closely paralleled that of the Roos family and their end was just as ignominious. John Beaumont, like Thomas Roos, supported Henry VI in his struggle against York and, in July 1460, he was killed at the battle of Northampton.[77] John's son, William, was unable to reconcile himself to the Yorkist regime. Although he managed to survive until the advent of the Tudors when he was restored to his honours, he, like Edmund, lord Roos, subsequently lost his reason.[78] The Beaumonts, therefore, one of Leicestershire's leading noble families, had no part to play in county politics once the Lancastrian dynasty was overthrown in 1461.

Unlike either the lords Roos or the lords Beaumont, the lords Ferrers of Groby appear to have confined their interests almost entirely to Leicestershire, at least until 1457. William, lord Ferrers of Groby, was appointed to every commission of the peace in the county between 1422 and the year of his death, 1445.[79] No doubt his influence on local affairs can be explained in terms of the extensive overlordships he held in each of the county's six hundreds, though the manors he held in demesne were confined to Groby in Sparkenhoe, Bradgate in West Goscote and Lutter-

74 See map 3.
75 *V.C.H. Leics.*, v, pp. 124, 206; Nichols, ii, p. 661; G.E.C. ii, p. 62.
76 Gartree: *V.C.H. Leics.*, v, p. 214; Nichols, ii, pp. 460, 568. Framland: *ibid.*, ii, pp. 18, 195. Guthlaxton: *ibid.*, iv, pp. 11. Sparkenhoe: *ibid.*, iv, *passim*. East Goscote: *ibid.*, iii, pp. 64, 366, 498. West Goscote: *ibid.*, iii, pp. 1114–16.
77 *Three Fifteenth-Century Chronicles*, ed. J. Gairdner, Camden n.s. 28, London, 1880, p. 74.
78 G.E.C., ii, p. 63.
79 *C.P.R.*, 1422–9, p. 565; *ibid.*, 1429–36, p. 619; *ibid.*, 1436–41, p. 584; *ibid.*, 1441–6, p. 473.

worth in Guthlaxton.[80] After 1445, Edward Grey, who held the title, lord Ferrers of Groby, in right of his wife, Elizabeth granddaughter and heir of William, assumed the latter's rôle in county politics until his own death in 1457.[81]

Henceforth, neither Edward Grey's son, Sir John Grey, nor his grandson, Thomas, maintained Ferrers involvement in Leicestershire politics. Sir John was killed fighting for the king at the second battle of St Albans in 1461 and, keeping in mind the consequence which befell the lords Roos and Beaumont for failing to predict Lancastrian defeat, one may be tempted, for the sake of symmetry, to explain the eclipse of the Ferrerses of Groby in similar national-political terms. However, symmetry is elusive in this case and an explanation for the loosening of Ferrers ties with Leicestershire must be sought elsewhere.

It may be recalled that Edward Grey held the title, lord Ferrers of Groby, and its attendant lands in Leicestershire in right of his wife, Elizabeth.[82] The heirs, therefore, would have to await Elizabeth's death before entering the Ferrers inheritance. By the time Elizabeth did eventually die in 1483, her son, John Grey, was himself long dead and Thomas Grey's local interests were already concentrated in Warwickshire where he had inherited the lands of his paternal grandmother, Joan Astley.[83] As a consequence neither John nor Thomas was in a position to involve himself in Leicestershire politics. Furthermore, sometime before 1462, Elizabeth took as her second husband, Sir John Bourchier, a younger son of Henry, earl of Essex.[84] Sir John's interests seem to have lain in Essex where he was certainly buried.[85] There is no evidence to suggest that he used his marriage to Elizabeth to extend his influence into the Midlands.

While the lords Ferrers of Groby, William Ferrers and Edward Grey, exercised their influence in Leicestershire from their *caput honoris* within the county, the seat of Lovel power lay beyond its boundaries at Tichmarsh in Northamptonshire.[86] Their consider-

---

[80] *V. C. H. Leics.*, v, *passim*; Nichols, II–IV, *passim*; *T.L.A.S.*, 14, 1925–6, p. 87; *ibid.*, 16 1929–31, p. 50. For manors held in demesne see Nichols, IV, p. 630; *ibid.*, III, p. 661.
[81] *G.E.C.*, v, pp. 357–60; *C.P.R.*, 1446–52, p. 590; *ibid.*, 1452–61, p. 669.
[82] See above, n. 54.
[83] *G.E.C.*, v, pp. 360–2; *ibid.*, IV, p. 419; *V. C. H. Warws.*, VI, p. 17; *ibid.*, IV, p. 179.
[84] *G.E.C.*, v, p. 360.
[85] *V. C. H. Essex*, II, p. 175; H. W. King, 'Ancient wills', *Transactions of the Essex Archaeological Society*, I, 146, 1878, pp. 147–50.
[86] *V. C. H. Northants.*, III, pp. 143–6.

able holdings, which extended even into Oxfordshire and Wiltshire, prompted one historian to refer to John, lord Lovel, as 'one
of the wealthiest of peers below the rank of earl'.[87] It is hardly
surprising, then, that the Lovels were consistently appointed to
the commissions of the peace in these three shires.[88]

However, in Leicestershire, Lovel holdings were relatively
minor, consisting mainly of two manors and land in Sparkenhoe
and the overlordship of a manor and lands in Gartree hundred.[89]
Nevertheless, William, lord Lovel, was regularly appointed to
Leicestershire commissions of the peace until his death in 1455,
and although his son and heir, John, appears not to have taken the
same interest in the county, the William Lovel, knight, who was
appointed to the commissions of the peace in 1456 and 1457 was
probably John's young brother, the lord Morley.[90]

After 1457, Lovel appointments to the bench of justices of the
peace in Leicestershire ceased. Furthermore, in May 1463 John
Lovel transferred his manors at Bagworth and Thornton and his
lands at Thornton and Desford to William, lord Hastings, in
return for a reciprocal transfer of Hastings' manors in Yorkshire
to Lovel.[91] Changes were also made to the Lovel overlordship
of the manor of Carlton Culieu some time after 1455. The nature
of these changes is unclear, but it seems that the overlordship
passed out of Lovel possession.[92] Taken together, such evidence,
sparse as it is, suggests that a conscious decision was made to
withdraw from the county, though whether this decision was
made voluntarily for sound economic reasons, or under pressure
from lord Hastings, is open to speculation.

Of the remaining noble families with lands in Leicestershire,
two, the Mowbrays and the Zouches, played little part in the
politics of the shire. Mowbray lands in the county were part of
the Segrave inheritance, acquired when Elizabeth Segrave, sole

---

87 Ross, *Edward IV*, p. 438. For Lovel manors in Oxfordshire and Wiltshire see *V. C. H.,
Oxon.*, IV, p. 367; *ibid.*, VI, *pp. 82, 127*; *ibid.*, VIII, p. 60; *ibid.*, X, p. 234; *V. C. H. Wilts.*, V,
p. 53; *ibid.*, IX, pp. 81, 176; *ibid.*, XI, p. 240; *ibid.*, XII, p. 112.
88 *C.P.R.*, 1429–36, pp. 622, 626; *ibid.*, 1436–41, pp. 587, 592; *ibid.*, 1441–6, pp. 476, 480;
ibid., 1452–61, p. 681.
89 H.M.C., *Report on the Manuscripts of . . . Reginald Rawdon Hastings . . .*, I, London, 1928,
p. 296; *V. C. H. Leics*, V, pp. 77, 257.
90 *C.P.R.*, 1429–36, p. 619; *ibid.*, 1436–41, p. 584; *ibid.*, 1441–6, p. 473; *ibid.*, 1446–52, p.
590; *ibid.*, 1452–61, p. 669. For lord Morley see G.E.C., IX, p. 219.
91 H. M. C., *Hastings*, I, p. 296.
92 *V. C. H. Leics.*, V, p. 77.

heiress of John, lord Segrave, married John, lord Mowbray.[93] These extensive Segrave estates were mainly confined to the hundreds of Framland and East Goscote, but as with most lords whose *caput honoris* lay outside the county, the Mowbrays would have become 'rentiers' by the fifteenth century rather than remaining demesne farmers.[94] The same applies to the lords Zouche who were consistently appointed to commissions of the peace in their native Northamptonshire, occasionally to those in Rutland, but only from 1478 onwards to those in Leicestershire.[95]

No list of Leicestershire nobility would be complete without mention of the family which produced one of the fifteenth century's most powerful peers, William, lord Hastings. In the fourteenth century, the main area of Hastings activity had been in the North Riding of Yorkshire where they held the manors of Slingsby and Allerton.[96] William's great-grandfather, Sir Ralph I, was twice pricked as sheriff of Yorkshire in 1337 and 1340, and in 1334 the earl of Lancaster appointed him as steward in the honor of Pickering.[97] Although Sir Ralph's son, also called Ralph, inherited the manor of Kirby Muxloe in Leicestershire from his maternal uncle, Sir Robert Herle, in 1365, he, too, maintained strong links both with Yorkshire, where he served as sheriff in 1376–7 and 1380–1, and with the house of Lancaster in the retinue of John of Gaunt.[98]

Despite the family's close association with the earldom and duchy of Lancaster in the fourteenth century, in 1405, Ralph II's eldest son, Sir Ralph III, joined archbishop Scrope's rebellion against the first Lancastrian king, Henry IV.[99] This revolt was

[93] G.E.C., XI, pp. 609–10.

[94] For the trend towards renting see *V. C. H. Leics.*, II, p. 182; G. A. Holmes, *The Estates of the Higher Nobility in Fourteenth-Century England*, Cambridge, 1957, pp. 112–16. For Mowbray holdings in Leicestershire see Nichols, II and III, *passim*.

[95] For Northants, see *C.P.R.*, 1429–36, p. 622; *ibid.*, 1436–41, p. 587; *ibid.*, 1441–6, p. 475; *ibid.*, 1452–61, p. 673. For Rutland see *ibid.*, 1429–36, p. 623; *ibid.*, 1452–61, p. 675. For Leics. see *ibid.*, 1476–85, p. 564.

[96] *V. C. H. Yorks. (N.R.)*, I, p. 559; *ibid.*, II, p. 422.

[97] Lists and Indexes, IX, p. 161; Somerville, I, p. 356.

[98] H. N. Bell, *The Huntingdon Peerage*, London, 1820, p. 11; H.M.C., *Hastings*, I, pp. 21–2; Lists and Indexes, IX, p. 162; *John of Gaunt's Register, 1371–1375*, ed. S. Armitage Smith, 2 vols., Camden, 3rd ser., 20 and 21, London, 1911, vol. 21, pp. 330–1, nos. 1759, 1760; *John of Gaunt's Register, 1379–1383*, ed. E. C. Lodge and R. Somerville, 2 vols., Camden, 3rd ser., 56 and 57, London, 1937, vol. 56, pp. 7, 56 no. 162, 185 no. 561.

[99] E. F. Jacob, *The Fifteenth Century, 1399–1485*, Oxford, 1961, repr. 1976, pp. 58–9; *C.P.R.*, 1405–8, pp. 88, 177, 478.

quickly suppressed, but Hastings' rôle must have been important and conspicuous, for in July 1405, he was tried and executed and his lands were confiscated.[100] Five years later, however, in May 1410, the family estate was restored to Ralph's brother and heir, Sir Richard Hastings, who, in 1422, was appointed steward of Knaresborough, thereby re-establishing the connection between the Hastingses and the duchy of Lancaster.[101] He also served as sheriff of Yorkshire in 1426 and 1434, was elected knight of the shire there in 1425 and 1429 and, until his death in 1436, received regular commissions to sit on the bench of JPs in the North Riding.[102]

Although it may appear that Sir Richard was merely emulating the careers of his father and grandfather, this is not entirely the case. No doubt mindful of the potential turbulence of northern politics, he also began the family's closer association with the affairs of Leicestershire where he served as sheriff in 1415, 1423, 1427 and 1434,[103] and as JP from 1424 to 1431.[104] Richard's brother and heir, Sir Leonard Hastings, a retainer of the duke of York, continued to play an active rôle in Leicestershire's local politics in the late 1440s and early 1450s. He served on commissions of the peace from 1448 until his death in 1455;[105] he was appointed sheriff of Leicestershire and Warwickshire in 1453;[106] and in 1455 he was elected to parliament as knight of the shire for Leicestershire.[107] Whereas Sir Richard divided his time and energy between Leicestershire and Yorkshire, it was probably Sir Leonard who finally established the family's *caput honoris* in Leicestershire where, in addition to the manor of Kirby Muxloe, they held the manors of Newton Harcourt, Kilby, Wistow and Fleckney.[108] They also possessed lands in the town of Leicester itself, in Glen Magna, Ravenstone, Ashby Parva, Appleby Magna and Braunstone.[109]

[100] *C.P.R.*, 1405–8, pp. 53, 54, 69, 261, 478.

[101] *Ibid.*, 1408–13, pp. 195–6; Somerville, I, p. 524.

[102] Lists and Indexes, IX, p. 162; *Return*, pp. 309, 317; *C.P.R.*, 1442–9, p. 572; *ibid.*, 1429–36, p. 628.

[103] Lists and Indexes, IX, p. 145.   [104] *C.P.R.*, 1422–9, p. 565; *ibid.*, 1429–36, p. 619.

[105] *Ibid.*, 1446–52, p. 590; *ibid.*, 1452–61, p. 669.

[106] Lists and Indexes, IX, p. 145.   [107] Wedgwood, *Register*, p. 653.

[108] H.M.C., *Hastings*, I, p. xiii.

[109] *Ibid.*, p. 294; Nichols, I, p. 273; *ibid.*, II, p. 575; *ibid.*, III, p. 932; *ibid.*, IV, pp. 21, 430, 616. (The move to Leicestershire had an additional advantage in that it gave the family closer access to its manors in Warwickshire and Northamptonshire, for which see H.M.C., *Hastings*, I, pp. 136, 149.)

Such extensive holdings assured the Hastings family a fore-most position among the county's leading gentry but it was Sir Leonard's son, William, who laid the foundations of the family's greatness. Like his father before him, William was a retainer of Richard, duke of York. He was present at the 'Rout of Ludford Bridge' in October 1459, but may have been among those who counselled against fighting the king and who after-wards, in response to an appeal to the king's grace, received 'mercy bothe of lyffe and lym'.[110] That such was the case is suggested by the fact that Hastings suffered in neither life nor limb. He was not attainted by the Coventry parliament which met the following month, but was instead fined £100 and, along with his brothers, Thomas and Ralph, was pardoned his misdemeanours.[111]

There is little conclusive evidence to indicate that Hastings played a major part in the events leading to the change of dynasty, though that he did so may be inferred from the rewards he subsequently received. He was not with the duke of York at Wakefield, but he was probably at the battle of Mortimer's Cross with the earl of March.[112] Allowing that he was at Mortimer's Cross, one would be surprised had he not attended the meeting at Baynard's Castle which approved the decision to make Edward king, though he is not specifically named as having been present.[113] At the end of March, however, he fought at the battle of Towton where his martial accomplishments were sufficiently marked for him to receive a knighthood.[114]

Thereafter, Hastings' rise in power and prestige was rapid. On the national level he was appointed councillor and created

[110] *Gregory's Chronicle*, p. 207.

[111] For the fine and pardon see *C.P.R.*, 1452–61, pp. 552, 577. W. H. Dunham, 'Lord Hastings' indentured retainers, 1461–1483', *Transactions of the Connecticut Academy of Arts and Sciences*, 39, 1955, p. 20, asserts that Hastings was attainted (no reference provided). That this was not the case see *Rot. Parl,,* v, pp. 349, 368.

[112] C. L. Scofield, *The Life and Reign of Edward the Fourth*, 2 vols., London, 1923, new impression 1967, I, p. 137. Charles Ross maintains that 'there is no evidence that Hastings was in Edward's company' (Ross, *Edward IV*, p. 31 n. 3). While it is true that William Worcester omits Hastings from his list of those present at Mortimer's Cross (see William Worcester, *Itineraries*, ed. J. H. Harvey, Oxford, 1969, pp. 203–5), Clement Paston's letter to his brother, John, dated 23 January 1461, strongly suggests that Hastings was present (see *Paston Letters*, I, p. 197).

[113] C. A. J. Armstrong, 'The inauguration ceremonies of the Yorkist kings, and their title to the throne', *T.R.H.S.*, 4th ser., 30, 1948, p. 56.

[114] *Paston Letters*, I, p. 197.

chamberlain of the king's household; on 8 May 1461, he was made receiver general of the duchy of Cornwall and this appointment was followed a few days later by the constableship and stewardship of Rockingham Castle; the same month he was appointed master of the mint in London; in June 1461 he was elevated to the peerage as baron Hastings; in July he added the chamberlainship of north Wales to his many other offices.[115] Moreover, within Leicestershire itself, his power was no less enhanced. Apart from the stewardship of the duchy of Lancaster possessions within the county, Hastings was granted the forfeited estates of Lancastrian supporters, lord Beaumont, lord Roos and the earl of Wiltshire. Thereby, a member of the gentry was transformed into the county's pre-eminent nobleman.[116]

As we have seen, noble authority in Leicestershire was diffuse until 1461. The Roos family, the Mowbrays and the Lovels all had major holdings outside the shire but, despite their economic interest within it, they took little active part in its politics. Although the Beaumonts were appointed to commissions of the peace, they were more powerful in Lincolnshire where they had their major residence. Only the lords Ferrers of Groby resided in Leicestershire. Yet, as indicated above, their influence in the county waned after 1457.[117] Now, after 1461, with the grant to William Hastings of the Leicestershire manors belonging to the Lancastrian lords, Roos, Beaumont and the earl of Wiltshire, the authority of the nobility within the shire became concentrated in the hands of one man.

Despite these changed circumstances, it would be unwarranted to assume that this authority automatically manifested itself in greatly increased noble control of the shire's administration and politics. The interests of the nobility were rarely, if ever, confined merely to a single county. Such interests tended to be at least regional, spanning a number of counties and, more often than not, were national as well. In fifteenth-century Leicestershire this was no less true of William Hastings than it was, say, of the lords Roos and Beaumont.

Leicestershire, therefore, provides us with an interesting area in which to study the fifteenth-century gentry. There were no great

[115] J. R. Lander, 'Council, administration and councillors, 1461–1485', *B.I.H.R.*, 32, 1959, p. 168; *C.P.R.*, 1461–7, pp. 9, 13, 26, 130; *C.C.R.*, 1461–8, p. 61.
[116] *C.P.R.*, 1461–7, pp. 103–4; *ibid.*, 1467–77, p. 26.
[117] See above, p. 22.

monasteries to dominate, and therefore complicate, local society and politics. The king, as duke of Lancaster, was an absentee landlord. There was no magnate of the first order who held the county in his thrall or pair of magnates who vied with each other for control. Most of Leicestershire's nobility were non-residents for whom the county was of secondary importance. In short, Leicestershire is just the sort of county in which we would expect to find an assertive local community, well attuned to assuming responsibility for its own administration and unlikely to accept gracefully what it may consider to be unwarranted outside interference in its affairs.

Of course, it may be pointed out that wherever we look, English government in the middle ages was essentially local government, carried on by those who lived in and knew the areas where they held sway.[118] It is equally true that by the fifteenth century, the battle for control of that government had already been fought between the nobility and lesser personages below the rank of baron with the latter, the gentry, emerging as the victors.[119] Nevertheless, it is inconceivable that a study of the gentry in Yorkshire, for example, could do justice to its subject without taking into account the pervasive presence of the Percies and Nevilles or that historians should ignore the dukes of Norfolk and Suffolk and the earls of Oxford in East Anglia when the Pastons certainly could not – at least not for long. We may agree with Cam that the gentry had their hands on the helm of local administration but only rarely had they the opportunity independently to plot the course as well. Leicestershire appears to offer one of these rare opportunities.

---

[118] A. B. Ferguson, *The Indian Summer of English Chivalry*, Durham, NC, 1960, p. 127.
[119] H. Cam, 'The legislators of medieval England', *Proc. Brit. Acad.*, 31, 1945, p. 144; H. M. Cam, 'Cambridgeshire sheriffs in the thirteenth century', *Liberties and Communities in Medieval England*, Cambridge, 1944, p. 28.

2

THE GENTRY IN THE FIFTEENTH
CENTURY

Who or what were the gentry is a question which has vexed many historians of the medieval and early modern periods. A few, whose concern is with the sixteenth and seventeenth centuries where debate about the gentry is almost unavoidable, obviously consider that the term, 'gentry', has passed sufficiently into the *lingua franca* of the discipline for it to require neither definition nor explanation.[1] More tentative scholars, while admitting that the term defies simple definition, are rarely more forthcoming.[2] Still others are content in the knowledge that the gentry filled the social and economic gap between the barons and the yeomen.[3] The latter view has the twin advantages of being disarmingly simple while at the same time being stamped with the authority of bishop William Stubbs.[4]

For historians of the sixteenth century, the gentry is seen to consist of landowners bearing the title, knight, at the group's uppermost level, followed in status by the esquire and, finally, the gentleman at the lowest stratum.[5] In the seventeenth century, this trio of status groups was joined by a fourth, the artificial Jacobean creation, the baronets, whose ostensible purpose was to fill that wide gap perceived to exist between the knights and the parliamentary peerage. Baronets, therefore, ousted the knights proper from their elevated position within the hierarchy of the

---

[1] See, for example, Trevor-Roper, *The Gentry*; A. Everitt, ed., *Suffolk and the Great Rebellion 1640–1660*, Ipswich, 1961.
[2] A. Fletcher, *A County Community in Peace and War: Sussex 1600–1660*, London, 1975, p. 22.
[3] See below n. 4 and n. 5.
[4] W. Stubbs, *The Constitutional History of England*, 5th edn, 3 vols., Oxford, 1903, III, p. 563.
[5] G. E. Mingay, *The Gentry. The Rise and Fall of a Ruling Class*, London, 1976, p. 3; R. B. Smith, *Land and Politics in the England of Henry VIII. The West Riding of Yorkshire: 1530–46*, Oxford, 1970, p. 65; L. Stone, *The Crisis of the Aristocracy 1558–1641*, abridged edn, Oxford, 1967, p. 28; J. Cornwall, 'The people of Rutland in 1522', *T.L.A.H.S.*, 37, 1961–2, p. 15.

gentry.[6] This is still the most widely held view of the gentry and it is the model which, it seems, is implicitly adopted even by those who shirk the task of providing the term with an explicit definition.

More adventurous spirits have sought a greater precision in their definitions, a precision based on land tenure and income. One sometimes finds the gentry defined as those landowners below the parliamentary peerage who held freehold land providing an income of at least £10 per annum.[7] While such a definition pretends to mathematical exactitude, we would do well to be cautious. R. H. Tawney has already pointed out that there were freeholders whose holdings were so insignificant that they had to sell their labour for wages in order to subsist. Moreover, and more apposite to our purposes, he has reminded us that not all members of the gentry held their lands by freehold.[8] Even R. B. Smith and J. Cornwall both admit that some £10 freeholders may have been yeomen and that some gentlemen had recorded incomes as low as £5 per annum.[9] These caveats would suggest that something more than form of tenure or mere income was involved in determining status.

Our picture of the gentry becomes further complicated when we learn that merchants, lawyers and office holders were accorded gentlemanly status. Also, a liveried retainer was regarded as a gentleman but may have ceased to be so once he doffed his livery.[10] These complexities have, of course, elicited comment from those historians who are forced to use the term, 'gentry'. Tawney admits that it is a group 'ragged at its edges'; Smith confesses to a degree of arbitrariness when drawing the line between gentry and yeomen; and Professor Stone, in an attempt to accommodate complicating material, has been constrained to resort to an inelegant construct which sets a rural-based hierarchy

---

[6] Stone, *The Crisis of the Aristocracy*, pp. 43–8.

[7] T. B. Pugh, 'The magnates, knights and gentry', in *Fifteenth Century England 1399–1509*, eds. S. B. Chrimes *et al.*, Manchester, 1972, pp. 96–7; Smith, *Land and Politics*, pp. 65–6; J. Cornwall, 'The early Tudor gentry', *Econ. Hist. Rev.*, 2nd ser., 17, 1964–5, pp. 460–70.

[8] R. H. Tawney, *The Agrarian Problem in the Sixteenth Century*, London, 1912, p. 37 and *passim*.

[9] Smith, *Land and Politics*, pp. 65–6; Cornwall, 'Early Tudor gentry', pp. 462–5.

[10] F. R. H. Du Boulay, *An Age of Ambition. English Society in the Late Middle Ages*, London, 1970, p. 72; E. W. Ives, 'The common lawyers of pre-Reformation England', *T.R.H.S.*, 5th ser., 18, 1968, p. 157; Tawney, 'The rise of the gentry, 1558–1640', p. 4; R. L. Storey, 'Gentlemen-bureaucrats', in *Profession, Vocation and Culture in Later Medieval England*, ed. C. H. Clough, Liverpool, 1982, pp. 91–5.

beside four occupational hierarchies.[11] Such concessions suggest a justifiable feeling of unease about the term, 'gentry'.

The only point of agreement is that the gentry consisted of knights, esquires and gentlemen who shared gentle status. Any movement beyond this point will produce provisos, qualifications and, eventually, disagreement. Unfortunately, if we look back beyond the sixteenth century, our single point of agreement ceases to hold as well, and we are still left with the question, who or what were the gentry? Perhaps the best way to resolve our problem is to adopt an atomistic approach and to trace the formation of the gentry as a status group through the development of its component parts.

The origins of the English gentry can be found in Anglo-Norman society as it developed after the Conquest and, particularly, in the Anglo-Norman knight whose knighthood indicated that he had successfully completed his military apprenticeship. At this stage, knighthood indicated a specialized form of military expertise; it had not yet provided a mark of social distinction.[12] This continued to be the case for as long as the knight's function remained essentially military and for as long as his equipment consisted of the mail shirt or hauberk, the simple conical helmet, the shield, lance, sword and axe and the comparatively light horse as depicted on the Bayeux Tapestry.[13] Although Sir James Mann suggests that the hauberk required skill and time to manufacture and was consequently an expensive piece of armour,[14] he perhaps over-estimates the cost of eleventh-century labour. In fact, a careful study of the evidence from Domesday Book reveals that serving knights could fund their profession from annual incomes of between 30s. and £2, that is, with the income from lands little more extensive than those of the wealthier peasants.[15]

By the late thirteenth century, however, the picture was quite different. The lightly armoured knight of the eleventh century

[11] Tawney, 'The rise of the gentry, 1558–1640', p. 4; Smith, *Land and Politics*, p. 65; L. Stone, 'Social mobility in England, 1500–1700', *Past and Present*, 33, 1966, pp. 17–21.

[12] Sir F. Stenton, *The First Century of English Feudalism 1066–1166*, 2nd edn, London, 1961, pp. 131–42; G. O. Sayles, *The Medieval Foundations of England*, 2nd edn, London, 1966, pp. 225, 230.

[13] Sir James Mann, 'Arms and armour', in *The Bayeux Tapestry*, ed. Sir Frank Stenton, London, 1957, pp. 56–69.

[14] *ibid.*, p. 63.

[15] S. Harvey, 'The knight and the knight's fee in England', *Past and Present*, 49, 1970, reprinted in *Peasants, Knights and Heretics*, ed. R. H. Hilton, Cambridge, 1981, pp. 145–51.

had been superseded by the knight bearing full body armour. First, the use of mail was extended to provide coverings for the legs, feet, arms and hands.[16] The conical helmet was replaced by the great helm which encased the entire head and face and most of the neck in iron. Plate metal was also used to provide additional protection to the elbows, knees and shins. The knight's horse, too, had become protected by armour so that it needed to be strong and heavy to carry the additional weight.[17] These developments raised the cost of equipping a knight by as much as fivefold to tenfold, which, one historian has suggested, was much faster than the rate of increase in the income derived from land.[18]

While the cost of military accoutrements was increasing, impositions did not end there. The actual ceremony of dubbing could be expensive, especially if it occurred at court, and the feudal incidents due from knights ensured that the financial demands were ongoing.[19] Furthermore, the burdens placed upon these later knights were never merely military and monetary. Increasingly, they were called upon to perform civil duties which, in the words of Stubbs, were 'severe and engrossing'.[20] Unlike his eleventh-century counterpart, the thirteenth-century knight needed wealth to support his calling, and his wealth, so the argument goes, transformed him into a man of considerable social standing.[21] His status was further enhanced by the administrative, judicial and police duties which fell to him. Look as we may for the gentry in the first one and a half centuries after the Conquest, we find only knights.

[16] A concise summary of armorial developments at this time may be found in H. M. Chew, *The English Ecclesiastical Tenants-in-Chief and Knight Service*, London, 1932, pp. 89–90. See, too, Sir James Mann, *European Arms and Armour*, 2 vols., London, 1962, I, pp. xxxii–li; C. J. Ffoulkes, 'European arms and armour', in *Social Life in Early England*, ed. G. Barraclough, London, 1960, pp. 126–7; C. Ffoulkes, *Armour and Weapons*, Wakefield, 1973, pp. 15–38.

[17] Harvey, 'The knight and the knight's fee in England', p. 170; Chew, *Ecclesiastical Tenants-in-Chief*, p. 90; J. E. Morris, *The Welsh Wars of Edward I*, Oxford, 1901, repr. 1968, p. 49.

[18] S. Painter, *Studies in the History of the English Feudal Barony*, Baltimore, 1943, pp. 41–2; N. Denholm-Young, *History and Heraldry 1254–1310*, London, 1965, pp. 19–20.

[19] M. Powicke, *Military Obligations in Medieval England*, London, 1962, pp. 69–70; F. M. Nichols, 'On feudal and obligatory knighthood', *Archaeologia*, 39, 1863, p. 214.

[20] Stubbs, *The Constitutional History of England*, III, p. 563; G. Lapsley, 'Buzones', *E.H.R.*, 47, 1932, pp. 193, 554, 565; McKisack, *The Fourteenth Century*, p. 189; Sir Maurice Powicke, *The Thirteenth Century, 1216–1307*, 2nd edn, London 1962, p. 539; R. F. Treharne, 'The knights of the period of reform and rebellion, 1258–1267: a critical phase in the rise of a new class', *B.I.H.R.*, 21, 1946–8, pp. 2–4.

[21] Harvey, 'The knight and the knight's fee in England', p. 172.

Nevertheless, by the mid-thirteenth century it was becoming increasingly clear that the knights alone were no longer equal to the tasks foisted upon them by the central government. Many, whose income would have supported knighthood, preferred to avoid the dignity, thereby escaping its more onerous obligations.[22] The resulting decline in the number of knights prompted government attempts to stem the tide by issuing writs of distraint.[23] No doubt, distraint of knighthood was initially designed to force men of substance to be dubbed in order to provide strenuous knights for the king's army. At the same time it ensured a supply of knightly officials, though it has been argued that at the outset the foremost consideration was to raise revenue from the fines.[24] Be that as it may, the major significance of distraint of knighthood is that it reveals official recognition of a group of men, akin to knights in wealth, but who were prepared to forego the status bestowed by knighthood. By the end of the thirteenth century these men were beginning to fill many of the administrative, judicial and legislative positions formerly reserved for belted knights.[25] In them we see the genesis of the later medieval esquires, though it was as late as 1370 before the notoriously conservative heralds gave esquires their own idiomorphic stamp of social approval.[26]

In the fourteenth century we therefore find knights and esquires whom historians sometimes refer to as 'the gentry'.[27] Yet, this medieval gentry patently fails to mirror the model created for the sixteenth century with its trinity of knights, esquires and gentlemen; the gentleman appears to be missing. Unfortunately, he is not to be found in the French *gentil-homme* either, for in the fourteenth century *gentilis* and *nobilis* were interchangeable terms

[22] Denholm-Young, *History and Heraldry*, p. 158; Powicke, *The Thirteenth Century*, pp. 539–41; Ferguson, *The Indian Summer of English Chivalry*, pp. 4, 13.

[23] Nichols, 'On feudal and obligatory knighthood', pp. 202–4; F. M. Stenton, 'The changing feudalism of the middle ages', *History*, n.s., 19, 1934–5, p. 299; N. Denholm-Young, 'Feudal society in the thirteenth century: the knights', *History*, n.s., 29, 1944, p. 116.

[24] A. L. Poole, *Obligations of Society in the XII and XIII Centuries*, Oxford, 1946, p. 4. For the opposing view see Powicke, *Military Obligations*, pp. 73–4; Powicke, *The Thirteenth Century*, p. 546.

[25] Nichols, 'On feudal and obligatory knighthood', pp. 201, 224.

[26] N. Denholm-Young, *The Country Gentry in the Fourteenth Century*, Oxford, 1969, p. 4.

[27] Stubbs, *The Constitutional History of England*, III, pp. 544–75; Saul, *Knights and Esquires*, p. 30 and *passim*.

which were equally applicable to an esquire and an earl.[28] Despite the claim that 'nobility had parted company with gentility' by the second half of the fifteenth century, the heralds, even as late as 1530, appear to have been unaware of the separation.[29]

'Gentleman', as a term of worship, does not, in fact, begin to appear until after the Statute of Additions of 1413 which stipulated that original writs and indictments should record the status of defendants.[30] But the Statute of Additions notwithstanding, as a description of rank and status, the use of the term, 'gentleman', was adopted haltingly and with some confusion, as the omission of status and the procession of *aliases* in the Pardon Rolls reveal.[31] We need to be wary, therefore, about welcoming too readily the newly found gentleman into the bosom of the fifteenth-century gentry.

This outline of the development of a status group, the gentry, should reveal that the term is exceedingly flexible in meaning. For historians of the fourteenth century, knights and esquires constituted the gentry; for historians of the sixteenth, the gentry consisted of knights, esquires and gentlemen. But the student of the fifteenth century is in a particularly invidious position. Should he, like his fourteenth-century counterpart, though with less justification, ignore gentlemen altogether? Or should he adopt the sixteenth-century model of the gentry and include gentlemen, even though they were only just beginning to join their superiors, the knights and esquires? Personal preference initially favoured the latter option but, as we shall see, the dilemma eventually resolves itself.[32]

If deciding what constituted the fifteenth-century gentry poses difficulties, the task of isolating the determinants of gentry status is even more perplexing. The Statute of Additions fails to shed light on the problem, as does the law in general. Indeed, it has long been recognized that there was no legal distinction between free men of

---

[28] G. R. Sitwell, 'The English gentleman', *The Ancestor*, 1, 1902, pp. 68–71; A. R. Wagner, *English Genealogy*, London, 1960, pp. 105–6.

[29] McFarlane, *The Nobility of Later Medieval England*, p. 275; A. R. Wagner, *Heralds and Heraldry in the Middle Ages*, 2nd edn, London, 1956, p. 77.

[30] Storey, 'Gentlemen-bureaucrats', p. 90; Sitwell, 'The English gentleman', pp. 64–5, 73.

[31] For omissions of status see, for example, the Pardon Roll of 1450, where the status of William Manston and John Septvans is unstated (*C.P.R.*, 1446–52, p. 373). That each may have been at least of esquire status see *P.P.C.*, VI, pp. 287–9. For the use of *aliases* see Storey, 'Gentlemen-bureaucrats', pp. 93–5.

[32] See below, pp. 43–4, 49.

gentle, and those of non-gentle, status.[33] While the laws were silent on the issue, Sir John Fortescue, that fifteenth-century repository of legal, constitutional and probably archaic wisdom, is no more forthcoming. His reference to the knight (*miles*), the esquire (*armiger*) and the non-gentle franklin as being 'well-off in possessions'[34] not only ignores the gentleman altogether but is also notable for its lack of precision.

Nevertheless, Fortescue does alert us to the dangers of relying on economic considerations as a determinant of social status. He considers £5 per annum to be 'a feyre lyvynge ffor a yoman',[35] but also draws attention to the many yeomen (*valetti*) who could spend in excess of £100 per annum.[36] Given that distraint of knighthood was levied on those with incomes of £40 and more, some yeomen, despite their social inferiority, were, by Fortescue's reckoning, economically superior to many knights. The point that income is an uncertain guide to status is reinforced by the Leicestershire material where we discover that in 1436 Robert Barnevile and John Blaby each had declared incomes of £6 per year. However, while Barnevile was regarded as a yeoman, Blaby was reported to be a gentleman.[37]

A herald's grant of coat armour is hardly a determinant of status either. While these grants announced that a family belonged to the gentry, the grant itself did not so much confer status but was, instead, a formal recognition of one's social position. Similarly, the proposition that if one lived like a gentleman and if one were reputed to be a gentleman, then one was a gentleman[38] would make just as much logical and historical sense were it turned on its head. But William Harrison's oft-quoted aphorism that whoever 'will bear the port, charge and countenance of a gentleman [will be] reputed for a gentleman ever after'[39] exposes the nub of the problem. It reveals that even in the late sixteenth century, a gentleman was recognized instinctively, intuitively. Objective

[33] Sir F. Pollock and F. W. Maitland, *The History of English Law before the Time of Edward I*, 2nd edn, 2 vols., Cambridge, 1923, I, pp. 407–11.

[34] Sir John Fortescue, *De Laudibus Legum Anglie*, ed. S. B. Chrimes, Cambridge, 1942, repr. 1949, pp. 68–9.

[35] Sir John Fortescue, *The Governance of England*, ed. C. Plummer, London, 1885, p. 151.

[36] Fortescue, *De Laudibus*, pp. 68–9. The term *valetti* could conceivably be translated as 'esquires', though, given the context, Chrimes' translation, 'yeomen', seems preferable.

[37] E179/192/59; C.P.R., 1446–52, p. 534; *ibid.*, 1436–41, p. 6.

[38] Mingay, *The Gentry*, p. 2; Du Boulay, *An Age of Ambition*, p. 70; Wagner, *English Genealogy*, pp. 111, 129.

[39] Quoted in Mingay, *The Gentry*, p. 2.

measures of status were elusive in the fifteenth century, too; they can scarcely prove to be less so to modern historians. This is not to suggest that there was no link between income and status but merely that the link can not be reduced to a simple mathematical equation.

The difficulties involved in delineating the gentry in theoretical terms are legion, but if we move to the concrete and attempt to isolate those families of fifteenth-century Leicestershire which were accorded gentle status, the undertaking is no less daunting. Heralds' visitations which, despite their shortcomings, may have provided a starting point, do not exist for the county in the fifteenth century.[40] In the absence of any contemporary or near-contemporary register of the shire's social elite, one must turn, therefore, to a variety of material the original intent of which was quite different from our own purposes.

As it was a function of the gentry to perform the duties of local government, one possible approach would be to recognize those who held local offices as constituting the country gentry. These would include sheriffs, knights of the shire, justices of the peace, escheators, commissioners of array, coroners and tax collectors. However, two problems immediately present themselves. In the fifteenth century, Leicestershire and Warwickshire shared a common sheriff and escheator so that although some of these officers were members of the Leicestershire gentry, others came from the neighbouring county. Also, there is always the danger that in concentrating upon the office holders alone, one will focus attention not on the representatives of the gentry as a whole but on a sub-set of the gentry, those work-horses of local administration, the *buzones*.[41] Furthermore, one must bear in mind that even substantial gentlemen may not have played a consistently active rôle in local government.[42]

In order to overcome the latter problem, it is necessary to turn to the tax returns surviving for Leicestershire in the period 1422–85. The most helpful of these is the graduated income tax of 1436 which was granted by parliament in December 1435 to finance the war effort in France.[43] The tax was levied on net incomes

---

[40] For the deficiencies of heralds' visitations see A. Everitt, *The Community of Kent and the Great Rebellion, 1640–60*, Leicester, 1966, pp. 33–4 n. 3.
[41] Lapsley, 'Buzones', *passim*.   [42] Richmond, *John Hopton*.
[43] For this and what follows, see *Rot. Parl.*, IV, pp. 486–7.

exceeding £5 per annum and derived not only from freehold land but also from annuities and offices. Contributions to the tax were scaled according to income. Those who earned £5 per year paid 2s.6d. plus 6d. for every pound between £5 and £100; income between £100 and £400 was taxed at 8d. in the pound while those who earned over £400 were taxed at 2s. in the pound on their entire income. The 1436 subsidy was therefore designed to tap the wealth of the nation and to provide a more equitable distribution of the tax burden than was achieved by the old fifteenths and tenths.

Although barons and other members of the nobility dealt directly with the chancellor and treasurer, the non-noble population was accountable to special commissioners appointed in the shires. These commissioners, 'certain sufficient persons by [the king's] counsel to be named',[44] were empowered to examine the county's freeholders and to assess and levy the subsidy. They were then required to make their returns to the Exchequer to which they also reported the names of defaulters.[45]

From the surviving returns to the Exchequer, it is clear that the commissioners or their clerks could exercise considerable discretion about the amount of information to be recorded and about the form in which that information was presented. For example, the return for the counties of Cambridge and Huntingdon includes names of freeholders arranged in columns, a list of the other counties where taxpayers held lands and an assessment of their net income.[46] The return for Derbyshire and Nottinghamshire is likewise arranged in columns and includes not only the taxpayer's net worth but also calculates the amount payable.[47] In this case, too, the clerk seems to have intended to include the names of other counties where the taxpayer held freehold land but, after doing so for Thomas Blount, he clearly recognized the extra effort such prolixity would involve; he did not provide the same information about the remaining taxpayers. The Lincolnshire return similarly omits mention of holdings in other counties but, once again, lists the names of freeholders in columns on the left hand side of the manuscript, followed by their

[44] *Ibid.*, p. 486.
[45] The names of defaulters are to be found in E179/240/269 where the clerk provided a note if payment had been made in another county.
[46] E179/240/268.
[47] E179/240/266.

net income and subsidy payable on the right hand side.[48] This return is also noteworthy in that it assesses many incomes down to shillings and pence whereas most returns, including that for Warwickshire and Leicestershire, report incomes rounded off to the nearest pound.

The commissioners for Warwickshire and Leicestershire were much less concerned about superfluous detail or even about the neatness of their return than the commissioners for Derbyshire, Nottinghamshire, Lincolnshire, Huntingdonshire or Cambridgeshire. Their return eschewed the use of columns; it failed to enrol other counties where taxpayers held land, and the calculation of the amount of subsidy levied on each freeholder was not recorded.[49] Nevertheless, the Leicestershire section of the return provides us with names of those persons in the county whose declared net income was at least £5 per annum from freehold land, annuities and fees. These names can be supplemented by those of the county's tenants-in-chief, found in the subsidy on knights' fees collected in 1428.[50] Unfortunately, details of the 1450 graduated income tax have not survived for Leicestershire.[51] Nevertheless, the family names gleaned from the 1428 and the 1436 subsidies, along with those who accepted the burdens of local government office, provide us with our starting point of 249 families of either gentry or potential gentry status. This total excludes sheriffs and escheators whose appointment was based on their standing in Warwickshire rather than Leicestershire; non-Leicestershire justices of the peace have also been omitted.[52]

It would be unwarranted to claim that all those of gentle status have been included in this number, that all who have found a place in the total belonged to the gentry or, even if their gentle status be accepted, that they can be counted specifically among the members of the Leicestershire gentry. For example, the Danvers family not only failed to aspire to government positions within

---

[48] E179/136/198.
[49] E179/192/59.   [50] *Feudal Aids*, III, pp. 118–26.
[51] R. Virgoe, 'The parliamentary subsidy of 1450', *B.I.H.R.*, 55, 1982, p. 125.
[52] Sheriffs: Lists and Indexes, IX, pp. 145–6. Knights of the shire: *Return*; Wedgwood, *Register*. Justices of the peace: *C.P.R.* Escheators: *List of Escheators for England*, A. C. Wood, compiler, typescript volume, P. R. O. Round Room, London, 1932, pp. 170–1. Commissioners of Array: *C.P.R.* Coroners: *C.C.R.*; *C.P.R.* Tax collectors: *Feudal Aids*, III, p. 106; E372/275 MS 45v; E179/241/368; E179/133/72, 82, 86; *C.F.R.*

the shire but also managed to avoid detection in the tax returns. Their inclusion among the 249 is based on the chance survival of a charter of 1458, to which John Danvers, esquire, of Swithland, acted as a witness.[53] His presence serves as a reminder that others of his status may have left no record whatsoever. Also, the Pykewell family is included because Margaret Pykewell was taxed on her income of £5 in 1436.[54] However, she was the widow of John Pykewell, the merchant and wool-packer from the borough of Leicester, and can not, therefore, be included among the county gentry.[55] Still others, about whose status there can be no such reservations, must be rejected on the basis that their holdings in Leicestershire were secondary to more extensive manors held in other counties. Sir Thomas Grene, for example, falls into this category. He derived an income, probably in excess of £15-6-8, from his manor of Kegworth and lands in Claxton and Long Whatton.[56] Nevertheless, his social interactions and political activities were confined to Lincolnshire and Northamptonshire where most of his lands were situated. He was certainly a gentleman, but not of the Leicestershire gentry. These considerations, combined with a paucity of contemporary references to some families, demand that the task of exclusion, already begun with non-Leicestershire sheriffs, escheators and justices of the peace, be extended to a further seventy-six families.

Of the remaining 173 families, listed in appendix 1, fourteen provided at least one knight in the period 1422–85 and another thirteen families were sufficiently wealthy for their heads to become knights had they wished to do so.[57] At least one of these distrainee families had provided a knight by 1487 when Thomas Pulteney was dubbed at the coronation of Elizabeth of York.[58] However, throughout the period under consideration, the Pulteneys must be counted among the potential, rather than actual, knights.

The incomes of twelve of the fourteen knightly families is known, with all earning at least £40 per annum. This sum was regarded at the time as the minimum required to support the dignity. Little can be said with certainty about the incomes of the

---

[53] L.R.O. 5D33/108/87.   [54] E179/192/59.

[55] *Calendar of Plea and Memoranda Rolls Preserved among the Archives of the Corporation of the City of London at the Guildhall*, A.D. *1413–1437*, ed. A. H. Thomas, Cambridge, 1943, p. 249; *Village Notes*, VI, p. 242.

[56] C140/13/21.   [57] E372/275; E372/284; E159/234; E159/242; E159/243.

[58] W. A. Shaw, *The Knights of England*, 2 vols., London, 1971, I, p. 142.

remaining two families, the Hastingses and the Neeles. Sir Richard Hastings held lands in Northamptonshire and Yorkshire as well as Leicestershire and Warwickshire.[59] In 1436, the tax commissioners for Northamptonshire reported to the Exchequer that he had failed to appear before them but a clerk later recorded that Hastings had been assessed in Yorkshire.[60] Unfortunately, the enrolled account for Yorkshire has not survived.[61] The inquisitions held after the deaths of Sir Richard Hastings and his brother, Sir Leonard, in 1436 and 1455 respectively, are no more helpful. Both inquisitions outline the extent of Hastings holdings but fail to indicate their value.[62] The most that can be said about Sir Richard's income is that he was wealthy enough to lend the king £106-13-4 in 1436 towards the cost of the wars in France and that this sum matched the amount lent by Bartholomew Brokesby whose income was £230 per annum.[63] The family, therefore, probably ranked as one of the wealthiest in Leicestershire, even before its windfall of grants made by a grateful Edward IV.

No such assumption can be made on behalf of the Neele family. Sir Richard Neele's association with the law was, doubtless, a lucrative source of income. In 1469, when he was justice of the king's bench, Richard was granted 110 marks yearly 'for the better maintenance of his estate'.[64] But, in the absence of any tax assessment, the most that can be said about the family's economic status, as opposed to Richard Neele's personal earnings, is that it enjoyed an income of at least £40 per annum.[65]

If we allow Sir Richard Neele and Sir Richard Hastings incomes of £40 and £200 respectively,[66] then the median income for the knightly families is £100 per annum with a mode of £103 per annum. It follows, therefore, that three knightly families, the Erdyngtons, the Shirleys and the Hastingses, possessed economic resources which set them apart from

---

[59] C139/83/58.   [60] E179/240/269.
[61] H. L. Gray, 'Incomes from land in England in 1436', *E.H.R.*, 49, 1934, pp. 610–11, 611 n. 1.
[62] C139/83/58; C139/162/22.   [63] *P.P.C.*, IV, pp. 323–4.
[64] *C.P.R.*, 1467–77, p. 176.
[65] The first reference to Richard Neele comes in 1442 when he served as knight of the shire and justice of the peace in Leicestershire (Wedgwood, *Register*, p. 31; *C.P.R.*, 1441–6, p. 437; E101/590/34). He later served on the king's bench and in the court of common pleas (E. Foss, cited in *T.L.A.S.*, 17, 1931–3, p. 3). For judges' incomes see below pp. 74–5.
[66] Statistically, the exact, amounts are irrelevant to the argument which can tolerate, in the case of Hastings, a deviation of between − 10 per cent and + 100 per cent (£180–400) and, in the case of Neele, a deviation of + 125 per cent (£40–£90).

the others. Their incomes were about twice that of their nearest rivals and their lofty economic position is partly reflected in the ties of marriage they formed with members of the nobility.[67]

Between the actual and potential knightly families there lay a wide economic gap. The median incomes for distrainees was £40 per annum which is less than half the median for their knightly counterparts. Nevertheless, it has to be admitted that the highest income recorded for any of the Leicestershire gentry, of whatever status, belonged to a member of this group. In 1436, Bartholomew Brokesby paid tax on £230 but he consistently refused to assume knighthood. The reasons for this deprecation remain uncertain. Obviously they were not economic. Nor can Brokesby be accused of attempting to shirk his political responsibilities. He represented the county as knight of the shire in five parliaments between 1422 and 1432, laboured on numerous commissions and was not only appointed to, but regularly served on, commissions of the peace.[68]

But although Bartholomew Brokesby was the equal of the greater knights in economic terms, it must be noted that in the 1436 return, his income of £230 was recorded in two separate amounts of £100 at the head of the list of Leicestershire taxpayers and of £130 at the very end.[69] One of these sums, probably the former, clearly refers to Brokesby's income from freehold land while the other amount may have derived from fees and annuities. Brokesby certainly had a long career of service to the social, political and even clerical elite. He had been executor to both Thomas Arundel, archbishop of Canterbury, and Joan Beauchamp, lady Abergavenny, and had also been one of the latter's feoffees and a beneficiary under her will.[70] In the late 1430s and early 40s we find him acting as a feoffee for James Butler, earl of Ormond.[71] Another Leicestershire taxpayer, Walter Keble,

---

[67] Thomas Erdyngton married Joyce, granddaughter and coheir of Hugh, lord Burnell (G.E.C., II, p. 435, n. f.). Sir Richard Hastings married Elizabeth, daughter of Henry, lord Beaumont, while his brother, Sir Leonard Hastings, married Alice, daughter of lord Camoys (Bell, *The Huntingdon Peerage*, p. 12). Ralph Shirley's second wife was Elizabeth, sister of Walter, lord Mountjoy (Nichols, II, pp. 716–17). The issue of gentry marriage with members of the nobility is discussed more fully in chapter 6.

[68] *Return*, pp. 302, 308, 313, 316, 321; C.P.R., *passim*; E101/590/34.

[69] E179/192/59.

[70] C67/38, MS 27; C.P.R., 1422–9, p. 486; Dugdale, II, p. 1032.

[71] C.P.R., 1429–36, p. 506; *ibid.*, 1436–41, p. 435.

whose income was also derived from, and recorded under, two separate sources, earned £100 as a feoffee for Butler's son and heir.[72] It is unlikely that Brokesby, acting in a similar capacity for the father, should have earned anything less. If this is the case, then at least £100 and possibly £130 of Brokesby's income was personal to himself; his reported income does not reflect the economic status of the Brokesby family in the long term. There is, therefore, no justification on the basis of wealth in allowing to the Brokesbys membership of the tiny elite of greater knightly families.[73]

More surprising than the wealth of Bartholomew Brokesby, however, is the discovery that four of the distrainee families whose representatives were taxed in 1436 admitted to incomes well below the anticipated £40 per annum.[74] Of course, Henry VI's government was not averse to using what Fortescue called 'exquysite meanes'[75] to raise revenue. Yet it is inconceivable that the authorities should have wished further to alienate the political nation by attempting to collect fines illegally from esquires earning less than £40. Parliamentary opposition to distraints was sufficiently vocal to ensure caution on that point.[76] Even if we concede that annual variations in income were inevitable, this provides an inadequate explanation for such a wide discrepancy between the £40 accepted as a minimum for distraint and the declared incomes of these four families.[77] One can only conclude that some commoners were, not surprisingly, as adept as the baronage at concealing their wealth from tax assessors.[78] The same conclusion is suggested by the rounded figures given for earnings and the suspiciously high cluster of incomes, about a third, of £5. The tax assessments should therefore be regarded as indicating minimum income.[79]

Once again, there is no justification for viewing the lesser distrainees along with the lesser knights as a distinct

---

[72] E179/192/59.
[73] As would occur under Gray's classification of greater knights, actual and potential (Gray, 'Incomes from land in England in 1436', p. 623).
[74] Astley, Hotoft, Malory and Wyvyll.
[75] Fortescue, *Governance of England*, p. 119.   [76] *Rot. Parl.*, v, p. 20.
[77] For their declared incomes see appendix 1.
[78] See T. B. Pugh and C. D. Ross, 'The English baronage and the income tax of 1436', *B.I.H.R.*, 26, 1953, pp. 1–28.
[79] Tax was payable in a single county though income may have derived from several. This arrangement enabled taxpayers to conceal the extent of their external income from the

group.[80] If we omit the greater actual and potential knightly families from our calculations,[81] then the median income for lesser potential knights was still less than half that for the lesser actual knights.

Although the distrainees were accorded the status term, 'esquire', there was just as wide an economic gap between them and ordinary esquires as existed between knights and potential knights. Forty-six families provided mere esquires in the period 1422–85 and the incomes of thirty of these, or just over 65 per cent, is known. Owing to the greater size of this group, the imperative to estimate the unknown incomes is not as categorical as it was with the knights and distrainees. The known incomes of the esquire families ranged from £6 to £54 per annum with a mode of £26 and a median of £20. The median income for mere esquires was therefore half that for distrainees.

This orderly regression down the social scale is destroyed once we move beyond the esquires. Most surprising of all is the economic chasm which separated them from the gentlemen. The highest recorded income for the latter group was the assessment of £8 for Thomas Herdewyn. The modal income was only £6, less than a quarter that for the esquires, and many gentlemen earned as little as £5. Indeed, one suspects that some gentlemen whose incomes were not recorded earned less than £5 per annum. In fifteenth-century Leicestershire there was, therefore, little economic distinction between gentlemen and the wealthier peasantry. For the purposes of comparison, this sub-gentry group has been included in appendix I.

A further unexpected revelation relates to the size of the group of mere gentlemen. Only fourteen families can be identified as belonging to this sub-set and, in the case of at least two, their status was equivocal. In 1416, Thomas Noveray was described as a husbandman, but by 1419 he was regarded as being of gentle status.[82] Also, in 1454, when Thomas Sampson received his pardon for not appearing before a court, he was referred to as a

---

local commissioners. There are, of course, other limits to using the 1436 tax return to establish a register of gentry families. Those whose annual income fell below £5 did not pay tax and are therefore not recorded. Furthermore, rarely do the returns record the status of taxpayers.

[80] Gray, 'Incomes from land in England in 1436', p. 623.
[81] That is, Erdyngton, Hastings, Shirley and Brokesby.
[82] *Village Notes*, III, p. 24.

yeoman.[83] Nevertheless, three years earlier, in a charter dated 1451, he had been termed a gentleman.[84]

Contemporaries in the fifteenth century were clearly uncertain about who should be admitted to the gentry at the group's lowest level. Indeed, for those aspiring to gentle status, the process of acceptance by their would-be peers may have taken some years and spanned more than one generation. But these considerations hardly explain why the number of mere gentlemen should appear so low. A more likely explanation is to be found in the nature of the evidence used. It will be recalled that our register of families was compiled from the subsidy on knights' fees collected in 1428, from the graduated subsidy on incomes collected in 1436, from those who were fined for failing to accept knighthood and from those who did accept the burdens of local administration. It is not so much the case, therefore, that our net has been cast insufficiently wide; it may be the case, however, that we have not trawled deeply enough or, perhaps, that the weave of our net has been too open to entrap the smaller fry, the lesser gentry. Either way, it appears that for practical reasons the fifteenth-century gentry must be regarded as encompassing knights and esquires. But we should be cavalier indeed were we to consign the mere gentlemen to historical oblivion solely on the basis of an analysis of their income. To add depth to our image we now need to examine the gentry's tenure of land.

[83] *C.P.R.*, 1452–61, p. 182.   [84] *C.C.R.*, 1447–54, p. 277.

3

LAND AND INCOME

The distribution of gentry estates within Leicestershire was very much a reflection of topographical realities.[1] The majority of their holdings were situated along the valleys of the Soar, the Wreake, the eastern Sence and the tributaries of these rivers and along the northern banks of the Welland in the south-east corner of Gartree hundred.[2] High concentrations of gentry estates also lay on the higher ground between Leicester and the Rutland border in the east and in southern Guthlaxton in the south. The region between Watling Street and the 400-foot contour east of Watling Street hosted modest concentrations of estates. But two areas of Leicestershire, Charnwood Forest, which spans the hundreds of Sparkenhoe and West Goscote, and the Vale of Belvoir, supported very few gentry holdings. In Charnwood's case, topographical features were the major determinant; its rocky outcrops, thin soils and poor drainage made early settlement and later subinfeudation unattractive, though the wastes of surrounding manors did extend into it.[3] The absence of gentry estates in the Vale of Belvoir was, however, a product of the region's domination by lord Roos's honor and lordship of Belvoir which included the manors of Barkestone, Plungar, Bottesford, Redmile and Harby and lands at Normanton and Easthorpe.[4]

Much of the gentry's wealth was derived from these lands, either in the form of rents or by the direct use or sale of the land's produce. The differentiation among the various gentry groups which we have already witnessed in relation to income should,

[1] See maps 1, 4–7.
[2] To confuse matters, Leicestershire has two rivers called Sence. The reference here is to the Sence which rises in the east of the county and flows westwards, entering the Soar about a mile from Blaby. The second, or western, Sence rises in the Charnwood region, flowing south-west into the Anker river. See map 1.
[3] Dury, *The East Midlands and the Peak*, p., 28; *T.L.A.S.*, 15, 1927–8, pp. 2–32.
[4] C139/104/39; *C.P.R.*, 1461–7, p. 352; *ibid.*, 1467–77, p. 27; Nichols, II, pp. 18, 38, 105, 300.

therefore, find further reflection in the extent and wider distribution of their estates. In order to test the validity of this assumption, one is forced to adopt the practice of counting manors. Of course, historians now recognize that the value of a manor depended not only on the variables of size and topography but also, to some extent, on the managerial skills of its lord.[5] But three further sources of difficulty have greater relevance to our present purposes. First, it is not always possible to determine whether a particular tract of land can be classed as a manor.[6] Second, an estate was rarely a static entity. It was added to through marriage, purchase or royal grant, while depletions resulted from sales, gifts to children, usually younger sons and daughters, or by confiscation.[7] Such changes to the estate can make the counting of manors a frustrating exercise. A third difficulty arises from the fact that the gentry often held manors in neighbouring or more distant counties. Any analysis of their Leicestershire properties will not, therefore, provide a complete picture of the landed foundations of their status within the shire. Despite these problems, a study of the gentry's manorial holdings reveals a close correlation between land distribution and status.[8]

Although the overwhelming majority of knightly, distrainee and esquire families possessed at least one manor in the county, the most extensive estates belonged mainly to the knightly families. Close to 60 per cent of this group held between three and seven manors in Leicestershire and all had additional manors in other counties. Usually, these 'foreign' manors were situated in two or three neighbouring shires but occasionally they were more widely scattered. The Shirleys, Ferrerses and Trussells owned estates spanning six, seven and nine counties respectively.

Among the distrainees and esquires, Thomas and John Boyville, Thomas Palmer, Thomas Everyngham and John Merbury controlled estates as extensive as those of some of the knights. Generally, however, both these groups lagged well behind their knightly superiors. The Boyvilles and Palmers excepted, of the remaining distrainees, over 83 per cent held between one and

---

[5] Cooper, 'The counting of manors'.

[6] The Belgrave family's holdings in Belgrave fall into this category. These holdings were classed as a manor by the early sixteenth century but there is no direct evidence that they were designated as such in the fifteenth.

[7] Thomas Palmer was associated with no fewer than six manors but he never held more than five at any one time and, for most of our period, he had only four manors in hand.

[8] Appendix 3 provides details of manorial holdings.

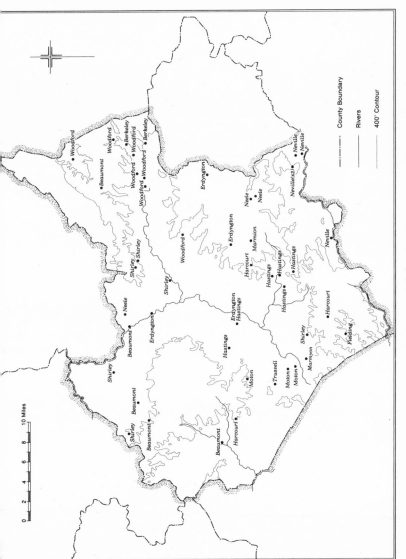

Map 4 Knightly Manors

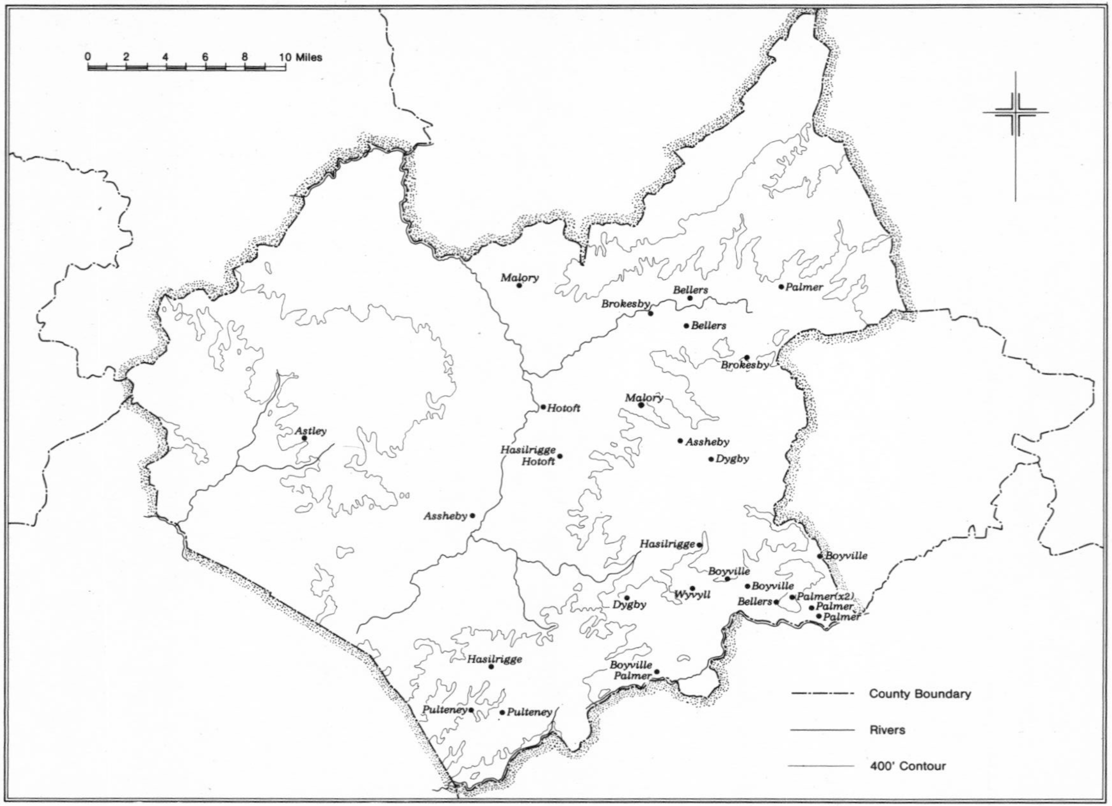

Map 4. Distinctive manors

Legend:
- — · — · — County Boundary
- ———— Rivers
- ———— 400' Contour

Scale: 0 2 4 6 8 10 Miles

Place names shown on map:
Palmer, Brokesby, Bellers, Bellers, Brokesby, Ashbeby, Digby, Malory, Malory, Boyville, Palmer, Palmer, Bellers, Boyville, Hasilrigge, Wyvill, Digby, Boyville, Palmer, Hotoft, Hasilrigge, Hotoft, Ashbeby, Hasilrigge, Pulteney, Pulteney, Astley

three manors in Leicestershire and only two-thirds of distrainee estates extended beyond the county boundary, invariably into a single neighbouring shire. The esquires were even less well endowed with landed possessions. Over 90 per cent of esquires held two manors or fewer in Leicestershire and in over 50 per cent of cases their estates were confined entirely to the county.

The most surprising feature to emerge from our analysis of the tenurial qualifications of the gentry relates to the gentlemen at the lower end of the social hierarchy. Only one family in this group held lands identifiable as a manor, namely the senior branch of Farnhams who held a manor at Over Hall in Quorndon. In part, the problem of determining the manorial status of some parcels of land may account for our unexpected revelation, though it seems odd that this particular difficulty should surface only in relation to the gentlemen. It is more likely that just as there was little economic distinction between mere gentlemen and the wealthier of their non-gentle social inferiors so, too, there was little tenurial distinction between them either.[9] In most cases, it was tenure of a manor and the exercise of lordship which such tenure involved that distinguished the gentry from non-gentry.

As a general rule, the greater the number of manors held by a family in Leicestershire, then the more scattered was the estate. As most knightly families had between three and seven manors, they therefore had a greater tendency to have scattered estates (arbitrarily defined as three or more manors or clusters of manors situated at least 6 miles from each other) than the non-knightly gentry. The Shirley family's holdings in Leicestershire fall into this category. Their manor at Staunton Harold formed one nucleus, Long Whatton a second; a third nucleus was a cluster of manors consisting of Ratcliffe-on-Wreake, Ragdale and Willows, while Dunton Bassett formed a fourth. Between a third and a half of knightly families held scattered estates though less than a tenth of distrainees and mere esquires did so.

About half the knightly and distrainee families held what may be termed a double-nucleated estate consisting of two manors or two clusters of manors at least 6 miles apart. The Malorys' manors of Walton-on-the-Wolds and Croxton, which were 9 miles apart, formed this type of holding. Also, twice during the fifteenth century, Thomas Palmer possessed a double-nucleated estate,

---

[9] See above, p.43. Leicestershire was, of course, part of the Danelaw which, in general, 'was a region full of small landholders' (*Documents Illustrative of the Danelaw*, p. xlviii).

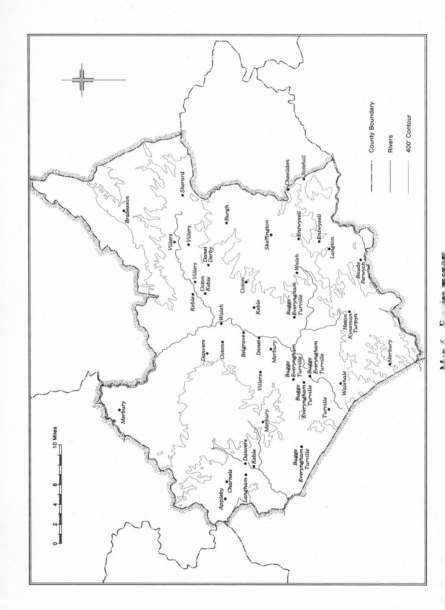

Map 6. Fenland manors

Legend:
- - - - - County Boundary
——— Rivers
——— 400' Contour

0 2 4 6 10 Miles

Brabeston
Sherrard
Villers
Villers
Villers
Burgh
Coton
Keble Danet
Keble Derby
Merbury
Coton
Walsh
Keble
Sheffington
Danvers
Cotone
Belgrave
Danet
Merbury
Villers
Merbury
Bugge
Everyngham
Turville
Bugge
Everyngham
Turville
Merbury
Danvers
Keble
Bugge
Everyngham
Turville
Appleby
Charnels
Longham
Walsh
Entwysell
Entwysell
Langton
Chesilden
Sotehill
Bugge
Everyngham
Turville
Bugge
Everyngham
Turville
Turville
Walshale
Heton
Kynnersman
Turpyn
Baude
Penwoch
Merbury

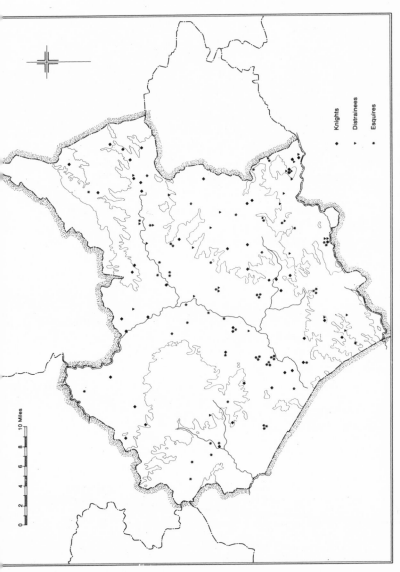

Map 7   Gentry manors – a collation of knightly, distrainee and esquire manors

Knights

Distrainees

Esquires

0 2 4 6 8 10 Miles

first, from 1442, when he purchased the manor of Lubenham, until 1450, when he then granted the manor to his daughter and son-in-law, Katherine and William Neville.[10] The second occasion was between 1462 and 1467 when the crown temporarily granted him lord Roos's confiscated manor of Freeby.[11] For most of his life, however, Palmer had a compact estate in Leicestershire consisting of four manors at Holt, Prestgrave and Drayton, all within 2 miles of each other. Most of the esquires possessed compact estates, too, though in their case these were often based on a single manor.

This admittedly 'bird's-eye' view of gentry holdings tells us nothing about how their estates were organized and managed. Nor does it indicate how the gentry were affected by, and reacted to, what has been variously described as a recession in agriculture, or, more extravagantly, as an economic crisis.[12] Especially after the Black Death, prices of some agricultural products fell, labour became scarce and rents were reduced to attract a dwindling pool of tenants.[13] In response to changed economic circumstances, the greater landlords, the nobility and larger religious institutions retreated from labour-intensive, and therefore expensive, demesne farming and either converted their arable to pasture or, more usually, leased out their demesne to tenants.[14]

The Leicestershire nobility were certainly not isolated from these economic problems. The Beaumonts' manor of Whitwick had been worth £52-13-4 net in 1396. By 1413, four messuages had become decayed and the manor was then worth £43-6-8.[15] Fourteen years later, in 1427, twelve of its thirty-one messuages

[10] L.R.O. DE220/58; *C.C.R.*, 1441–7, p. 117.

[11] *C.P.R.*, 1461–7, p. 182; *ibid.*, 1467–77, p. 43.

[12] C. Dyer, *Warwickshire Farming 1349–c. 1520. Preparations for Agricultural Revolution*, Oxford, 1981, p. 1; M. M. Postan, *The Medieval Economy and Society*, London, 1972, p. 174.

[13] Dyer, *Warwickshire Farming*, pp. 1–10; M. M. Postan, 'Medieval agrarian society in its prime: England', *The Cambridge Economic History of Europe*, 2nd edn, Cambridge, 1966, I, pp. 595–600.

[14] Hilton, 'Medieval agrarian history', pp. 181–5; F. R. H. Du Boulay, 'Who were farming the English demesnes at the end of the middle ages', *Econ. Hist. Rev.*, 2nd ser., 18, 1965, pp. 443–55; B. Harvey, 'The leasing of the abbot of Westminster's demesnes in the later middle ages', *Econ. Hist. Rev.*, 2nd ser., 22, 1969, pp. 17–27; J. T. Rosenthal, *Nobles and the Noble Life 1295–1500*, London, 1976, p. 70; Hilton, *The Economic Development of Some Leicestershire Estates*, pp. 79–88.

[15] *T.L.A.S.*, 15, 1927–8, p. 238.

were in the hands of the lord for lack of tenants.[16] But Whitwick's decline in value did not end there; in 1464 it was said to be worth a mere £24-6-8.[17] In almost seventy years, the manor had dropped in value by about 54 per cent. Whitwick was not the only Beaumont manor to witness diminishing receipts. By 1413, the site of the manor of Loughborough, which formerly returned £4, was worth only £2 per annum and in the same year, four messuages which had once returned £4 were in a state of decay and worth nothing.[18] Other landlords besides the Beaumonts were also experiencing declining returns from their estates. In the year spanning 1399–1400, the minister's account for the duchy of Lancaster manor of Castle Donington showed a sum of £5-4-11½ for reduction and decay of rents, and a rental for the same manor in 1462 regularly reveals reductions in customaries of over 30 per cent.[19] At Enderby, the duke of Somerset's water mill which had once yielded £1-6-8 per year was reported to be in total ruin and therefore, one assumes, was worthless.[20] In order to compensate for declining rents and to reduce their rising labour costs, the nobility released further lands onto the rental market. Henry, lord Beaumont, was letting the site of the manor of Loughborough and his capital messuage at Ernesby by 1413 while William Zouche's entire manor of Claybrooke was leased by the middle of the century.[21]

Leicestershire religious houses were also affected by the changed economic climate. During the fifteenth century, Leicester Abbey retreated from demesne farming on most of its eleven manors in the county. By 1477 only the home farm and three nearby demesnes were still being cultivated; the demesnes of all the other manors had been leased. One would therefore expect a rise in rental returns but such was not the case. In 1341 the abbey's rents had yielded £266; in 1408 yields were down to £207; by 1477 rents returned only £177.[22] The abbey also declined as a wool producer. The treasurer's receipt roll of 1297–8 shows that wool sales amounted to £220-3-10 which Hilton calculates as equivalent to 35 per cent of the institution's income. In the mid-fourteenth century, sales of wool yielded about £200; by 1477

[16] C139/35/49 MS 6; E149/140/6.   [17] E153/1880 MS 2.
[18] *Quorndon Records*, p. 129.   [19] *T.L.A.S.*, 14, 1925–6, pp. 54, 59–61.
[20] H.M.C., *Hastings*, 1, pp. 346–7.   [21] L.R.O.5D33/177, fos. 4, 82.
[22] Hilton, 'Medieval agrarian history', pp. 182–4; Hilton, *Economic Development of Some Leicestershire Estates*, pp. 79–86 and *passim*.

this figure had dropped to £70 and by 1493 Leicester Abbey had ceased wool production altogether.[23] R. H. Hilton's conclusion that the economic situation of landlords was critical seems well-founded.[24] However, the question arises whether the economic situation of the lesser landlords, the gentry, was equally as critical as it appears to have been for the greater.

As it was their directly cultivated lands which provided the nobility with the flexibility to respond to the new economic dispensation, we should, perhaps, start with the demesne. Hilton has shown that for the early fourteenth century, the typical lay estate in Leicestershire consisted of manors which had small demesnes.[25] This feature continued into the fifteenth century and, although there was some room for isolated variations, generally there was little distinction between the size of noble and gentry demesnes. Lord Ferrers of Groby's manor at Lutterworth contained no demesne lands whatsoever.[26] But apart from Lutterworth, few manors had demesnes as small as the 30 acres at Braunstone or the 60 acres at each of Cotesbach and Hemington.[27] Most demesnes consisted of at least one carucate.[28] Lord Roos's manor of Bottesford had 150 acres (about $1\frac{1}{2}$ carucates) of demesne lands; Margaret Burgh's manor of Allexton, which passed to Anne Chesilden on Margaret's death, had 140 acres of arable in demesne; Richard Hastings' manor at Newton Harcourt had six virgates, or about 144 acres, of demesne while lord Ferrers' *caput* at Groby had a demesne consisting of 300 acres of arable.[29] The manor of Hallaton, part of a non-noble estate, had as many as 4 carucates (almost 400 acres) of arable but demesnes of this size, or larger, were rare.[30]

[23] Hilton, *Economic Development of Some Leicestershire Estates*, pp. 25, 28, 87.
[24] Hilton, 'Medieval agrarian history', p. 185.
[25] Hilton, *Economic Development of Some Leicestershire Estates*, p. 15.
[26] C139/119/33 MS 18. [27] C139/87/43 MS 16.
[28] Hilton takes a Leicestershire carucate to equal 96 acres ('Medieval agrarian history', p. 154) but as a carucate consisted of the amount of land which an eight-ox ploughteam could plough in a year, the measurement depended very much on contours and the heaviness of the soil. A carucate could equal as much as 120 acres; Sir Thomas Blount's virgate (4 virgates is taken as the equivalent of 1 carucate) at Allexton consisted of 30 acres of arable and $2\frac{1}{4}$ acres of meadow (*Village Notes*, 1, p. 14). The Hospital of Burton Lazars was given a half carucate of 35 acres in Newton Burdet in the twelfth century (*Documents Illustrative of the Danelaw*, p. xxxvii), making a 70-acre carucate.
[29] C139/140/39; L.R.O.5D33/177, fo. 15; C139/83/58 MS 5; C139/119/33 MS 18; C139/170/40 MS 7.
[30] L.R.O.5D33/176, fo. 57. In 1507, John Villers' manor of Hoby (Howby) consisted of

Hilton also concludes that in early fourteenth-century Leicestershire, labour services were light and that landlords therefore
relied heavily on wage labour.[31] This was also the case in the
fifteenth century. At Woodthorp there were thirty-two works,
sixteen relating to haymaking and sixteen for reaping corn in
August each year. Twenty-six works at Woodhouse were also
confined to reaping at harvest time, as were the eighteen works
on 4 virgates at Quorndon.[32] Admittedly, all of these works were
confined to lands belonging to the Beaumonts, a noble family,
but they cannot be considered as onerous. For the rest of the year
the Beaumonts needed to employ wage labour to perform such
farm tasks as driving stray animals off their waste at
Beaumanor.[33]

On gentry estates, villeinage was sufficiently rare to warrant
special mention when it occurred. Out of ten tenants on the
Ingleby fee of the manor of Hoby, only one, Thomas Webster, is
recorded in a rental as holding his messuage and single virgate by
villein tenure.[34] The gentry, like the nobility, relied overwhelmingly on wage labour. Ralph Shirley I's wage bill on the manor
of Barrow in Nottinghamshire amounted to 46s. 8d. in 1413–14,
and when John Farnham ploughed, planted and harvested crops
on his leased lands at Woodhouse he had to employ the labour to
do it.[35]

The gentry used their arable to produce a selection of grains and
leguminous crops. In addition to the spring crops of peas, beans,
oats and barley, John Farnham grew wheat, which is a winter
crop.[36] The pulses were probably used as winter feed for
Farnham's stock while the barley was important to gentry
households for producing malt for brewing.[37] A greater proportion of arable seems to have been devoted to spring crops than to
wheat, thereby making the three-field rotation of crops imposs-

---

800 acres of land (arable), 100 acres of meadow and 140 acres of pasture (*C.I.P.M.*, 22
Hen. VII, no. 329).

[31] Hilton, *Economic Development of Some Leicestershire Estates*, p., 15.

[32] C139/35/49 MS 6.   [33] *Quorndon Records*, p. 126.

[34] Bodl. Lib. Wood Empt. 7, fo. 143v.

[35] L.R.O.26D53/2194; *Quorndon Records*, p. 124.

[36] *Quorndon Records*, p. 124.

[37] For the Farnham family's stock, see below, p. 63. The manor at Staunton Harold
consisted of a kiln house containing a 'heyre', a horse-hair fabric used for drying malt
over the kiln, and a brewhouse (L.R.O.26D53/1949). It is not unusual to encounter
references to kilns or brewhouses in inquisitions *post mortem* (L.R.O. 5D33/176, fo. 57).

ible.[38] On the manor of Groby, however, the three-field system of rotation was practised; of the 300 acres of arable, 100 acres were allowed to lie fallow each year.[39] In this case the Ferrerses must have regularly reduced the extent of their spring planting which suggests that they had few stock to be carried over the winter or, perhaps, that they were able to buy fodder on the open market.

In the absence of consecutive runs of manorial documents relating to gentry estates, it is impossible to reconstruct a reliable representation of how they exploited their landed resources over an extended period. At best, as we have seen, we may occasionally glimpse some aspects of the economy of the estate or of some part of it for a particular year but it must be stressed that the picture we receive for that year is a static image which, in the long term, may be atypical. However, the little evidence at our disposal suggests that the gentry were experiencing the same difficulties as, and adopting similar strategies to, the greater landlords.

The knightly families, but particularly those who held scattered estates, were, like the nobility and monastic houses, retreating from direct demesne cultivation. As early as 1413–14, the demesnes of the Shirley manors at Shirley, Hope and Hoon in Derbyshire, Ettington in Warwickshire, Colston in Nottinghamshire, Barnham in Suffolk and Ragdale in Leicestershire had all been leased.[40] An indenture of 1457 reveals that Thomas Erdyngton's demesne at Braunstone was being leased by Richard Reynold of the same place. Reynold was not the first to farm the demesne there. Before 1457, the lessee was Thomas Clerk and Clerk's predecessor on the demesne had been William Hatter.[41] Erdyngton had evidently withdrawn from direct agricultural exploitation at Braunstone for many years. This policy of withdrawal from cultivation applied, too, to Erdyngton's manor of Barrow-on-Soar. The entire manor was leased in 1435 to Richard Harcourt, Thomas Farnham and three others for twenty years at an annual rent of £40.[42] The lessees' intention may have been to sub-let the demesne in smaller portions or they may have hired

---

[38] See *Quorndon Records*, p. 117; W. G. Hoskins, *The Midland Peasant*, London, 1957, p. 69; Hilton, *Economic Development of Some Leicestershire Estates*, pp. 52–3. Hilton argues in favour of a four-field system of rotation.

[39] C139/119/33 MS 18; C139/170/40 MS 7.   [40] L.R.O. 26D53/2194.

[41] L.R.O. DG5/2.   [42] H.M.C., *Hastings*, I, p. 72.

labour to work the land, thereby deriving their profits from its produce.[43] Either way, the arrangement reveals that the fifteenth-century gentry possessed the same capitalistic opportunism which is so highly valued in our own rapacious age. Richard Hastings was another who was leasing his demesne early in the century. In 1415 his capital messuage on the manor of Braunstone was farmed to two local husbandmen for nine years at an annual rent of £5.[44] It was not, then, just the distant demesne of scattered estates that was being leased. Braunstone was only about 2 miles from Hastings' *caput* at Kirby Muxloe.

For most of the gentry who held compact estates or single manors, leasing of the demesne, at least in its entirety, cannot have been a serious option. Their households still needed supplies of wheat for bread, barley for brewing and stock for meat and, of course, their stock required winter fodder. During times of uncertain prices, these needs could best be supplied by the direct exploitation of the demesne. Evidence for continued demesne cultivation and grazing is found in wills and inventories which frequently mention farm implements and stock.

In his will, John Hotoft referred to his 'crops in the ground' at Knebworth and his bequests included a cart, harness, carthorses, plough-horse, sheep and cattle.[45] Ralph Shirley III's manor at Staunton Harold carried two wains, nine horses, twelve draught oxen, two other oxen and a number of sheep and cattle.[46] In addition to wains and draught animals, a cryptic reference to two 'window sheets' and twenty-eight sacks stored in the kiln house suggests that Shirley was growing wheat. Window sheets may have been coverings for unglazed windows, though the need for such coverings in a kiln house seems unusual. They were more likely winnowing sheets used for separating chaff from grain. The sacks would have then been used to store the grain. Everard Dygby's estate also carried a wain as well as a plough, a pair of cart wheels, six plough-horses and various stock, while Ralph Woodford, Geoffrey Sherard, Thomas Pulteney and Thomas Keble all had sheep and cattle on their farms.[47] Although these references provide ample indication of continued cultivation and grazing of

---

[43] For the Farnhams' involvement in this sort of activity, see above, p. 55.

[44] H.M.C., *Hastings*, I, p. 25.   [45] PROB11/1/15/118.

[46] L.R.O. 26D53/1949.

[47] PROB11/16/11/81–1v; PROB11/11/23/183–3v; PROB11/9/23/176v–7; PROB11/15/24/193v; PROB11/12/3/22v–3v.

the demesne, the gentry's detailed and intimate knowledge of their implements and livestock testifies to the close interest they took in their agricultural capital.[48]

While the twin difficulties of the rising cost and shortage of labour could be alleviated by leasing demesnes, the gentry also encountered the problem of declining rents. Between 1414 and 1431, the Shirleys' receipts from rents were either stable, as on their manor of Hope, or else declined.[49] At Hoon, rents which had returned £18-18-4 in 1413–14, yielded only £17-18-6 by 1431, a fall of about 5 per cent. The decline in rents on the manors of Sheldon and Ratcliffe-on-Soar was 8 per cent and 11 per cent respectively. The two accounts of 1414 and 1431 fail to cover the same manors but if we omit returns for those manors which are not common to both, then total receipts had diminished by about 30 per cent in under twenty years. In six years, the rent on Margaret Flaunders' manor at Sheepy Parva declined from £2-16-8 in 1435 to £2-3-4 in 1441, a drop of about 24 per cent.[50] On the manors of Pippewall and Woodcote in Ashby de la Zouch, a decline in rent was accompanied by a longer lease. In 1410, the manors 'with all woods [and] demesne lands' were leased for twelve years at £2-6-9 per annum. At the end of these twelve years, the same lands were leased for twenty years at an annual rent of £1-4-0, a startling drop in return of 48 per cent.[51]

Longer leases were, of course, in the interests of the lessees who, if their leased lands required capital improvements, would expect security of tenure in order to reap the full benefits of their investments. That landlords expected improvements to be carried out can be seen in the abbot of Geronden's lease of the abbey's lands and tenements in Alton to Thomas Barwell of Odstone.[52] This lease was for sixty years but the first four years' rent was a nominal red rose per year followed by £1-18-4 in the fifth year and £3-1-0 each year thereafter. The low initial rent acknowledges capital outlay and minimal profits in the early stages of the lease.

Long leases could be in the lessor's interest, too. During times of

---

[48] For the personal concern of landlords with manorial administration see R. H. Britnell, 'Minor landlords in England and medieval agrarian capitalism', *Past and Present*, 89, 1980, pp. 7–8.

[49] L.R.O. 26D53/2194, 1980.   [50] *C.A.D.*, VI, C6536, C6529.

[51] H.M.C., *Hastings*, I, p. 6.

[52] *Ibid.*, p. 8. See, too, C. Dyer, 'A small landowner in the fifteenth century', *Midland History*, I, 3, 1972, p. 10.

falling rents it was preferable to have a tenant paying an agreed sum which was assured and would not be gradually reduced over a period of years. The alternative of empty tenements or falling rents with each new lease was an unattractive option. But long leases had serious disadvantages as well. Rents had to be sufficiently low to attract lessees. There was also a greater risk with long leases that the lessee would try to over-exploit his tenement. Edith Waryn, who leased lands in Thorpe Arnold for life from William Assheby of Welby, was charged with causing wastes and destruction to houses there.[53] Furthermore, the lessor needed to consider whether a long lease would reduce his flexibility if the economic pendulum were to swing back in favour of higher prices for demesne produce or of higher rents.

It appears, therefore, that the financial plight of the gentry was as critical as that of the nobility. But appearances can be deceptive. Given the relatively small size of the gentry demesne, a greater proportion of its produce was destined for consumption within the household rather than for the market. The conventional wisdom is that the gentry were therefore less likely to feel the effects of falling prices for demesne produce.[54] This argument has much to commend it. Rarely does one form the impression that the gentry were seriously affected by any economic recession and, except in the unusual case of Thomas Erdyngton who leased out the demesne on his *caput* at Barrow-on-Soar, rarely do we find the entire demesne on home farms being leased.[55] Nevertheless, the gentry's comparative prosperity cannot be explained solely in terms of a buffer provided by demesne cultivation for home consumption.[56] Prosperity and subsistence farming rarely, if ever, co-exist.

We should not assume that rents or demesne produce constituted the only source of profit from land. In the *de banco* rolls, pleas of damage to trees and woods reveal that timber was an important economic resource. In 1428, John Bellers claimed that his oaks, ash, whitethorns and blackthorns on his land at Sutton Cheney had been damaged to the value of 40s. by four husbandmen from nearby Cadeby.[57] Earlier in the century, John Farn-

---

[53] *Village Notes*, IV, p. 273.
[54] Postan, 'Medieval agrarian society in its prime', pp. 596–7, Postan, *Medieval Economy and Society*, p. 174.
[55] H.M.C., *Hastings*, I, p. 72.
[56] For gentry expenditure, an indicator of prosperity, see below, chapter 7.
[57] L.R.O. 5D33/172.

ham's loss had been even greater. Trees worth £20 had been cut down and carried away from Quorndon in 1405.[58] The Farnhams in fact seem to have been uncharacteristically careless with their timber, though their losses are also an indication of the difficulties involved in protecting this particular resource. About thirty years later, Robert had £5 worth of trees stolen from Quorndon in 1434, and the following year Robert's uncle, Thomas, accused his life tenants at Loughborough, Robert and Eleanor Walker, of making wastes, sales and destruction of land, houses, woods and gardens contrary to law.[59] Among their numerous crimes, the Walkers had felled twenty ash trees, ten pear trees and ten apple trees worth a total of 40s. Of course, it was in the claimant's interest to exaggerate the value of his loss but his plea at least had to be credible.

When the gentry were able to realize their profits from timber before it fell prey to the criminally inclined, the rewards could be substantial. In 1459, John Shirley sold to Thomas Stokes and John Forster for £20 the right to cut and cart wood and underwood between Staunton Harold and Ashby de la Zouch.[60] While sales of this order may not have provided a regular income, it is worth noting that £20 was the equivalent of about two years' income from Shirley's manor of Whatton. Sir Roger Swillington of Nottinghamshire also found his oaks in Priorwood in Leicester Forest an occasional, but highly lucrative, source of income. He sold the right to cut branches of oak there for two years, earning himself in the process the notable sum of 50 marks.[61] On the manor of Barrow-on-Soar, the sale of 3,700 faggots, *lez polles* (poles), underwood, toppings and clippings of trees, bark and hedge grossed £11-14-0, or over 13 per cent of the manor's total receipts.[62] References to branches, poles, toppings, clippings and underwood indicate the practice of coppicing or harvesting rather than wholesale destruction of stands of timber.[63]

---

[58] *Quorndon Records*, p. 123.

[59] L.R.O. 5D33/172; *Quorndon Records*, pp. 139, 140.

[60] L.R.O. 26D53/504. John Forster, yeoman, had been appointed James Ormond's bailiff for Ashby de la Zouch in 1445 during pleasure at 2d. *per diem*; the appointment was later made for life. Forster was also one of Bartholomew Brokesby's feoffees while Thomas Stokes acted as feoffee for Thomas Erdyngton (H.M.C., *Hastings*, I, pp. 1, 2, 155, 300; Bodl. Lib. Wood Empt. 7, fos. 164v–5r, mispaginated as 183v–4r).

[61] H.M.C., *Hastings*, I, pp. 22–3.

[62] *Quorndon Records*, p. 164.

[63] For the long survival of coppicing see J. Creasey, 'Industries of the countryside', *Seasons of Change. Rural Life in Victorian and Edwardian England*, ed. S. Ward, London, 1982, pp.

Almost all references to sales and thefts of timber apply to the area west of the Soar, especially on the edges of Charnwood and Leicester Forests. Stands of trees in the east of the county tended to be small. One of the largest of these stands was Thomas Palmer's 80 acres of wood centred on his cluster of manors around Holt in the far south-east.[64] The manor of Hallaton in the same area had 15 acres while Allexton boasted a mere 4 acres of wood.[65] Further north, the Dygby's manor of Tilton had 30 acres of woodland and there were also 30 acres on the Shirley manors of Willows and Ragdale.[66] The economic value of these small eastern woods was measured in shillings rather than pounds.[67]

Minerals were another source of income exploited by the gentry, though returns from these were considerably more modest than from timber. Ralph Shirley I's stone quarry (*minera petrarum*) at Barrow in Nottinghamshire made 8s. from sales in 1413–14.[68] Within Leicestershire itself, the range of minerals was more varied and included stone, coal, lime and slate. Coal had been mined in the county as early as the thirteenth century but even by the fifteenth, its economic significance had not yet become apparent.[69] On the manors of Pippewall and Woodcote the lessee's rights to coal seem to have been added to his lease as an afterthought and were lumped together with rights over stone.[70] Clearly, the area's ample supplies of wood reduced the attractiveness of coal, and professional colliers, whose presence would indicate increasing mining activity, do not appear in the records until the 1490s.[71] Limestone, however, was more valuable. The manor of Barrow-on-Soar supported eighty-five lime pits which in 1481 returned £2-16-8 from sales.[72] There were also slate pits at Barrow but in 1481 they returned no profit. Nevertheless, back

81–3. I am indebted to Mr David Kent for drawing my attention to this reference.

[64] L.R.O. 5D33/174, fo. 263.

[65] L.R.O. 5D33/176, fo. 57; L.R.O. 5D33/177, fo. 15.

[66] L.R.O. 5D33/177, fo. 24; L.R.O. 5D33/86, fo. 1.

[67] The 15 acres of wood at Hallaton returned 8s. 4d. per year (L.R.O. 5D33/176, fo. 57).

[68] L.R.O. 26D53/2194.

[69] C. Owen, *The Leicestershire and South Derbyshire Coalfield, 1200–1900*, Ashbourne, 1984, p. 20.

[70] H.M.C., *Hastings*, I, p. 6.

[71] Owen, *The Leicestershire and South Derbyshire Coalfield*, p. 22.

[72] *Quorndon Records*, p. 164. Lime from Barrow was being sold to build lord Hastings' new residence at Kirby Muxloe (M. W. Beresford and J. K. S. St Joseph, *Medieval England. An Aerial Survey*, Cambridge Air Surveys, II, Cambridge, 1958, p. 57).

in 1428, William Richmount, slater of Leicester, had been paid £1 per year over twenty years to re-roof with slate all the buildings on Thomas Beaumont's manors of Overton and Goadby.[73] Richmount's slate could have been bought from either Barrow or Swithland. As in the case of timber, the shire's mineral resources were confined to the region west of the Soar.

In the east of the county and along the Soar and other river valleys, the numerous rivers, brooks and streams provided fish as well as sites for water mills. Once again, as with timber, the worth of fishing rights occasionally appears through the charges of theft brought before the court of common pleas. At Long Whatton, on one of the Soar's tributaries, fish valued at £5 was stolen from Thomas Assheby, while Hugh Boyville helped himself to £10 worth of fish from Elizabeth Scrope's 'separate fishing' at Great Bowden on the Welland.[74] Early in the century, on the manor of Castle Donington, fishing rights were let to farm together with mills, probably on the river Trent, for £12-4-4 per annum.[75] Thomas Palmer also owned two mills at Holt which he leased to a local miller for £3-16-8 per annum, though in this case the indenture of lease fails to specify whether the mills were water, wind, or horse powered.[76]

The enterprising Hastings family managed to acquire a water mill where none had existed before. In 1439, Sir Leonard Hastings leased a site for a water mill at Ravenstone to John Hyne for life at a yearly rent of 6s.8d. and two capons. In return, Hyne was to erect a mill with flood gates. Just over eighteen years later, by which time the parties to the original agreement were both dead, we find Sir Leonard's son, William, leasing the now-completed water mill for eighteen years at an annual rent of 13s.4d.[77] The sums involved were admittedly a miniscule proportion of Hastings' total income, but to acquire an economic asset which returned an increasing income without making any capital outlay whatsoever calls not only for business acumen but also for imagination.

Sales or leases of timber, minerals, fishing rights and mills never rivalled receipts from rents. Nevertheless, they did provide an additional dimension to the gentry's income. At the same time

---

[73] H.M.C., *Sixty-Ninth Report (Middleton)*, London, 1911, p. 109.
[74] L.R.O. 5D33/172.   [75] *T.L.A.S.*, 14, 1925–6, p. 54.
[76] L.R.O. DE221/4/1/101.   [77] H.M.C., *Hastings*, I, p.11.

they reveal the gentry's readiness to tap diverse sources of revenue in order to maintain their flexibility in uncertain economic times. Diversity, flexibility and opportunism are particularly apparent in the gentry's willingness to channel their activities towards animal husbandry, most notably sheep, but also cattle and pig, farming. A combination of horses and oxen had always been needed to work the demesne arable while a small number of cows and ewes and fat cattle were kept to supply the household with milk, cheese, butter and meat.[78] These draught animals and milch cows continued to feature in wills and inventories until the end of the century and beyond.[79] However, there are few references to larger herds and flocks until around the middle of the century when the gentry must have begun to convert to grazing on a more commercial scale.

Compared to the size of some monastic flocks which were numbered in thousands, the scale of the gentry's enterprise was apparently small.[80] Even by the early sixteenth century, Ralph Shirley III's entire flock at Staunton Harold numbered only 140 sheep.[81] Thomas Farnham was grazing 200 sheep at Woodhouse in 1448.[82] Three years later, Farnham's nephew, Robert, appears to have been breeding sheep for he had 200 'little lambs' at Hoton, Prestwold, Burton-on-the-Wolds and Cotes.[83] Thomas Pulteney was also breeding sheep, and bequeathed in his will a total of seventy ewes and lambs.[84]

Although the gentry's conversion to pastoralism would at first have been tentative, these figures probably underestimate the full extent of gentry sheep farming. Robert Farnham's 200 lambs indicate a flock of at least 400 if we assume one ewe for every lamb. Furthermore, wills refer to only a proportion of the testator's livestock. For instance, Geoffrey Sherard bequeathed sixty ewes 'of my best' but made no reference to lambs, rams, wethers or lesser quality sheep whose existence is nevertheless implied.[85] Similarly, Everard Dygby refers to twelve ewes, sixty

---

[78] Ewes' milk as well as cows' milk was used to make cheese (R. Trow-Smith, *A History of British Livestock Husbandry to 1700*, London, 1957, p. 119).

[79] See, for example, L.R.O. 26D53/1949; PROB11/16/11/81.

[80] Hilton, *Economic Development of Some Leicestershire Estates*, p. 67.

[81] L.R.O. 26D53/1949.   [82] *Quorndon Records*, p. 144.

[83] *Ibid.*, pp. 145–6.   [84] PROB11/15/24/193v.

[85] PROB11/9/23/176v–7.

of his best sheep and to 'the residue' but he provides no indication of how extensive that residue may have been.[86]

T. H. Lloyd's study of the wool trade in the late middle ages reveals that throughout the first half of the fifteenth century, wool prices were depressed.[87] Net losses on the duchy of Lancaster and Burton Priory's sheep farms in Berkshire and Gloucestershire in the 1430s and 40s warn us that conversion to sheep pasture was therefore by no means a panacea for the economic ills which beset landlords. But we should not assume that the Leicestershire gentry turned to sheep farming in desperation or that they suffered from the vagaries of the market in the same way as large-scale wool growers.[88] Initially producing on a more limited scale, the gentry had less to lose if wool prices fell, and by breeding their own stock they were well placed to increase or decrease the size of their flocks according to the demands of the market. By the later decades of the fifteenth century we find the gentry responding to those market demands by greatly increasing their involvement in animal husbandry.

According to an inventory taken at Thomas Keble's death in 1500, he had flocks totalling over 3,600 sheep on his Leicestershire lands and manors.[89] These flocks, together with wool-clips in hand, were estimated to be worth £228-10-1, or about 70 per cent of the total value of Keble's stock, equipment and farm produce in store. The scale of his enterprise obviates any suggestion that Keble was turning to sheep farming in desperation. Throughout the 1470s, 80s and 90s, he single-mindedly and vigorously pursued a deliberate policy of investing heavily in his chosen venture by buying land to support his flocks.[90]

Under the terms of Richard Hotoft's putative will, Keble had first inherited lands in Stretton but thereafter he extended his holdings by purchase and lease.[91] The Hotoft manor of Humberstone was originally alienated to John Staunton after Richard

[86] PROB11/16/11/81v.
[87] T. H. Lloyd, *The Movement of Wool Prices in Medieval England*, Economic History Review Supplement 6, Cambridge, 1973, pp. 24–9.
[88] Lloyd argues that 'a healthy rent roll was ... preferable to the risky business of sheep farming' and that landlords turned to pastoralism in desperation (*ibid.*, p. 29).
[89] The inventory (Wilts. Rec. Off., 88:5/17a MSS 1–4) is printed in *Common Lawyers*, pp. 432–47.
[90] *Ibid.*, pp. 332–9.   [91] C1/42/89–92.

Hotoft's death but Thomas Keble later purchased it from John's brother, Thomas.[92] Another Staunton manor, Congerstone, was bought from Thomas Staunton's 'cousin' and heir, Edward Churche.[93] Lands in Hamilton, where the village had been abandoned as early as 1450 and later enclosed for pasture by the Willoughbys of Wollaton, probably in the 1470s, were sold to Keble in 1495.[94] About ten years before Hamilton was acquired, Keble had leased Potters Marston from the Benedictine priory of St Mary in Coventry.[95] By 1500, this manor was stocked with 429 wethers.

In converting to pasture, Keble was both imitator of, and an example to, other landlords.[96] He was certainly not the first to recognize the profitability of pastoralism. As early as 1461, Thomas Assheby's manor of Lowesby had 600 acres of pasture and 230 acres of meadow.[97] The acreage of pasture was extended in 1487 when the village of Lowesby itself was enclosed.[98] Much the same process occurred on the Turpyns' manor of Knaptoft where the 100 acres of meadow and 600 acres of pasture referred to in a fine of 1507 were the product of enclosure of the village.[99] John Turpyn acquired the manor by marriage in 1465 and the process of change must have begun shortly after that date for, in 1482, he had 150 head of stock grazing there.[100] But the extent and obvious fruitfulness of Keble's conversion to pasture must also have acted as a beacon to attract others to adopt his policy. On Sir Thomas Pulteney's two manors of Misterton and Pulteney there was no arable land by the early sixteenth century. Misterton consisted of 100 acres of meadow and 800 acres of pasture worth £45-2-0 per annum, while the manor of Pulteney had 1000 acres of pasture worth £40.[101]

The procedure adopted by Thomas Pulteney to effect the changeover to pasture is unknown but evidence relating to other manors indicates that there were two basic patterns of change. On

---

[92] C1/58/322. [93] *C.I.P.M.*, 17 Hen. VII, no. 497.
[94] W. G. Hoskins, *Essays in Leicestershire History*, Liverpool, 1950, pp. 74–5.
[95] *Common Lawyers*, p. 344.
[96] For the gentry's readiness to imitate their neighbours' practices see M. Beresford, *The Lost Villages of England*, London, 1954, p. 211.
[97] L.R.O. 5D33/174, fo. 264v. [98] Hoskins, *Essays*, p. 81.
[99] *Ibid.*, p. 96.
[100] *Village Notes*, v, pp. 391–2; *Pedigrees*, pp. 44–6; L.R.O. 5D33/172.
[101] *C.I.P.M.*, 22 Hen. VII, no. 204.

the countess of Shrewsbury's holdings at Bittesby, the process was gradual until, in 1488, the last remaining 150 acres of arable were converted to pasture.[102] On John Villers' manor of Brooksby, however, action was taken quickly and decisively on 6 December 1492. On that day, four farms, involving 160 acres of arable, were enclosed.[103]

Of course, not all pasture was devoted to sheep farming. Thomas Keble owned 158 assorted bullocks, steers, cows and heifers pastured at Lubenham, Potters Marston, Thrussington, Hamilton and on his *caput* at Humberstone.[104] The presence of cows and heifers indicates that Keble was also breeding his own stock. Ralph Shirley III grazed 60 steers at Staunton Harold, and John Turpyn, in addition to his 100 sheep at Knaptoft, kept 50 steers there, too.[105] William Belgrave had a herd of unknown size but its existence was a source of annoyance and financial loss to Belgrave's neighbours whose crops were dispastured and trampled.[106]

It is doubtful that these cattle herds were intended for the London market. First, the herds were too small and, second, professional drovers whose presence in large numbers might indicate a thriving cross-country trade were not particularly numerous in Leicestershire.[107] Small herds suggest that the cattle were intended to feed the household and to supply the local markets at Market Harborough and Leicester where there was a growing demand for hides to sustain the expanding leather industry.[108]

Despite even this later fifteenth-century scramble to convert to

---

[102] Hoskins, *Essays*, p. 93; Beresford, *Lost Villages*, p. 210 citing E368/314 Eas. m.15.

[103] Hoskins, *Essays*, p. 98; *The Domesday of Inclosures 1517–1518*, ed. I. S. Leadam, 2 vols., London, 1897, Kennikat repr., Port Washington, NY, 1971, I, p. 237. It is impossible to say how much of Leicestershire had been enclosed by the time the commissioners of enclosures visited the county in August 1517. Leadam calculates that in the hundred of Gartree, for which the commissioners' returns are fullest, 1.32 per cent of the land had been enclosed, all of it for pasture (*Domesday of Inclosures*, I, p. 222). In Framland, for which the record is incomplete, 330 acres were enclosed, all of it for arable. These Framland enclosures account for only 11 per cent of total enclosures recorded by the 1517 commission, the remaining 89 per cent being for pasture (88.9 per cent) and parks (0.1 per cent).

[104] *Common Lawyers*, pp. 440–2.

[105] L.R.O. 26D53/1949; L.R.O. 5D33/172.

[106] *Village Notes*, VI, p. 85; *T.L.A.S.*, 16, 1929–31, p. 60.

[107] For Leicestershire drovers see, for example, *C.P.R.*, 1436–49, p. 327; *ibid.*, 1461–7, p. 318.

[108] *V. C. H. Leics.*, IV, pp. 37, 41–2.

pasture, the gentry still did not totally abandon direct cultivation. At Potters Marston, Thomas Keble maintained two draught oxen, though his inventory makes no mention of a plough there.[109] If he had to lease a plough then it is unlikely that more than a few acres were devoted to cultivation. On his eastern property at Hamilton, however, more extensive cultivation is indicated by the ten pairs of draught oxen and seven working steers. About a mile away, on Keble's *caput* at Humberstone, there were three wains, two ploughs and six horses. As efficient ploughing was achieved by hitching a combination of horses and oxen to the plough, there must have been exchanges of draught animals and equipment between Hamilton and Humberstone.[110] Keble's crops included 18 acres of barley in the ground at Humberstone and a quarter of malt in 'the gardener'. A 'litell stakke' of wheat, estimated at four quarters, was stored in the barn. However, as one would expect, most arable was devoted to the production of pulses for fodder. Fifteen quarters of peas worth 30s. were already in storage at Humberstone in July. The Pulteneys, too, in spite of the lack of arable land on their main manors at Misterton and Pulteney, were able to continue cultivation at nearby North Kilworth, South Kilworth, Cotesbach and Cotes Devil, all within a 3-mile radius of Pulteney.[111]

Evidence for swine herding is less plentiful than it is for pastoralism. As pigs are notoriously destructive of both pasture and arable, we would expect herds to be confined to the wastes of Charnwood and Leicester Forests where acorns were in plentiful supply.[112] John Farnham of Quorndon kept swine at Barrow-on-Soar on the edge of Charnwood but the size of his herd, if indeed it was a herd, is not recorded.[113] We do know, however, that Sir Robert Moton of Peckleton owned a swine herd. In 1462, Sir Robert's brother, Richard, quitclaimed to his widowed sister-in-law, Elizabeth, forty pigs on the Motons' manor of Cheadle in Staffordshire.[114] But there is no sign that the Motons reared pigs in Leicestershire, too. Nevertheless, circumstantial evidence

[109] *Common Lawyers*, p. 441.
[110] For ploughing, see Walter of Henley, 'Husbandry', in *Walter of Henley's Husbandry*, ed. E. Lamond, London, 1890, pp. 11–13.
[111] *C.I.P.M.*, 22 Hen. VII, no. 204.
[112] For sound advice on pig husbandry see Walter of Henley, 'Husbandry', p. 29; 'Seneschaucie', in *Walter of Henley's Husbandry*, pp. 113–15.
[113] *Quorndon Records*, p. 122.
[114] *C.C.R.*, 1461–8, p. 147. See, too, *T.L.A.S.*, 17, 1931–3, p. 129.

points to more widespread swine herding than these examples suggest. In 1492, a subsidy roll for the borough of Leicester refers to an area in the town called 'le swyne market'.[115] That a number of gentry were taxed on tenements in this area is hardly conclusive evidence of commercial pig production, but it certainly is suggestive of such.

Although the gentry's problems of declining rents, empty tenements and falling prices for arable produce were ameliorated by diversification and ultimately solved by those who expanded their pastures, a further response to dwindling receipts was to increase the size of the estate. There were a number of ways of achieving this solution but one of the quickest and least expensive was through marriage. Of five succeeding generations of Shirleys in the late fourteenth to the late fifteenth centuries, only one, John Shirley, failed to marry an heiress. Ralph I's father, Hugh, Ralph I himself, Ralph II and Ralph III all married heiresses, thereby extending the Shirley estate and, of course, adding to their income. Many other examples could be cited to illustrate the point but to avoid needless repetition we may confine ourselves to one further case, that of Margaret Bugge.[116]

Margaret, sister and heir of Baldwin Bugge, first married Richard Turville. The Turvilles held land at Normanton but their manor of Aston Flamville was a recent acquisition, gained through the marriage of Richard's father to the Flamville heiress. At the time of Margaret's marriage to Richard, probably some time before 1430, she had not yet succeeded to her brother's manors and lands. In fact, Richard Turville's premature death ensured that he never enjoyed the Bugge estate but he did sire a son, William, by Margaret. Having proved her capacity to bear children, Margaret next attracted the attention of Reginald Moton whom she later married. Reginald was more fortunate than Richard in that he had the use and profits of Margaret's five Leicestershire manors and extensive lands until his death in 1445. The twice-widowed Margaret, with an obvious aversion to solitary and celibate life, but also probably conscious of the need for a protector to secure the rights of her daughters by Reginald Moton against the chicanery of Reginald's father, Robert, then

---

[115] Bateson, II, pp. 332–4. Among those taxed in the swine market were Thomas Keble, Everard Fielding, Richard Belgrave, Everard Dygby, Thomas Villers, John Danet and Nicholas Temple.

[116] Other examples and references for the following may be found in appendix 3.

took Thomas Everyngham as her third husband. Everyngham also enjoyed the use and profits of his wife's inheritance until he, too, died in 1461. Her duty to wedlock and her daughters now fulfilled, Margaret lived on in widowhood until her own death in 1474. Her son, William Turville, at last entered on the Bugge inheritance.

In the course of the fifteenth century, two members of the gentry, Reginald Moton and Thomas Everyngham, had, through marriage, enjoyed the benefits and profits of the Bugge estate, albeit temporarily. The economic rewards of marriage for the Turvilles were less immediate but more durable. There can be no doubt that Margaret's long-postponed endowment of her first husband's family was responsible for the inclusion of her grandson, John, among the worthiest men of the shire in the reign of Henry VII, though it took another generation before the Turvilles attained the dignity of knighthood.[117]

Holdings were sometimes inherited from more distant kin. Richard Hotoft's kinsman, John Hotoft, who was possibly Richard's brother but more likely an uncle or a cousin, left him his lands in Stretton. Richard, in turn, bequeathed the same lands, so his beneficiary claimed, to his first cousin twice removed, Thomas Keble.[118] However, it was not a common practice for distant kin to be so charitable.

Those gentry who failed to secure an heiress or who lacked generous kinfolk could still expand their estate by purchase or lease or, as we have already witnessed in the case of Thomas Keble who bought the manor of Humberstone and leased the manor of Potters Marston, by a combination of both. The Palmers actually bought their way into the county in the early fifteenth century when Thomas's father, William, purchased the Trussel manor at Holt. Thomas later added to the estate by buying the second manor at Holt and manors at Drayton and Prestgrave with appurtenant lands at Cranoe, Bringhurst, Easton, Medbourne, and Burrough-on-the-Hill.[119] Palmer was still buying land in 1439 and 1442 when he acquired lands at Tugby, Goadby and

---

[117] B. L. Harl. 6166, fo. 60v; *W.H.R.*, no. 267. It will be appreciated that our intention here is primarily to show how the estate was extended through marriage. There can be no suggestion that marriages were contracted only in order to extend the estate. Marriage involved a wide range of motives which are discussed below, chapter 6.

[118] PROB11/1/15/118; C1/42/89–92. Also, see above, p. 64.

[119] L.R.O. 5D/33/174, fo. 255. See appendix 3 under Palmer.

Billesdon and the manor of Lubenham, about 2 miles west of Market Harborough.[120]

The Woodfords also owed their position among the county gentry to land purchases. In their case, the Leicestershire branch of the family was founded in the fourteenth century by John Woodford.[121] According to fifteenth-century family tradition, John, who lived to the ripe age of 'five score years and seven', was the son of a gentleman of Salisbury but had gone to Melton Mowbray where he married a merchant's daughter and heir. No doubt his wife's inheritance enabled John to buy his lands and manors in Melton, Brentingby, Burton St Lazars, Thorpe Arnold and Wyfordby. Capital was also probably amassed during John's war service in France where, again according to fifteenth-century tradition, he had fought at Poitiers and been present at the capture of Calais. For the remainder of the fourteenth century both John and his son, William, 'a fulle discrete man and sufficiently learned in the law', built on John's earlier foundation, adding the manor of Knipton and many smaller parcels of land in Framland hundred.

It was clearly not beyond the gentry's reach to buy entire manors. That they were able to do so suggests either the possession of liquid assets or access to credit or, perhaps, a combination of both. There was £22-10-6 in ready money at Staunton Harold when Ralph Shirley III died.[122] John Hotoft had even greater liquidity; in his will he could refer to 50 marks at his place in London and a further 200 marks stored in an 'iron bownden coffer' at Knebworth.[123] Hotoft also referred to 'all the dettys that be owyng in Essex' but failed to specify whether these debts were owed to him or whether he, himself, was the debtor. For the sake of his wife, who was bequeathed these debts, we can only hope that the former was the case. That most of the work of the court of common pleas involved the recovery of debts also points to the ready availability of loans.[124]

While some gentry could afford to buy whole manors, there can be no concealing the fact that such purchases were expensive. The manor of Humberstone, worth £20 per year, cost Thomas

[120] L.R.O. 5D/33/174, fos. 259, 260.
[121] B. L. Cotton Claudius, A XIII, fos. 3, 3v, 6, 9, 10v, 11, 8v–53v, 175 and *passim*.
[122] L.R.O. 26D53/1949.   [123] PROB11/1/15/118.
[124] See M. Hastings, *The Court of Common Pleas in Fifteenth Century England*, Ithaca, NY, 1947, pp. 8, 26–7, 237.

Keble 400 marks, or £266-13-4.[125] Many purchases of land were therefore on a less grand scale. In the fifteenth century, Sir Robert Woodford continued the policy of buying land begun by his great-grandfather and grandfather but his purchases were often of small plots, clearly designed to consolidate and round off the estate.[126] In 1433 he bought from Thomas Chancellor a croft and 3 selions of land in Wyfordby and half an acre in the fields at nearby Stapleford. Some years earlier, Woodford had also bought lands in Wyfordby from Geoffrey Poutrell.[127]

Bartholomew Brokesby similarly purchased small blocks of land, many of which abutted his own tenements. In 1428 he bought a toft lying between his own land and that of the prior of Launde in Frisby, and another toft was added to the first in 1435.[128] He also acquired five messuages, two tofts, 160 acres of land, 20 acres of meadow, 4 of pasture and 4d. rent in Frisby for 100 marks.[129] Brokesby made piecemeal acquisitions at Gaddesby as well. He first bought land there in 1431, adding 17 acres of land and pasture bought from John Swift in 1433.[130] In 1434 another 3 acres of land were purchased and then 'a place built on a site' bought from Alice Brokesby (obviously a relative) for 20s.[131] Small purchases continued to be added to the holding in Gaddesby until, by 1445, Brokesby's tenements there were returning £4-11-9 gross or £4-4-9 net in annual rent.[132]

We should not assume, therefore, on the basis of the incontrovertible evidence which points to falling rents, neglected and decaying tenements and declining receipts from sales of grain from individual manors that the gentry were financially embarrassed, let alone facing an economic crisis. Owning smaller and more compact estates than the nobility or large religious houses, they were better placed to take a direct interest in their affairs and to react to changing economic demands. By increasing the size of their estates, they were able to mitigate the consequences of declining rents; by fully exploiting whatever resources were

---

[125] C1/58/322.
[126] This process of consolidation and rounding off can also be seen in an arrangement between Richard Langham and John Marchall of Kilby. Richard granted John 'a little land, in exchange for other land there' (H.M.C., *Hastings*, 1, p. 100).
[127] B. L. Cotton Claudius, A XIII, fos. 57–7v.
[128] Bodl. Lib. Wood Empt. 7, fos. 160v–1 (mispaginated as fos. 180v, 182v), 163v.
[129] *Ibid.*, fo. 170.   [130] *Ibid.*, fos. 106, 132–2v.
[131] *Ibid.*, fo. 137v.   [132] *Ibid.*, fo. 139v. For additions, see *ibid.*, fos. 138–9v.

specific to their own manors and lands, they were protected against falling prices in other areas of the economy; and by converting their arable to pasture to graze both sheep and cattle, they not only solved the twin problems of empty tenements and shortage of labour, but they were also in the best position to benefit from the growing demand for wool and hides in the later decades of the fifteenth century.

Even if our study of the financial plight of the gentry were confined to a consideration of their estates, we should have good reason to feel confident about their economic well-being. However, although the estate was the gentry's major source of income, it may not have been the only source. K. B. McFarlane, in his analysis of the financial position of the higher nobility, cogently argues that it is a fallacy to propose that 'falling rents meant a poorer family'.[133] McFarlane's main concern was to illustrate the fact that among the nobility, their pool of estates became concentrated into fewer hands and that, therefore, 'their landed incomes were rising, not steadily but, more accurately, by leaps'.[134] As we have seen, some gentry families, such as the Shirleys and the Turvilles benefited in a similar way through advantageous marriages to heiresses. But McFarlane also draws attention to the nobility's extra-landed sources of income, particularly the rewards of war service abroad and of royal patronage at home.[135] We therefore need to consider whether the gentry, too, received income from beyond the confines of their own acres.

During the first half of the fifteenth century, the rewards falling to those who followed Henry V or the duke of Bedford to France could be substantial. William Worcester claimed that Sir John Fastolf won 20,000 marks in 1424 at the battle of Verneuil.[136] Even if Fastolf received only a small proportion of this glittering prize, he was still well recompensed for his efforts. Although it is impossible to provide an accurate tally of his receipts as a professional soldier, the remittances he regularly sent from France to his agents in England during the 1420s and 30s amounted to several thousand pounds. In the 1450s, Sir John claimed from Henry VI's treasury a further £11,000 as his due for war

---

[133] McFarlane, *The Nobility of Later Medieval England*, p. 186.
[134] *Ibid.*, p. 59.   [135] *Ibid.*, pp. 182–4, 194–5.
[136] McFarlane, *England in the Fifteenth Century*, p. 178.

services.[137] For such as he, 'the fortunes of war' clearly had a literal, as opposed to the more usual metaphorical, meaning.

There is no evidence, however, that the war enriched the Leicestershire gentry on the same scale that it advantaged Sir John Fastolf. Nevertheless, we may assume that the twenty-two members of the Leicestershire gentry who served in France between 1409 and 1475 received their share of the pickings.[138] For instance, Thomas Everyngham, like Fastolf, was also present at the battle of Verneuil where thirty-six prisoners were taken.[139] But even if the benefits of booty and ransom were denied to some, and there is no evidence for that claim either, then less spectacular gains were assured through wages. In April, 1419, Sir Richard Hastings received £42-9-4½ in wages for himself, five men at arms and eighteen archers for one eighth of a year's service.[140] Hastings was serving regularly in France; in 1416 he had agreed to take nine men at arms and eighteen archers for a quarter year at £2 per day for himself, 1s. for his men at arms and 6d. for his archers; and in 1421 his military services were again secured at the same fee for six months.[141] Ralph Shirley was also paid war wages of £111-1-0½ for himself, seven men at arms and twenty-three archers for a quarter year.[142] Admittedly, such sums did not make fortunes but they helped to ensure the gentry's continuing participation in a war in which riches could be found through ransoms and booty.

Although war indentures reveal that the Leicestershire gentry agreed to serve mainly for limited periods, the chances for reward needed to balance even these temporary periods of neglect of their estates. After Bedford's death, when the tide of war began to turn in France's favour, the prospect of large-scale gain diminished. The Leicestershire gentry became less willing to venture across the Channel, as revealed in the paucity of indentures and payments from the 1440s. But all passion for glory and,

---

[137] *Ibid.*, pp. 179–81.
[138] In 1409, Robert Woodford settled his affairs at home before heading for France (B. L. Cotton Claudius, A XIII, fo. 223). In 1475, William Trussell II indented to serve Edward IV, also in France (E101/71/6 MS 987). For fuller details of the twenty-two see appendix 3.
[139] *Letters and Papers Illustrative of the Wars of the English in France during the Reign of Henry the Sixth*, ed. J. Stevenson, Rerum Britannicorum Medii Aevi Scriptores, Rolls Series, 2 vols., London, 1861–4, II, pp. 394–5.
[140] Dunham, 'Lord Hastings' indentured retainers 1461–1483', p. 137.
[141] *Ibid.*, pp. 136, 139–40.   [142] *Stemmata Shirleiana*, p. 42.

73

perhaps, riches, was not entirely spent by 1453. At least one Leicestershire knight, Sir William Trussell, accompanied Edward IV to France in 1475.[143]

A more regular and secure income than that yielded by the uncertain outcome of war was provided by royal service at home. The Wardrobe Books of both Henry VI and Edward IV reveal routine payments of gifts and wages to gentry members of the household but the greatest gains were the result of occasional grants.[144] The king's knight, Sir Thomas Erdyngton, and his wife, Joyce, received James earl of Wiltshire's confiscated manor of Bordesley in Warwickshire from a grateful Edward IV.[145] Ralph Shirley II's office as esquire of the chamber also probably helped to secure him the duchy of Lancaster's wardenship of the forest of High Peak in Derbyshire which, in 1443, he farmed out for nine years at an annual rent of 40s.[146] Thomas Everyngham, another esquire of the chamber, was granted in 1460 the stewardship of Cottingham, *alias* Cottingham Soke, in Yorkshire and 10 marks per year as wages.[147]

While royal grants provided welcome additions to the gentry's income, the crown could resume them with ease. We have already seen how Thomas Palmer enjoyed the profits of lord Roos's confiscated manor of Freeby for five years.[148] However, the original grant had been for ten years.[149] Similarly, Thomas Everyngham's grant had been for life but, as the Yorkist regime exempted him from the pardon of 1461, it is clear that he did not long have the use of Cottingham's income.[150]

A third, and probably the most lucrative, source of non-landed income was through the legal profession. Over thirty Leicestershire gentry can be identified as having either legal training or legal knowledge.[151] One of these lawyers, Richard Neele, was appointed serjeant-at-law in 1463, king's serjeant in 1464 and a judge on the king's bench just before the readeption. When Edward IV returned to his realm in 1471, Neele was then transferred to the court of common pleas.[152] As early as July, 1461, the king had

---

[143] E101/71/6 MS 987; E101/70/6 MS 725.
[144] Wardrobe Books: E101/408–12, *passim*. For the fifteen Leicestershire gentry who were members of the household, see appendix 3.
[145] *C.P.R.*, 1461–67, p. 186.   [146] *Stemmata Shirleiana*, p. 43; Somerville, I, p. 568.
[147] *C.P.R.*, 1452–61, p. 580.   [148] See above, p. 52.
[149] *C.P.R.*, 1461–7, p. 182.   [150] Wedgwood, *Biographies*, p. 308.
[151] See appendix 3.
[152] E. Foss, *Biographia Juridica. A Biographical Dictionary of the Judges of England 1066–1870*, London, 1870, p. 474; *C.P.R.*, 1461–7, p. 387; *C.C.R.*, 1461–8, p. 173.

granted him a life annuity of £40 from the farm of Derby for unspecified service.[153] Thomas Keble was another who rose to the upper pinnacles of the law. He was appointed serjeant-at-law in 1486 and king's serjeant in 1495 and he served as justice of assize on the northern circuit.[154] Ives argues that a very junior judge might earn about £250 per year from fees, retainers and practice, while a king's serjeant earned in excess of £300.[155] Given these substantial rewards, it is not surprising that Thomas Keble could add so extensively to his estate.[156]

Except for Neele and Keble, the aspirations or abilities of most of the Leicestershire lawyers were more modest. Three men, Henry Sotehill, Richard Hotoft and Everard Fielding, were retained by the duchy of Lancaster, and Sotehill even rose to become king's attorney.[157] But most lawyers probably drew their fees from relatives, neighbours and acquaintances. Thomas Berkeley acted as his father's attorney, and Thomas Hotoft used his niece's in-laws, Robert and Thomas Staunton, as pleaders before chancery in his dispute with Thomas Keble.[158] As revealed in deeds, charters and wills, lawyers were also widely used by other gentry as feoffees, witnesses and executors. No doubt, in addition to their fees they received *douceurs* either as tokens of gratitude or, perhaps, as symbols of more sinister intent. Ralph Shirley II's gifts of a doe to Thomas Chatterley, clerk of the justice of assize, and a buck to the justice's son, arouse one's suspicions on that point.[159]

By grasping whatever economic opportunities were available, whether in war, in royal service or in the legal profession, many of the gentry were able further to augment their income from land and, in fact, to add to their holdings. This opportunism and diversity in their financial interests, combined with the flexible management of their estates, ensured that the gentry survived better than most, and certainly better than the major religious

---

[153] *C.P.R.*, 1461–7, p. 96; *C.C.R.*, 1461–8, p. 20.
[154] *Common Lawyers*, pp. 64–7. Keble had been retained by the duchy of Lancaster as legal advisor from 1478 before becoming the duchy's attorney-general in 1483 (Somerville, I, p. 406). He was also retained by the city of Coventry for an undisclosed fee and acted on its behalf in a dispute with Coventry Priory. The city later offered Keble the recordership – a post which he declined (*The Coventry Leet Book*, ed. M. D. Harris, London, 1907–8, Kraus repr., New York, 1971, pp. 477, 524–8).
[155] *Common Lawyers*, p. 323.   [156] See above, pp. 64–5.
[157] Somerville, I, pp. 425, 454, 564, 569, 570; *C.P.R.*, 1461–7, p. 475.
[158] C1/9/189; C1/40/290.   [159] L.R.O. 26D53/293.

houses, the economic rigours of the early fifteenth century. But the accumulation of capital and its investment in land and livestock promised not merely survival but burgeoning expansion during the century's closing decades. With a strengthening of the gentry's economic position we would also expect some flexing of their political muscle. Perhaps the audacity of the late sixteenth- and seventeenth-century gentry does not merely have its roots in the great plunder and redistribution after 1540 but can be traced back to the more prosaic realm of careful husbandry in the fifteenth.[160]

[160] See W. G. Hoskins, *The Age of Plunder*, London, 1976; Trevor-Roper, *The Gentry*.

4

A COUNTY COMMUNITY AND THE
POLITICS OF THE SHIRE

A possible hazard facing the historian who studies the gentry within the boundaries of a single shire is that the county itself may assume a greater significance in his thinking than it in fact possessed for the knights and esquires of the time. To express the problem another way, we may be tempted to assume that beyond the confines of their households and manors, the gentry saw themselves as part of a wider shire community. Yielding to such temptation is not entirely a self-indulgence, for the concept of a shire community was by no means foreign to contemporaries in the fifteenth century. From the point of view of the central government, the county was an administrative unit.[1]

In most cases, each of these units had its own sheriff. Admittedly, the sheriff was appointed by the king and accountable at the Exchequer but he was also drawn from the local community and, therefore, was sensitive to its needs. Even in those instances where two counties shared a sheriff, each had its own shire court to which members of the community owed suit. As the shire court's judicial function waned, local men still retained control over the administration of justice in their counties by being appointed to commissions of the peace. But the shire court continued to have a political rôle. Here, the county came together to receive information about government policy and to elect their representatives who would sit in parliament *pro communitate comitatus*.[2] These MPs were responsible for conveying the community's political voice to London, while the county in its turn assumed responsibility for paying their expenses. In addition, the county was taxed as a unit, with local men assessing individual taxpayers within its

---

[1] For the following see H. Cam, *Liberties and Communities in Medieval England*, Cambridge, 1944, pp. 236–47; Pollock and Maitland, *The History of English Law*, I, pp. 532–6; J. R. Maddicott, 'The county community and the making of public opinion in fourteenth-century England', *T.R.H.S.*, 5th ser., 28, 1978, pp. 27–43.

[2] Cam, *Liberties and Communities*, p. 236.

borders, collecting the levy and ensuring the safe delivery of monies to Exchequer officials.

Although there is no doubt that the county formed a clearly defined administrative unit, some historians have taken the matter further to argue in favour of a cohesive shire community. Sir Frederick Pollock and F. W. Maitland view the county as 'not a mere stretch of land, a governmental district; it is an organized body of men; it is a *communitatus*'.[3] Helen Cam also rejects any notion that the shire community was merely a convenient administrative construct designed to serve the needs of the central government. Instead, she sees it as 'an organism, a unit held together by proximity, by local feeling and above all by common living traditions and common responsibilities'.[4] J. E. A. Jolliffe similarly believes that 'common obligation created common outlook'.[5] Writing of the decades leading up to the 'Period of Reform' in the thirteenth century, J. R. Maddicott can point to 'the self-confident communities of the counties' whose assertiveness 'possessed an internal dynamic of its own, derived largely from the strength of the local community and from the leadership provided by a powerful knightly class'.[6] For these historians, the community of the shire had a real existence.[7]

However, that the gentry considered themselves to have been part of this shire community, let alone its leaders, is a proposition upon which opinion is now divided. Recent studies have suggested that the county had little or no part to play in determining the gentry's social or political affiliations.[8] According to these studies, social horizons were determined by the pattern of land-holding and by the kinship network, neither of which was influenced by administrative divisions. At the same time, the fundamental political unit was the aristocratic affinity which, depending on a magnate's territorial holdings, may or may not have coincided with the county boundary.[9] Nigel Saul, on the

---

3   Pollock and Maitland, *The History of English Law*, I, p. 534.
4   Cam, *Liberties and Communities*, p. 247.
5   J. E. A. Jolliffe, *The Constitutional History of Medieval England*, 4th edn, London, 1961, p. 307.
6   J. R. Maddicott, 'Magna Carta and the local community 1215–1259', *Past and Present*, 102, 1984, pp. 64, 63.
7   See Cam, *Liberties and Communities*, p. 236.
8   Wright, *The Derbyshire Gentry*, pp. 56–9; Astill, 'The medieval gentry', pp. 81–129.
9   Wright, *The Derbyshire Gentry*, pp. 57–8, Astill, 'The medieval gentry', pp. 120–2; M. Cherry, 'The Courtenay earls of Devon: the formation and disintegration of a late

other hand, while recognizing that retaining was inimical to the gentry's sense of identity with the shire, nevertheless argues that it was the idea of community which had triumphed by the end of the fourteenth century.[10] Michael Bennett similarly argues that for most of the gentry 'the county . . . provided the fundamental source of cohesion', though he also admits that among the upper gentry in particular, their interests and affiliations were sometimes wider than the county.[11]

Despite these diametrically opposed ideas, historians have eschewed giving vent to those vitriolic humours which devastatingly burned their mark on, but enlivened, the 'Storm over the Gentry'. In fact, hitherto there has been small need to resolve a conflict which can be easily accommodated by appeal to regional differences.[12] Were the issue merely a question of two types of communities then such restraint might be justified; but the problem cuts deeper than that. At its core lies the prospect of two kinds of gentry. On the one hand, we see a gentry, if not entirely parochial in its outlook, at least restricted in its social horizons and constrained politically within the confines of a magnate affinity. On the other hand, we may view the gentry as forming part of a wider social community, the shire community, in which they find a more independent political voice. In short, our perception of the gentry as social and political entities will depend largely on whether or not they considered themselves to have been leading members of the community of the shire. In order to address this issue we shall need first to determine the associations forged among the gentry. In the absence of personal correspondence, these relationships are best revealed through documents relating to land transactions which were an integral part of estate management.

As we have seen in the previous chapter, a gentry estate was rarely a static entity. It was usually subject to the twin processes of disintegration and consolidation. Depletion could result from sales, gifts for charitable or pious purposes or to younger children and, temporarily, from a widow's claim to her dower rights. Additional lands might be acquired by inheritance, through marriage to an heiress, by royal grant from a forfeited estate or by

medieval aristocratic affinity', *Southern History*, 1, 1979, pp. 71, 76ff; Carpenter, 'Political society in Warwickshire', pp. 94–8.
[10] Saul, *Knights and Esquires*, pp. 258, 259.
[11] Bennett, *Community, Class and Careerism*, pp. 21, 26 and *passim*.
[12] *Ibid.*, pp. 238–9.

a simple process of purchase.[13] These changes to a landlord's holdings were seldom the sole concern of the contracting parties. As others, either spuriously or justifiably, might discover dormant rights to the lands in question, it was necessary to involve a wider group of people as witnesses to deeds and charters. This need is not to suggest that the witnesses all had to be present at the sealing of a charter but their permission had to be sought, probably in writing, before their names were used.[14] We may therefore assume, at the very least, an acquaintance between the principals and their witnesses. These witnesses could vouch for the authenticity of the agreement were it ever to become the subject of dispute or of litigation between hostile claimants. The disposal of personal property in wills similarly required the assistance of executors, supervisors and witnesses.

Furthermore, the fifteenth-century gentry recognized the value of entrusting their lands to feoffees to the use of the feoffor. The origins of enfeoffments to uses are obscure but it seems that the gentry themselves were the first to employ the device and that only from the 1340s onwards did the nobility increasingly follow the example set by their social inferiors.[15] Thereafter, the growth of enfeoffments was rapid.[16] Given the flexibility they afforded the feoffor and the financial savings for his heir, such growth is not unexpected. The *cestui que use* was able to enjoy the benefits of his estate during his lifetime and he could then direct his feoffees to deliver seisin according to his will after his death. In this way, younger sons or daughters could be provided for at the expense of the heir without their benefactor having to make a gift while he was still alive. Alternatively, the feoffees could be directed to deliver seisin to the heir who thereby would escape the burdens of feudal incidents such as wardship, marriage and entry fines.[17] The

---

[13] See above, p. 46 and *passim*.

[14] *Transcripts of Charters Relating to the Gilbertine Houses of Sixle, Ormsby, Catley, Bullington, and Alvingham*, ed. F. M. Stenton, Horncastle, 1922 for 1920, p. xxxi.

[15] Enfeoffments to uses are discussed at length by S. F. C. Milsom, *Historical Foundations of the Common Law*, London, 1969, pp. 169–88; J. M. W. Bean, *The Decline of English Feudalism, 1215–1540*, Manchester, 1968, pp. 104–79; T. F. T. Plucknett, *A Concise History of the Common Law*, 4th edn, London, 1948, pp. 544–55.

[16] Bean, *The Decline of English Feudalism*, p. 120.

[17] For the benefits of enfeoffment to use see J. L. Barton, 'The medieval use', *The Law Quarterly Review*, 81, 1965, pp. 572–4; McFarlane, *The Nobility of Later Medieval England*, pp. 68–73; Milsom, *Historical Foundations of the Common Law*, pp. 176–80; Plucknett, *A Concise History of the Common Law*, pp. 546, 550–2; Bean, *The Decline of English Feudalism*, pp. 136ff.

estate, therefore, was not simply a source of economic profit; the gentry's need for witnesses and feoffees ensured that it was also a source of social interaction. If we can unravel the relationships and affiliations which this interaction produced, we may be better placed to understand the internal politics of the shire.

The most immediate relationships were those provided by a network of kinfolk.[18] As we would expect, members of the immediate family were often called upon to act as feoffees, witnesses to deeds and charters or as executors of, and witnesses to, wills. Sir Robert Moton I used his brother, Alan, as a feoffee for his manor of Peckleton in Leicestershire and another brother, Richard, as feoffee for his lands in Staffordshire.[19] When Thomas Hasilrigge and his son, William, leased lands at Noseley to the warden and chaplains of the chantry there, the witnesses to the indenture included two members of the Hasilrigge family, one from Noseley and another from nearby Rolleston.[20] The executors of Everard Fielding's will were his brother, Martin, and his son and heir, William, while Ralph Woodford's three younger sons, Mathew, John and Robert, were his executors.[21]

In-laws also served as executors and business associates. John Shirley's executors included his brother-in-law, Henry Willoughby, whose selection for the task may have been designed to safeguard the interests of his sister, John's wife, Eleanor Shirley.[22] Willoughby subsequently became a feoffee of John and Eleanor's son, Ralph III, as did William Littleton, the husband of Ralph's wife's sister.[23] When the widowed Margaret German leased her water mill and fishing rights at Cossington, her brother-in-law, Ralph Butler, husband of Margaret's sister, Elizabeth, acted as a witness to the agreement.[24] John Bellers II selected as feoffees for his manors of Eye Kettleby and Sysonby, his brother-in-law, Nicholas Griffin, and Ralph Woodford who was the husband of Bellers' niece, Elizabeth.[25] Two members of Ralph Shirley II's council were Thomas Staunton, a cadet of Ralph's first wife's

---

[18] Gentry family relationships are discussed at greater length in chapter 6 below.

[19] C1/13/163; C1/15/124; *C.C.R.*, 1461–8, p. 147.

[20] L.R.O. DG21/28.

[21] PROB11/18/5/30; PROB11/11/23/182v–3v.

[22] L.R.O. 26D53/1947.   [23] L.R.O. 26D53/315, 543.

[24] L.R.O. 44′28/116. For Margaret's relationship to Butler, see L.R.O. 44′28/115.

[25] C1/56/236.

family, and Sir Thomas Blount, Ralph's father-in-law by his second marriage.[26]

However, despite evidence which points to co-operation within families, it is quite clear that the family did not constitute a power-bloc or a sodality whose members were steadfast in their loyalty to one another. The Leicestershire gentry had sufficient reminders to impress upon them the truth of this fact. For example, among those who stole twenty-six sheep from Sir Robert Woodford's manor at Ashby Folville, was Sir Robert's own grandson and ultimate heir, Ralph Woodford.[27] Rights to property were later at the centre of a ten-year feud between Ralph and his uncle, Walter Woodford, and a dispute between Sir Robert Moton and his daughter-in-law, Margaret, was the subject of protracted proceedings before chancery.[28]

The growth in chancery's activity as a court of equity to adjudicate in disputes between feoffors or their heirs and feoffees further reveals that the trust placed in feoffees was often misplaced.[29] As often as not, it seems, family members were as adept at abusing that trust as non-family members were. Jane Staunton enfeoffed her father- and brother-in-law with manors bought from the proceeds of the sale of her inherited lands. These men then sold the manors for their own profit without any compensation to Jane.[30] Ellen Bellers similarly entrusted her manors to her father-in-law who in turn proceeded to treat the property as if it were his own.[31] While associations through marriage certainly extended the pool from which the gentry might draw their feoffees, the experiences of the Woodfords, Jane Staunton and Ellen Bellers reveal that members of both the immediate family and the wider kin still required rigorous vetting before appointment to positions of trust. It is hardly surprising, then, that the gentry should call on the services of a wider network of associates than could be supplied by the family and kin.

The limits to the gentry's reliance upon family members is revealed by Thomas Palmer's transfer of his manor of Lubenham

---

[26] L.R.O. 26D53/344.   [27] L.R.O. 5D33/172.
[28] C1/13/10; C1/13/162–3; C1/15/125–6; C1/22/114a–d.
[29] For the fifteenth-century growth in appeals to chancery concerning enfeoffments to use, see M. E. Avery, 'The history of the equitable jurisdiction of chancery before 1460', *B.I.H.R.*, 42, 1969, pp. 130–2.
[30] C1/58/322.   [31] C1/9/356.

to his daughter and son-in-law, Katherine and William Neville.[32] Palmer had enfeoffed nine men with his manor and the deed of transfer was witnessed by a further seven named men and unspecified 'others'. None of the named witnesses and only one of the feoffees, a John Palmer, was a relative of Thomas. In Thomas Erdyngton's lease of his capital messuage in Braunstone, none of the nine named witnesses was a relative.[33] When Erdyngton later sold his interests in Braunstone, the thirteen named witnesses to his quitclaim again did not include relatives.[34] Six witnesses were, in fact, small-scale landholders, probably tenants, in Braunstone. No doubt their involvement was to safeguard the future interests of the purchaser. Limited reliance upon family members is also revealed in an enfeoffment made by Bartholomew Brokesby in April 1445. Brokesby enfeoffed ten men in all his lands and tenements in twelve villages scattered within the area bounded by Dalby-on-the-Wolds, Little Dalby and Barkby.[35] Of the ten feoffees, only one, John Brokesby of Frisby, was a relative. Obviously, as with Thomas Palmer and Thomas Erdyngton, the expectation of family solidarity was not Bartholomew's foremost criterion for the selection of his associates.

Two of Brokesby's feoffees, William Wright of Gaddesby and John Bret of Rotherby, were his neighbours in these villages and their local knowledge of who owned which lands and by what right would have been an important consideration in their election. Brokesby may even have bought some land from the Brets a few years earlier, for in 1442, Agnes Bret, John's wife, delivered seisin to Bartholomew Brokesby of a piece of meadow in Ashby Folville.[36] John's brother, William, had certainly bought lands from Brokesby, for he specifically refers to this purchase in his will.[37]

The reason for Nicholas Gerveys' selection as one of Brokesby's feoffees is not so immediately apparent. At Harby, he was 5 miles distant from Brokesby's outlying tenement at Holwell. However, in 1440, Gerveys had acquired a messuage, seven tofts and 180 acres of land at Chadwell and Wycomb as his share of the

---

[32] L.R.O. DE220/58 (bundle MTD/54).
[33] L.R.O. DG5/2.   [34] L.R.O. DG5/5.
[35] Bodl. Lib. Wood Empt. 7, fos. 164v–5 (contemporary mispagination 183v–4).
[36] *Ibid.*, fos. 103v–4.   [37] L.R.O. 5D33/180.

Hauberk inheritance.[38] As these lands were only about 3 miles from Holwell, we may classify Nicholas Gerveys as a neighbour, too.

A further two feoffees, John Dansey senior and his son, John junior, lived at Somerby, just over 2 miles from Brokesby's manor and lands at Little Dalby. The Danseys also held lands of their own in Little Dalby and at Frisby, near Brokesby's *caput honoris*.[39] It may appear, therefore, that, as in the cases of William Wright and John Bret, the Danseys were chosen as feoffees because they were Brokesby's neighbours. But the relationship between the two families goes deeper than that. Bartholomew and John senior were acting as feoffees in the manor of Ashby de la Zouch for Joan Beauchamp, lady Abergavenny, as early as 1417.[40] Brokesby was one of Joan's trusted servants who became an executor of, and a beneficiary under, her will. As Dansey also received a bequest, it is clear that he, too, was a Beauchamp retainer.[41] After Joan's death in 1435, the two men delivered seisin of the manor of Haselbeche in Northamptonshire to James Butler, earl of Ormond, husband of Joan's daughter, Joan.[42] A few months later, they conveyed lady Abergavenny's manor of Ashby de la Zouch to Humphrey, duke of Gloucester.[43] By 1440, Brokesby and Dansey were enfeoffed with lands in Essex with a reversion to Ormond, so it seems that when Joan Beauchamp died, they had promptly transferred their services to her son-in-law.[44]

None of the remaining four feoffees was a neighbour. Why Thomas Neele of Owston or Robert Neuton of Belgrave were enfeoffed must remain a mystery, though Neuton was later a juror at Brokesby's inquisition *post mortem*, a fact which suggests that he was knowledgeable about the disposition of the family's lands.[45] He may even have been a servant. Richard Byngham of Nottinghamshire and John Forster of Knighton, south-east of Leicester, were more distant still from Brokesby's lands. Byngham was a justice of the king's bench and it is possible that his

[38] *Pedigrees*, p. 80; *W.H.R.*, no. 1136.   [39] *C.I.P.M.*, 14 Hen. VII, no. 133.
[40] *T.L.A.S.*, 15, 1927–8, p. 93.
[41] C67/38 MS 27; Dugdale, II, pp. 1031–2.
[42] *C.P.R.*, 1429–36, p. 506; G.E.C., X, p. 125.
[43] H.M.C., *Hastings*, I, p. 1.   [44] *C.P.R.*, 1436–41, p. 435.
[45] C139/136/43 MS 2.

nvolvement with Brokesby, also a lawyer, was through the law.[46] However, it is more likely that Byngham's and Forster's association with Bartholomew was a product of their attachment to the Butlers. Byngham, like Brokesby, was a feoffee of James Butler junior by 1447, and two years earlier, John Forster, yeoman, had been granted the office of the bailiwick of Butler's manor of Ashby de la Zouch.[47]

In addition to listing feoffees, Brokesby's indenture of 1445 was witnessed by seven named men and 'many others' unnamed. Six of these men came from the same general area where Bartholomew held his estate in the north-east of the county. Some, such as Robert Woodford of Ashby Folville and Thorpe Arnold, William Villers of Brooksby, Walter Keble of Rearsby and Rotherby and Thomas Derby of Gaddesby, were Brokesby's very close neighbours in these villages. Only John Aubrey of Osgathorpe in West Goscote, about 16 miles from Frisby, was not a neighbour. Like the Danseys, Richard Byngham and John Forster, Aubrey's association may have been through service to Joan Beauchamp. A William Aubrey, possibly John's father or some other relative, had been one of Joan's feoffees in the manor of Ashby de la Zouch before 1421.[48]

Bartholomew Brokesby, therefore, seems to have had a number of criteria in mind when he selected his feoffees and witnesses. The first, most important criterion was that he should include men from his own area whose local knowledge about the owner's rights would assist in the estate's protection. As a bonus, these neighbours, by the fact that they were party to the indenture, were thereby removed from the pool of possible claimants or disputants who might threaten Brokesby's peaceful possession of his lands. A second criterion was that associates with whom he had worked closely in other fields, in this case in the Beauchamp and Butler affinities, should be approached for their help. The overlord could be requested to exert his or her influence were any of the feoffees or witnesses tempted to abuse their trust. Third, it was clearly a good idea to include lawyers such as, in this case, Richard Byngham, Thomas Berkeley and Walter Keble. These men could ensure that the documents were 'good, true and

---

* H.M.C., *Hastings*, I, p. 1; C66/414 MS 20v.
? H.M.C., *Hastings*, I, p. 1. Byngham was sufficiently close to Brokesby to be made one of the executors of his will (*C.C.R.*, 1447–57, p. 358).
* *T.L.A.S.*, 15, 1927–8, p. 93.

lawfully made'.[49] Finally, the inclusion of John Brokesby as a feoffee indicates that trusted family members could be called upon for their assistance. Of course, these categories were not mutually exclusive; John Brokesby was both a relative and a neighbour; the two John Danseys were neighbours and John senior was also an associate in the retinue of lady Abergavenny; Richard Byngham was a lawyer and possibly an associate, too, in the retinue of Jame Butler.

Furthermore, in Brokesby's selection of his helpers, we can discern two circles of association, one narrow and parochial, the other, while neither national nor regional, certainly much more diffuse than the former. This fact raises a number of important questions. First, we need to consider whether Brokesby's experience was typical of the rest of the gentry. Second, if the forces of localism were uppermost, as is implied by the gentry's reliance upon neighbours, then their social horizons may be dismissed as being exceedingly narrow. We therefore need to test the relative strength of these forces. A third question relates to the degree of diffusion in gentry relationships for it is upon this that the vexed question of whether there was a county community will largely depend.

A closer scrutiny of the associates of other gentry reveals that they, like Bartholomew Brokesby, relied heavily on neighbours as witnesses to their transactions. The witnesses to John German's grant to Robert Hanson of his mill at Cossington included Thomas Erdyngton of Barrow-on-Soar, Richard Walsh of Wanlip, Richard Neele of Prestwold, Thomas Farnham of Quorndon and Robert Chamberlain of Seagrave.[50] The most distant of these men was Richard Neele, who lived 5 miles from Cossington. All the others lived well within a 3-mile radius of Cossington. That the selection of associates was partly determined by the distribution of their estates can be seen, too, in Thomas Erdyngton's own lease of his capital messuage in Braunstone.[51] One of the witnesses, William Hastings, lived at Kirby, about 2 miles from Braunstone. William Babthorpe, another witness, came from Nottinghamshire, but his wife's manor of Aylestone was less than 2 miles from Braunstone. Two further witnesses, John Nicol and John Tailor, were non-gentry neighbours in

[49] As did Robert Moton in another context (C1/14/24).
[50] L.R.O. 44'28/110.   [51] L.R.O. DG5/2.

Braunstone itself. Similarly, in a quitclaim by Sir John Trussell to Thomas Palmer's father, William, of his manor and lands in Holt and Prestgrave, the four named witnesses came from Holt, Drayton and Bringhurst, all within a mile or so of Prestgrave.[52] The almost universal reliance upon neighbours seems to confirm the triumph of localism in the gentry's business dealings. As we have already suggested, there were very good practical reasons for involving neighbours in land transactions. Given that one of the gentry's prime concerns was the protection of the estate, their choice was not one of whether neighbours would participate in their affairs but rather of which neighbours would do so.

Thomas Erdyngton's lease and Sir John Trussell's quitclaim further reveal that witnesses were often drawn from non-gentle landholders. Very rarely, though, did such men fill the higher position of trust, that of feoffee.[53] Instead, the gentry preferred their social equals to act in this capacity. Thomas Palmer's feoffees in his purchased manor of Lubenham included John Boyville, Everard Dygby and John Bellers.[54] Boyville came from Stockerston, about $2\frac{1}{2}$ miles from Palmer's *caput*. Dygby's Leicestershire manor of Tilton was about 9 miles from Holt but his Rutland manor of Stoke Dry was only 1 mile from the county border and about 3 miles from Palmer's residence. Bellers came from Eye Kettleby in the Wreake valley, 16 miles from Palmer's manors but he also held a manor at Medbourne, less than 2 miles from Holt.

However, the gentry's social horizons were not quite as parochial as this evidence might lead us to believe. All of the knightly families, about two-thirds of the distrainees and just over 40 per cent of the esquires held lands in other, usually neighbouring, counties. These families often used outsiders as witnesses, feoffees and executors. Marriage also helped to extend the gentry's body of associates, not only beyond their immediate neighbourhoods but also beyond the county boundary. John Coton of Thurcaston and Keyham used four of his Fitzherbert relatives, three of them brothers-in-law, as feoffees for his Leicestershire manors.[55] His only Leicestershire feoffee was Robert Moton of

[52] L.R.O. DE221/4/1/36.
[53] A notable exception was John Belgrave's enfeoffment of John Reynold with all his lands in Leicestershire (*C.I.P.M.*, 4 Hen. VII, no. 419).
[54] L.R.O. DE220/58.   [55] C140/66/34.

Peckleton who was not a neighbour. The Shirleys were another family who regularly relied on the services of their Derbyshire neighbours and kin.[56] Although the pattern of landholding and marriage helped to broaden the gentry's social horizons beyond the parochial, our evidence thus far suggests that there was no sense of a community of the shire which both determined, and was reflected by, gentry associations.[57]

Nevertheless, as John Coton's use of Robert Moton as a feoffee reveals, localism, the pattern of landholding and family networks, all had their limits as determinants of gentry associations. Moton was not one of Coton's neighbours; nor was he a relative. John Beller's feoffees included Richard Neele and John Farnham, each of whom lived about a dozen miles from Bellers manors of Eye Kettleby and Sysonby.[58] Neither Farnham nor Neele was a relative of Bellers. Richard Boyville, a nephew of Thomas Boyville, held a double-nucleated estate at Odstone and Turlangton but two of his feoffees, Thomas Palmer and Thomas Farnham, neither of whom was related to Boyville, lived about 7 and 12 miles respectively from the closest nucleus.[59] One of the witnesses to John Trussell's quitclaim of Trussel manor at Holt to Thomas Palmer was Richard Hastings of Kirby Muxloe.[60] Once again, there was no family relationship between Hastings and Trussell or Palmer. Hastings did, however, also hold manors at Fleckney, Kilby, Newton Harcourt and Wistow which, like Holt, were all in the hundred of Gartree. The closest of these manors to Holt was Fleckney, over 10 miles distant. Clearly, in these cases, the pattern of landholding and the kinship network had little part to play in the selection of associates. One is led to wonder, therefore, what these men, Hastings, Palmer, Farnham and Neele, may have had in common.

A survey of available deeds and charters and of inquisitions *post mortem* in fact reveals these men or their heirs in high demand as witnesses or feoffees. Furthermore, in many cases they had no geographical or kinship links with the persons they were assisting.

---

[56] See, for example, Ralph Shirley II's feoffees for his manor of Whatton, Edward Longford from Derbyshire and Ralph's brothers-in-law, Walter and Thomas Blount, also from Derbyshire (L.R.O. 72′30/1/37).

[57] This is the conclusion reached by Wright, *The Derbyshire Gentry*, p. 58; Astill, 'The medieval gentry', pp. 81ff.

[58] C140/52/27.   [59] C140/17/23.

[60] L.R.O. DE221/4/1/66.

Nor were they alone in appearing as associates with almost tedious regularity. In addition to the Neeles and Hastingses among the knightly families, appear the Woodfords, Motons, Berkeleys, Trussells and, to a lesser extent, Thomas Erdyngton II. Palmer's fellow distrainees who were in demand included Boyvilles, Bellerses, Brokesbys, Asshebys, Dygbys, Hotofts and, less often, Pulteneys, Wyvylls and Hasilrigges. Esquire families who regularly associated with other gentry were the Stauntons, Villerses, Kebles, Whattons and Sherards. Less regular associates included Walshes, Skeffingtons and Entwysells.

There is no single thread which unifies each and every entry on this list of twenty-six individuals and families. However, a sizeable minority, over 46 per cent, provided the workhorses of county administration as justices of the peace, commissioners, sheriffs or escheators. About 54 per cent represented the shire in parliament. Over 61 per cent were lawyers.[61] But before we consider the significance of these figures or try to draw conclusions from them one further piece of evidence, which may have a bearing on the debate about whether there was a community of the shire, must be produced.

On 11 May 1446, a declaration was drawn up to the effect that Elizabeth, wife of Robert Sherard, had given birth to a daughter, 'christened and called Joan'.[62] This strange document has survived among the Sherard papers but, given its contents, it is possible that other copies were made for wider circulation. Joan, we are told, lived for only two hours. After her death, her body was taken to the parish church at Stapleford and buried in the churchyard there. No doubt such personal tragedies were commonplace in fifteenth-century Leicestershire. Less commonplace was the perceived need to trumpet the Sherards' loss through a declaration 'unto all Christian people [whom] these presents here to see or hear'. From oblique hints in the declaration itself, however, we are in a position to hazard an explanation.

The declaration states that Robert was the son and heir of Laurence Sherard 'that now is deceased' and that he 'wedded a gentlewoman that *was* called Elizabeth Durant, daughter and heir of John Durant late of Cottesmore in the county of Rutland'.[63] Had their daughter, Joan, lived, she would have been heir general

---

[61] See chapters 3 and 5 and appendices 1 and 3.
[62] L.R.O. DG40/481.   [63] My emphasis.

to the Sherard and Durant estates. The declaration is at pains further to point out that the child was 'of many divers persons herd loud crie'. It also stresses that it is reporting truthfully and that anyone doubting its veracity would be placing his soul in peril. At first glance, it may appear that this document was designed to forestall some dispute about the heir to the Sherard or Durant inheritance or, indeed, to both. However, closer inspection reveals that Robert Sherard was protecting his own life-interest in his wife's real property under the rules governing the 'law or courtesy of England'.

In order for a husband to have tenancy of an estate by courtesy, four conditions had to be satisfied: he had to be lawfully married; his wife must have had seisin of her property as there could be no courtesy of a reversion or a remainder; there needed to be lawful issue of the marriage, born alive; and finally, the wife had to be dead.[64] If we return to the Sherard declaration we find that each of these four conditions is dealt with either explicitly or implicitly. First, the document explicitly states that Robert Sherard and Elizabeth Durant were married. Second, as John Durant is referred to as 'late of Cottesmore', we may safely assume that Elizabeth did have seisin of her inheritance. Third, the reference to Elizabeth in the past tense (see n. 63 above), strongly suggests that she, too, had died, most probably in childbed while giving birth to Joan. Fourth, we are expressly told that Joan lived for two hours and her loud cries, heard by numerous people, provided proof of the fact.

Although this document may provide an interesting footnote to the practical application of 'the courtesy of England' in the fifteenth century, our prime concern is with the thirty-five men, the professed authors of the declaration, who were lending their support to Robert Sherard's claims. It is unlikely that fifteenth-century childbirth had become such a public spectacle as to warrant the presence of thirty-five shire worthies. Obviously, these men had been informed by trustworthy witnesses of the circumstances of Joan Sherard's birth, brief life and untimely death. Nevertheless, their involvement does reveal the breadth of social contacts available to a member of the gentry.

---

[64] Sir William Holdsworth, *A History of English Law*, 5th edn, 12 vols., London, 1942, III, pp. 185–8, esp. pp. 187–8. See, too, Pollock and Maitland, *The History of English Law*, II, pp. 414–20; S. Painter, 'The family and the feudal system in twelfth-century England', *Speculum*, 35, 1, 1960, p. 13.

Nine of the thirty-five were clerics, mainly Leicestershire abbots and priors. One was a lord, namely Edward Grey, lord Ferrers of Groby. Three, Robert Bagoutt, John of Bothe and John of Stanley (or Stoneleigh, near Belvoir?), have eluded my researches but the remaining twenty-two belonged to the gentry and overwhelmingly to the Leicestershire gentry. Only three men, Robert and John Browe and Thomas Tunstall, can be positively identified as outsiders, while a fourth, Thomas Flower, may have been an outsider, too. The Browes held the manor of Teigh in Rutland, about $3\frac{1}{2}$ miles from the Sherards' *caput* at Stapleford.[65] The two Roberts, Browe and Sherard, had also fought together at Agincourt in 1415.[66] By 1446, therefore, their relationship was long-standing. The relationship between Sherard and Tunstall was equally long-standing, for Tunstall had also fought at Agincourt.[67] Thomas Flower, though, poses a problem. As early as 1422, a Roger Flower, father of Thomas, had acquired lands in Leicestershire at Leesthorpe, less than 4 miles from Stapleford.[68] These Flowers came from Oakham and were one of Rutland's leading gentry families.[69] But there was also a Thomas Flower of Edmundsthorpe in Leicestershire who witnessed Margaret Chitlow's quitclaim of lands to Thomas Berkeley in 1459.[70] The two Thomases may, of course, have been the same person, in which case our problem disappears. But even were they not, regardless of whether Robert Sherard's associate came from Leesthorpe or Edmundsthorpe, he was still a Sherard neighbour.

Of the remaining eighteen Leicestershire gentlemen, half were either relatives or neighbours or both. They included Sir Robert Woodford, Sir Laurence Berkeley and his son, Thomas, Bartholomew Brokesby, Anthony and John Malory and Thomas Assheby. All of these men were related to Sherard by marriage; Woodford, the Berkeleys and Brokesby were neighbours, too. John Bellers was also party to the declaration. He was not a relative but he was a neighbour. Surprisingly, none of Robert Sherard's brothers was associated with the pronouncement. Perhaps this was a deliberate ploy to preclude any suggestion by

---

[65] *V.C.H. Rut.* I, p. 178; *ibid.*, II, p. 153.   [66] *Ibid.*, I, p. 178; E101/69/5 MS 419.
[67] *D.K.R.*, 44th report (Calendar of the French Rolls, 1–10 Hen. V), London, 1883, p. 560.
[68] *V. C. H. Leics.*, V, p. 278.   [69] *V. C. H. Rut.*, I, p. 178.
[70] B. L. Harl. 265, fo. 135.

Elizabeth Sherard's collateral heirs that the claims being made were merely a Sherard family plot. But their exclusion may also suggest that the involvement of Thomas Assheby, for example, or Sir Robert Woodford or the Berkeleys was not dictated by their familial relationship to Sherard but by some different consideration.

The other signatories to the declaration, however, are of greater significance to the argument. These men, who included William Villers of Brooksby, Walter Keble of Rearsby, Richard Hotoft of Humberstone and Everard Dygby of Tilton, were drawn from much further afield and none was closely related to Sherard. Sir Robert Moton from distant Peckleton was also involved, as was Sir William Trussell from even more distant Elmesthorpe. It may be recalled that these gentry were among those who, time and time again, keep appearing as associates of their peers from all over the county; that they provided the workhorses for county administration and that the majority were lawyers.[71] Sherard himself was one of their number. Collectively, they appear to have constituted a shire establishment whose appeal may have resided in a combination of their administrative ability and legal training. Not only did they defend the gentry's interest within the county but their fellows also displayed a marked readiness to entrust them with the shire's voice in parliament. If this establishment provided the shire with an idea of community then that fellowship was something that was taken for granted; it did not need to be constantly reaffirmed in commonplace transactions but, as Robert Sherard's associates in 1446 reveal, it could surface in times of difficulty or crisis. Had Sherard merely been looking for powerful allies, he could have found them closer to hand in Rutland which was only about 1 mile distant from his *caput*, or in Lincolnshire or even Nottinghamshire which were about 5 and 10 miles respectively from his residence. Instead, he almost exclusively turned his gaze inwards into his native county. He sought the assistance of Leicestershire allies, specifically men of his own shire community.

In part, this social cohesion may have been the product of Leicestershire's compactness. Leicester, the administrative centre of the shire, was also the geographical centre. Apart from the Vale of Belvoir, which formed an isolated wedge between

[71] See above, p. 89.

Nottinghamshire and Lincolnshire and where gentry holdings were sparse anyway, few areas of the county lay beyond 15 to 20 miles of the county borough. Here, the meetings of the shire court were held, meetings which, for parliamentary elections, could attract as many as seventy representatives of the county's leading families.[72] In Leicester, too, a number of these families owned tenements.[73] No doubt, some of the produce of their farms was sold in the town's markets. Leicester and its shire court could provide a focus for social interaction among the gentry from all over the county and thereby help to broaden their social horizons beyond the immediate neighbourhood or kinship network.

However, this emphasis on Leicestershire's compactness should not be interpreted as an endorsement of the view that geographic peculiarities were uppermost in providing its gentry with a concept of the community of the shire. Nor is there any suggestion that the social experiences of the Leicestershire gentry were radically different from those of the gentry in other counties. In fact, the argument about Leicestershire has a more general application. It need not be the case that the gentry saw themselves as members of one community rather than another; they were not either narrowly parochial or members of a wider shire community; they were both. Rather like the ellipses in a Venn diagram, the social circles of the fifteenth-century gentry sometimes overlapped and sometimes one circle engulfed another. If we emphasize the purely local community at the expense of the community of the shire, then that emphasis is partly the product of the nature of the evidence which tends to focus attention on entirely local concerns. Not so well documented are those rarer moments of special need when, as the Sherard declaration shows, men could request and be granted the support of the wider shire community.[74]

Although we may argue in favour of a community of the shire in social terms, whether the county also constituted a political unit is less clear. Historians have discerned political cohesion in Devonshire and Warwickshire but in both instances, that cohesion was imposed from above, by the Courtenays in Devon and

---

[72] C219/14/1 pt 2 MS 102.   [73] Bateson, II, pp. 331–4.
[74] It is worth remarking that the argument for a county community in Cheshire and Lancashire similarly hinges upon exceptional circumstances (Bennett, *Community, Class and Careerism*, pp. 21–6).

by Richard Beauchamp in Warwickshire.[75] In neither case did unity survive the death or incapacity of its creators.[76] It is clear that in Devon and Warwickshire, the strongest political force was the affinity rather than the county. In these shires powerful resident magnates composed the political score which the gentry, if not always in perfect pitch and harmony, then played to order. Leicestershire, however, at least during the first sixty years of the century, was not subject to magnate domination. If the gentry there regarded the affinity as the natural political unit then they would need to look outside the county for good lordship and to find it either among the magnates at large or with the king who, as duke of Lancaster, was the most important, albeit absentee, lay landholder in the shire. In the former case, political cohesion within the county would be unlikely.

The social horizons of the Leicestershire gentry were certainly not so narrow as to preclude associations with the nobility from outside the county. Some of the more strenuous gentry followed noble captains to France in war retinues. Thomas Beaumont, Thomas Everyngham and Sir Richard Hastings all served under the duke of Bedford, while Everyngham may also have served with lord Scales and the earl of Shrewsbury.[77] Everyngham and Hastings were both professional soldiers whose long careers in the field would have brought them into contact with an even wider group of lords than merely the military commanders they indented to follow.[78] Robert Moton, John Shirley and Thomas Walsh fought respectively in the retinues of Richard, lord Grey of Codnor, Richard Beauchamp, earl of Warwick, and Thomas Montague, earl of Salisbury.[79] Lord Grey was related to Moton through marriage to the uterine sister of

---

[75] Cherry, 'The Courtenay earls of Devon', pp. 71, 76ff; Carpenter, 'Political society in Warwickshire', pp. 94–8.

[76] Cherry, 'The Courtenay earls of Devon', pp. 92–7; Carpenter, 'Political society in Warwickshire', pp. 98–9, 144–50.

[77] B. L. Harl. 6166, fo. 69v; *Letters and Papers Illustrative of the Wars of the English in France*, II, pp. 412, 434–5, [629]. There is some doubt about the identity of Shrewsbury's retainer. At least three Everyngham families held land in south Yorkshire, including the Everynghams of Newhall in Leicestershire. A. J. Pollard believes that Shrewsbury's follower was Thomas Everyngham of Stainbrough (A. J. Pollard, *John Talbot and the War in France, 1427–1453*, London, 1983, p. 76 and n. 33).

[78] *Letters and Papers Illustrative of the Wars of the English in France*, II, pp. 394, 412, 435, [629]; E101/70/6 MS 725; Dunham, 'Lord Hastings' indentured retainers 1461–83', pp. 136, 137. For Everyngham see below chapter 5, n. 79.

[79] J. S. Roskell, *The Commons in the Parliament of 1422*, Manchester, 1954, pp. 93, 205; *Stemmata Shirleiana*, p. 51; E101/71/2 MS 833.

Moton's wife and he also had modest landed interests in Leicestershire.[80] But most of these military alliances were of short
duration and with members of the nobility who had little or no
landed interest in Leicestershire. They were therefore politically
insignificant for the county. It is worth noting that lord Roos's
retinue at Agincourt, despite his manors and lands in the
hundred of Framland, contained no members of the Leicestershire gentry.[81]

The Leicestershire gentry provided their social superiors
with non-military service, too. We have already seen that Bartholomew Brokesby, Walter Keble and John Dansey were servants
of Joan Beauchamp, lady Abergavenny.[82] Reginald Moton
was probably also one of her servants as he, like Brokesby, Keble
and Dansey, received a bequest of 100 marks under Joan's
will.[83] These associations might suggest that lady Abergavenny
was welding together a minor sodality in Leicestershire but an
alternative interpretation is possible. Keble and Dansey were
Brokesby's neighbours and Moton was married to Brokesby's
cousin, Margaret Bugge.[84] Rather than Joan providing the link
between these men, it is just as likely that Brokesby himself
introduced his own associates and kin to the Beauchamp
affinity.[85]

Bartholomew Brokesby and his fellows were not alone in
entering noble service. Humphrey Stafford, earl of Stafford, and
later, from 1444, duke of Buckingham,[86] had at least four
Leicestershire men in his employ. In 1440, Richard Hotoft was
retained at £2 per annum, and two years later, when he became a
member of the earl's council, he was granted a further £5 a year.[87]
Another Stafford servant, William Heton, acted as steward of the earl's lands in Nottinghamshire and Rutland in 1440–1,
and Robert Staunton was steward in Nottinghamshire and
Leicestershire from 1453 to 1457.[88] Thomas Whatton of Mount-

[80] Roskell, *The Commons in the Parliament of 1422*, p. 205. See map 3.
[81] Sir Nicholas Harris Nicolas, *History of the Battle of Agincourt*, 2nd edn, London, 1832, p.
343.   [82] See above, p. 84.
[83] Dugdale, II, p. 1032.   [84] C1/22/114a.
[85] Cf. Pollard, 'The Richmondshire community of gentry during the Wars of the Roses',
pp. 53–4, where it is suggested that Sir John Conyers may have selected Richard duke of
Gloucester's early retainers at Middleham for him.
[86] G.E.C., II, p. 388.
[87] C. Rawcliffe, *The Staffords, Earls of Stafford and Dukes of Buckingham*, Cambridge, 1978,
pp. 220, 234.   [88] *Ibid.*, p. 204.

sorrel was Humphrey's bailiff at Maxstoke in Warwickshire in 1452–3.[89] Lord Zouche of neighbouring Northamptonshire also used the services of Leicestershire men. Thomas Palmer was one of his feoffees for his manor of Bushby and, as a reward for 'good counsel', was granted the stewardship of Zouche's Leicestershire manor of Thorpe Arnold for life.[90]

There can be no suggestion, however, that these affiliations provide accurate indicators of the gentry's political loyalties. Humphrey Stafford was, of course, an enthusiastic supporter of the Lancastrian regime. His son, also named Humphrey, was killed fighting for the king at St Albans in 1455 while the duke himself died in the same cause at Northampton in 1460.[91] Nevertheless, two of the elder Humphrey's Leicestershire servants, Richard Hotoft and Robert Staunton, continued to be appointed to local administrative positions after the dynastic change in 1461, Hotoft as commissioner of arrest in 1461, as tax assessor in 1463 and as justice of the peace for Rutland in 1464. Staunton sat on various commissions and on the bench of JPs during the 1460s, 70s and into the 80s.[92] Heton and Whatton may have died before it became necessary for them to decide their political allegiances. With Heton's last appointment as justice of the peace in 1456 and Whatton's much earlier, in 1448, they had at least retired from public life.[93]

More important to the argument is the fact that each of Stafford's four Leicestershire servants was a lawyer. Lord Zouche's feoffee, Thomas Palmer, was also learned in the law. Indeed, of twenty-three Leicestershire men who served the nobility as feoffees, executors, stewards or counsellors, over 65 per cent can be identified as lawyers. As such, they were selling their professional skills but not necessarily their political independence. Furthermore, as professional men, their services were called upon by a number of good lords. Richard Hotoft, besides being retained by the earl of Stafford, also acted as feoffee for Henry, lord Grey of Codnor.[94] William Heton, Stafford's steward, had earlier been executor of William, lord Roos's, will

[89] *The Account of the Great Household of Humphrey, First Duke of Buckingham for the Year 1452–3*, ed. M. Harris, Camden Miscellany, 4th ser. 29, London, 1984, pp. 11, 28.
[90] L.R.O. 5D33/177, fo. 82.   [91] G.E.C., II, p. 389.
[92] See appendices 1 and 3.   [93] See appendix 3.
[94] *Village Notes*, II, p. 228; *Nichols*, II, p. 557.

which was drawn up in February 1412.[95] Thereafter, Heton continued his association with the Roos family as steward and receiver for William's son, John, and as feoffee for both William's widow, Margaret, lady Roos, and a Sir Thomas Roos in Sussex.[96] Henry Sotehill, another lawyer, acted as feoffee for Richard, duke of York, Richard Neville, earl of Warwick, and, later, for George, duke of Clarence.[97]

That service is an unsure guide to political affiliations is further revealed by Everard Dygby I's career. In 1443, Dygby was a member of John Beaufort, duke of Somerset's, retinue in France.[98] By the end of the decade he was acting on behalf of Beaufort's enemy, Richard, duke of York, as the latter's feoffee for lands in Rutland.[99] Dygby's neighbour, Thomas Palmer, was also one of York's feoffees on the same occasion. After the change of regime, Palmer was referred to as 'the king's servant' when he received his reward for good service to both Richard of York and to his son, Edward IV.[100] Relations between Dygby and Palmer appear to have been close. They sat together on the Rutlandshire bench of JPs in 1446, 1448, 1456 and 1458 and on various Rutland commissions between 1448 and 1459.[101] Dygby was one of Palmer's feoffees for the manor of Lubenham until 1450, becoming involved in the business side of the marriage of Palmer's daughter, Katherine, to William Neville when this manor was transferred to the young couple.[102] He was also feoffee for Palmer's manors and lands around Holt and Medbourne and was regularly called upon to act as witness to Palmer's charters and quitclaims.[103] Nevertheless, despite Dygby's former service to the duke of York and despite his close associations with York's servant, Thomas Palmer, he fought against Edward IV

[95] *Early Lincoln Wills*, ed. A. Gibbons, Lincoln, 1888, p. 137.
[96] E372/275 MS 52v; C67/42 MS 40; *C.P.R.*, 1429–36, p. 62.
[97] Richmond, *John Hopton*, pp. 162, 184; *C.P.R.*, 1467–77, p. 530.
[98] *D.K.R.*, 48th report (Calendar of the French Rolls, Hen. VI), London, 1877, pp. 357, 360.
[99] *C.P.R.*, 1446–52, p. 218.   [100] *Ibid.*, 1461–7, p. 182.
[101] *Ibid.*, 1441–6, p. 477; *ibid.*, 1446–52, p. 593; *ibid.*, 1452–61, p. 675; *ibid.*, 1446–52, pp. 140, 319; *ibid.*, 1452–61, p. 557.
[102] L.R.O. DE220/58; DE220/60. The right-hand side of the latter manuscript is torn but the reference to Everard, an uncommon name in the county in 1450, is almost certainly to Everard Dygby.
[103] L.R.O. DE221/4/3/60; L.R.O. DE221/4/1/59; L.R.O. DE221/4/1/96; L.R.O. DE221/2/178/2 MS 144.

at Towton where he was killed. He was later attainted by Edward IV's first parliament which declared his lands forfeited.[104]

Although the gentry pursued service with lords from outside the county, two considerations indicate that these associations did not lead to political factionalism within it. First, most of the gentry served the nobility in a professional capacity, as lawyers providing 'good counsel', as stewards, bailiffs and, occasionally, as feoffees. The subsequent careers of Richard Hotoft and Robert Staunton reveal that in political terms, these associations could count for little.[105] Second, the good relations between Thomas Palmer and Everard Dygby show that whatever conflict may have divided their superiors, partisanship was not necessarily allowed to poison gentry relationships within the shire where these men had to live and work together in its administration.

That contemporaries themselves recognized the limits of gentry loyalty to their noble masters can be seen, of all places, in William Hastings' actions in late 1459 and the subsequent attitude towards him adopted by Henry VI's government. Hastings, whose basic loyalty to the Yorkist cause has never been questioned, may have been among those who counselled against taking the field at Ludford.[106] Whatever his rôle on that occasion, after the Rout of Ludford when his Yorkist companions were scattering to Ireland and Calais, William made his peace with Henry VI, paid a fine of £100 and received a royal pardon.[107] Given the choice between self-preservation or loyalty to his master and exile, Hastings, on this occasion, chose the former. Like Henry Vernon who, over a decade later, received, and wisely ignored, repeated summonses to join with his lord, Clarence, and with Warwick against Edward IV,[108] Hastings knew when to trim his political sails. R. L. Storey's assertion that a lord's 'retainers had no choice but to follow him into battle'[109] seems to attribute to lords a greater authority than they possessed and to retainers a lesser degree of independence than they in fact had.

While gentry–magnate associations did not lead to a fracturing of the shire's political mould, neither is it the case that the crown

[104] *Rot. Parl.*, v, p. 477; *C.P.R.*, 1461–7, p. 153.
[105] See above, p. 96.   [106] *Gregory's Chronicle*, p. 207.
[107] *C.P.R.*, 1452–61, pp. 552–77.   [108] H. M. C., *Rut.*, i, pp. 2–4.
[109] R. L. Storey, *The End of the House of Lancaster*, London, 1966, p. 16.

provided the cement of political cohesion. In fact, the crown's policy in the shire, and particularly duchy of Lancaster policy, though not designed to do so, resulted in a weakening of royal control. In 1415 before his departure for France, Henry V entrusted certain of his Lancastrian lands, including the manors of Foxton, Smeeton and Langton in Leicestershire, to feoffees for the performance of his will.[110] Despite repeated attempts under Henry VI to prize these enfeoffments from the grasp of the feoffees, the lands were not returned to the duchy until May 1443. After 1422, queen Katherine's dower of 10,000 marks was also a charge on the duchy. Her assignment included the castle, town and honor of Leicester, comprising the manors of Hinckley, Earl Shilton, Desford, Glenfield, Sileby, Belgrave, Swannington and Stapleford which remained in the dowager queen's hands until her death in 1437. In 1445, the honor of Leicester was again granted out, this time as part of queen Margaret's dower, and the following year, the king's remaining Leicestershire manor, Castle Donington, was granted to feoffees for the performance of his will.[111] Apart from the loss of revenue which Henry VI suffered as a result of these grants, of greater importance for his relationship with the county gentry was his loss of directly disposable patronage.

Moreover, in the course of the fifteenth century, some of the honor's offices became sinecures for the nobility. In 1437, the stewardship was granted to John, lord, and later viscount, Beaumont, who retained it until 1460 when he was replaced by Richard, earl of Warwick.[112] Warwick's tenure was short-lived but he was succeeded by another nobleman, William, lord Hastings, in July 1461. Very briefly in 1485, a member of the Leicestershire gentry, Everard Fielding, was steward but the office soon reverted to noble control in the person of Edward, lord Hastings. The master forestership and stewardship of Castle Donington similarly passed into noble hands. Sir Ralph Shirley had been appointed master-forester for life in 1414 but in 1442 he was joined in office by the newly elevated viscount Beaumont. After Shirley's death in 1443, Beaumont retained the master-forestership alone until 1460. He was replaced by the earl of Warwick who in turn was succeeded by lord Hastings.

[110] For this and what follows, see Somerville, I, pp. 199–212, 339–40.
[111] *Ibid.*; *T.L.A.S.*, 14, 1925–6, pp. 42–3.
[112] For the remainder of this paragraph, see Somerville, I, pp. 563–4, 568, 572, 573.

These same men succeeded each other in the stewardship of Castle Donington from 1437 onwards. Although the constable-ship of the castle managed to remain longer in gentry hands, it, too, became a noble sinecure from 1461 to 1484.

For the most part, the other honorial offices, those of receiver, feodary and bailiff of Leicester, were granted to non-nobles. Nevertheless, these offices were not always reserved for the local gentry. Peter Barewell, sometime receiver between 1402 and 1407, had been mayor of Leicester.[113] Arnold Holker, receiver between 1407 and 1422, was a household official, though his deputy, William Belgrave, belonged to a minor Leicestershire gentry family. Thomas Staunton, also a member of the Leices-tershire gentry, had been a household official before his appoint-ment to the receivership in 1449.[114] The only Leicestershire gentlemen appointed as feodary and bailiff of Leicester were Richard Hotoft who was granted both offices in 1441, Alexander Villers, who was Hotoft's deputy bailiff from 1443, and Everard Fielding who was bailiff for a short time in 1485.

Occasionally, the distribution of gentry lands allowed for the appointment of some men to duchy offices outside the shire. Sir Richard Hastings, who held manors and lands in Yorkshire, became steward of Knaresborough in 1422, remaining in office until his death in 1436.[115] Thomas Staunton, whose family held lands in Leicestershire, Nottinghamshire and Derbyshire, was constable of Melbourne in Derbyshire in 1418 and steward there from 1437.[116] Thomas's kinsman, Robert Staunton, was bailiff of Allerton, Plumtree and Risley wapentakes in 1438–9 and again in 1473–4.[117] Like Melbourne, these wapentakes were part of the honor of Tutbury in Derbyshire. Leicestershire lawyers also found employment with the duchy. Henry Sotehill was a duchy apprentice-at-law between 1456 and 1466, and became deputy chief steward of the north parts in 1459.[118] Thomas Keble was also retained as an apprentice-at-law and later rose to become the duchy's attorney general.[119] Nevertheless, appointments to of-

[113] For references to honorial offices, see *ibid.*, I, pp. 565, 566, 569–71.
[114] See appendix 3.   [115] Somerville I, p. 524.
[116] *Ibid.*, I, pp. 558, 557.   [117] *Ibid.*, I, p. 558.
[118] *Ibid.*, I, pp. 454, 425.
[119] *Ibid.*, I, pp. 454, 406; *Grants, etc. from the Crown during the Reign of Edward the Fifth*, ed. J. G. Nichols, Camden o.s. 60, London, 1854, p. 65.

fices outside the shire cannot have been designed to enhance the king's political control within the county.

After the change of regime in 1461, there was no significant alteration of policy regarding appointments to duchy offices in Leicestershire. As we have seen, the stewardships of the honor and of Castle Donington and the master-forestership remained in noble hands. In 1463, the receivership went to Thomas Palmer, no doubt as a further reward for his earlier good services to Richard and Edward of York.[120] William Moton's appointment to the receivership in 1480 was also probably made as a reward for services; he had been lord Hastings' retainer since 1475.[121] Piers Curtis, a household official and sometimes alderman, mayor and burgess of Leicester, was bailiff there from 1461 and became feodary in 1471.[122] Another bailiff, Richard Reynold, was a non-gentry lawyer who, like William Moton, had close affiliations with the Hastings family.[123] Emulating crown policy under Henry VI, Edward IV continued to use honorial offices to reward his supporters and household officials, some of whom did not belong to the gentry, rather than as a means politically to weld together the county's social elite.

A further potential source of royal patronage, the household, was no more effective a tool than the duchy of Lancaster for imposing political unity on the shire from without. In fact, for professional bureaucrats such as John Hotoft, controller of Henry V's household when he was prince of Wales and, from 1423, Henry VI's keeper of the wardrobe, employment in London only served to weaken his ties with his native county.[124] Hotoft retained his landed interest in Leicestershire but around 1412 he began to invest in property closer to the capital in Hertford-shire.[125] By 1428 he had become sufficiently settled there to be pricked as the county's sheriff.[126] John's newly acquired commit-ments in Hertfordshire, combined with his long absences in

---

[120] Somerville, I, p. 566; *C.P.R.*, 1461–7, p. 182.
[121] Somerville, I, pp. 566–7; Dunham, 'Lord Hastings' indentured retainers 1461–1483', p. 119.
[122] Wedgwood, *Biographies*, p. 244; Wedgwood, *Register*, pp. 438, 461, 654; Bateson, II, pp. 296, 300, 304; Somerville, I, pp. 571, 569–70.
[123] Somerville, I, p. 571; H.M.C., *Hastings*, I, pp. 143, 145.
[124] *Handbook of British Chronology*, ed. Sir F. M. Powicke and E. B. Fryde, 2nd edn, London, 1961, 3rd edn, 1986, p. 79; *Warrants for Issues, 1399–1485*, p. 144.
[125] PROB11/1/15/118; *V. C. H. Herts.*, III, pp. 115, 196, 391, 469.
[126] Lists and Indexes, IX, p. 44.

London, ensured that he had little or no political involvement in Leicestershire as an agent of the crown.

For most of the gentry who served Henry VI either as king's knights or as esquires of the chamber, attendance in court was less regular than for bureaucrats such as Hotoft.[127] Dividing their time between the king's presence and their own estates, they were in a position to keep him informed of events and concerns in their shires.[128] But we should not assume that the traffic in information was two-way or that these members of the king's affinity acted as agents for the crown when they returned to their respective counties. Of the eleven Leicestershire men who were either retained as king's knights or who were attracted to the royal household during Henry VI's reign, three, Thomas Hotoft, John Merbury and Ralph Shirley II, played no part in the administration of the shire as sheriff, escheator, justice of the peace or on *ad hoc* commissions.[129] Four others, Henry Beaumont, Thomas Staunton, John Whatton and Thomas Walsh, had very limited rôles in local government both during and after their periods of service. Walsh was pricked once as sheriff in 1456. John Whatton was returned to the Coventry parliament in 1459 and was also made escheator in the same year but his political career in the county was otherwise undistinguished. Henry Beaumont and Thomas Staunton were also returned to parliament in 1446 and 1447 respectively but they, too, were political lightweights. Neither man became sheriff or escheator or secured an appointment to the bench of JPs. Beaumont, in fact, never held any other shire office and Staunton's services in Leicestershire were not used again until 1457 when he was appointed to a commission of array.

Another household official, John Bellers II, had been MP in 1432, 1435 and 1450 and a justice of the peace since 1444 before he became an esquire of the chamber, but royal service notwithstanding, he was never pricked as sheriff and only infrequently was he appointed to *ad hoc* commissions. Royal service similarly brought few advances to the political career of Thomas Erdyngton who was king's knight by 1443. Admittedly, Erdyngton was pricked as sheriff in 1445 and elected knight of the shire for Leicestershire in 1446 but he had been sheriff there before, in 1434,

---

[127] Griffiths, *The Reign of King Henry VI*, pp. 296–7.
[128] Cf. Ross, *Edward IV*, pp. 326–7.
[129] This and subsequent information about household officials and local government experience is drawn from appendix 3.

and had been elected to parliament for Warwickshire in 1440. The careers of these men suggest that if the household were intended to be a political recruiting office and training ground for gentry who would carry the king's authority back into their shires, then the success of its Leicestershire cohort was singularly lacking.[130]

Furthermore, only three of Henry VI's personal retainers and household officers with Leicestershire connections, Henry Beaumont, Thomas Everyngham and William Grymmesby, remained sufficiently loyal to fight in his cause either at Wakefield or Towton.[131] A fourth, John Bellers II, must have been regarded with suspicion by the new regime for he was dropped from all Yorkist commissions of the peace but by 1463 he was commissioned as a tax assessor. Most of the others who had been politically obscure under Lancaster remained so after the Yorkists seized power. Thomas Erdyngton alone continued as a king's knight under Edward IV and in 1462 received a grant for life of one of the earl of Wiltshire's confiscated manors in Warwickshire.[132] He at least had not been transformed into a loyal son of Lancaster by his membership of Henry VI's retinue.

Under Edward IV, the knights and esquires of the household were not used to weld together a political community of the shire either. In the early years of the reign when the size of the household was drastically reduced,[133] two Leicestershire men, John Staunton and Thomas Erdyngton, entered the king's service

[130] A contrary view of the impact of members of the king's affinity on shire offices is taken by C. A. Robertson, 'Local government and the king's "affinity" in fifteenth-century Leicestershire and Warwickshire', *T.L.A.H.S.*, 52, 1976–7, pp. 37–45. Three aspects of Robertson's study tend to exaggerate the extent of royal interference in local appointments. First, the inclusion of Warwickshire in his study leads to generalizations which may apply to that county but not to Leicestershire. Warwickshire was dominated by magnates with strong court connections; Leicestershire was not so encumbered. Second, too much emphasis has been placed on the bonds formed between lords and retainers who entered indentures to serve in France. As we have already seen, these associations were politically insignificant (see above, pp. 96–8). Third, too little attention had been paid to the chronology of central and local service, thereby leading Robertson to assume a causal connection between household service and local government appointments when no such assumption is warranted.

[131] *Rot. Parl.*, v, p. 477. I am assuming that the William Grymmesby late of London who fought at Wakefield and the William Grymmesby late of Grimsby who fought at Towton were the same man. His connection with Leicestershire was through marriage to Anne, daughter and coheir of Reginald Moton.

[132] *C.P.R.*, 1461–7, p. 186.

[133] D. A. L. Morgan, 'The king's affinity in the polity of Yorkist England', *T.R.H.S.*, 5th ser., 23, 1973, pp. 4–5.

as a page and king's knight respectively. Later, John Shirley, Sir William Trussell and William Villers also made their way to court. Of these five, only Trussell played any further part in the administration of his shire. The inescapable conclusion is that neither Henry VI nor Edward IV had a coherent policy of interference in Leicestershire's internal affairs. Such aloofness on the part of the crown yields to no ready explanation. It is possible though, that in the absence of magnate domination in Leicestershire for most of our period, there was little need for the king to use members of his own affinity as a makeweight in the county's political scales.

Even after 1461, when William Hastings was elevated to the peerage and granted the confiscated Beaumont and Roos estates to add to his own already extensive Leicestershire manors, very few of his retainers were drawn from his home county.[134] Of the sixty-seven retainers who can be identified with the midland shires of Derby, Stafford, Nottingham, Warwick and Leicester, thirty-two were from Derbyshire, fourteen from Staffordshire, five from Nottinghamshire, two from Warwickshire and, according to Dunham, fourteen from Leicestershire. However, the latter figure is almost certainly an exaggeration. Given Hastings' obvious attempts to extend his influence into Derbyshire, many of his Leicestershire retainers, especially John and Ralph Shirley, the three members of the Staunton family and possibly Sir William Trussell as well, were chosen because of their landholdings in the former county. Trussell held extensive lands in Staffordshire, too, where Hastings was also building up his affinity. Sir Robert Harcourt was another retainer whose estate partly lay in Staffordshire. Once again, it may have been these Staffordshire connections which made Trussell and Harcourt attractive as retainers.

Of the eight Leicestershire gentry whose indentures to serve Hastings have survived,[135] five, John and Ralph Shirley, John Harcourt, John Danvers and William Neville, played no part in the county's government; two, William Trussell and William Moton, had already served the county as MP (Trussell) and sheriff (Moton) before being retained. Thomas Entwysell alone may have owed his advancement to the shrievalty in 1482 to his association with Hastings but as he had sealed his indenture eight years earlier in 1474, there was clearly no haste either on

[134] Dunham, 'Lord Hastings' indentured retainers 1461–1483', pp. 28–9.
[135] *Ibid.*, pp. 119–20.

Entwysell's part to claim his reward or on Hastings' part to assert political influence through his retainer.[136] Once again, the reasons for Hastings' forbearance are speculative. He may have regarded the expenditure in fees to his own neighbours as an unnecessary extravagance. Being closer to hand, the Leicestershire gentry would have been more susceptible to informal influence in any case. But perhaps, too, Hastings knew when to leave well enough alone.[137] Blatant interference in the internal affairs of a county which, for at least the previous sixty years, had not been overburdened with magnate or crown authority, could have offended local sensibilities.

We may confidently conclude that Leicestershire was not forged into a political unit by outside magnate intervention, by the king, or, indeed, after 1461 by its own resident magnate, lord Hastings. Hastings' reluctance openly to meddle in the county's internal affairs further reveals that in Leicestershire the retinue was not an important political unit. Of course, some gentry did display an acute awareness of the political issues of the day. As we have already seen, Henry Beaumont, Thomas Everyngham and William Grymmesby not only took an interest in national politics but were also prepared to fight for their chosen cause.[138] And they were not the only Leicestershire gentry to do so. Henry Beaumont's kinsman, John Beaumont, Everard Dygby I, William Fielding and John Danet all fought for Henry VI in 1460–1.[139] About ten years earlier, in 1450, the county had also produced an active opponent of the Lancastrian regime when Sir William Trussell, grandfather of Edward IV's knight of the same name, participated in Cade's Rebellion.[140]

However, we should not assume that these partisan activists were typical. In fact, they constituted a very small minority of the county gentry. For men such as Thomas Erdyngton, who as one of Henry VI's knights became closely associated with the losing side, the key to survival was flexibility. Pope Pius II's perception of John Lex, a Lancastrian agent in Rome during the troubled year of 1460, was equally applicable to Erdyngton and his like.

---

[136] See I. Rowney, 'The Hastings affinity in Staffordshire and the honour of Tutbury', *B.I.H.R.*, 57, 1984, pp. 35–45, where it is argued that Hastings' political influence in Staffordshire was similarly used sparingly.

[137] Cf. *ibid.*, p. 45.   [138] See above, p. 103.

[139] *Rot. Parl.*, v, p. 477; Wedgwood, *Biographies*, p. 314; Scofield, *The Life and Reign of Edward the Fourth*, I, p. 156.

[140] *C.P.R.*, 1446–52, pp. 355–6.

Pius believed that Lex 'will do as others generally do nowadays, and acclaim the victors, and though at first he sided with the others he will now side with those in power.'[141] Henry VI and Edward IV not only would have recognized this sentiment as a fact of political life but they also relied upon it for their own survival, Henry in 1470–1 and Edward in 1461.

More numerous than the politically ambidextrous Erdyngton were those gentry who maintained their neutrality. In fact, most of the Leicestershire gentry showed a marked reluctance to become overly involved in the dangerous national politics of the day. Indeed, this reluctance itself amounts to a widespread political attitude. Nevertheless, a widespread attitude hardly equates with a county political community. But although we are not yet in a position to say that the gentry saw themselves as part of a shire political community neither are we in a position to jettison the proposition. If such a concept existed, then it is more likely to find expression not in national, but in purely local, county concerns. Only by focussing on county government may we be in a position to understand county politics.

[141] *Calendar of State Papers and Manuscripts Existing in the Archives and Collections of Milan*, i, ed. A. B. Hinds, London, 1912, p. 35.

5

THE GENTRY AND LOCAL GOVERNMENT,
1422–1485

Medieval county administration performed four major functions. It provided the central government with some of its finance; it protected the king's feudal rights and revenues within the shire; it was responsible for providing the military support demanded by the crown and, through its judicial activities, it maintained the king's peace. In the generation following the Conquest, the official most responsible for performing these duties was the sheriff who, unlike his Anglo-Saxon forebear, was drawn from the ranks of the regional magnates, the baronage.[1] The baronial sheriffs were powerful men indeed, occasionally holding the office in a number of shires at once, often treating the shrievalty as an hereditary fief and, at times, using their vice-regal authority to launch rebellions against the crown.[2]

Nevertheless, by the fifteenth century two developments had occurred. First, the powers of the sheriff had been trimmed by the appointment of additional, more specialized, officials.[3] Second, the great baronial families had ceased personally to fill the offices of local government. Instead, these offices had passed to lesser men of gentle status who, for the most part, held lands and lived in the counties where they served.[4] During

---

[1] W. A. Morris, 'The office of sheriff in the early Norman period', *E.H.R.*, 33, 1918, pp. 145–75; A. L. Poole, *From Domesday Book to Magna Carta 1087–1216*, Oxford, 1951, pp. 387–8.

[2] Morris, 'The office of sheriff', *passim*; Ch. Petit-Dutaillis, *The Feudal Monarchy in France and England*, London, 1936, p. 70; H. R. Loyn, *The Norman Conquest*, 2nd edn, London, 1967, pp. 148–51; H. M. Cam, *The Hundred and the Hundred Rolls. An Outline of Local Government in Medieval England*, London, 1930, p. 2.

[3] R. B. Pugh, 'The king's government in the middle ages', in *V. C. H. Wilts.*, v, pp. 5ff; M. H. Keen, *England in the Later Middle Ages*, London, 1973, p. 6; Pollock and Maitland, *The History of English Law*, I, pp. 533–5.

[4] R. F. Treharne, 'The knights in the period of reform and rebellion, 1258–1267', esp. pp. 3, 7; Cam, 'The legislators of medieval England', p. 144; P. R. Coss, *The Langley Family and its Cartulary. A Study in Late Medieval 'Gentry'*, Dugdale Occasional Papers, 22, Oxford, 1974, p. 5; Denholm-Young, *History and Heraldry*, p. 158; Powicke, *The*

the Angevin and Plantagenet periods, government became not only local rather than regional but it also became self-government.[5]

The first limitation to the powers of the sheriff came at the end of the twelfth century with the arrival of the coroner whose office, from 1246 onwards, was filled by election for life in the county court.[6] Usually, four coroners were elected for each county. In addition, some boroughs were served by their own coroners. This was the case with the borough of Leicester which had two.[7]

The various duties performed by the coroner have been well documented.[8] Attention needs to be drawn only to his principal responsibility which was to act as keeper of the pleas of the crown. Although the coroner did not hear and determine cases, his record of all that transpired in the county court and in the tourn served as a check on the activities of the sheriff.[9]

Early in the thirteenth century the sheriff and coroner were joined by the escheator who inherited the sheriff's responsibility for assessing, administering and delivering escheats.[10] At first there had been merely two escheatries for the entire kingdom, one for each side of the Trent. Later, Edward III experimented by establishing eight regional officials who were assigned groups of counties. Finally, from 1341, escheators

Thirteenth Century, p. 539; A Harding, *The Law Courts of Medieval England*, London, 1973, p. 92. There were, of course, notable exceptions even as late as the fifteenth century. For example, Richard Beauchamp, earl of Warwick, was hereditary sheriff of Worcestershire from 1403 to 1439 (*Early Treatises on the Practice of the Justice of the Peace in the Fifteenth and Sixteenth Centuries*, B. H. Putnam, Oxford Studies in Social and Legal History, VIII, Oxford, 1924, p. 67). However, the earl did not personally perform the shrieval duties.

5 See A. B. White, *Self-Government at the King's Command*, Minneapolis, 1933, pp. 1–2. Also, see below, pp. 133–4.

6 *Ibid.*, pp. 1, 91; Poole, *From Domesday Book to Magna Carta*, pp. 390–1; Cam, *Hundred Rolls*, p. 128; R. F. Hunnisett, *The Medieval Coroner*, Cambridge, 1961, p. 150.

7 Hunnisett, *The Medieval Coroner*, pp. 134–7.

8 *Stat. Realm*, I, pp. 40–1; H. M. Jewell, *English Local Administration in the Middle Ages*, Newton Abbot, 1972, pp. 154–5; H. M. Cam, 'Shire officials: coroners, constables and bailiffs', in *The English Government at Work 1327–1336*, III, ed. J. F. Willard *et al.*, Cambridge, Mass., 1950, pp. 143–65; Hunnisett, *The Medieval Coroner*, pp. vii–viii.

9 Pollock and Maitland, *The History of English Law*, I, p. 534; Cam, 'Shire officials', pp. 153–4.

10 Cam, *Hundred Rolls*, pp. 199–202; Jewell, *English Local Administration*, pp. 99–100.

were appointed to each county, or pair of counties, to coincide with the shrievalties.[11]

Furthermore, the policing and judicial powers attached to the sheriff's office were eroded, first by the keepers and, subsequently, by the justices, of the peace.[12] An act of 1361 recognized the right of justices to hear and determine 'all manner of felonies and trespasses' in their sessions.[13] Thereafter, a justice's duties were expanded to include hearing cases involving weights and measures, rates of pay under the Statute of Labourers and Artificers and breaches of the sumptuary laws, thereby assigning to him economic and social, in addition to his well-established criminal, competence.[14] Despite evidence to suggest that sheriffs resented and actively opposed the growing power of the justices, their opposition merely served to draw official attention to their own shortcomings and corrupt practices.[15] As a result, from 1461, indictments which had formerly been brought to the sheriff's tourn had to be sent instead to the sessions of the justices of the peace.[16] Thereafter, the sheriff could present indictments but he could no longer hear and determine them.

One historian, Professor Putnam, has claimed that the statute of 1461 completed 'the downfall of the sheriff'.[17] Indeed, we cannot deny that the fifteenth-century sheriff had become a mere shadow of his Norman counterpart. Not only had the coroners, escheators and justices of the peace assumed many of his police,

---

[11] S. T. Gibson, 'The escheatries 1327–41', *E.H.R.*, 36, 1921, pp. 218–25; T. F. Tout, *The Place of the Reign of Edward II in English History*, 2nd edn, revised H. Johnstone, Manchester, 1936, pp. 321–2; E. R. Stevenson, 'The escheator', in *The English Government at Work 1327–1336*, II, ed. W. A. Morris and J. R. Strayer, Cambridge, Mass., 1947, pp. 113–20. As with its sheriff, Leicestershire shared its escheator with Warwickshire.

[12] B. H. Putnam, 'The transformation of the keepers of the peace into the justices of the peace 1327–1380', *T.R.H.S.*, 4th ser., 12, 1929, pp. 19–48; A. Harding, 'The origins and early history of the keepers of the peace', *T.R.H.S.*, 5th ser., 10, 1960, pp. 85–109.

[13] *Stat. Realm*, I, pp. 364–5, c. 1.

[14] *Ibid.*, p. 365, c. 5; *ibid.*, II, p. 63, c. 8; *ibid.*, II, p. 402, c. 5; *Proceedings before the Justices of the Peace in the Fourteenth and Fifteenth Centuries, Edward III to Richard III*, ed. B. H. Putnam, London, 1938, pp. xxviii, xlvi, xlviii; B. Osborne, *Justices of the Peace 1361–1848*, Shaftesbury, 1960, pp. 8–9; Harding, *Law Courts*, p. 95; R. Sillem, 'Commissions of the peace, 1380–1485', *B.I.H.R.*, 10, 1932–3, pp. 81–104.

[15] For example, the sheriffs of Herefordshire had been illegally hearing cases in their tourn dealing with the Statute of Labourers and Artificers (*Stat. Realm*, II, p. 266, c. 7; *ibid.*, p. 281, c. 7). See, too, *Proceedings*, p. xxxvi.

[16] *Stat. Realm*, II, pp. 389–91, c. 2.   [17] *Proceedings*, p. lv.

feudal and judicial functions, but his military duties had also, in part, been superseded by the appointment of commissioners of array.[18]

Yet, the fifteenth-century sheriff was a man of considerable local standing who could still wield great power and influence. No longer to be regarded as 'the very pulse of the machine' of local government,[19] as addressee and server of writs he nonetheless did have his fingers on that pulse.[20] As empaneller of juries he could control their composition, thereby affecting the outcome of indictments.[21] As the official responsible for organizing the election of knights of the shire in the county court, he could secure the election of his own friends, or, failing that, return members who had not been elected at all.[22] Coroners were also chosen in the county court, so it seems reasonable to assume that their election, too, could have been the subject of shrieval sharp practice. As late as 1481, John Shynner was urging Sir William Stonor to labour to become sheriff, 'for hyt ys a presentabell offise' which appealed to the 'worcheppefollyst yn ye sher'. He further reminded his correspondent that 'hyt ys beter to goveryn then to be goveryed'.[23] Shynner's letter indicates that the sheriff was still a force to be reckoned with in local affairs and that, whatever the perception of later historians, his 'downfall', to borrow Professor Putnam's word, was not at all apparent to contemporaries.

Although our attention has been focussed on those officials whose business came to circumscribe the work of the sheriff, they by no means constituted the total of shire officers. The central government also relied on local men to assess and collect taxes.[24] Various *ad hoc* commissions, such as commissions of array or of oyer and terminer, contained a leaven of county residents and

---

[18] Cam, 'Shire officials', p. 143. [19] Cam, *Hundred Rolls*, p. 59.

[20] For sheriffs' duties, see W. A. Morris, 'The sheriff', in *The English Government at Work 1327–1336*, II, ed. W. A. Morris and J. R. Strayer, Cambridge, Mass., 1947, pp. 53–73. For the bureaucratic side of the sheriff's office see M. H. Mills, 'The medieval shire house', in *Studies Presented to Sir Hilary Jenkinson*, ed. J. C. Davies, London, 1957, pp. 254–71.

[21] Morris, 'The sheriff', p. 68.

[22] See *P.P.C.*, VI, pp. 183–4; *Stat. Realm*, II, p. 340, c. 14; H. G. Richardson, 'The Commons and medieval politics', *T.R.H.S.*, 4th ser., 28, 1946, pp. 39–42.

[23] *The Stonor Letters and Papers 1290–1483*, ed. C. L. Kingsford, 2 vols., Camden 3rd ser., 29–30, London, 1919, vol. II, pp. 134–5.

[24] C. Johnson, 'The collectors of lay taxes', in *The English Government at Work 1327–1336*, II, ed. W. A. Morris and J. R. Strayer, Cambridge, Mass., 1947, pp. 201–26.

landholders.[25] There were, too, the knights of the shires and burgesses who, by a statute of 1413, were expected to be residents of their shires or boroughs.[26] Admittedly, the shire and borough representatives were not directly involved in local government. However, they did act as links between the centre and the localities, carrying to parliament the petitions formulated in the county court, conveying back to their constituencies reports of the assembly's proceedings and binding their communities to provide the taxes which they had granted.[27] They should therefore be included in our considerations.[28]

But our aim here is not to concentrate on the offices themselves but upon the men who filled them. What was the relationship between the economic and social status of the office holders and the positions they filled? Did those who were appointed or elected satisfy the statutory requirements pertaining to their office? Did local government fall into the hands of a few select families or did most of the shire gentry families play their part? How experienced in local government were those who were selected for, or elected to, positions of authority? To what extent did national politics impinge upon the selection or election of local office holders? In order to attempt an answer to the last question it will be necessary to keep in mind the background of political upheavals at the centre; the revolt of the Commons in parliament in 1449–50, the dynastic tensions of the mid- to late 1450s, the Lancastrian coup and Yorkist counter-coup of 1470–1, the fall of the duke of Clarence in 1478 and the brief minority of Edward V followed by the duke of Gloucester's usurpation of 1483. However, one of our major concerns will be with the dynastic change of 1461 to see if the polity of Yorkist England differed significantly from that of its Lancastrian predecessor. Most importantly of all, we are also in search of evidence which may point to the concept of the shire as a political unit.

From appendix 1 it can be seen that there was a clear

---

[25] Putnam, *Proceedings*, pp. xlix–l; *C.P.R.*, 1429–36, pp. 126, 424, 520, 529 and *passim*.

[26] *Stat. Realm*, II, p. 170, c.1.

[27] Maddicott, 'The county community', p. 29; H. M. Cam, 'The relation of English members of parliament to their constituencies in the fourteenth century: a neglected text', in *Liberties and Communities*, pp. 223–35; Richardson, 'The Commons and medieval politics', pp. 21–45.

[28] The king also relied on justices of assize and gaol delivery to maintain law and order. However, these men tended to be professional lawyers sent out from the central courts rather than local gentry and therefore must be discounted (M. M. Taylor, 'The justices of assize', in *The English Government at Work*, III, pp. 231–2).

correlation between status and office holding and that the social hierarchy within the county gentry coincides with a hierarchy of offices. Knightly families had a virtual monopoly of the shrievalty within the shire.[29] Only two of the thirteen potential knightly families and a mere five of the forty-six esquire families produced sheriffs. None of the gentlemen became a sheriff. The Leicestershire experience, therefore, shows that the shrievalty had not lost its attraction to members of the upper gentry, despite a reduction of the sheriffs' powers.

Slightly below the sheriffs in status were the knights of the shire. Knightly, and potential knightly families dominated. Only six of the mere esquire families produced knights of the shire, while gentlemen were never elected.

Office holding became more open to the middling gentry, the esquires, with the commission of the peace and escheatorship. In the case of the former, knights and distrainees were regularly appointed. Nevertheless, as the century progressed and the size of the commissions increased, places were found to accommodate the mere esquires. Close to a third of these families were represented on the commissions of the peace.

The escheatorship, on the other hand, failed to be attractive to knights. The only representative of the Leicestershire knightly families appointed to the escheatorship was William Moton in 1467, although his selection for the office predated his acquisition of knighthood.[30] There was less reticence on the part of distrainee families to accept the escheatorship. Five distrainees, representing four families, were appointed escheator on six occasions.

If we considered the Leicestershire material alone we should discover that while the escheatorship had lost its appeal to knights, it was not yet regarded as an office suitable for mere esquires, only eight of whom were appointed. However, it must be remembered that Leicestershire shared its escheator with Warwickshire and, of the sixty appointments made to the office between 1423 and 1485, only sixteen were of Leicestershire personnel. Given that the sample is so small we need to consider some of the Warwickshire appointees if we are to reach any meaningful conclusions about the status of those appointed. To this end, the period 1441–52 was selected for closer scrutiny, primarily because

---

[29] For the moment our concern is with Leicestershire offices. Those members of the gentry who held offices in neighbouring counties will be dealt with only in passing.

[30] *List of Escheators*, p. 171.

it provides a consecutive run of Warwickshire appointments and with the added advantage of falling close to the middle of our period. Of the twelve appointments made between 1441 and 1452, two were categorically designated as 'esquire'.[31] Of the remaining ten, eight are readily identifiable as esquires. Despite the shortage of specifically Leicestershire evidence on this point, therefore, the escheatorship was, in fact, regarded as mainly the preserve of esquires rather than of knights.

Within this hierarchy of offices the commissioners of array fell part-way between the knights of the shire and the justices of the peace. Between 1422 and 1485, ten commissions were appointed in Leicestershire.[32] In each of these commissions, esquire families were represented, but the chances of receiving a commission increased the higher one's status. Preference was given to members of the knightly, and potential knightly, families.

In contrast to these major offices, the coronership and tax commission attracted men of more lowly status. The early medieval coroner had been a man of high rank, coming from the same social stratum as the sheriff.[33] The First Statute of Westminster stipulated that coroners be chosen from among the 'most wise and discreet knights'.[34] Nevertheless, the statute also recognized that even at this early date (1275) the election of 'mean persons and undiscreet' had been common. Notwithstanding the act's attempt to call a halt to this development, the election of non-knights must have continued because in 1340 the knightly provision was dropped altogether and the coroners' qualifications reduced to having 'sufficient' land in fee in the county where they held office.[35] How much land in fee was 'sufficient' was not defined, though land worth £20 per annum was probably intended.[36] A further act of 1354 was even more vague, the electors being exhorted to choose 'the most meet and most lawful people that shall be found in the said counties'.[37] By this date, the

---

[31] *Ibid.*, pp. 170–1.

[32] *C.P.R.*, 1429–36, pp. 520, 523; *ibid.*, 1452–61, pp. 402, 560; *ibid.*, 1467–77, pp. 196, 199, 284, 405; *ibid.*, 1476–85, pp. 400, 489.

[33] Cam, *Hundred Rolls*, p. 128; Jewell, *English Local Administration*, p. 156; Hunnisett, *The Medieval Coroner*, p. 173.

[34] *Stat. Realm*, I, p. 29, c. 10.   [35] *Ibid.*, p. 283, stat. 1, c. 8.

[36] Cf. *ibid.*, II, pp. 309–10, c. 11, where justices were expected to have sufficient land in fee and 'sufficient' was defined as land worth £20 a year.

[37] *Ibid.*, I, p. 346, c. 6; see, too, Hunnisett, *The Medieval Coroner*, pp. 173–5.

government at last recognized and bowed to the reality that the coronership was no longer attractive to the upper gentry. Perhaps they found the clerical side of the coroner's duties as recorder just too laborious.

The lack of precision evident in the statutory qualifications for coroners presents one difficulty, but there are others. For example, the writs *de coronatore eligendo*, which ordered the replacement of insufficiently qualified or incapacitated coroners, fail to say whether the person being removed, though elected, had actually performed the duties of his office.[38] Furthermore, the writs fail to specify whether the coroner in question was a county, or a borough, coroner. The major problem, however, is that of discovering who held the office.

For the period 1422–85, only eight coroners have been identified.[39] Almost certainly, three of these were coroners for the borough of Leicester.[40] Of the remaining five, none was a knight or distrained of knighthood. Two, Richard Acton and John Danet, were members of esquire families. Acton must have been elected in or before 1430 when a writ *de coronatore eligendo* was issued to the sheriff on the grounds that the coroner was insufficiently qualified.[41] The efficacy of such writs may be judged from the fact that another had to be issued ordering Acton's removal in 1433.[42] Nevertheless, he was still performing his coronial duties in May 1442.[43] Later the same year, two further attempts at his removal were made, one on the grounds that, for certain unspecified reasons, the king wished it, the other using the well-worn excuse that Acton was insufficiently qualified and unable to perform his duties.[44]

No such imputation attached itself to John Danet who was elected coroner in, or sometime before, 1422.[45] Two years later, his removal was ordered because of his appointment as under-

---

[38] Pugh, 'The king's government in the middle ages', p. 24; Hunnisett, *The Medieval Coroner*, p. 156.

[39] Richard Acton, John Danet, John Blaby, Nicholas Joye, Henry Othehall, John Reynold, Richard Yates and William Hynde (Hande).

[40] John Reynold, Richard Yates and William Hynde. John Reynold and Richard Yates were acting as coroners in 1466 (KB9/313/29) and William Hynde was coroner in 1470 (KB9/327/39, 40). Reynold had been mayor of Leicester in 1459, Yates witnessed a borough lease in 1462, while Hynde acted as witness to a grant of land to the borough in 1452 (Bateson, II, pp. 258, 269, 278).

[41] *C.C.R.*, 1429–35, p. 75.   [42] *Ibid.*, p. 216.

[43] KB9/241/84.   [44] *C.C.R.*, 1441–7, p. 85.

[45] JUST3/31/12 MS 5; *C.C.R.*, 1422–9, p. 165.

sheriff. The incompatibility of the dual rôle is understandable.[46] But despite the crown's concern on this matter, Danet must have either ignored the conflict of interests or else managed to get himself re-elected to the coronership after he ceased to be under-sheriff. He was certainly acting as coroner as late as 1444.[47]

Of the remaining three coroners, one, John Blaby, was a gentleman, but the other two, Nicholas Joye of Stathern and Henry Othehall of Sutton, were never accorded gentle status.[48] Nicholas Joye may well have come from one of those ambitious families who found the coronership a convenient stepping stone to social advancement.[49] His social interactions were by no means confined to the sub-gentry for he acted as godfather at the baptism of William Villers in 1405.[50] But it is impossible to determine whether fifteenth-century ambition would have brought social reward to this particular family in the sixteenth for early in the century the Joyes died out in the male line. What the limited Leicestershire material does reveal, however, is that the decline of the coronership, which gathered momentum in the fourteenth century, continued throughout the fifteenth.[51]

The tax collector was another county official whose status had declined since the early fourteenth century.[52] Knights were never appointed, and only once, at the very beginning of our period, was a member of a distrainee family appointed.[53] Nine esquires did become tax collectors between 1422 and 1446, but not thereafter. Of these nine, the Walsh family alone stands apart from the general run of collectors. Although Richard Walsh had been collector in 1422, he himself subsequently failed to serve in any other capacity.[54] Nevertheless, his son, Thomas, rose to be sheriff in 1456 and to be appointed to commissions of the peace

---

[46] See above, p. 108.   [47] *C.P.R.*, 1441–6, p. 319; KB9/247/44.

[48] *C.C.R.*, 1422–9, pp. 170, 174; *Quorndon Records*, p. 135.

[49] Hunnisett, *The Medieval Coroner*, p. 171.

[50] C139/42/74 MS 2. The word used is *sponsalia* but it is clear from the context that godfather is intended.

[51] For the coroner's decline see Cam, *Hundred Rolls*, p. 128; Cam, 'Shire officials', p. 156; Hunnisett, *The Medieval Coroner*, pp. 171–4, 197.

[52] See Johnson, 'The collectors of lay taxes', pp. 201ff; J. R. Strayer, 'Introduction', in *The English Government at Work*, II, pp. 17–19. Throughout, I have confined my statements ⸱o the collectors, rather than the assessors, of taxation. The latter were drawn from the ranks of the upper and middle gentry families and, as they were always experienced in other local government offices, they can, with justification, be omitted here.

[53] Richard Hotoft, the elder, in 1422 (*C.F.R.*, 1422–30, p. 5).

[54] *Ibid.*, 1422–30, p. 5.

and of array between 1456 and 1460.[55] The other eight cases reveal that tax collecting was not considered a route to further advancement. The only other office filled by Richard Acton was the coronership, a post he had held since at least 1430. John Danet, tax collector in 1445 and a man of greater substance than Acton, had been appointed escheator in 1438, but otherwise his experiences, too, were limited to the lesser offices.[56] Members of the other six esquire families failed to attain higher office in the county.

By far the greater number of tax collectors was drawn from the mere gentry and sub-gentry families.[57] A few collectors became experienced through repeated appointment. For example, William Weston of Carlton served five times between 1422 and 1432 and John Attewell of Foxton was appointed four times.[58] However, the vast majority, seventy-four in all, served only once, suggesting not only that there was a large pool of available personnel from which to draw, but also that perhaps the office was unpopular and therefore to be avoided.

This initial analysis of office holders reveals that local government positions can be divided into two groups, the major and the minor. The former group, which includes the sheriff, the knight of the shire, the justice of the peace, the commissioner of array and the escheator, attracted men who were drawn from the ranks of the upper and middle gentry. The minor shire offices, the coronership and the office of tax collector, were filled by men of much lesser status, most of whom were not members of the gentry at all. As non-gentry office holders fall outside the scope of this study, we shall concentrate our attention on the major county offices and on the men who filled them but especially on the offices of sheriff, knight of the shire and justice of the peace.

Chief among these county officials was the sheriff. Although Leicestershire and Warwickshire were linked to form a single shrievalty, no attempt was made to ensure an even-handed division of the office between the two shires. Between 1422 and 1485, sixty-five appointments were made but Leicestershire men were pricked on only twenty-four occasions. This discrepancy

---

[55] Lists and Indexes, IX, p. 145; *C.P.R.*, 1452–61, p. 669, *ibid.*, p. 560.

[56] Coroner, 1424 (*C.C.R.*, 1422–9, p. 165); under-sheriff, 1424 (*ibid.*); escheator, 1438 (*List of Escheators*, p. 170); tax collector, 1445 (*C.F.R.*, 1437–45, p. 329).

[57] Between 1422 and 1485, a total of ninety families.

[58] *C.F.R.*, 1422–30, pp. 5, 220, 292, 329; *ibid.*, 1430–7, pp. 69, 107, 191, 358.

cannot be explained in terms of either the county's wealth or population, for on both counts Leicestershire marginally outstripped its western neighbour.[59] The explanation is more likely to be found in Leicestershire's lack, or, more accurately, Warwickshire's surfeit, of powerful magnates, whose contacts with central government could be used to draw the Exchequer's attention to men of their affinity.[60] For example, at least four Warwickshire appointees between 1425 and 1431, Richard Clodesdale, John Harewell, William Peyto and William Mountford, had close links with Richard Beauchamp, earl of Warwick.[61] While it is impossible to prove that the earl's influence secured their appointment, as king's counsellor and, from 1428, governor of the boy-king, he was certainly in a position to do so.[62]

Both the Leicestershire and Warwickshire sheriffs satisfied the fourteenth-century statutory provisions which provided for annual appointments.[63] Even in the early 1420s, when the twin pressures of war and pestilence demanded a relaxation of the rule, no Leicestershire or Warwickshire sheriff served for longer than a year at a time.[64] A few Leicestershire gentry did, nevertheless, avail themselves of the regulation which permitted subsequent appointment after a lapse of three years.[65] Sir Richard Hastings was sheriff in 1423, 1427 and again in 1433, and Thomas Erdyngton and Thomas Ferrers served twice, in 1434 and 1445 and in 1460 and 1468 respectively. However, there was a greater propensity towards re-selection among the Warwickshire personnel, with thirty individuals serving on forty-one occasions.[66] In two instances, though, the appointment of Richard Hastings was contrary to the spirit, though not the letter, of the law. In the first case he was pricked for Leicestershire in December 1426, immediately after serving as sheriff in Yorkshire, and he was pricked as sheriff of Yorkshire again in 1433, the year after he had been selected as sheriff of Leicestershire.[67]

[59] Russell, *British Medieval Population*, p. 132; Schofield, 'The geographical distribution of wealth in England, 1334–1649', p. 504.

[60] For the importance of the sheriff to magnate control of the shire see Jacob, *The Fifteenth Century*, p. 448.

[61] B. L. Eg. Roll, 8773; Dugdale, I, p. 476; *ibid.*, II, pp. 809, 1009.

[62] Wolffe, *Henry VI*, pp. 45–6.

[63] *Stat. Realm*, p. 283, stat. I, c. 7; *ibid.*, p. 346, c. 7.

[64] *Ibid.*, II, p. 206, stat. I, c. 5; Lists and Indexes, IX, pp. 145–6.

[65] *Stat. Realm*, II, p. 4, c. 11.   [66] Lists and Indexes, IX, pp. 145–6.

[67] *Ibid.*, pp. 145, 162.

Further regulations required that sheriffs not only hold sufficient land within their shires but also that they be residents of their
bailiwicks.[68] Some of the Leicestershire sheriffs such as Richard,
Leonard and William Hastings, Thomas Erdyngton and Thomas
Ferrers did, indeed, hold land in both counties but, in practice, it
was acceptable if the incumbent held in only one county. For
example, Laurence and Thomas Berkeley held lands in Leicestershire and Rutland but not in Warwickshire.[69]

The majority of the twenty Leicestershire sheriffs had previous
experience in at least some local government office either in
Leicestershire itself or in another county. Five, Lawrence Berkeley, Robert Moton, William Trussell, Thomas Fouleshurst and
Thomas Walsh, had formerly been elected as knights of the shire,
and a further four, Thomas Berkeley, Everard Fielding, Leonard
Hastings and William Moton, had been commissioners of the
peace.[70] Four of these nine, Laurence Berkeley, Leonard Hastings, Thomas Fouleshurst and Robert Moton, had served additional apprenticeships on *ad hoc* commissions as tax assessors,
raising loans or as commissioners of array. Another two, Richard
Hastings and Laurence Sherard, had never been knights of the
shire or justices of the peace but they had been appointed to *ad hoc*
commissions in Leicestershire. Sherard had also been sheriff of
Rutland.

Although the Exchequer displayed a bias in favour of men with
experience, this was clearly not the sole criterion it adopted when
selecting candidates to be presented for the king's approval.
William Moton, the only Leicestershireman who came to the
office after serving as escheator, may have owed his selection in
November 1471 to the influence of William, lord Hastings.
Moton was a feoffee for the manor of Belvoir, acquired by
Hastings in 1467, and the association between the two men was
later strengthened when Moton entered the Hastings retinue in
1475.[71] But he was probably the same William Moton who was
knighted after the battle of Tewkesbury in May 1471, and
therefore received his shrieval office from a grateful king as an

---

[68] *Stat. Realm*, I, p. 174, stat. 2; *ibid.*, p. 283, stat. 1, c. 7; *ibid.*, II, p. 134, c. 5.

[69] See appendix 3.

[70] Thomas Assheby, sheriff in 1440, has been omitted from these calculations. The
Thomas Assheby who was knight of the shire in 1414 and 1419 and justice of the peace
between 1422 and 1431 was probably the father of the sheriff.

[71] H.M.C., *Hastings*, I, p. 296; *C.P.R.*, 1467–77, p. 26; Dunham, 'Lord Hastings'
indentured retainers 1461–1483', p. 144.

additional reward for services rendered directly to the crown.[72] William Trussell was another of Hastings' retainers. In his case, Trussell's appointment as sheriff did follow the sealing of his indenture by a few months.[73]

Of course, Moton and Trussell were both sufficiently qualified to be selected on their own merits and without magnate or crown interference. However, a surprisingly large proportion of the Leicestershire sheriffs, nine in all, were new to local office at the time of their appointment. In these instances, the prime consideration must have been not only demonstrable loyalty to the regime but also, in some cases, the possession of powerful sponsors. It is difficult not to suspect the duke of York's involvement in the employment of the young and inexperienced William Hastings, whose writ of appointment in November 1455 came just ten days after York assumed the Protectorate.[74] Another newcomer to local government, Thomas Entwysell, was, in turn, a Hastings retainer for eight years before being pricked as sheriff in 1482.[75]

Obviously, the crown was also in a position to exert its influence over appointments. For example, Sir William Trussell was a knight of the body in the royal household at least a year before he was pricked as sheriff. Furthermore, in November 1474 he had indented to serve Edward IV both personally and with six spears and sixty archers in the war with France.[76] We have already seen that the king was generous towards those who served him well.[77] One is therefore convinced that Trussell's appointment owed more to his household affiliations than either to his earlier experience as knight of the shire or to his indenture with lord Hastings.[78] Similarly, Thomas Everyngham's close court connections probably secured his appointment to the shrievalty in

[72] Shaw, *The Knights of England*, II, p. 15; *Paston Letters 1422–1509*, V, p. 105.

[73] Dunham, 'Lord Hastings' indentured retainers 1461–1483', p. 144.

[74] Lists and Indexes, IX, p. 145; J. R. Lander, 'Henry VI and the duke of York's second protectorate, 1455 to 1456', *B.J.R.L.*, 43, 1960–1, p. 57. The Hastings family had close ties with the house of Mortimer, of which York was the heir, since the days of William's uncle, Sir Ralph, who was executed for his part in the rebellion of 1405 (*C.P.R.*, 1405–8, pp. 69, 88, 177, 478).

[75] Dunham 'Lord Hastings' indentured retainers 1461–1483', p. 144.

[76] E101/71/6 MS 987.

[77] See, for example, references to Sir William Moton above p. 118 and chapter 4.

[78] Professor Dunham's opinion that in the indenture of March 1475 between Hastings and Trussell the chamberlain is cultivating Trussell rather than vice versa seems well considered (Dunham, 'Lord Hastings' indentured retainers, 1461–1483', p. 35).

1446. He is revealed in the wardrobe account books to have been an esquire of the chamber since at least 1442.[79]

Both Trussell's and Everyngham's military careers show them to have been men sound in limb, fully capable of performing the onerous duties required of the sheriff.[80] In fact, the Exchequer clearly preferred men such as they, mature enough to demand respect, but sufficiently youthful to withstand the rigours of a position which involved long hours in the saddle. The ages of twelve of the Leicestershire sheriffs are known. Six of these, Thomas Berkeley, Thomas Erdyngton, Thomas Ferrers, Robert Harcourt, Ralph Woodford and Thomas Pulteney, were in their thirties, and a further three, William Moton, William Trussell and Thomas Everyngham, were in their early to midforties. But in the unsettled, early 1450s other considerations took priority over age. Leonard Hastings was fifty-seven when he was selected and Robert Moton was seventy-six.[81] The youngest Leicestershire sheriff was the twenty-four-year-old William Hastings.[82]

The appointment of Sir Leonard and William Hastings closely followed advances in the political career of the duke of York.[83] One therefore suspects not only that York used his influence to secure their selection but also that both men welcomed this opportunity to advance their own careers. For the aged Sir Robert Moton, however, the appointment came as an unwanted honour.[84] He felt himself unequal to the task and, understandably, tried to obtain a discharge on account of his great age and feebleness. Clearly, Moton's previous loyal service to the regime counted for more than any decline in agility; his request was refused. Nevertheless, in deference to his advancing years and to

---

[79] E101/409/9, fo. 36v. Everyngham was also closely connected with a number of the Lancastrian lords. He had been a feoffee of the duke of Somerset (Wedgwood, *Biographies*, p. 308); later, he was standard bearer for John Talbot, earl of Shrewsbury, at Castillon (Thomas Basin, *Histoire de Charles VII*, II, 1445–50, ed. Charles Samaran, Paris, 1944, p. 195); and both John viscount Beaumont and John lord Lovell thought highly of him. To Beaumont, Everyngham was his 'wilbeloved Thomas Everyngham', and Lovell considered him to be 'right a good and a feithfull gentilman' (*Paston Letters 1422–1509*, III, p. 143, no. 381). See, too, Griffiths, *The Reign of King Henry VI*, p. 341.

[80] For these duties see Morris, 'The sheriff', pp. 105–7; Cam, *Hundred Rolls*, pp. 67ff.

[81] Wedgwood, *Biographies*, p. 433; E149/161 MS 3; C139/83/58 MS 5; *Pedigrees*, p. 62.

[82] C139/162/22 MS 5.

[83] York was summoned to the great council in October 1453 following the onset of the king's mental collapse (*P.P.C.*, VI, p. 163) and appointed to his second Protectorate in November 1455 (Lander, 'Henry VI and the duke of York's second protectorate', p. 57). [84] E199/45/10 MS 3.

obviate the need for unnecessary travel, he was granted permission to account at the Exchequer by deputy rather than in person. No doubt, most of the burdens of office were performed by deputies, the under-sheriffs, too. Unfortunately, these under-sheriffs remain rather shadowy figures. Apart from John Danet, the others who have been discovered belonged to the mere gentry.[85]

We have already seen that five of the Leicestershire sheriffs had previously served as knights of the shire in parliament. But the flow of personnel from office to office was not all one-way. Five of the Leicestershire sheriffs subsequently represented the county in parliament.[86] These shire representatives were elected in the county court held in the borough of Leicester. Of course, the appointment of the sheriff lay with the central administration and was therefore open to direct magnate interference, but there can be no suggestion that the election of members was a matter entirely in the hands of the local freeholders. As convenor of the county court, the sheriff was in a position to meddle in the election process, either on his own account or at the behest of the more powerful. The Paston letters amply reveal that the electors themselves were also not immune from magnate pressure.[87]

The central government was not unmindful of shrieval shortcomings and its response in the fourteenth century had been to forbid the return of active sheriffs.[88] A further act of 1413 insisted that the representatives be residents of their counties on the date of the writ of summons, thereby ensuring some link between electors and elected.[89] In order to avoid the election of men of small substance and, therefore, of little independence, a statute of 1445 required that 'the knights of the shire . . . shall be notable knights of the same counties for which they shall be chosen or otherwise such notable esquires, gentlemen of birth . . . as shall be

---

[85] Thomas Sampson, under-sheriff of Laurence Berkeley (C1/9/189), Thomas Herdewyn, under-sheriff to Thomas Erdyngton (C1/12/131) and Thomas Farnham, who was probably the son of Robert of Over Hall rather than his more elevated uncle of the same name (*Index of Ancient Petitions of the Chancery and the Exchequer*, Lists and Indexes, I, revised edn, London 1892, Kraus repr., New York, 1966, p. 122).

[86] Thomas Erdyngton, Thomas Everyngham, Leonard Hastings, William Trussell and Thomas Berkeley. Bartholomew Brokesby, representative in the first parliament of Henry VI, had been sheriff in 1419 and 1410 but he had served as knight of the shire before that, in 1409.

[87] *Paston Letters*, I, pp. 95–6, 284, 577–8; *ibid.*, II, pp. 48, 50, 54, 117.

[88] *Stat. Realm.*, I, p. 394.   [89] *Ibid.*, II, p. 170, c. 1.

able to be knights and no man to be such knight which standeth in the degree of a yeoman and under'.[90] As can be seen, electors were not expressly forbidden to return representatives drawn from the ranks of the mere esquires or even the mere gentry, although in the latter case they baulked at doing so. Nevertheless, they were clearly expected to return members selected from the knightly, or potential knightly, families.

Between 1422 and 1483, writs for thirty-one parliaments were issued.[91] However, for three of these parliaments, those of 1460, 1463 and January 1483, not only have the Leicestershire returns failed to survive but the names of the county representatives cannot be found among the records of payments made to MPs. Another parliament, that of 1469, never met, and for a further two elections, in November 1461 and for the aborted parliament of June 1483, the name of only one county representative can be deduced.[92] These gaps reduce the number of known shire knights to fifty-two out of a possible total of sixty-two.

As the law required, all of the Leicestershire members were residents of the shire and none of the county's sheriffs was ever elected during his year in office. Thomas Berkeley, though, was in breach of the legislation when he was elected in September 1472 while still serving as sheriff of Rutland.[93] William Fielding was similarly sheriff of Cambridge and Huntingdon when elected to the readeption parliament.[94] Nor was the law of 1445 governing the status of MPs strictly adhered to. Almost a fifth of those returned were drawn from esquire families. In fact, the statute itself appears to have had little effect on electors, for as many mere esquires were elected in the twenty-three years after its enactment as had been in the preceding twenty-three years.

Although about a fifth of MPs were mere esquires, this must be set against an equal proportion who were belted knights at the time of their election. There was, indeed, a notable preference for belted knights during the second reign of Edward IV, when all five members between 1472 and 1483 bore that distinction. This was a presage of the situation in the early sixteenth century when over

---

90 *Ibid.*, p. 342, c. 7. 91 *Return*; Wedgwood, *Register*.
92 Among the parliamentary writs and returns (C219) the missing Leicestershire returns are for the parliaments of 1439, 1445, 1460, 1461, 1463, 1469 (which never met) 1470 and the January and June parliaments of 1483.
93 Lists and Indexes, IX, p. 113. 94 *Ibid.*, p. 13; Wedgwood, *Register*, p. 386.

half of Leicestershire's MPs were belted knights.[95] A further four members were drawn from knightly families, though they themselves were not knights at the time of election, and the remaining twenty-eight belonged to distrainee families. The statute of 1445 was therefore complied with in just over 80 per cent of elections.

Despite the fifty-two parliamentary seats available to the Leicestershire gentry between 1422 and 1483, knights of the shire were chosen from a much more exclusive group than this number suggests. Of the seventy-three upper and middle gentry families, only twenty-two provided MPs, involving a total of twenty-four individuals. Twelve of these men represented the county once and another six sat twice. Therefore, over half of Leicestershire's representation (about 54 per cent) was monopolized by six individuals sitting on three or more occasions. Foremost among these six was Thomas Palmer. He was elected to seven parliaments between 1433 and 1467. Bartholomew Brokesby was another experienced shire knight whose parliamentary career began with his election in 1409. He was returned to five of the eight parliaments called between 1422 and 1432. John Boyville was also elected five times, while Richard Hotoft II and John Bellers II were returned four times. William Fielding sat in three parliaments. If we also take into account those who entered parliament before 1422[96] and those who had represented other constituencies before being elected in Leicestershire,[97] then on thirty-four occasions out of fifty-two the shire knight was a man with previous parliamentary experience.

This high level of re-election indicates that the demand for a place in parliament outstripped the supply of available seats. Some sought to satisfy that demand by securing election in another county, while a few were content to represent a parliamentary borough. In all instances, election in another county merely reflected wider territorial interests and the pattern of landholding as those who were elected in another county also held land there. Election to a borough seat was quite a different matter, however.

[95] S. T. Bindoff, *The House of Commons, 1509–1558*, 3 vols., London, 1982, I, p. 128. For the Elizabethan period see J. E. Neale, *The Elizabethan House of Commons*, revised edn, Harmondsworth, 1963, pp. 289–307.

[96] Bartholomew Brokesby (1409), Laurence Berkeley (1421), John Burgh (1421).

[97] Henry Beaumont, MP Dunwich, 1429, 1432; Thomas Erdyngton, MP Warwickshire, 1440; Robert Staunton, MP Grimsby, 1447.

In each case, the individual concerned either had close personal links with the crown or had powerful court friends who could labour the electors on his behalf.[98] If such pressure was also applied to the electors of the borough of Leicester, the sole parliamentary borough in the county, it was never successful in securing the return of a member of the shire gentry. Such political independence suggests that the town enjoyed some economic strength in the fifteenth century.

The majority of Leicestershire's MPs, fifteen out of twenty-four, had previously served in local government office before their first election as shire knight. Occasionally, that background of service was wide-ranging. Thomas Berkeley had been sheriff, justice of the peace and had been appointed to various commissions in Leicestershire and Rutland, including five commissions of array, before he was first elected to parliament in 1472. William Moton, too, had been justice of the peace, escheator, sheriff and commissioner of array before his election.[99]

Nevertheless, there were others who were much less qualified. Robert Moton had served on a single commission of oyer and terminer sixteen years before his election to parliament, and John Whatton's election followed by thirty-seven years his only other appointment as commissioner of weights and measures. Our definition of the term must be exceedingly flexible were we to consider these men as 'experienced'. Nor must we neglect the ten shire knights whose first sortie into local government office came with their election to parliament.[100] What the Leicestershire evidence reveals is that appointment to shire offices was more likely to follow an earlier electoral success at the shire court. Election marked not so much the zenith of a career in local government, but was, instead, an early stepping stone towards further advancement. The demand for seats is therefore understandable.

[98] Henry Beaumont: MP Dunwich, 1429, 1432; younger brother of John, lord (later viscount) Beaumont; king's squire. Robert Staunton: MP Grimsby, 1447; deputy of John, lord Beaumont as steward of Castle Donington. Richard Hotoft: MP Warwick, 1453, 1455; feodary and bailiff of duchy of Lancaster lands in Warwickshire. Thomas Keble: MP Lostwithiel, 1478; member of lord Hastings' affinity (Hastings was receiver-general of the duchy of Cornwall).

[99] See appendix 3.

[100] Bartholomew Brokesby (1409), Laurence Berkeley (1421), Thomas Fouleshurst (1423), John Boyville (1423), Baldwin Bugge (1425), Everard Dygby (1429), John Bellers II (1432), Thomas Astley (1436), Richard Neele (1441), William Trussell (1472).

While personal ambition can explain why members of the gentry should have sought election, it does not account for their success in that quest. The high rate of re-election further indicates that the electors themselves preferred their representatives to be experienced, to be men who would know how best to protect the county's interests as well as their own. When they did elect a novice, that is, a man who had never before served either in parliament or in any other local government office, they usually selected as co-member a man of some experience. The sole exception was in the parliament of 1423 when the two novices, Thomas Fouleshurst and John Boyville, were elected. There was also a propensity on the part of electors to turn to successive generations of certain families. Between 1422 and 1483, two MPs, Robert Moton and Laurence Berkeley, were succeeded as shire knights by their respective sons, William Moton and Thomas Berkeley. If we look back beyond 1422 we find earlier generations of Trussells (1421), Hotofts (1421, 1414), Bellerses (1420, 1414, 1413), Berkeleys (1411, 1404, 1402), Brokesbys (1403) and Bugges (1403, 1397) serving as MPs.[101]

Whatever criteria were used by the electors in choosing shire knights, there is no record to indicate that they were consistently subjected to magnate or crown pressure. At times, however, national, rather than regional, considerations did dictate that the composition of the Commons could not be left to the whim of the shire electors. On these occasions, circumstantial evidence suggests that the shire court was laboured in order to ensure the return of members sympathetic to the crown. To the parliament of 1447, which was the occasion of the downfall and death of Humphrey, duke of Gloucester, the Leicestershire electors returned Richard Hotoft and Thomas Staunton. Hotoft had represented the shire on two previous occasions but this was the first time in the fifteenth century that the county had returned two duchy of Lancaster officials to the one parliament.[102] To the crisis parliament of 1449–50 Hotoft was again returned together with the Lancastrian partisan, William Fielding. The depth of Fielding's pro-Lancastrian sentiments may be gauged by the fact that he was elected again to the Coventry parliament of 1459, called to attaint the Yorkist lords, and also, it is argued, to Henry

[101] *Return*, pp. 300, 297, 284, 295, 279, 276, 267, 263, 265, 253.
[102] Somerville, I, pp. 557, 558, 569, 570, 573.

VI's readeption parliament of 1470–1.[103] He was eventually killed fighting for queen Margaret at the battle of Tewkesbury.[104] Later, when parliament was called in 1478 to attaint the duke of Clarence, Leicestershire returned Sir William Trussell and Sir William Moton, both of whom were, by this stage, indentured retainers of lord Hastings.[105] These examples indicate that electoral freedom could be circumvented when it was thought necessary to do so.[106]

The circumstantial evidence is also supported by referring to the sheriffs' returns for parliamentary elections.[107] The elections for both shire knights and burgesses were held in the county court in Leicester. It is clear that sheriffs were allowed, or perhaps arrogated to themselves, a certain amount of latitude when making their returns. Sometimes, a sheriff, such as Thomas Erdyngton in 1435, would make a separate return for elections of knights of the shire and for burgesses, despite the elections having been held in the same place on the same day.[108] Other sheriffs considered a single return to be sufficient but distinguished between shire and borough electors.[109] Some sheriffs, for whom a single return was deemed adequate, failed to make any distinction between shire and borough electors, though the latter do always appear at the end of the list.[110] There are differences, too, in the numbers of electors recorded. William Peyto listed seventy electors as being present at the election of August 1429, such large numbers suggesting that the election may have been contested,[111] while Richard Hastings considered his duty fulfilled by naming merely six electors in September 1423.[112] The usual practice, however, was to record between one and two dozen of

---

[103] Wedgwood, *Biographies*, p. 314.

[104] *Paston Letters 1422–1509*, V, p. 104; John Warkworth, *A Chronicle of the First Thirteen Years of the Reign of King Edward the Fourth*, ed. J. O. Halliwell, Camden o.s. 10, London, 1839, p. 18.

[105] Dunham, 'Lord Hastings' indentured retainers 1461–1483', p. 141 and *passim*.

[106] See Roskell, *The Commons in the Parliament of 1422*, p. 27.

[107] What follows is based on parliamentary writs and returns C219/13/1–C219/17/3.

[108] C219/14/5 pt 2 docs. 102 and 103.

[109] A practice adopted by, for example, Richard Hastings in 1422 (C219/13/1).

[110] For example, Thomas Everyngham at the 1447 election (C219/15/4 pt 2 doc. 103).

[111] Cf. R. Virgoe, 'An election dispute of 1483', *B.I.H.R.*, 60, 1987, p. 24. For other disputed elections, see R. Virgoe, 'The Cambridgeshire election of 1439', *B.I.H.R.*, 46, 1973, pp. 95–101; R. Virgoe, 'Three Suffolk parliamentary elections of the mid-fifteenth century', *B.I.H.R.*, 39, 1966, pp. 185–96.

[112] C219/14/1 pt 2 doc. 102; C219/13/2 pt 2 doc. 94.

the most important electors by name and to allude to anonymous 'others' as having been present. Nevertheless, the sheriff's return of February 1449 fails to specify any electors at all by name.[113] The return was therefore in breach of the 'majority rule' clause of the act of 1429 which specified that the sheriffs should make their return 'by indentures sealed betwixt the said sheriffs and the said choosers'.[114]

The February 1449 return provides a possible insight into how lax the electoral system could be. The election, which was held on Thursday 6 February, returned Thomas Everyngham and Thomas Palmer whose names were duly recorded on the sheriff's return. Later in the return, the shire knights are referred to, not as Thomas and Thomas but as Thomas and Richard. The mistake could be dismissed as a slip of the quill by an inattentive clerk but comparison of the Leicestershire return with that for Warwickshire may reveal a more sinister explanation.[115]

The Warwickshire election was held on Monday 10 February, four days after the Leicestershire election.[116] Apart from two scribal errors, the location and date of the election and the names of those elected, the wording of each return is identical, even to the extent of failing to name any electors. The successful candidates for Warwickshire were Thomas Bate and Richard Hotoft. Here, then, is a clue to why the Leicestershire return makes reference to Thomas and Richard instead of Thomas and Thomas. Although the Leicestershire election is reported to have taken place before the Warwickshire, the sheriff's return was, in fact, drawn up some time after the election of Thomas Bate and Richard Hotoft. The supposedly earlier Leicestershire return is a copy of the later Warwickshire return.

In itself, this anomaly may signify nothing more than a clerical convenience. But considered together with the omission of named electors and the fact that one of those elected, Thomas Palmer, by this stage had, in local government, a record second to none of loyal service to the regime and that the other three had strong Lancastrian affiliations, one suspects that both elections were less

---

[113] C219/15/6 pt 2 doc. 106. [114] *Stat. Realm*, II, p. 243, 8 Hen. VI, c. 7.
[115] C219/15/6 pt 2 doc. 104.
[116] The days have been worked out using *Handbook of Dates for Students of English History*, ed. C. R. Cheney, London, 1978.

free than they might have been, if they were held at all.[117] Sheriffs normally named the electors in order to spread the burden of responsibility if the return were called into question at a later date.[118] The assumption behind the idiosyncratic return of February 1449 must be that it would not be questioned and such an assumption would be warranted only if the crown had meddled in the matter. If this conclusion is accepted then the Leicestershire return of early 1449 provides us with an example of the denial of that democratic principle which was so much in evidence in the Nottinghamshire election of 1460.[119]

Much the same conclusion about crown interference can be drawn from the election of 1459 which returned the staunch Lancastrians, William Fielding and John Whatton, to the Parliament of Devils at Coventry. In his return, the sheriff was at pains to stress that all the electors were residents who held freehold land worth at least 40s. yearly beyond outgoings.[120] This was the only occasion during the period when the sheriff in Leicestershire thought it necessary to be so precise and to publicize his conformity to the proper practices. The reason for his concern becomes apparent when we turn to the list of electors.

The list, providing twelve names in all for both the shire and borough elections, is noteworthy in that not a single member of the upper- and middle-ranking gentry is recorded as being present. All of the electors were lesser folk whose status, in some cases, was probably determined by holdings worth little more than that required for them to exercise the franchise. These were not the sort of men who traditionally took the lead in county politics and one must resist any suggestion that they took the lead on this occasion either. As it is inconceivable that the presence of the shire's natural leaders would have passed unnoted, their absence

---

[117] For Thomas Palmer see appendix 3. Thomas Everyngham was an esquire of the chamber (E101/409/9, fo. 36v). Also, see above p. 120 n. 79. Richard Hotoft was feodary of duchy of Lancaster lands in Warwickshire, Leicestershire and Northamptonshire and also bailiff of Warwick and Leicester (Somerville, I, pp. 569–71, 589). Thomas Bate had early attracted the notice of the queen to whom he was 'oure welbeloved T. Bate'. In 1445 Margaret asked the mayor, bailiff and commons of Coventry to reserve the recordership for Bate whom she considered to be 'suffisiant of cunnying and habilite' (*Letters of Queen Margaret of Anjou*, p. 140).

[118] See Virgoe, 'An election dispute of 1483', p. 27.

[119] S. J. Payling, 'The widening franchise – parliamentary elections in Lancastrian Nottinghamshire', in *England in the Fifteenth Century. Proceedings of the 1986 Harlaxton Symposium*, ed. D. Williams, Woodbridge, 1987, pp. 167–86.

[120] C219/16/5 doc. 62. See *An English Chronicle*, p. 83, where it is claimed that those elected in 1459 were enemies of the Yorkist cause.

suggests not only that they considered the 'election' to be a mere endorsement of candidates already selected outside the county, an endorsement which could be left to their social inferiors, but also that none wished to be too closely associated with the impending action against the duke of York and his supporters. Furthermore, in the election of 1459 we seem to be witnessing an early manifestation of the disintegration of support for Lancaster within the shire; the gentry were indicating their discontent by boycotting the 'election' at the shire court.

Given that membership of parliament was an important route towards furthering one's political career, the successful candidate could only have welcomed magnate or crown interference on his behalf, though the electors themselves probably had a less indulgent attitude towards such meddling. But the number of parliamentary seats was limited and, as we have seen, only an exclusive group was permitted to take that path. Since Warwickshire and Leicestershire shared their sheriff, the shrievalty, too, offered restricted scope to Leicestershire personnel who wished, in the words of John Shynner, 'to goveryn [rather] then to be goveryed'.[121] A potentially broader avenue leading to political advancement lay with the commission of the peace which, in practice if not in law,[122] could include as many justices as the council wished to appoint.

The justices of the peace were to be 'the most sufficient knights, esquires and gentlemen of the law' of their counties.[123] Any doubts about the flexibility of this requirement were countered by subsequent legislation which stipulated that justices of the peace who were not also lords or justices of assizes should be residents of their shires.[124] In 1439, a further act defined 'sufficient' as possession of an income of at least £20 per annum, though this particular regulation could be waived by the chancellor if the appointee were learned in the law.[125] On the whole, the economic qualification was complied with. Of the Leicestershire justices whose economic status is known, only four had declared incomes below the statutory £20 per annum.[126] Nevertheless,

---

[121] *Stonor Letters*, II, p. 135.
[122] *Stat. Realm*, I, p. 364, c. 1; *ibid.*, II, p. 58, c. 10; *ibid.*, II, p. 77, c. 11; *Proceedings*, pp. lxxix–lxxx.
[123] *Stat. Realm*, II, p. 63, stat. 1, c. 7.   [124] *Ibid.*, II, p. 187, stat. 2, c. 1.
[125] *Ibid.*, II, pp. 309–10, c. 11.
[126] John Bellers II, Thomas Whatton, Thomas Walsh and Thomas Farnham.

each of these four played an active rôle on the bench and must therefore have been well versed in the law.[127]

Between 1422 and 1485, 41 commissions were issued for Leicestershire, involving a total of 643 individual appointments.[128] Of course, by no means all of these positions were made available to members of the local gentry. Each commission contained nobles, most of whom had at least some territorial interest in the shire. The practice of commissioning ecclesiastics, too, which began in other counties in 1424,[129] was adopted haltingly in Leicestershire but, from 1456 onwards, it became the rule for either the bishop of Lincoln or the Master of the Hospital at Burton Lazars or both of them together to be included. Two assize judges, usually justices of the common pleas, but occasionally a justice of the king's bench, were also added to each commission and the bench's legal expertise was sometimes further strengthened by the inclusion of a king's serjeant or a king's attorney.[130] Outsiders were, at times, commissioned, most notably in the first decade of our period and again from 1483 to 1485. In the 1420s and early 30s, before the chief stewardships of the duchy of Lancaster passed into the hands of the nobility, it was customary to appoint the chief steward of the northern parts as a justice of the peace in Leicestershire.[131] Richard III also appointed outsiders who were closely associated with his regime.[132] In the 60s, Edward IV's cousins, Humphrey and John

[127] Bellers: KB9/248/36; KB9/262/87; E101/590/34 MS 10. Whatton: KB9/229/4/11; KB9/230B/191; KB9/235/11; KB9/253/11; E101/590/34 MSS 6,7,8,9. Walsh: KB9/284/8; KB9/288/29. Farnham: KB9/237/57; KB9/248/36; KB9/251/14; KB9/253/11; KB9/256/118; KB9/262/87; KB9/269/66; KB9/270A/19; KB9/284/8; KB9/286/25; E101/590/34 MSS 8,9,10,11,12.

[128] The printed calendars yield only 640 appointments. A further three, Richard Hotoft (July 1444; C66/457 MS 25v), Thomas Littleton (1481; C66/545 MS 25v) and Guy Fairfax (1482; C66/548 MS 20v), can be found on the dorse of the original rolls where the names of members of the *quorum* are recorded.

[129] *Proceedings*, p. lxxxi.

[130] Common pleas: James Strangways, William Ascogh, John Portyngton, Robert Danby, Peter Ardern, John Nedeham and Thomas Littleton. King's bench: Guy Fairfax, John Markham, John Nedeham. King's serjeant: John Vavasour. King's attorney: William Babthorp. (Foss, *Biographia Juridica, passim*; Somerville, I, *passim*.)

[131] Roger Flore, John Tyrell, John Cokayn, ex-chief-steward (*Somerville*, I, pp. 419–20).

[132] Richard Radcliff, William Catesby, Robert Harington and Gervase Clifton. There was also a Robert Harington of Exton in Rutland who was appointed to commissions of array in Leicestershire in May and December 1484 (Wedgwood, *Biographies*, p. 426). However, in view of the company he kept, the JP was more likely the Sir Robert Harington (Harrington) who held lands in Lancashire and Yorkshire and who played a part in the execution of William Hastings (C. Ross, *Richard III*, London, 1981, pp. 51, 57, 85, 156 and *passim*).

Bourchier, appear in the calendared lists of justices, but John Bourchier at least had a territorial interest in the shire in right of his wife, Elizabeth, lady Ferrers of Groby.[133]

These appointments aside, there were still 333 positions on the bench of JPs made available to members of the shire gentry. In statistical terms, therefore, the chances of securing a seat on the bench were over six times greater than being elected as a knight of the shire and about fourteen times greater than being pricked as sheriff. But these figures alone can give an altogether misleading picture. Despite the large number of available places on the bench, the local JPs selected to serve amounted to only thirty-eight individuals drawn from twenty-nine families. Furthermore, not all of those appointed would have actually sat on the bench. From the records of payments made to JPs and of those whose cases were called before the court of king's bench, the active justices appear to have numbered no more than twenty-three individuals.[134] The commission of the peace certainly provided an additional outlet for those who wished to play a part in the government of the shire but, as with the shrievalty and member-ship of parliament, it was an outlet made available to a select few.

This stricture notwithstanding, and despite the fact that the size of commissions and the proportion of local gentry appointed to them fluctuated throughout the century, the general trend was towards larger commissions with greater local involvement. In 1423, the commission contained eleven JPs, only two of whom, or just over 18 per cent, were members of the shire gentry. By 1485, the largest commission in our period boasted twenty-two members, half of whom were local men. In the 1440s and again in the 70s and early 80s, the proportion of local gentry on the commissions regularly reached and often exceeded 60 per cent. Furthermore, the bulk of the work of the bench fell to the gentry members. The only lord for whom there is evidence of his having sat, was William, lord Ferrers of Groby.[135] The ecclesiastics never participated in the work of the bench and the lawyers of the central courts and other outsiders played a very minor rôle in its deliberations.[136]

---

[133] G.E.C., III, pp. 552–4; *ibid.*, V, p. 360.
[134] See above n. 127; E101/590/34 MSS 1, 3–12; KB9/335/51; KB9/341/8; KB9/345/10; KB9/354/13, 18; KB9/355/41, 57; KB9/358/12; KB9/360/75; KB9/951/52.
[135] KB9/229/4/11; KB9/230B/191.   [136] E101/590/34 MSS 1,3,4.

Although the work of the bench was left largely in the hands of the local justices we need to consider whether their appointment was politically motivated by external forces. Unfortunately, as with the pricking of sheriffs, there is no body of direct evidence we can turn to. Nevertheless, occasionally, we can discern political pressures playing a part, either in the appointment of individuals to, or their removal from, the commissions of the peace. William Fielding and John Bellers II served as justices throughout the 1450s but were conspicuously absent in the 1460s. During Henry VI's readeption they were again appointed to the bench. Fielding's career was cut short at the battle of Tewkesbury but Bellers was subsequently dropped from the commission when Edward IV returned to power. Sir Ralph Woodford and Richard Perwych were also appointed to the readeption commissions but neither man had previously served on the Leicestershire bench and, as with John Bellers II, their services were dispensed with on the return of the Yorkists. As it was unusual for commissions to be so short-lived we may assume that the reason for the brevity of their careers in local government was political. In contrast to these Lancastrian sympathisers, William Moton, Robert Staunton and Thomas Palmer were dropped from the readeption commissions but were back on the bench by 1474.

Despite these indications of political influence on the composition of the commissions of the peace, it must be admitted that for most of our period the bench was generally a stable institution. The dynastic tensions and conflicts of the 1450s brought little change to its internal structure other than the usual variations one would expect to see over a period of years as JPs retired or died. Minor modifications were made in 1460 and again at the readeption but the upheavals caused by the attainder of the duke of Clarence and the usurpation of Richard III found little reflection in the Leicestershire personnel appointed.

This analysis of the composition of the commissions of the peace nevertheless confirms what we have already seen as applying in the case of sheriffs and knights of the shire, namely, that in the fifteenth century, local government was the preserve of a select group within the county gentry, Lapsley's *buzones*.[137] Not only were there individual workhorses such as Bartholomew Brokesby, Thomas Palmer, Robert Staunton, John Bellers II and

[137] Lapsley, 'Buzones', pp. 177–93, 545–67; *Proceedings*, p. lxxxiii.

John Boyville but, throughout the period, we find succeeding generations of Berkeleys (Laurence and Thomas), Fieldings (William and Everard), Hastingses (Richard, Leonard and William), Motons (Robert and William), Asshebys (Thomas and William), Pulteneys (John and Thomas) and Hotofts (Richard I and Richard II), seven families in all, being appointed or elected time and again to the major county offices. What is more, all of these men were drawn from the knightly or potential knightly families.

We have seen, too, that even in the absence of strong, local magnates during most of our period, the selection or election of officials may occasionally have been the subject of both crown and magnate interference, but especially so after the readeption when lord Hastings' power in the area was supposedly paramount. Yet, even then, in the 1470s, pressure was not consistently applied. There were certainly examples of political careers being advanced or cut short by external manipulation but the general impression is that advancement was as much dictated by an official's standing within his local community, by the limits of his ambition and by his personal aptitude as it was by the result of the workings of good lordship. The career of Thomas Berkeley, who served in local government offices under Henry VI, under Edward IV, under the readeption government as commissioner of array and again under the restored Yorkist regime, reveals that the Leicestershire gentry could, if they were flexible enough in their allegiances, weather any political storms raging at the centre. The more partisan gentry, such as Sir William Fielding, could be, and were, called upon to pay a heavy price for being steadfast in their support for the losing faction. But the sins of the father were not visited upon succeeding generations; the name of Sir William's son, Everard, appears on the list of JPs by 1477. It seems that the right of the superior local families to govern in their counties could not be denied indefinitely.

Whereas local government was 'self-government at the king's command', the fifteenth-century evidence further reveals that the king's command had to be responsive to local sensibilities. The king certainly had the final say when it came to appointing sheriffs, justices of the peace, escheators and various *ad hoc* commissioners. He could also interfere in the electoral process, as Henry VI or one of his agents seems to have done in Leicestershire in the election to the first parliament of 1449. But there were limits to the royal power. In the case of appointments, the choice of local officials was constrained by statute, not only to residents, but to the socially and economically superior residents of the shire. At election time, too, the county gentry could display their concern about undue interference, as they appear to have done in Leicester in 1459, by boycotting proceedings in the shire court. Even when a family fell from royal favour, the king's grace could rarely be withheld indefinitely. It seems unreasonable to assume that the gentry were any less self-assertive in their own shires than they were, for example, in the second parliament of 1449–50. Here, the Commons foisted a sweeping act of resumption on an unwilling monarch and, in the face of both royal and noble opposition, they also tried to impeach the king's chief adviser, the duke of Suffolk.[138] Men such as these were unlikely to be overawed on their home territory.

Just as there was a social establishment of superior gentry families in Leicestershire,[139] so, too, there was a political establishment, an oligarchy of family members who not only governed but expected to govern, in the county.[140] In selecting officials and electing MPs from their number, the king and the local shire community alike constantly deferred to these men who would therefore feel assured of their own county-wide importance. It was they who welded the county together into a coherent political community. Self-government may have been at the king's command[141] but, in fifteenth-century Leicestershire, the officers in the field, the gentry, wielded a more immediate authority over the governed. Perhaps our earlier simile of a Venn diagram, which we used to illustrate the gentry's interlocking social circles, may be equally applicable to their political affiliations.[142] These affiliations were with the king, with local and neighbouring magnates and with other members of the county gentry. While political circles often overlapped, it was the last mentioned, the political community of the shire, which provided the strongest cohesive force in Leicestershire.

[138] See *Rot. Parl.*, v, pp. 176–99, which outlines the Commons' moves against Suffolk, the act of resumption and Henry's liberal list of exemptions from the act.
[139] See above, pp. 92–3.　　[140] See above, p. 133.
[141] White, *Self-Government at the King's Command*, p. 2.
[142] See above, p. 93.

6

HOUSEHOLD, FAMILY AND MARRIAGE

Just as the gentry are often seen as the political pawns of their social superiors, the nobility, so too has the gentry family been presented as subject to the external agencies of the wider kin and the 'good lord'.[1] Any treatment of the attitudes, concerns and ambitions of the Leicestershire gentry must therefore necessarily consider the more intimate aspects of their lives. It must deal with the household which provided the setting for family life itself and the relationships formed within it between husband and wife and between parents and children, and with the ties of kinship which bound one gentry family to another. Throughout this chapter our major concern will be with the extent to which the personal lives of the gentry were, indeed, subservient to external agencies.

The setting for family life was, of course, the household. Unfortunately, private correspondence, diaries and the more important domestic account books which can provide such valuable material about the size and organization of gentry homes have not survived for Leicestershire. Nevertheless, light may be thrown on gentry households by looking first at the manor houses which contained them. While the finest remaining examples of fifteenth-century secular architecture in the county were built by lord Hastings at Ashby de la Zouch and Kirby Muxloe, only fragments of the relatively less grand gentry houses now stand as testimony to their own former dignity. Perhaps the most architecturally striking of these surviving fifteenth-century structures can be found at Holt, the home of Thomas Palmer and his family.[2]

The manor house of Holt (now Neville Holt) has been much

---

[1] L. Stone, *The Family, Sex and Marriage in England 1500–1800*, abridged edn, Harmondsworth, 1979, p. 69.

[2] N. Pevsner, *The Buildings of England: Leicestershire and Rutland*, 2nd edn, Harmondsworth, 1984, pp. 26–8. The most complete example of a medieval manor house is the manor house at Donington-le-Heath which dates from the late thirteenth century (T. L. Marsden, 'Manor House farm, Donington-le-Heath, Leicestershire c. 1280', *Transactions of the Ancient Monument Society*, n.s., 10, 1962, pp. 33–43).

changed by later accretions but the medieval hall, sandwiched between more recent constructions to its east and west, still remains, essentially unaltered.[3] In form, the hall seems to differ little from that at Penshurst Place in Kent or of Haddon Hall in Derbyshire.[4] Like them, it is two storeys in height, reaching up to an open timber roof. Screens at the eastern end of the hall probably separated it from the service quarters of kitchen, buttery and pantry but the screens have since been removed and all traces of the service quarters have been effaced by the building projects of subsequent generations. A spiral stairway in the south-east corner leads to a doorway which, before the removal of the screens, would have opened onto a minstrels' gallery above the screens and along the hall's eastern wall. The playing of music was clearly an integral part of at least more formal occasions such as Christmas or New Year.[5]

During the fifteenth century, Thomas Palmer made additions to the earlier structure. A fine bay window, or oriel, was built at the hall's south-west corner and this was balanced by a porch at its south-east corner.[6] The latter acted as protection against draughts while the oriel provided more light at the lord's end of the hall. However, as both bay and porch were divided into upper and lower floors, the prime concern seems to have been the need for additional private living space. At about the same time, the house was also crenellated. That the crenellations were intended to be decorative rather than defensive is suggested by the expanse of glass in the bay windows and by their closeness to ground level.

Thomas Palmer's extensions and decorative flourishes cannot be dated precisely. Certainly, they were undertaken before 1475, the year of Thomas's death.[7] Nevertheless, even if the work had

---

[3] For what follows, I am indebted to the detailed description provided by G. F. Farnham and A. H. Thompson, 'The manor, house and chapel of Holt', *T.L.A.S.*, 13, 1923–4, pp. 232–5.

[4] See D. Yarwood, *The Architecture of Britain*, London, 1976, pp. 74–9. For the general lay-out of medieval gentry houses see, too, D. Starkey, 'The age of the household: politics, society and the arts c. 1350–c. 1550', in *The Later Middle Ages*, ed. S. Medcalf, London, 1981, p. 244.

[5] Cf. Dame Alice de Bryene who played host to a harpist from Christmas Day 1412 until 2 January 1413. Another of Dame Alice's guests, Sir Richard Waldegrave, arrived on 10 January 1413 with a minstrel of his own. (*The Household Book of Dame Alice de Bryene*, ed. V. B. Redstone, Suffolk Institute of Archaeology and History, Bungay, 1984, pp. 25–8, 30.)

[6] The balance provided by oriel and porch was a fifteenth-century architectural convention (M. Wood, *The English Medieval House*, London, 1965, pp. 104–5).

[7] C140/55/9 MS 2.

not yet begun, it is likely that Palmer was already planning a regime of beautification and extension as early as 1448. In that year he was granted permission to empark 300 acres of land, meadow and wood in Holt and Keythorpe and it was not unusual for such changes in land-use on the manor to be associated with modifications to the manor house itself.[8]

Whether Thomas Palmer extended the family's private apartments which would have been situated to the west of the hall, it is no longer possible to say. Later building-work has made it difficult to reconstruct the original lay-out. However, the survival of the upper part of a stairway near the oriel indicates the former presence of a solar. There would have been a chamber or chambers beneath this, too; but further than this, the archaeological evidence is silent. Yet, despite a shortage of evidence, the stone-built hall at Neville Holt still testifies both to the degree of domestic comfort demanded by a member of the fifteenth-century gentry, and to his pretensions.

That Thomas Palmer's building activities can be attributed to his pretension rather than to a need for extra space becomes even more apparent when we examine the family circumstances. He married twice and by these marriages he fathered four daughters, Elizabeth, Margaret, Joan and Katherine.[9] At its most extensive, therefore, his family numbered six people. The dates of Palmer's marriages are unknown but he was certainly married to his second wife, Elizabeth Bishopsden, by 1429.[10] In 1448, when, it has been argued, Palmer was planning his building projects, his daughters were either at, or approaching, marriageable age. One of the younger pair of daughters, Katherine, married two years later, in 1450. That she and her husband were granted the manor of Lubenham, indicates, despite Katherine's tender age, her move to a separate establishment.[11] It is highly probable that the older daughters were also married by this date. In the absence of a son, and with a contracting family, Palmer's alterations at Holt were a proclamation of his own personal wealth and status. No doubt, too, he and his wife, Elizabeth, would enjoy the extra comfort.

While detail of the private and service quarters of Neville Holt

---

[8] *C.Ch.R.*, 1427–1516, VI, p. 100. See, for example, permission granted to lord Hastings to crenellate and empark at Ashby de la Zouch and Kirby Muxloe (*ibid.*, p. 242).

[9] *Pedigrees*, pp. 36, 93; C140/55/9 MS 2; E149/232/10; L.R.O. DE220/58; *C.C.R.*, 1441–7, p. 117.

[10] L.R.O. DE221/4/1/96.   [11] L.R.O. DE220/58.

is lacking, we are better served for the manor house of Staunton Harold. After the death of Sir Ralph Shirley in 1516, the archbishop of Canterbury's apparitor, John Rudding, made an inventory of Shirley's goods and chattels for the purpose of probate. Rudding was clearly a meticulous bureaucrat for he apparently wandered through the house, room by room, jotting down the items in each and noting their value. Little would have escaped his professional eye and his labours have provided us not only with a list of rooms but also with an image of how they were furnished.[12]

Rudding began his inventory in the hall. It was sparsely furnished, containing only a cupboard, four short tables and an equal number of forms attached to the floor. This was where members of the household dined; but although Alice de Bryene of Acton Hall in Suffolk regularly ate in the company of her household early in the fifteenth century, by the early sixteenth century, the relatively few pieces of furniture in the hall at Staunton Harold support the view that the family had retreated from this communal room into the greater intimacy of its own apartments.[13]

The inventory fails to explain how Staunton Harold's private rooms were arranged in relation to each other but they included a great parlour, an inner parlour, a great chamber underneath the hall, a countinghouse and various other chambers amounting to ten rooms in all. Unfortunately, John Rudding listed cushions and stools separately, so we are unable to say whether most of these rooms had assumed specialized functions or if they doubled up as bedrooms at night and living quarters during the day. Certainly, the countinghouse, which contained only a 'cupboard with evidences', must have been reserved solely for transacting estate business. The great parlour, too, had a specialized function. The Flemish carpet and red sey hanging seem to have been designed for day-time comfort, and the trestle table indicates that some meals were eaten here.

Seven of the rooms contained beds of various types, ranging in size and comfort from a cradle in the wardrobe chamber to the

---

[12] L.R.O. 26D53/1949.
[13] *Alice de Bryene*, p. 1 and *passim*. Langland was already complaining in the late fourteenth century that the lord and lady 'liketh noght to sitte' in the hall but preferred 'to eaten by hymselve / In a privee parlour' (William Langland, *The Vision of Piers Plowman*, ed. A. V. C. Schmidt, London, 1978, passus x, lines 97–9, p. 103).

great feather bed in the inner parlour.[14] There was also a number of pallets in four of the rooms. In total, this array of cradles, beds and pallets provided permanent sleeping arrangements for at least fourteen people, including infants. Possibly some of the beds and probably all of the pallets were reserved for the more important household servants such as personal attendants and, perhaps, a chaplain.[15]

The more menial servants were confined to the service quarters. This part of the house consisted of a kitchen, brewhouse, pantry, buttery, larderhouse, 'a great parlour for servants', a 'great chamber for weyne men' (waggoners), a kiln house and further chambers off each of the kitchen, brewhouse and buttery. Including a bed in the stable, there was sleeping accommodation for ten menial servants. Rudding also noted the existence of twelve additional bedsteads, 'great and small', though he neglected to mention where they were stored. No doubt they could be trundled out, either above or below stairs as the need arose, when guests arrived or when the number of servants increased such as at harvest time.[16]

Of course, Sir Ralph Shirley's establishment as described in 1516 bears little resemblance to the Staunton Harold of John Staunton's day almost a century earlier. When John Staunton died in 1421 the manor was said to consist of a hall, two chambers, a kitchen, a stable, two barns or granaries (*orria*) and a dovecote.[17] Like

---

[14] Rudding refers to a total of four feather beds (L.R.O. 26D53/1949).

[15] Alice de Bryene's household included chaplains, and her visitor, Morgan Gough, brought with him a chaplain of his own (*Alice de Bryene*, pp. 16–17, 174). Sir Richard Graystoke used his chaplain to carry messages to William Stonor (*Stonor Letters*, II, p. 23) and Robert Littester was chaplain and domestic servant to Sir William Plumpton (*The Plumpton Correspondence*, ed. T. Stapleton, Camden o.s. 4, London, 1839, p. lxxiv). The regular dispensations granted to the Leicestershire gentry to hear mass before daybreak, to have a portable altar and to have their personal household confessors show that Leicestershire households often contained chaplains (*Calendar of Entries in the Papal Registers Relating to Great Britain and Ireland*, VI–XIII, London, 1904–55, 1427–47, VIII, pp. 42, 362; *ibid.*, 1431–47, IX, pp. 231, 233 and *passim*). Of course, a chaplain performed other tasks besides conducting religious services. Walter Norton, who was chaplain to Adam Warde of Shulton, acted as the latter's attorney in land transactions (L.R.O. 72′30/II/11).

[16] That the size of households fluctuated, see *The Household of Edward IV. The Black Book and the Ordinance of 1478*, ed. A. R. Myers, Manchester, 1959, p. 21. During the August harvest in 1413, Alice de Bryene often provided supper for over forty people and breakfast for thirty. Many of her boonworkers must therefore have stayed at, or near, the manor house overnight (*Alice de Bryene*, pp. 85–91).

[17] E149/127/12. Farnham is incorrect in placing Staunton's death in 1406 (*Pedigrees*, p. 101). He died on 12 September 1421, five months before the death of his son, Thomas, on St Valentine's Day 1422 (C139/1/21 MS 2; E149/127/12).

Thomas Palmer at Holt, the Shirleys must have undertaken extensive building works during the fifteenth century or even very early in the sixteenth. The question therefore arises of how typical was Staunton Harold of gentry houses for the fifteenth century.

The little that remains from the fifteenth century at Neville Holt shows that Staunton Harold was not unique either in form or in that it was built of stone. But not even two swallows make a summer. That so few examples of Leicestershire gentry houses remain from the fifteenth century may, of course, testify to the vigour with which later generations demolished the old and built anew. However, a more likely explanation for the paucity of archaeological evidence is that the Leicestershire gentry, like their urban cousins in Leicester and Loughborough, built their houses of timber which is less likely to endure.[18] We should also keep in mind that both Shirley and Palmer belonged to the upper gentry, to knightly and potential knightly families respectively. Their houses would, therefore, have been more substantial than most, neither typical for the gentry as a whole nor atypical of the houses of others of their elevated status.

The houses of the middle-ranking gentry, the esquires and prosperous gentlemen, were, we may assume, smaller than those of the Shirleys at Staunton Harold and the Palmers at Holt. They probably differed little from Thomas Walsh's manor houses at Burton Overy and Wanlip. Burton Overy consisted of a hall, two chambers, a kitchen, two barns and a stable, while Wanlip boasted a hall, three chambers, a kitchen, two barns, two stables and a dovehouse.[19] Furthermore, the manor house at Wanlip was either wooden framed or built entirely of wood for it had become unroofed sometime before 1440 thereby exposing its timbers to the elements and causing them to rot.[20]

Little can be said with certainty about the households which these manor houses contained. Obviously, the size of the household depended on the capacity of the house itself and this in turn was determined by the wealth and status of the particular gentry family.[21] Size was also controlled by the composition of

---

[18] *The Itinerary of John Leland*, I, p. 14; *The Illustrated Journeys of Celia Fiennes*, p. 145.

[19] C145/309/47; L.R.O. 5D33/177, fo. 77.

[20] *Ibid.* The manor house at Wanlip appears to have been no larger than Munden's chantry at Bridport which consisted of a hall, kitchen, pantry, two chambers (and possibly one or two other guest rooms) and a dovecote (*A Small Household of the Fifteenth Century*, ed. K. L. Wood-Legh, Manchester, 1956, p. xx).

[21] J.-L. Flandrin, *Families in Former Times*, trans. R. Southern, Cambridge, 1979, pp. 61–2.

the family, by whether its head was single, married or widowed and by the presence or absence of offspring who required nurses during infancy and tutors during childhood. The widowed Alice de Bryene's household consisted of a lady's maid, a chamberlain and an unspecified number of squires, chaplains, grooms, clerks of the chapel and boys.[22] Judging by the number of meals served each day and by subtracting named guests from the total, we can calculate that her regular household may have amounted to approximately fifteen people.

However, the only clue to the size of specifically Leicestershire gentry households is provided by John Rudding's inventory. Although Rudding's mandate did not run to listing servants, a household of twenty-four is suggested by the number of beds at Staunton Harold. Significantly, this figure coincides exactly with the size of household envisaged by the author of Edward IV's *Black Book* for a knight banneret worth over £200 per year.[23] The same author considered a household of sixteen as suitable for a knight bachelor worth over £100 and a household of ten for an esquire with an income of over £50 per year.[24] It seems reasonable to accept these figures as a rough guide to the size of households in Leicestershire.

Perhaps the most important point to emerge from our brief study of the Shirley and Palmer building programmes is that they highlight a paradox. On the one hand, the emphasis upon external grandeur at Neville Holt is a public affirmation in stone of Palmer's status within county society. Inside both Neville Holt and Staunton Harold, the maintaining of the traditional medieval hall is an only slightly less public affirmation of the family's position within the household. But a further emphasis upon smaller, intimate and more comfortably furnished rooms for the sole use of the family also attests to a growing demand for privacy. If these two examples of fifteenth-century gentry architecture, Neville Holt and Staunton Harold, may be taken as our guide, they suggest a developing dichotomy between the public household and a private or personal family life, a distinction between the public *persona* and the private person but with the concerns of the latter assuming increasing importance. A closer analysis of the

---

[22] *Alice de Bryene*, pp. v, 124.   [23] *The Black Book*, pp. 107–8.
[24] *Ibid.*, pp. 108, 110, 129–30.

family which occupied the core of the household should indicate whether such an hypothesis is justified.

It is now recognized that the late medieval family was a nuclear, rather than an extended, multi-generational or joint, family.[25] The Leicestershire evidence tends to confirm this view. By the time Ralph Woodford died he had already given lands to his younger sons, Mathew, John and Robert, an action which suggests that they possessed independent establishments.[26] In 1450, John Chesilden I's sons, William and John II, also had separate households at Allexton and Uppingham respectively.[27] Joint families, if they occurred at all, must have been exceedingly rare.

Very occasionally, however, we do encounter extended and multi-generational families. When John Brokesby married Joan, daughter of Sir Leonard Hastings, Hastings agreed to maintain the couple, presumably in his own household, until they came of age.[28] Much the same arrangement must have applied to the young John Sotehill and Elizabeth Plumpton after their marriage. Elizabeth was only three years old when her grandfather delivered her to John's father, Henry Sotehill, in Leicestershire, and no doubt the infant pair continued to reside with Elizabeth's in-laws for some years after the wedding.[29] In each case, the multi-generational arrangement was dictated by the extreme youth of the second generation. But child marriages were the exception and most marriage settlements reveal parents providing endowments for their children to establish separate households.

Although contemporaries recognized the obvious need for very young married children to share a household with one or other set of parents, the sheltering of aged or widowed parents by their married children was a responsibility not lightly to be shouldered. The formal indenture between Sir Robert Plumpton and his son, William, whereby William agreed to allow both his father and mother 'to take their ease and reast, and to be at board with the said William', is a curiosity.[30] It is especially curious because

[25] P. Laslett, *The World We Have Lost*, 2nd edn, London, 1979, pp. 93–4; R. A. Houlbrooke, *The English Family 1450–1700*, London, 1984, p. 18; M. Mitterauer and R. Sieder, *The European Family. Patriarchy to Partnership from the Middle Ages to the Present*, trans. K. Oosterveen and M. Hörzinger, Oxford, 1982, p. 13; Stone, *The Family, Sex and Marriage*, p. 69.

[26] PROB11/11/23/183–3v.   [27] C1/19/473.

[28] H.M.C., *Hastings*, I, pp. 300–1.   [29] *Plumpton Correspondence*, p. lxxi.

[30] The full text of the indenture is printed in *ibid.*, pp. cxxiii–cxxv.

neither Sir Robert nor his son had any illusions about the sufficiency of paternal and filial affection to maintain domestic harmony between the generations. They agreed in advance that 'any break or varience' be submitted to the arbitration of the local clergy. As they were fully aware of the potential problems, we may safely assume that the arrangement was not seen as inherently desirable but was, instead, imposed by the age and probable infirmity of the older generation.

Special conditions applied, too, in the case of the widowed Alice Plumpton. Her son, also called Robert, granted his mother *sa table sufficaunt et convenable a son degre* and *une chambre, appelle le closetts, ou une petit chambre fait enhaut deincs le dit closett, au son propre use, et sufficaunts luminere et fououk.*[31] Alice had a brood of young children and Robert's sense of duty as head of the family was directed as much towards his younger siblings as it was towards his mother.

Predictably, it was the older generation which recognized the dangers inherent in outstaying its welcome. Elizabeth Pole, daughter and coheir of Reginald Moton of Peckleton, stood *in loco parentis* to her teenaged grandson, German, and temporarily shared a household with him and his young wife at Radburne. However, as soon as German came of age, although he was prepared, if not happy, for his grandmother to remain in the household, the astute Elizabeth understood that the time had come for her to move elsewhere and, as she put it, 'to get me into a little cornner'.[32] Although there is more than a hint of Mrs Gummidge in the tone of Elizabeth's letter, her instincts were basically sound. The condition for her continued residence at Radburne, that she 'be as kynd to my sayd son [*sic*] Germyne as he intendeth to be to me', was easier to promise than to honour. German may have been naive enough to believe that good intentions would suffice. His grandmother knew better.

Similarly, Eleanor Shirley knew her hard-nosed son, Ralph III, only too well to delude herself that they would be able to sort. As it was, their dispute over her dower rights required the mediation of, among others, the legal-minded Thomas Keble, serjeant-at-law, and William Littleton, eldest son of the justice of common pleas.[33] By the time agreement was reached, Eleanor had taken

---

[31] *Ibid.*, pp. xxvii–xxviii.   [32] *Ibid.*, p. 190.

[33] L.R.O. 26D53/83, 315; *D.N.B.*, XI, p. 1253.

herself well away from Ralph at Staunton Harold to the family's manor of Middleton in Warwickshire.

Even more rare than the multi-generational family was the extended family. A notable exception of very limited scope is provided by the Walsh family. Thomas Walsh, variously described as 'a person of unsound mind', 'a lunatic with lucid intervals', 'demented' and as 'an idiot', lived first with his sister, Margaret, and her husband, Sir Thomas Gresley.[34] The precise nature of Thomas's disability or of the problems it may have caused to those around him is unclear. What is clear is that no innate sense of charity prompted the Gresleys to become Good Samaritans. It was probably Thomas Walsh's heir, his brother, Richard, with his eye on the value of his future inheritance, who realized that in clutching Thomas to the bosom of their family, the Gresleys were motivated less by fraternal devotion than by mercenary considerations. They were accused and found guilty by a royal commission of enquiry of having caused 'great wastes and destructions' on Thomas's lands. As a result of this finding, the unfortunate Thomas, along with his wasted lands, was removed from the doubtful care of Sir Thomas Gresley and assigned to the custody of Walsh's nephews, the sons of his other sister, Elizabeth Boyville.[35]

In the few instances, therefore, where we can find multi-generational or extended families these unusual arrangements had stemmed from distinctive circumstances. When child marriages were contracted, the children, as a matter of course, would continue to live with their in-laws until they came of age; aged parents might cohabit with married offspring if the vexations of age were compounded with burdensome infirmities; or a disabled person might be provided with shelter of sorts in the household of a sibling or of a more distant relative. But the rarity of such examples indicates that the nuclear family was the norm. Certainly, the problems anticipated by Elizabeth Pole and actually encountered by Eleanor Shirley show that the nuclear family was recognized as desirable by contemporaries for very good, personal reasons.

Having established that the typical Leicestershire gentry family consisted of mother, father and children, we are now confronted with the problem of how many children.[36] The question is more

[34] *C.P.R.*, 1422–9, p. 4; *ibid.*, 1436–41, pp. 371, 424.
[35] *Ibid.*; C145/309/47; L.R.O. 5D33/177, fo. 77.
[36] It will be appreciated that our primary concern is with specific families rather than with population in general. Little is to be gained, therefore, by taking into account those who

intractable than it seems. The most obvious difficulty is the absence of parish registers of baptisms but although this deficiency can be partly balanced by recourse to other material, the nature of that material can produce results which are not altogether satisfactory. For example, inquisitions *post mortem* name the heir to the patrimony. They are particularly helpful, therefore, such as in the case of Thomas Palmer, where the family consisted of daughters only. As joint heirs, all daughters are named in the inquisition.[37] Nevertheless, inquisitions are much less helpful when a male heir had younger siblings. Given that the latter had no legal claim on the patrimony, they were ignored in the escheator's return. Nor, of course, do inquisitions recognize the former existence of children who had died.

Wills also pose problems of their own. Naturally, they concentrate on those children who have survived until the time that the will was made. They therefore ignore not only children who died in infancy but also more mature offspring who died even a short time before their parent or parents. Furthermore, when a testator had already provided settlements of land and dowries for married sons and daughters he may justifiably have considered that these children had no further claim on his benevolence after his death. Like the dead, previously endowed children could be ignored in wills. Even the expectant heir was often omitted. Ralph Woodford, for example, made bequests in his will to his younger sons, Mathew, John and Robert, and to his daughter, Joan Neville, but he saw no need to donate gifts to his heir, William, who would, in any case, inherit the bulk of his father's estate as a matter of course.[38] Similarly, as the time approached for Robert Moton II to settle his worldly affairs, his largesse extended to his four sisters while his son, Edward, and his daughter, Elizabeth, receive not so much as a mention in his will.[39] If Elizabeth were married, then her dowry was obviously considered to have been sufficient provision, but she may, in fact, have been dead. Her brother, Edward, however, was still alive. Once again, there was no

---

did not marry or by trying to establish an acceptable multiplier. (See Russell, *British Medieval Population*; J. Kraus, 'The medieval household: large or small?'.)

[37] Pollock and Maitland, *The History of English Law*, p. 260. For Palmer's daughters, see C140/55/9 MS 2; E149/232/10. The same consideration applies where the joint heirs are sisters or the offspring of sisters of the deceased as in the case of John Bellers II (C140/52/27).

[38] PROB11/11/23/183v.

[39] PROB11/11/25/201.

pressing need to name him in the will as the property would devolve on him anyway.

These problems inherent in the more important evidence demand that the discovery of 325 children of gentry families should be regarded as the absolute minimum number of offspring. As we would expect, therefore, the figures yield a very low average of 2.5 children per family.[40] Little, apart from guessing, can be done to compensate for the under-recording of children who were not heirs but at least some compensation can be made to accommodate child mortality. If we take into account a mortality rate of 30 per cent among children up to the age of fifteen years then the average size of the family increases to 3.6 children while a mortality rate of 40 per cent yields 4.2 children per family.[41] Nevertheless, it is worth noting that about 20 per cent of Leicestershire gentry families consisted of five or more children.

The largest of these families, those of Thomas Neville who had nine children and of John Shirley who had twelve, belonged to the knightly group.[42] This fact may tempt us to propose that family size, like household size, was determined by wealth and status.[43] However, a closer inspection of the figures reveals no such correlation. Just over 22 per cent of knightly families consisted of five or more children while the proportion for esquire families was also about 22 per cent. Nor can we find any significant correlation between early marriage and fertility rates.[44] Certainly, two of our large families, Thomas Neville's and John Sotehill's, followed early marriages; but Ralph Shirley III's child marriage produced a single daughter while Thomas Erdyngton II's marriage appears to have been barren. In fact, although five teenage marriages produced five or more children, six resulted in families of two or fewer.[45]

[40] The offspring of William Hastings have been excluded from all calculations. Hastings married after his elevation to the peerage and his five children therefore fall outside the scope of this aspect of the study.

[41] For mortality rates see Starkey, 'The age of the household', p. 230. Children of the first and subsequent marriages are counted as one family.

[42] L.R.O. DE220/90–1; PROB11/13/27/229; *C.I.P.M.*, 19 Hen. VII, no. 691; L.R.O. 26D53/1947, 1948; *Stemmata Shirleiana*, p. 51.

[43] For the relationship between household size and wealth and status see above p. 140. See, too, D. Herlihy and C. Klapisch-Zuber, *Tuscans and their Families. A Study of the Florentine Catasto of 1427*, New Haven, CT, 1978, p. 286.

[44] See Russell, *British Medieval Population*, p. 164; Starkey, 'The age of the household', p. 230. It must be admitted here that the sample is very small, eleven families in all.

[45] Ralph Shirley II is included in the latter figure though he did subsequently sire six children by his second wife.

It would be interesting to determine the relationships forged between these children and their parents and among siblings. In the case of the Pastons in East Anglia their personal correspondence has proved both illuminating and rewarding in this regard but, in the absence of such material for the Leicestershire gentry, our statements about their relationships must be impressionistic and somewhat tentative. This caveat aside, the Leicestershire evidence suggests that attempts to portray our medieval forebears as lacking in affection are presenting only part of the picture.[46]

Of course, discord within families was by no means unusual. Mention has already been made of the strained relationship between Ralph Shirley III and his mother, occasioned by a dispute over her dower rights.[47] Ralph also withheld his sister, Jane's, marriage portion which she had been granted under the terms of her father's will.[48] He justified his actions on the grounds that Jane had had an incestuous relationship with, and borne a child to, her father-in-law.[49] Whatever the legal merits of Ralph's case there can be no concealing the tones of priggish conceit in his revelations about Jane's alleged peccadilloes. Lacking

---

[46] See Du Boulay, *An Age of Ambition*, p. 116; Stone, *The Family, Sex and Marriage*, pp. 82, 87; Starkey, 'The age of the household', pp. 231, 235.

[47] See above, p. 143.   [48] L.R.O. 26D53/1947.

[49] C1/289/48–52. Dr Susan Wright follows *Stemmata Shirleiana* and gives Jane's husband as Richard Kniveton of Bradley (*The Derbyshire Gentry*, p. 217). However, a Sir William Brown petitioned the chancellor, William Archbishop of Canterbury, claiming that he had married 'Johanne', daughter of John Shirley. 'Johanne' was dead by the time of the petition but Brown's complaint was that her brother, Ralph, had failed to pay her marriage portion of 100 marks, allowed for in John Shirley's will (C1/289/48–52). The reference to William Archbishop of Canterbury dates Brown's appeal to the years 1504–15 (*Handbook of British Chronology*, p. 88). 'Johanne' is a common variant of Jane and Sir Ralph's reply to Brown's bill of complaint also refers to the lady in question as 'Jane', thereby countering any suspicion that Johanne and Jane were not the same person. As Ralph did not deny that there had been a marriage between his sister and Sir William Brown and as Brown would not have been entitled to the 100 marks had he been Jane's second husband, it seems that the claim in *Stemmata Shirleiana* of a marriage between Jane and Richard Kniveton is incorrect. Of course, the author of the *Stemmata* may have been privy to evidence which suggested an intention to marry Jane to Richard Kniveton, even though the marriage never took place. We should also keep in mind that, as a member of the Shirley family himself whose audience would include other members of his family, the author had a vested interest in not drawing attention to Sir Ralph Shirley's sordid accusations against the virtue of his dead sister (C1/289/52). One problem remains, however. Ralph refers to his sister's father-in-law, William Trussell. If we accept 'father-in-law' in its usual sense this would preclude a marriage between Jane and either Richard Kniveton or Sir William Brown. We can only assume that Ralph had in mind some other form of relationship between Jane and Trussell, the nature of which is elusive.

respect for his sister's honour, Ralph could have had little
affection for her person.

In the Moton family, variance resulted from the conflicting
claims of brothers of the half-blood. Robert Moton I had first
married Margery Malory, producing a son, Reginald, who in turn
had two daughters, Anne and Elizabeth. Robert later married
Elizabeth Mulso who also produced a son, William. We can
understand Robert's desire to provide as lavishly as possible for
William who would, after all, perpetuate the family name.
Similarly, we can understand Reginald's determination to ensure
that his brother of the half-blood was not provided for at the
expense of his own daughters. The clash of interests resulted in a
bitter dispute between Robert and his elder son, Reginald,
involving the forgery of deeds and hints of blackmail.[50] There can
be little wonder that this particular dispute became the topic of
gossip in the county.

There may have been tension, too, in the Keble family between
Thomas Keble and his son, Walter, though Thomas's early death
probably prevented these tensions from developing into outright
hostilities. Nevertheless, it is clear from Thomas's will that he was
well aware of his son and heir's delinquent tendencies which made
the father apprehensive about the future.[51] Apart from bequea-
thing Walter his books of scripture 'to the entent that he shall the
rather apply him to virtue and conning' and exhorting him to
'eschew all vice and misrule', Thomas arranged for his executors
to keep possession of his lands and goods until Walter reached the
relatively mature age of twenty-four years. During the intervening period the executors were closely to monitor Walter's moral
development and if he failed 'to amend and apply him to virtue,
truth and goodness then he [was to] have no part thereof' until he
did amend.

But against these examples of internal family friction we can
cite instances of harmonious co-existence, loyalty and, occasionally, affection and love. Thomas Keble was certainly apprehensive
about his son's juvenile shortcomings but his tone is one of
disappointment rather than despair. He still had sufficient faith in
his son to hope for a reformation and that he took such pains to
make that reformation possible points to paternal concern and
affection rather than bitterness or animosity. Once he was made

---

[50] C1/13/162–3; C1/15/125–6; C1/22/114a–d.   [51] PROB11/12/3/22v–3v.

privy to the strictures of Thomas's will, the immature Walter may, of course, have viewed his father's well-intentioned endeavours with a more jaundiced eye.

Although Thomas Keble's feelings for his son may not have been reciprocated, there can be no gainsaying the mutual respect evident between Robert Woodford and his mother, Mabil. The two worked in tandem. Mabil's dower property was granted to her without apparent quibble or rancour. Later, we find the pair jointly farming out tenements in Melton Mowbray, and the trust between them developed sufficiently for Mabil to make Robert her attorney and for Robert to make his mother one of his feoffees for his manors and lands before he headed for the wars in France.[52] No doubt, it was during this time that Mabil's reputation as matriarch of the family was established. Her fame was such that her great-grandson, Ralph, remembered her by name in his will, leaving money to provide prayers for the repose of her soul, though it must be admitted that the passage of time had made him unsure of their exact relationship.[53]

Wills also provide evidence of loyalty to, and concern for, siblings. Robert Moton II left bequests of money to each of his sisters, and Edmund Appleby generously left his sister 20s. per year for life.[54] John Sotehill arranged for the division of his goods among his wife, mother and three brothers while Ralph Woodford's gift to his sister, Katherine, was a practical assortment of livestock and some money.[55] As none of the beneficiaries had any legal claim on the testator's benevolence, these bequests speak of the bonds between the donors and the recipients.

Something much stronger than mere bonds, harmony, loyalty or affection can be glimpsed in the will of Elizabeth Sotehill.[56] Perhaps it was the early age at which she had been wrenched from the supposed security of her biological family in Yorkshire and transferred to the Sotehill household in Leicestershire that explains the strength of her attachment to the Sotehill family.[57] But whatever the psychological reasons may have been, only the depth of Elizabeth's love for both her husband and her eldest son can explain her solution to the emotional dilemma which she

[52] B. L. Cotton Claudius, A XIII, fos. 59v–60, 93v–4, 102v, 174–5, 223.
[53] PROB11/11/23/183–3v.   [54] PROB11/11/25/201; PROB11/15/1/7.
[55] PROB11/10/15/121; PROB11/11/12/183v.   [56] PROB11/15/19/151v.
[57] *Plumpton Correspondence*, p. lxxi.

faced as her own death approached. Her husband, John Sotehill, and their son, Henry, had already died by the time Elizabeth made her will. John had been buried at Stockerston in Leicestershire but Henry was interred at the Grey Friars in London. Wishing to be as close to these men in death as she had been in life, Elizabeth arranged for her body to be buried beside her son while her heart was to be removed and laid to rest with her husband. Other endearments in her will directed towards her daughter-in-law, Joan, Henry's widow, suggest that in their mutual grief at Henry's death, the two women found solace in each other's company and further reveal Elizabeth Sotehill as one of the more likeable characters of the fifteenth century, rivalled only, perhaps, by the better known Margery Paston.[58]

In the sensitive Elizabeth Sotehill we are confronted, therefore, with the antithesis of the unattractive Ralph Shirley III – her tenderness and love contrasting with his selfishness and spite – and between these two extremes we find a field of family feeling ranging through respect, loyalty and affection. In fact the array of sentiment found in the nuclear family was no less varied and rich in the fifteenth century than it is today. Then, as now, some families could live harmoniously, caringly and lovingly; some could not. How irritating, then, are studies which dwell on the latter at the expense of the former, thereby implicitly denying the immutability of human nature.[59]

Relationships among the wider kin are less well documented than those between siblings or between parents and children. In part, this lack of evidence may be explained by the greater geographical distance separating kinfolk, leading to less physical contact, and in part by the greater emotional distance between kin. As absence does not necessarily make the heart grow fonder, these two conditions are closely linked. Nevertheless, when we can, occasionally, determine relationships amongst kinfolk we find, once again, a range of sentiment.

For example, the breach between Ralph Woodford and his uncle, Walter, was so complete that the latter feared for his life at his nephew's hands.[60] The source of their conflict can be traced back to the 1430s or 40s when Sir Robert Woodford,

---

[58] See H. S. Bennett, *The Pastons and their England. Studies in an Age of Transition*, 2nd edn, Cambridge, 1968, pp. 42–6.

[59] See, for example, Stone, *Family, Sex and Marriage*, pp. 82, 87 and *passim*.

[60] C1/33/10.

Walter's father and Ralph's grandfather, was endowing his younger sons with purchased lands to the detriment of his heir.[61] After Sir Robert's death, Ralph determined to seize his uncle's portion and, if necessary, to hold it by force. Walter was unable to defend his rights as he lived 'far out' of Leicestershire, so Ralph's illegal entry onto the property endured for over ten years.

Property rights also lay behind a dispute between Thomas Keble and his cousin, Thomas Hotoft, the brother and heir of Richard Hotoft the younger.[62] Relations between Richard and Thomas Keble had been close enough for Keble later to request to be buried in the chapel where 'my kind cousin Richard Hotoft . . . lieth',[63] and, apparently, for Richard to have made Keble one of the executors of his will.[64] In this will, Richard had charged Thomas Keble to use the profits of certain lands to pay for prayers in the church of Humberstone. However, when Richard died, his feoffees, acting on the promptings of Thomas Hotoft, refused to release the lands into Keble's hands on the grounds that the latter wished personally to profit from the arrangement. Keble, in turn, accused Thomas Hotoft of being motivated by envy and malice.[65] The dispute is interesting in that it reveals how affection for, and a sense of duty towards, one relative could lead to friction with another, especially in cases where the division of property was involved.

Although signs of affection such as existed between Richard Hotoft and Thomas Keble are rare among the wider kin, we do find at least a sense of duty binding them together. While Ralph Woodford was antagonistic towards his uncle Walter, he could still be modestly generous to other kin. He provided money and livestock to a tribe of nieces and nephews, including a nephew ('cousin') from Staffordshire. Woodford himself had earlier received a present of a primer from his wife's maternal uncle, 'my cousin', John Bellers.[66] Everard Dygby II left his nephew, Rowland, eleven cows, a black steer and six ewes.[67] Thomas Keble's bequests included considerable sums of money to nieces,

[61] B. L. Cotton Claudius, A XIII, fo. 175v.
[62] The term, 'cousin', encompassed a variety of relationships. Thomas Keble's maternal grandfather and Richard and Thomas Hotoft were full cousins, making Keble and the Hotofts first cousins twice removed.
[63] PROB11/12/3/22v–3v.
[64] The will itself has not survived but for references to it see C1/42/89–92.
[65] C1/42/90. [66] PROB11/11/23/183v. [67] PROB11/16/11/81–1v.

nephews and cousins.[68] Even the parsimonious Ralph Shirley III was uncharacteristically generous towards his niece, Elizabeth Hasilrigge, to whom he gave 100 marks towards her marriage. He made other bequests to his nephew, Ralph, and a 'cousin', Richard Sacheverell. Sacheverell and another cousin, John Port king's solicitor, along with Ralph's brother-in-law, Robert Hasilrigge, were just trustworthy enough to be made his executors. Shirley did not neglect, however, to invoke God's curse on these executors if they failed to follow his will.[69] Trust could, after all, be misplaced. A sense of duty may also lie behind John Hotoft's bequests of property at Stretton to Richard Hotoft II and of £20 towards the marriage of Richard's daughter, 'little Joan', but 'little Joan' is also sufficiently familiar to indicate John's affection for her.[70]

Of course, one of the distinguishing features of late medieval society was its increasing concern about status and about the livelihood which maintained it.[71] As that livelihood largely depended on landed property, it is hardly surprising that most family disputes revolved around the estate. This fact holds for disputes both within the nuclear family and among the wider kin. Sir Robert Woodford's standing in Leicestershire resulted in part from John Woodford's judicious marriage to the Leicestershire heiress, Mabil Folville, who provided the family with its *caput* at Ashby Folville, and in part from a policy of land acquisition by purchase, pursued by Robert's father and grandfather.[72] But by endowing his younger sons with estates, Robert came to threaten the wealth, and therefore the status within county society, of his heir, Ralph. Hence, we can comprehend Ralph's violent attitude towards his uncle Walter who was unfortunate enough to have been given lands in Leicestershire where he could not defend them, rather than beyond his nephew's reach.[73]

[68] PROB11/12/3/22v–3v.   [69] PROB11/19/1/8v; L.R.O. 26D53/1948.

[70] PROB11/1/15/118. John's relationship to Richard is unknown. He may have been an uncle. He was the same John Hotoft who was treasurer of the household (E404/46/241).

[71] See, for example, the Statute of Additions (*Stat. Realm*, II, p. 171) and the attitude of Salisbury, Warwick and March to the *parvenu*, lord Rivers (*Paston Letters*, I, p. 162). See, too, John Russell's injunctions on the relative worth of the various estates in John Russell, 'The Boke of Nurture', *The Babees Book*, ed. F. J. Furnivall, London, 1868, Greenwood repr. New York, 1969, pp. 186ff.

[72] B. L. Cotton Claudius, A XIII, fos. 18v–43v, 47v–8v, 116v, 175.

[73] Cf. John Frende's advice to Thomas Stonor either to go to Devon to defend his property there or, failing that, to sell his lands in the county (*Stonor Letters*, I, pp. 55–7).

Similar extenuating circumstances help to explain Ralph Shirley III's squabbles with his mother and sister. Throughout much of the fifteenth century, the Shirley lands were encumbered with the claims of a succession of long-lived dowagers. Ralph I's mother, Beatrice, lived as a widow for thirty-seven years until 1440, just three years before the death of her son.[74] Ralph II's step-mother, Alice, survived her husband by twenty-three years, drawing her income from manors and lands in Leicestershire and Nottinghamshire and being provided with over £4 yearly in lieu of her rights to other manors and lands in Derbyshire and Leicestershire.[75] When Alice died in May 1466, Ralph could at last retrieve her dower property but he enjoyed its benefits for a mere seven months before his own death in December.[76] Ralph II's son, John, fared little better. At least his step-mother, Lucy, had already agreed in 1458 to confine her claims to the manors of Brailsford, Borowes and Thurvaston and not to make further demands on Alice's property whenever it should become available.[77] Nevertheless, she, too, was a drain on the patrimony for fifteen years after the death of her husband.[78]

When Ralph III eventually succeeded his father, his prospects must have appeared bleak indeed. His mother, Eleanor, was provided with the manors of Hoon, Brailsford, Bradley and Edington in Derbyshire, Ratcliffe-on-Wreake in Leicestershire and with manors in Nottinghamshire to the value of £80 yearly.[79] Under the terms of their father's will, each of his six brothers was entitled to 8 marks per annum for life while four of his five sisters were to receive sustenance until their marriage and then marriage portions of 100 marks apiece, the money to be set aside from landed income at the rate of £40 yearly.[80] With his mother and siblings acting as a drain on his inheritance, we can understand Ralph's attempts to lighten his financial burden at their expense.

Disputes about property were more likely to involve kindred of the blood or widows, each of whom contended for a share of finite resources. The affinal kin, on the other hand, had no claim on the family estate, a fact which has led to the contention that ties

---

[74] C139/101/65 MS 2; *Stemmata Shirleiana*, pp. 37, 43.
[75] E149/219/9; L.R.O. 26D53/344.   [76] C140/19/18 MS 3.
[77] L.R.O. 26D53/195.   [78] *Stemmata Shirleiana*, p. 39.
[79] L.R.O. 26D53/315.   [80] L.R.O. 26D53/1947; 26D53/83.

with them tended to be stronger than with consanguineous kin.[81] There is certainly much evidence to support this view. Time and again, testators turned to members of the affinal kin in preference to closer blood-relatives to execute, supervise or witness their wills. Rather than entrust the disposition of her daughter, Anne's, jointure to her surviving sons, Elizabeth Sotehill turned, instead, to her daughter-in-law, Joan.[82] Although the supervisor of John Turville's will was Robert Fouleshurst, a relative of his mother's, one of the witnesses was his wife's nephew, Thomas Hasilrigge.[83] Thomas Pulteney's will was witnessed by, among others, William Assheby who was either the brother or nephew of Pulteney's wife, Agnes.[84]

The apparent preference for appointing members of the affinal kin to positions of trust extended to the selection of feoffees, too. John Bellers' feoffees were his brother-in-law, Nicholas Griffin, and his niece's husband, Ralph Woodford.[85] Ralph Shirley II also used his brothers-in-law, Walter and Thomas Blount, as feoffees for his manor of Long Whatton.[86] One of Laurence Sherard's feoffees was his wife's nephew, Sir Thomas Berkeley, the son of Isabel Sherard's sister, Jane.[87] That the protection of the estate was a prime consideration when selecting feoffees can be seen in the case of Thomas Farnham. Farnham justifiably came to suspect his son, John's, intention to dissipate his inheritance. He therefore made his 'cousin', John Danvers, one of his feoffees in preference to his spendthrift son.[88]

But, despite the wealth of evidence pointing to close ties with the affinal kin, we find that members of the consanguineous kin were also appointed to positions of trust. John, Thomas and Hugh Boyville acted as feoffees to his use for their cousin, Richard Boyville.[89] Geoffrey Sherard, Ralph Woodford, Richard Perwych, Everard Dygby II and Richard Belgrave all used their sons as executors of their wills.[90] Everard Fielding turned to both his son, William, and his brother, Martin, to execute his will.[91] The strength of one's trust depended, it seems,

---

[81] Houlbrooke, *The English Family*, p. 19.   [82] PROB11/15/19/151v.

[83] PROB11/15/15/119v.   [84] PROB11/15/24/193v.

[85] C1/56/236.   [86] L.R.O. 72′30/1/37.

[87] C1/10/198.   [88] *Quorndon Records*, pp. 155–6.

[89] C140/17/23 MS 2.

[90] PROB11/9/23/176v–7; PROB11/11/23/182v–3v; PROB11/14/30/233; PROB11/16/ 11/81–1v; PROB11/16/17/127.

[91] PROB11/18/5/30.

more on the perceived personal merits of one's kin, regardless of whether they were consanguineous or affinal, and the conventions were flexible enough to permit a degree of personal choice. The variety and choice available to members of the gentry when forming relationships either within the nuclear family or among the wider kin indicate that individuals were not so much subject to external influences but, instead, merely adopted the universal maxim that they follow their own self-interest.[92] Of course, self-interest and the interest of others may coincide but in those cases where it did not, it was the former which prevailed. It remains to be seen, however, if the most important relationship of all, that between husband and wife which joined gentry families, one with another, was subject to less personal constraints.

The present study is based on a total of 194 marriages. Of these, 157 involved Leicestershire males, mostly family heads and their heirs male, while 57 involved gentry daughters. In order to avoid double counting, the cases of overlap where Leicestershire gentry married daughters of other Leicestershire gentry have been omitted from the total of 194. These 194 marriages reveal the way in which the Leicestershire gentry were interrelated through marriage but, being confined to a limited period, they do less than justice to the extent of matrimonial ties.[93]

---

[92] See J. Butler, *Fifteen Sermons Preached at the Rolls Chapel and a Dissertation upon the Nature of Virtue*, ed. W. R. Matthews, London, 1967, *passim*.

[93] A. J. Pollard has revealed a similar kinship network through marriage in Richmondshire (Pollard, 'The Richmondshire community of gentry during the Wars of the Roses', pp. 47–8). To illustrate the Leicestershire relationships more graphically, two genealogical tables are provided in appendix 2 (a) and (b). In each case an individual was chosen and the marriage links extended as far as space would permit. No significant criteria were used in making this choice and it is clear that similar tables would result from the selection of almost any other individuals. The starting point for (a) was Robert Woodford and that for (b) was Margaret Bugge. By the third and fourth generations in (a), the Woodford network encompassed Palmers, Skeffingtons, Villerses, Berkeleys, Sherards, Neeles, Bellerses, Asshebys, Nevilles, Pulteneys and Malorys. By the third generation in (b) the Bugge network embraced Motons, Turvilles, Grymmesbys, Fouleshursts, Hotofts, the two branches of Stauntons, Shirleys, Hazilrigges, Entwysells, Wyvylls, Danverses, Boyvilles, Perwyches, Brokesbys, Walshes, Sotehills and Pulteneys. Neither network can claim to be complete. For example, Thomas Berkeley in (a) married as his first wife, Emma Brokesby whose family has proved difficult to reconstruct (see appendix 3). If a relationship could be established between Emma Brokesby and Robert Brokesby (b) and between Agnes Pulteney (a) and John Pulteney (b), then the networks could be combined at two points.

These interrelationships were the product of a slight though distinct preference for selecting marriage partners from within the county. In 53 per cent of cases, gentry males married women from Leicestershire while 59 per cent of gentry daughters married within the shire. At times, spouses were chosen from among near neighbours such as in the cases of Robert Farnham's marriage to Margaret Whatton, both of whose families held land at Quorndon, and of Thomas Boyville's marriage to Elizabeth Walsh. Boyville held land at Ilston-on-the-Hill, only 2 miles from the Walsh manor of Burton Overy. Geographical proximity also seems to have played a part in the marriage bonds forged between Berkeleys, Woodfords and Sherards who all held lands in the east of the county close to the border with Rutlandshire. There can be little doubt that such families were well acquainted long before the sealing of marriage agreements.

Horizons were not always quite so narrow as these examples suggest. The search for marriage partners ranged county-wide and beyond. John Pulteney, who came from Miserton in the far south of the county, married Margaret, daughter of Thomas Walsh from Wanlip, north of Leicester, and Alice Shirley from Staunton Harold, close to the Derbyshire border in the north-west, married into the Brokesby family whose lands were north-east of Leicester at Frisby. Nor must we neglect the 46 per cent of gentry males or the 41 per cent of females whose respective wives and husbands came from beyond the county boundary from as far away as Devonshire in the south, Carmarthen in the west and Northumberland in the north.[94]

However, distance does not preclude prior social intercourse between families which were later to be connected by marriage. Admittedly, both the Stonor and the Paston letters reveal that prospective grooms relied upon a network of friends to gather information about, and procure introductions to, eligible partners hitherto unknown to them or to their families.[95] No doubt some Leicestershire marriages resulted from similar pre-nuptial manoeuvrings. Nevertheless, the need for such assistance should not necessarily be considered as universal. Within the county

---

[94] Everard Dygby II married Jacquetta, daughter of Sir John Ellis of Devonshire (*Pedigrees*, p. 131); Elizabeth Hastings married Sir John Donne of Carmarthen (*C.P.R.*, 1461–7, pp. 430–1; PROB11/7/10/77v); and Elizabeth Kynsman married John Turpyn of Northumberland (*Pedigrees*, p. 44).

[95] *Stonor Letters*, II, p. 126; *Paston Letters*, II, p. 96.

itself, points of contact among the wider community were provided by shire elections and the local bench of justices of the peace. Thus, at the election of 1422, among the electors were Richard Turville and Thomas Fouleshurst whose children were later to marry, Baldwin Bugge, whose sister was already married to Richard Turville, and Alan Moton, who was the uncle of one of Margaret Bugge's later husbands, Reginald Moton.[96] Similarly, the commission of the peace of 1448 included Leonard Hastings and Bartholomew Brokesby whose children were to marry five years later.[97] Thomas Palmer and Richard Neele sat on the same bench as members of the *quorum*, though their professional paths had crossed as early as 1442, again on the bench as members of the *quorum*.[98] Palmer and Neele were still acting as justices of the peace on the commission of 1475, the year of Thomas Palmer's death.[99] When Palmer's granddaughter married Richard Neele's son, the families were therefore already well acquainted.

The more informal points of contact which could bring eligible partners together must not be neglected, either. It is that same informality which explains why these occasions usually pass unrecorded but in the case of Alice de Bryene one is confronted by the extent of entertaining that occurred in medieval households.[100] Among her regular guests can often be counted a brood of sons and daughters. While it is impossible to say whether any of these specific gatherings resulted in matrimony, they certainly supplied the requisite opportunities.

Although the families of Leicestershire spouses, whether close neighbours or not, were probably already well known to each other at the time of a marriage, we are still left with a large proportion of partners who came from outside the county. The majority of outsiders, 82 per cent, in fact came from neighbouring counties. Invariably, one or other or both families held lands in the other's county. The Willoughbys who married into the Belgrave family also held land in Leicestershire at Wymeswold and Cossington, just a few miles from the Belgrave holdings at Thurmaston and Belgrave.[101] Anketin Malory, the father of Margery who married Robert Moton I, held a quarter

[96] C219/13/1.   [97] *C.P.R.*, 1446–52, p. 590; H.M.C., *Hastings*, I, pp. 300–1.
[98] C66/465 MS 29v; C66/451 MS 29v.   [99] C66/535 MS 31v.
[100] *Alice de Bryene*, p. 28 and *passim*.   [101] *Feudal Aids*, III, pp. 104, 120.

of a knight's fee at Kirkby Mallory, less than a mile from the Motons' manor of Peckleton.[102] Thomas Sherard already possessed land in Rutland before he married Margaret Hellewell from that county.[103] Even in the case of Elizabeth Hastings, who married Sir John Donne from Kidwelly in distant Carmarthenshire, there had been close links between the two families dating back to as early as 1415. In that year Elizabeth's father, Leonard Hastings, and Sir John's father, Griffith Donne, had fought together at Agincourt where both were probably members of the earl of March's retinue.[104] Contacts between the two families were subsequently maintained through mutual attachment to the house of York and through service in the French wars.[105] Taking these links into account, we can conclude that approximately 80 per cent of marriages involved families which were either already acquainted or were in a position to be so. We may assume that neighbours, friends and acquaintances maintained a keen interest in each other's growing families from which to select wives and husbands for their own offspring.

Service in France may also have been instrumental in furthering marriage alliances between the Hastingses and the nobility. Richard Hastings married a daughter of Henry, lord Beaumont, while his brother, Leonard Hastings, married a daughter of lord Camoys.[106] Thomas Erdyngton's wife, Joyce, also came from a noble family; she was the granddaughter and coheir of lord Burnell.[107] Their marriages lend support to the claim, based on a study of Richmondshire gentry marriages, that 'there was no rigid barrier between gentry and peerage'.[108]

In Leicestershire, however, marriage between gentry daughters and members of the nobility was totally unknown. Furthermore, William Hastings' marriage to Katherine Neville, daughter of the earl of Salisbury and widow of lord Bonville, followed his own

---

[102] *Ibid.*, III, p. 125. [103] E179/240/269.

[104] Wedgwood, *Biographies*, p. 433; T. W. Newton Dunn, 'The Dwn family', *Transactions of the Cymmrodorion Society*, 1946–7, pp. 273–5.

[105] Newton Dunn, 'The Dwn family', p. 274; E101/70/6/725; Somerville, I, pp. 242, 640.

[106] Service in France: Richard Hastings; E404/31/312; E101/70/725. Thomas and Henry Beaumont: E404/43/159; E404/52/165; E404/52/15; B. L. Harl. 6166, fo. 69v. Leonard Hastings: Wedgwood, *Biographies*, p. 433. Lord Camoys: E404/31/357.

[107] G.E.C., v, p. 90; *ibid.*, II, p. 435.

[108] Pollard, 'The Richmondshire community of gentry during the Wars of the Roses', p. 48.

elevation to the peerage, while Ralph Shirley's marriage to a sister of Walter Blount predated the latter's elevation to the peerage in 1465. Even were we to admit the Shirleys into this exclusive group which formed marriage alliances with the nobility, it is clear that there certainly were barriers, possibly not rigid but nonetheless real, separating gentry and peerage. The nobility selected partners from no lower than the knightly group and even within that group their marriages were confined to the wealthiest.[109] A similar reticence on the part of the gentry to marry beneath them can be seen at the lower end of the social scale. The only certain example of a marriage involving gentle and non-gentle spouses was that between Joyce Langham and Robert Jakes who, in status, may have occupied that grey area separating gentry and yeomen. These exceptions apart, most gentry marriages were endogamous.

According to the traditional view, one of the purposes of medieval marriage was to provide a male heir who would ensure the continuation of the lineage and preserve the integrity of inherited property. A judicious marriage could also bring additional property to extend the estate, thereby maintaining, or even enhancing, one's social standing within the community. Marriage had a further attraction in that it could cement political alliances not only between gentry and their social superiors but also among the gentry themselves.[110] Whether marriages were arranged by the parents or kin of the intended partners or by the partners themselves, these considerations of preserving the lineage or of pandering to social, economic or political ambitions make of marriage a commercial enterprise with the intended spouses constituting the bills of exchange.[111] Presented thus, medieval marriage, it seems, was governed by the head and the purse rather than by the heart and showed little or no concern for the prospects of connubial happiness. First impressions of Leicestershire marriages suggest that they conformed to this pattern.

The apparently least contentious purpose of marriage was the need to preserve the lineage through the production of sons. It is

---

[109] See chapter 2 above.
[110] Du Boulay, *An Age of Ambition*, pp. 92–6; Houlbrooke, *The English Family*, p. 75; P. M. Kendall, *The Yorkist Age*, London, 1962, pp. 364ff; Pollard, 'The Richmondshire community of gentry during the Wars of the Roses', pp. 27–59, esp. p. 47; Starkey, 'The age of the household', p. 232; Stone, *Family, Sex and Marriage*, p. 37.
[111] Pollard, 'The Richmondshire community of gentry during the Wars of the Roses', p. 47; Starkey, 'The age of the household', p. 235; Flandrin, *Families in Former Times*, p. 1; Mitterauer and Sieder, *The European Family*, p. 122.

clear from his subsequent attitude towards his son, Reginald, who sired daughters only, that Robert Moton's expectations from his second wife had been for another son.[112] The much married Ralph Shirley III also seems to have been hoping for a son, though only by his fourth and last wife, Joan Sheffield, was he able to produce one. John Bellers II's wives were not so accommodating and with him the Leicestershire branch of the family died out in the male line. Sir Thomas Erdyngton anticipated that a similar fate probably awaited his family. By 1444, his wife, dame Joyce, was already past child-bearing age and was showing no signs of embracing death to clear the way for a second wife. Rather than await the day when his manor at Barrow-on-Soar would escheat to the chief lord, Sir Thomas paid 40 marks into the hanaper for a licence to sell the reversion of his manor to John, viscount Beaumont, in exchange for 1,000 marks.[113] Nevertheless, he still hoped for children and arranged that if he were so blessed then his agreement with Beaumont would be void.[114]

However, we should not too readily assume that in failing to produce male heirs, the gentry themselves exaggerated what must have been a personal disappointment into a family disaster. No doubt, Sir Thomas Erdyngton derived some consolation from his windfall of 1,000 marks but others adopted a more emotionally satisfying way of filling the vacuum caused by the lack of a son. John Hotoft clearly found in his son-in-law, John Barre, an adequate substitute for a biological son. Throughout his will, Hotoft refers to Barre as 'my sonne' and lavishes upon him treasured family possessions. But the true indicator of Hotoft's obvious affection for his son-in-law lay in his bequest that Barre should have the reversion of certain lands at £100 below their market value even if his wife should die without issue.[115] Alternatively, in default of legitimate heirs, an illegitimate son could retain the family name. John Bradgate arranged for an estate of all his lands and tenements in Bradgate, Cropston, Thurcaston, Barkby, Thorp, Hamilton and Busby to be made to his bastard son, John Bradgate.[116] In time, the circumstances of John II's

[112] See above, p. 148.
[113] *C.P.R.*, 1441–6, pp. 279–80; H.M.C., *Hastings*, I, pp. 72–3.
[114] For the text of the indenture, see L.R.O. 5D33/108/98.
[115] PROB11/1/15/118–18v.   [116] C1/27/205.

birth would be forgotten and at least the appearance of continuity of the lineage preserved.

The limited significance of the lineage to the gentry is, in fact, placed in perspective by the fate of property devolving on coheirs rather than a single heir. The attempt by the last lord Basset of Drayton to disinherit his heirs general is already well known.[117] To prevent his estate from being divided between the descendants of his grandfather's sisters, namely, Thomas, lord Stafford, and Alice Chaworth, Ralph Basset devised all his lands on his nephew, Hugh Shirley, son of Basset's uterine, or possibly illegitimate, sister, Isabel, with remainder to William Stafford, younger brother of Thomas. As Hugh Shirley had no rights by inheritance to the property and as William Stafford's claim was secondary to that of his elder brother, it is clear that lord Basset's device was intended to preserve the estate intact.[118] Thomas Palmer's coheirs, his four daughters, were not treated as cavalierly as lord Basset's coheirs had been. Nevertheless, the core of the family property at Holt, rather than suffering a fourfold division, passed entirely to one daughter, Katherine, and her husband, William Neville.[119] The integrity of the Walsh family's *caput* at Wanlip was similarly preserved, in its case by agreement between the husbands of the coheirs. Ralph Shirley III, husband of Elizabeth Walsh, received Wanlip, while William Littleton, husband of Elizabeth's sister, Ellen, was compensated by grants of other lands of equal value.[120] It was, therefore, the preservation intact of the core of the estate rather than the maintenance of the lineage that taxed the ingenuity and was the prime concern of the gentry.

It is a simple matter, too, to exaggerate the importance of marriage to the advancement of political alliances.[121] That there were marriages involving political allies cannot be gainsaid, the most notable being William Hastings' marriage to Katherine

---

[117] G.E.C., II, pp. 3–6; McFarlane, *The Nobility of Later Medieval England*, p. 76.

[118] Ralph Basset's feoffees released the Basset manors and lands in Nottinghamshire, Leicestershire, Warwickshire and Worcestershire to Hugh Shirley's son, Sir Ralph, in August 1424. (*C.A.D.*, V, A11388.) Humphrey earl of Stafford and Sir Thomas Chaworth later forcibly disseised Sir Ralph of lands in Nottinghamshire and Warwickshire, prompting Shirley to petition both the king and parliament to assist in their recovery (L.R.O. 26D53/64, 65).

[119] *T.L.A.S.*, 13, 1923–4, p. 217.　　[120] L.R.O. 26D53/543.

[121] Cf., for example, C. Carpenter, 'The Beauchamp affinity: a study of bastard feudalism at work', *E.H.R.*, 95, 1980, p. 522, where a contrary view is adopted.

Neville, sister of the earl of Warwick. Mention has also been made of the political affiliations shared by Leonard Hastings and Griffith Donne before the marriage of their children.[122] Nevertheless, as William Hastings was later to learn, political alliances could be fluid and membership of a lord's retinue did not automatically lead to harmonious association. Geoffrey Sherard and William Lacy were both servants of lord Hastings yet fell to 'variance and discord' over the manor of Teigh in Rutlandshire.[123] In fact, marriages involving political allies may be seen more as a reflection of the opportunities that pre-existing alliances presented rather than as attempts to form new alliances or to strengthen old.

The same conclusion holds even at the more mundane level where members of the gentry required local allies to witness deeds, charters and wills or to act as executors or feoffees. That in-laws performed these tasks is undeniable but to assume that the aim of marriage was to acquire their services is to confuse the purpose of marriage with its result.[124] After the marriage between John Brokesby and Joan Hastings, for instance, we find Brokesbys acting as feoffees for their Hastings kin.[125] However, a Brokesby had been acting as feoffee for a Hastings as early as 1427, many years before the families became allied through marriage.[126]

Although doubts may be cast on the importance of the lineage and of advancing political alliances in the formation of marriages, it is the mercenary side of the arrangements that particularly galls the sensibilities of historians.[127] There is nothing edifying in Agnes Paston's violent, but unsuccessful, attempt to marry her daughter, Elizabeth, to the ageing and disfigured, albeit wealthy, Stephen Scrope.[128] Sir William Plumpton's disposal of his infant granddaughters and putative coheirs is also open to censure.[129] If Agnes and Sir William were typical in their concern for financial gain then we can fully understand the blanket condemnation of

---

[122] See above, p. 158. [123] L.R.O. DG40/282.
[124] For the use of in-laws in this capacity see above pp. 81–2. A contrary view is to be found in Wright, *The Derbyshire Gentry*, p. 54.
[125] H.M.C., *Hastings*, I, pp. 4–5, 291, 309, 310.
[126] *Ibid.*, p. 83; L.R.O. 5D33/108/105.
[127] See Bennett, *The Pastons and their England*, pp. 27–41; Mitterauer and Sieder, *The European Family*, p. 122; Kendall, *The Yorkist Age*, pp. 369–75.
[128] *Paston Letters*, II, pp. 31–2. [129] *Plumpton Correspondence*, pp. lxx–lxxi.

those who 'were ready to traffic in their flesh and blood to serve their own ends'.[130]

Most marriage agreements which set out the terms of this unseemly traffic tended to be settled between the parents of the prospective partners rather than between the partners themselves. The father of the bride provided the groom's father with a marriage portion while the groom's father promised a jointure for the bride's maintenance during her widowhood. The value of the marriage portion and jointure were set by negotiations, during which, if the Stonor correspondence is a reliable guide, the negotiators could indulge in brinkmanship, either to secure the best deal or, perhaps, to fend off an unwanted suitor. When William Stonor showed matrimonial interest in Margery Blount, her demand for a jointure of between £100 and £133-6-8 was sufficient to cool his ardour.[131] Some years later, when Walter Froste wished to marry Stonor's kinswoman, probably his sister, William replied that a jointure of £20 worth of land should be forthcoming otherwise all communication between them should cease.[132]

Although Margery Blount's demands indicate that negotiations provided some room for manoeuvre, the sums of money involved were determined more by a family's wealth and the perceived value of the intended spouse. In 1436 the Belgraves of Belgrave admitted to the modest annual income of £13.[133] Three generations later, Richard Belgrave could set aside only £6-13-4 per annum to build up a fund 'for the putting forth of my children...in marriage and other preferments'.[134] With four younger children to be 'put forth', the resulting fund would have been meagre enough. In contrast, among the upper gentry, Anne Vernon's father provided a marriage portion of £433-6-8 while her husband, Ralph Shirley III, promised a jointure consisting of £50 yearly from land, £60 from rent and a further £10 yearly once Ralph's mother, Eleanor, died.[135] Clearly, both Ralph Shirley and Sir Henry Vernon were keen on the match but the sums agreed upon are as much an affirmation of the perceived status of the two parties.

---

[130] Bennett, *The Pastons and their England*, p. 28.   [131] *Stonor Letters*, I, p. 125.

[132] *Ibid.*, II, pp. 75–6.   [133] E179/192/59.

[134] PROB11/16/17/127.   [135] L.R.O. 26D53/2552.

Less worthy was Anne Warner, Ralph's third wife. Whether her father's status was not so elevated as that of the Shirleys, whether he had less to offer with his daughter as a portion or whether Anne's personal charms were found wanting, is not recorded. But whatever the reasons, at £47, her jointure was considerably below half that of Anne Vernon.[136] Similarly, Sir Leonard Hastings gave £300 as a marriage portion with his daughter, Anne, who married Thomas Ferrers II.[137] Five years later, when another daughter, Joan, married John Brokesby, her marriage portion was only £200.[138] With Joan Hastings we see that fine balance which had to be achieved during negotiations. The Brokesbys were a substantial county family but they hardly compared to the Ferrerses whose landholdings spanned seven counties and who were direct male descendants of the last Ferrers, lord Ferrers of Groby. On the other hand, to have provided Joan with a much smaller portion would have been not only to her disparagement but also a reproach to Sir Leonard himself.

As the amount spent on marriage portions was often considerable, in many cases some financial difficulty must have resulted. In 1467, Vernon property had been valued at about £171.[139] It would have been virtually impossible, therefore, for Anne's father to have paid her sizeable portion in a lump sum. Instead, Henry Vernon agreed to pay £166-13-4 down and a further £33-6-8 each year for eight years until the debt was paid.[140] The marriage portion of Ralph Shirley's fourth wife, Joan Sheffield, was also paid in stages for when Ralph died, his father-in-law still owed £33-13-8 'for marriage money'.[141] Nicholas Griffin, too, opted to pay his daughter's portion of £233-6-8 in instalments, in his case, over three years.[142] Alternatively, one's kin sometimes agreed to lend financial assistance, especially if they were wealthy enough to do so. The aforementioned Joan Brokesby's brother, William lord Hastings, bequeathed his sister's daughter £133-6-8 towards her marriage.[143] Elizabeth Hasilrigge's uncle, Ralph Shirley III, left her £66-13-4 towards her portion which, given that John Shirley had provided no more

---

[136] L.R.O. 5D33/86, fos. 1–2.   [137] H.M.C., *Hastings*, I, p. 300.
[138] *Ibid.*, I, p. 301.   [139] Wright, *The Derbyshire Gentry*, p. 7 citing C140/24/24.
[140] L.R.O. 26D53/2552.   [141] L.R.O. 26D53/1949.
[142] L.R.O. DE220/90–1.   [143] PROB11/7/10/77v.

for each of his own four daughters, must be seen as very generous.[144] Robert Sotehill supplied his niece, Elizabeth Sotehill, with £100 as part of her marriage portion, though in his case he was discharging a long-standing family debt.[145] Failing all else, the gentry could always adopt Thomas Stonor's solution. In 1431, Stonor arranged for his son's marriage to be sold to raise capital towards the marriage of his daughters.[146]

It was evidently felt that money invested in marriage portions was well spent, provided it attracted the right sort of husband. Among the nobility, other nobles were the preferred choice. In 1455, William lord Lovell left his granddaughter, Anne, £200 towards her marriage 'if she be married worshipfully and to such as is or shall be a lord of name'.[147] A similar concern about status exercised the minds of the gentry. John Shirley's bequest of 100 marks towards the marriage of each of four daughters was to be paid only if they remained virtuous and eschewed marriage 'to suche persones as shalbe to them disparyssement'.[148] Gerard Danet also wished to ensure that his daughters' husbands were selected wisely by making payment of their marriage portions contingent upon their choice being ruled by his widow.[149]

For gentry males, the simplest way to maintain or enhance their status was to acquire additional lands through marriage to an heiress. In part, the Neele family owed its advancement to Sir Richard Neele's legal career in the king's service but, from relatively humble beginnings in Shepshed, it owed its manor in Prestwold to Richard's marriage to Isabel, daughter and coheir of William Ryddyngs. Sir Richard's son, Christopher, added to the estate by marrying another heiress, Margery Rokes, from whose maternal grandparents, Thomas Palmer and Elizabeth Bishopsden, he acquired the manor of Keythorpe and lands in Keythorpe, Tugby, Goadby and Billesdon and her share of the Bishopsden inheritance in Warwickshire.[150] Another legal family, the Kebles, came by its *caput* at Rearsby through Walter Keble's marriage to the heiress, Agnes Folville.[151]

---

[144] L.R.O. 26D53/1947; PROB11/19/1/8v.
[145] PROB11/15/19/151v.   [146] *Stonor Letters*, I, p. 47.
[147] L.A.O. Epis. Reg. XX [Chedworth], fo. 22v.
[148] L.R.O. 26D53/1947.   [149] L.R.O. 5D33/180.
[150] *T.L.A.S.*, 18, 1934–5, pp. 5–6.   [151] C1/72/24; *Pedigrees*, p. 79.

But the number of Leicestershire heiresses was limited and the shire gentry had to compete with outsiders in order to secure them. In fact, it was through marriages between heiresses and husbands from outside Leicestershire that the county gentry was replenished. The Shirleys, Sotehills, Turpyns, Hasilrigges and Nevilles all owed their arrival in the county to marriages with Leicestershire-born heiresses.[152] By the same token, native gentry married heiresses from other counties. In this way, Thomas Palmer and Everard Dygby I were able to extend their interests into Warwickshire and Rutland respectively.[153]

So great was the demand and so limited the supply that widowed heiresses were also valued. Margaret Bugge had already been married to Richard Turville by whom she had a son, William, before she married Reginald Moton. A child's hold on life was tenuous, as Thomas Neville recognized in his will.[154] Reginald Moton would have been no less perceptive when he married Margaret Bugge. William Turville's life was the sole barrier between Reginald's future offspring and the Bugge inheritance. Heiresses were, therefore, highly prized commodities in the marriage market and this fact helps to explain why almost two-thirds of Leicestershire marriages involving minors aged eighteen years and under also involved an heiress.[155] Any delay in laying claim to an heiress may have resulted in losing her to another contender.

Although the major point at issue during marriage negotiations was the size of portions and jointures, expenditure on the wedding celebration itself was also negotiable and would some-times be formally recorded in the indenture of agreement. Then, as now, the bride's father usually shouldered most of the costs. When Sir Leonard Hastings' daughter married Thomas Ferrers II, Hastings agreed to 'bear the expenses' of the wedding except for Thomas's apparel.[156] Bartholomew Villers also paid for his

---

[152] *Stemmata Shirleiana*, p. 39; *Pedigrees*, p. 102; *ibid.*, p. 44; *T.L.A.S.*, 12, 1921–2, p. 229; L.R.O. DE220/58; 'Medbourne Deeds', p. 9.

[153] *Pedeigrees*, p. 36; *T.L.A.S.*, 13, 1923–4, p. 216; *V.C.H. Rut.*, II, p. 223.

[154] L.R.O. DE220/94.

[155] F. J. Furnivall concedes that property arrangements were a factor in child-marriages but suspects that attempts to evade wardship were the chief cause (*Child-Marriages, Divorces and Ratifications etc. in the Diocese of Chester*, A.D. *1561–6*, ed. F. J. Furnivall, London, 1897, Kraus repr., New York, 1978, p. xxxix).

[156] H.M.C., *Hastings*, I, p. 300.

daughter's wedding but there was a limit to his largesse. He agreed to supply food and drink for his future son-in-law's friends 'provided that only such as were named by Bartholomew should come'.[157] At times, though, a wedding might call for greater financial resources than the gentry could muster. When Anne, daughter of Richard Harcourt of Oxfordshire, married Henry Fiennes, son and heir apparent of Lord Saye, the presence of nobles at the wedding dictated the need for additional splendour. In this case, both sets of parents equally bore the cost of the occasion.[158]

It is this apparently tasteless emphasis on the commercial side of marriage, the concern for portions, jointures and miscellaneous costs, that has understandably produced the belief that the selection of spouses in the middle ages was determined not by notions of love and affection but by social and economic needs.[159] This view is further supported by the fact that marriage agreements were often settled between the parents of the intended spouses and sometimes involved unions between children who, if they at all understood the nature of the arrangements, were hardly in a position to protest effectively.[160] Whether partners in marriage were the pawns of their parents or subject to social and economic imperatives, our vision of their predicament remains depressing.

Yet, alongside these cheerless images stands the Knight of La Tour-Landry's attitude towards his wife. By the time he wrote his educational works for the benefit of his children, Geoffrey de la Tour was already a widower; but there can be no concealing the intensity of his love for his wife during her lifetime. It is worth quoting him at length.

y delited me so moche in her that y made for
her love songges, balades, rondelles, virallës,
and diuerse nwe thinges in the best wise that
y couthe – but dethe – toke her frome me, the
whiche hathe made me haue mani a sorufull
thought and grete heuuinesse – for a true

[157] *Ibid.*, I, p. 141.
[158] L.R.O. DE221/3/2/31.
[159] Mitterauer and Sieder, *The European Family*, p. 122: Kendall, *The Yorkist Age*, pp. 364, 369.
[160] K. Dockray, 'Why did fifteenth-century English gentry marry?: the Pastons, Plumptons and Stonors revisited', in *Gentry and Lesser Nobility in Late Medieval Europe*, ed. M. Jones, Gloucester, 1986, pp. 64–5.

loveris hert forgetith neuer the woman that
enis he hathe truli loued.[161]

In Geoffrey's words we find none of the cold calculations of
courtly love, no evidence of the poet's conceits. He writes from
the heart and, in so doing, reminds us that medieval marriage
could be a source of great warmth and delight.

Happily, his voice is not solitary. When Sir Richard Harcourt
wrote to Thomas Stonor shortly before the marriage of Stonor's
daughter to John Cottesmore, he prayed God 'to graunt them
bothe moche Joy togeder',[162] thereby revealing that marital
bliss was a natural expectation; and Elizabeth Stonor's letter to
her 'ryght enterly and – most specyall belouyd husband' shows
that these expectations were sometimes fulfilled.[163] Two years
earlier, in an otherwise quite formal letter dealing with business matters, Elizabeth had confided in her husband, William,
that 'I longe sore ffore you, to se you her in London'.[164] The
economy of expression in her plea fails to mask the pains of
separation. Thomas Betson was another who suffered prolonged
periods of separation from his loved one, in his case his
future wife, Katherine Ryche. Nevertheless, his letter to her
shows him to have been both attentive to, and caring about, her
welfare.[165] But the most famous of all fifteenth-century love
matches is provided by the clandestine marriage between Margery Paston and Richard Calle. Their love withstood the opposition and active hostility of Margery's family.[166] Neither must
we forget the love between John Sotehill and his wife,
Elizabeth.[167]

Historians are, therefore, presented with a paradox. On one
side, we can call on evidence to indicate that medieval marriages
provided scope for the expression of strong affection and love
and that partners were expected to attain joy together. On
the other side, there is a mass of evidence that apparently points
to marriage as a purely business transaction with little or no
interest in the future happiness of the married couple. The latter
view is further supported by private letters which reveal the

[161] *The Book of the Knight of La Tour-Landry*, ed. T. Wright, London, 1906, Greenwood
rev. edn, New York, 1969, pp. 1–2.

[162] *Stonor Letters*, I, p. 114. [163] *Ibid.*, II, p. 66.

[164] *Ibid.*, II, p. 16. [165] *Ibid.*, II, pp. 6–8.

[166] *Paston Letters*, I, pp. 342, 541; *ibid.*, II, pp. 498–500; Bennett, *The Pastons and their
England*, pp. 42–6. [167] See above, pp. 149–50.

appeal of present wealth and future economic prospects of the chosen partner rather than of his or her more personal qualities.[168] While not wishing to disparage Katherine, duchess of Norfolk, we can assume that, to her twenty-year-old husband, the attractions of this *juvencula, aetatis fere iiijxx annorum*, were other than carnal.[169] Elizabeth Paston's marriage to Robert Poynings seems to have been equally loveless. She wrote to her mother: 'As for my mayster, my best beloved that ye call, and I must nedes call hym so now, for I fynde noon other cause, and as I trust to Jesu never shall'.[170] Her words are pregnant with bitter irony and whatever her motives were for marrying Poynings, we may deduce that they did not include affection.[171]

Admittedly, historians have made some attempt to resolve the paradox by claiming that, as an unexpected bonus, love could develop during a marriage.[172] Although there can be no quibble with the second part of this proposition, it leaves the essential elements of the paradox untouched. It still accepts that marriages were contracted for worldly reasons and that affection played little or no part in the arrangements.

Literary evidence, however, suggests that economic considerations were not the only criteria used in the selection of marriage partners. The anonymous author of 'How the Wise Man Taught his Son', while implicitly recognizing that there were marriages 'for coueitise', also advocates a higher ideal.[173] Despite his counsel, the lesson not to marry for money was lost on Margery Blount who demanded a jointure of between £100 and 200 marks. Nevertheless, her suitor's suspicion 'that she then had loved [his] londe better than [him]self' must have contributed to his dropping of his suit.[174] Money was, in fact, a secondary consideration in Sir William Stonor's quest for a wife. One unnamed contender had an income of 500 marks from

[168] *Paston Letters*, II, p. 32; *Stonor Letters*, I, pp. 123–4.
[169] William Worcester, 'Annales Rerum Anglicarum', in *Letters and Papers Illustrative of the Wars of the English in France*, II, pt II, p. 783.
[170] *Paston Letters*, I, p. 206.
[171] Surprisingly, the normally sensitive H. S. Bennett says 'it is difficult to judge whether or no she had at last found happiness' (Bennett, *The Pastons and their England*, p. 33). The measured coldness so apparent in Elizabeth's letter indicates that she had not.
[172] Starkey, 'The age of the household', p. 233; Du Boulay, *An Age of Ambition*, p. 102; Kendall, *The Yorkist Age*, p. 369.
[173] *Babees Book*, p. 50, lines 73ff.   [174] *Stonor Letters*, I, p. 126.

land but reports that she was 'fowle ... but lytyll and sumwhat rownde' were deemed sufficient handicaps to make her an unsuitable match.[175] John Paston and Margery Brews also refused to overrate the significance of wealth to their future happiness. They both fully understood that the financial side of their marriage arrangements was a matter for their parents to haggle over but, despite major, albeit temporary, problems in that sphere, the couple were, nonetheless, determined to marry. Margery's letter to her 'good, trewe, and lovyng Volentyne' signals the strength of her affection and one feels certain that in their case the financial cloth was eventually cut to fit the emotional suit rather than the other way round.[176]

John and Margery's success highlights the fact that although parental control over jointures and portions provided them with some voice in the selection of their children's marriage partners, ultimately, a marriage was made by the consent of the partners themselves.[177] Still greater independence of choice could be exercised in second, third or fourth marriages. In Leicestershire, over a fifth of all marriages fell into this category. Jane Shirley's marriage to Sir John Brown seems to have been an affair entirely of her own handling. Jane's father was already dead by the time she married and, if her brother, Ralph III's, later attitude is any guide, he was not altogether pleased with the match.[178] Perhaps, like Miss Frances in *Mansfield Park*, Jane married, 'in the common phrase, to disoblige her family'. Even child marriages allowed for the exercise of choice once the parties came of age. The number of annulments granted in the ecclesiastical courts

---

[175] *Ibid.*, II, p. 126. It is worth bearing in mind that even the pious Henry VI, of whom one finds it hard to imagine his being overly concerned with the pleasures of the flesh, ordered his ambassadors to survey a selection of prospective brides rather than just one 'to the intent that we may have choice' and for them to pay particular attention to looks and physique. He was also well aware that the latter could be enhanced by the use of artificial devices either to restrain a spreading waist-line or to improve an unfashionably large or small bosom and, to counter any attempted deception on that score, the ladies were to parade before the ambassadors in plain kirtles (*E.H.D., 1327–1485*, no. 137); the scene would have been pure Utopian (Sir Thomas More, *Utopia*, Harmondsworth, 1965, p. 103).

[176] *Paston Letters*, I, pp. 662–3.

[177] M. M. Sheehan, 'Choice of marriage partners in the middle ages', *Studies in Medieval and Renaissance History*, I, o.s., 11, 1978, p. 7: C. N. L. Brooke, 'Marriage and society in the central middle ages', and M. Ingram, 'Spousals litigation in the English ecclesiastical courts c. 1350–c. 1640', in *Marriage and Society. Studies in the Social History of Marriage*, ed. R. B. Outhwaite, London, 1981, pp. 27, 48–9.

[178] C1/289/48–52.

indicate that children were well aware of their rights in this matter.[179] That parents, too, were conscious of the need to allow their children to escape from an unwanted marriage is shown in William Hastings' will which made provision for the dissolution of his daughter, Anne's, child marriage to George, earl of Shrewsbury.[180]

But our negative impression of fifteenth-century attitudes towards marriage has been moulded by, and owes the greatest debt to, indentures of agreement which dwell on the settlement of jointures and portions. At least in private correspondence we often find the cash motive tempered by less mercenary concerns. In indentures, on the other hand, the business aspect of marriage finds triumphant expression. The indenture which preceded the marriage between Henry Vernon's daughter, Anne, and Ralph Shirley III, supplies us with a particularly fulsome example. Apart from settling the amounts payable as a portion and jointure, the indenture allows for the enfeoffment of Vernon's friends and sons with lands held in jointure, from which position of trust they could best guarantee Anne's interests. It covered, too, such matters as the deliberate wasting of property jointly held by Anne, bequests to be made to daughters born of the union and the repayment of part of Anne's marriage portion if she were to die prematurely.[181] Henry Vernon was clearly trying to cover every possible pecuniary contingency.

Apart from Ralph Shirley's shoddy treatment of his mother and sister, indications are that Anne Vernon needed all the legal protection her father could provide.[182] Despite the fact that some women, such as Mabil Woodford, could act as partners in estate management and that many were appointed to positions of trust as feoffees and executors, few can have been versed in the intricacies of the law in the way that Margaret Paston or Elizabeth Stonor were.[183] There must have been many such as Jane, second wife of John Staunton, who, after the death of her husband, was too naive to prevent her father- and brother-in-law from defrauding her of part of her inheritance.[184] Ellen, widow of

[179] *Child-Marriages . . . in the Diocese of Chester*, pp. 1–55; *The Register of Thomas Langley Bishop of Durham 1406–1437*, ed. R. L. Storey, 3 vols., London, 1956–9, II, p. 92.
[180] PROB11/7/10/77v.   [181] L.R.O. 26D53/2552.
[182] See above, pp. 143, 147.
[183] Bennett, *The Pastons and their England*, pp. 63–6; *Stonor Letters*, II, pp. 66–7.
[184] C1/58/322.

James Bellers, was another who foolishly ordered her feoffees to make an estate of her dower property to her father-in-law, Ralph. Ralph, in turn, derived the profits from these lands without making any compensation to Ellen.[185] Wives and their children also needed protection against wastrel husbands whose spendthrift ways could leave their dependants destitute. Ellen Bellers' predicament stemmed from her husband's accumulation of debts. John Farnham also falls into this category though in this case, to his credit, John's father, Thomas, defended the rights of his daughter-in-law against the younger Farnham's attempt to alienate his livelihood.[186]

These are the sorts of problems that marriage indentures attempted to anticipate and counteract. Henry Vernon's indenture, therefore, was not simply setting out the terms of a 'traffic in his flesh and blood'; he was displaying a natural paternal concern for his daughter's future welfare. Given that both spinsters and married women lacked any economic independence it was incumbent, first, upon fathers to ensure that their daughters would be suitably provided for during their widowhood and, second, upon fathers-in-law to ensure that this dependence did not constitute a drain on finite resources. It is unreasonable, therefore, for us to expect terms of endearment or signs of affection in what is, after all, a business document designed to strike a balance between these conflicting claims.

We can only conclude that in the formation of marriages, the fifteenth-century gentry were less subject to external constraints than at first appears. Beyond seeking out partners of comparable social status, there was sufficient scope for them to follow the dictates of the heart rather than the purse. To emphasize the latter at the expense of the former is to present only part of the picture and, in the cases of John Paston and Margery Brews, of Margery Paston and Richard Calle and, in Leicestershire, of John Sotehill and Elizabeth Plumpton, that would be a very small part of the picture indeed. Certainly there were mothers such as Agnes Paston and her equally unprepossessing daughter-in-law, Margaret, or fathers and grandfathers such as Sir William Plumpton, who mercilessly manipulated their children and grandchildren to further their own selfish purposes. But we should not assume that Agnes, Margaret and Sir William were archetypes of their age.

[185] C1/9/356.   [186] *Quorndon Records*, pp. 155–6.

Fortunately, the human mould allows for greater diversity than that.

The relative unimportance of external constraints in the formation of many marriages applies equally to family strategy as a whole. As we have seen, the demands of the wider kin or of the lineage were hardly a consideration when selecting feoffees, executors or witnesses or in the disposal of one's property. Nor did the formation of political alliances, whether with a 'good lord' or with one's social equals, greatly impinge upon the gentry's personal lives. In short, if we wished to depict the medieval gentry family as a cock-boat tossed in a sea of external agencies then Leicestershire will not provide us with our canvas.[187] Individualism, or that emphasis upon the private person which, we have argued, was reflected in the domestic architecture at Neville Holt and Staunton Harold,[188] is equally revealed by an independence of spirit in family relationships.[189]

---

[187] See S. Ozment, *When Fathers Ruled. Family Life in Reformation Europe*, Cambridge, Mass., 1983. In claiming that 'humankind is more the master of its fate than mastered by it' (*ibid.*, p. vii), Ozment is not so much expressing his bias, as he humbly puts it, but proclaiming a truism.   [188] See above, p. 141.

[189] A. Macfarlane seems to anticipate that the gentry may not have been individualistic (*The Origins of English Individualism*, Oxford, 1978, repr. 1985, p. 206). However, they were clearly just as 'ego-centred in kinship and social life' (*ibid.*, p. 163) as their social inferiors.

7

LIFE AND DEATH

Life began for John Chesilden II on St Valentine's Day, Wednesday 14 February, 1425 at Seaton in Rutlandshire.[1] Although the Chesildens normally resided in Rutland, they had landed interests in Northamptonshire and, after 1428, in Leicestershire, too, when John II's grandmother, Anne or Amice, inherited the manor of Allexton from her mother, Margaret Burgh.[2] Within a few hours of John II's birth, the stage had been set for his first public appearance in the near-by parish church of All Hallows.[3] Before the day was out, John would be baptised here and given the name which his father also bore. But first, John senior despatched a rider, William Baxter, to fetch lady Elizabeth Longford to be his son's godmother.[4] Meanwhile, the church was made ready; John Club carried fire to light the candles and John Murdok brought water to fill the font. Once these preparations were complete and Elizabeth Longford had arrived, a procession set out from the Chesilden's house to travel the short distance to All Hallows. Apart from John Chesilden senior and Elizabeth Longford, most of those present were probably neighbours, household servants and local tenants. There is no indication that the infant's mother attended the baptismal service. Her presence was not required and her first post-natal visit to the church would follow some days later for the ceremony known as 'churching'.[5] Thomas Carter bore the child in his arms until the first sacrament was administered and then John Bartville's wife, who may have been the

---

[1] C139/129/41; *Handbook of Dates*, p. 118.
[2] E149/141/20; C139/118/14 MS 6; *T.L.A.S.*, 11, 1919–20, pp. 419–21; *Village Notes*, I, pp. 14–15.
[3] Pevsner, *The Buildings of England: Leicestershire and Rutland*, pp. 505–6, plate 91.
[4] The following is based on the inquisition into John II's age, taken in 1446. See n. 1 above.
[5] *The Catholic Encyclopedia*, ed. C. G. Herbermann *et al.*, 16 vols., New York, 1907–17, III, p. 761; M. Warner, *Alone of All Her Sex. The Myth and the Cult of the Virgin Mary*, London, 1976, p. 75; B. Hamilton, *Religion in the Medieval West*, London, 1986, p. 113.

midwife at the birth or, perhaps, John II's newly appointed nurse, carried him back to his father's house where important guests almost certainly celebrated the occasion with a feast.[6]

No doubt, simple tableaux very similar to that at Seaton were regularly enacted in Leicestershire, too. William Villers, who was born in 1405 at Brooksby, was also carried from his father's house there to the parish church of St Michael to be baptized.[7] This sacrament did not ensure a place in heaven but entry to that Kingdom was denied to those who did not receive it.[8] Given the high rate of infant mortality, delays between birth and baptism were therefore necessarily brief. But although birth and baptism provide a convenient introduction to the more personal side of the life of a fifteenth-century gentleman, our main concern is with what happened afterwards, with how the gentry lived their lives and, ultimately, with how they approached death. We have already met the Leicestershire gentry as land-holders and farmers, as professional men, whether as soldiers or lawyers or both, as administrators and governors of their shire and as members of families. Illuminating as these aspects of their lives undoubtedly are, they provide a very limited image of the gentry as people. Indeed, it seems most unlikely that we shall ever know them as fully rounded individuals.[9] In the case of John Chesilden II, for example, we are better informed about the day of his birth than about any other day in his life.[10] Nevertheless, by piecing together fragments of information relating to a number of gentry, we may glimpse a little of the lives they led and thereby, perhaps, reach some understanding of the men they were.

The least illuminated period of the lives of the Leicestershire gentry is their childhood. Children were often mentioned in wills but only as the recipients of bequests, usually sums of money to be set aside towards their marriage.[11] We learn nothing

---

6   See Bennett, *The Pastons and their England*, p. 194.   7   C139/42/74.

8   *The Catholic Encyclopedia*, II, pp. 258–9ff.

9   Cf. Richmond, *John Hopton*. Despite Dr Richmond's sensitive and probing treatment of his subject, John Hopton remains a rather 'wooden' figure. It is no consolation that the difficulties attached to fifteenth-century biography apply equally to members of the nobility (see M. A. Hicks, *False, Fleeting, Purjur'd Clarence. George, Duke of Clarence 1449–78*, Gloucester, 1980).

10 John's younger brother, William, seems to have lived on the family's Leicestershire manor of Allexton until about 1450 when John conveyed it to John Boyville before its sale to Walter Blount of Derbyshire (C1/19/473; *T.L.A.S.*, 11, 1919–20, p. 421).

11 See, for example, PROB11/16/17/127; PROB11/1/15/118; PROB11/13/27/229.

of their play, training or early education. Nevertheless, some generalizations are possible. Infants were initially entrusted to the care of nurses, and women probably continued to dominate their upbringing until they attained the age of seven or so years.[12] Thereafter, a resident tutor may have been employed to deliver more formal instruction.[13] For example, John Still, a priest in the service of the Pastons, was expected 'to be good mastyr to lytyll Jak and to lerne hym well'.[14] Similarly, in those Leicestershire households which supported a chaplain, the rôle of tutor was no doubt added to his religious and other duties.[15]

The course of instruction designed for these children can also be only dimly perceived. One foreign observer, while allowing that the English did not lack intellectual capacity, admitted that few, the clergy excepted, were 'addicted to the study of letters'.[16] Sixteenth-century claims that the gentry were 'brought vp ignorantly and voide of good educac[i]ons' and that they considered the study of letters to be an occupation befitting rustics are even more censorious.[17] Although we may be tempted to dismiss such parodies as reflecting the prejudices of later humanists in particular and the artifice of educational reformers in general, they do suggest that the study of Latin was not a major feature of gentry education. In fact, fifteenth-century books of courtesy place greater emphasis on the development of good manners than they do on more academic pursuits.[18] Nevertheless, Caxton's *Book of Curtesye* added the study of Gower, Chaucer, Occleve and Lydgate to the curriculum, and an inventory of Thomas Keble's library, which contained books in French and Latin, further reveals that fifteenth-century education, despite the biases of its later detractors, was capable of producing highly cultivated laymen.[19]

[12] *Italian Relation*, p. 24. Cf. the early upbringing of Henry VI (Wolffe, *Henry VI*, pp. 35–6; Griffiths, *The Reign of King Henry VI*, pp. 51–3).

[13] See Sir Thomas Elyot, *The Gouernour*, introd. F. Watson, London, 1937, pp. 18–23.

[14] *Paston Letters*, I, p. 540. [15] See above, p. 139, n. 15.

[16] *Italian Relation*, p. 22.

[17] Sir Humphrey Gilbert, 'Queene Elizabethes Academy', in *A Book of Precedence etc.*, ed. F. J. Furnivall, London, 1869, Kraus, repr., New York, 1975, p. 10; *Babees Book*, p. xii.

[18] See, for example, 'The Babees Book', 'Urbanitatis', 'The Young Children's Book', 'Stans Puer ad Mensam' and 'John Russell's Boker of Nurture', all in *Babees Book*, pp. 1–9, 13–15, 17–25, 27–33, 117–99.

[19] *Caxton's Book of Curtesye*, ed. F. J. Furnivall, London, 1868, Kraus repr., New York, 1975, pp. 31–7; *Common Lawyers*, pp. 445–7.

Education at home was not the only option available to the gentry. A late fifteenth-century Italian visitor to England draws attention to the general practice of sending boys and girls, from about the age of seven, 'to hard service in the houses of other people'.[20] Alice de Bryene's household certainly included a number of boys and, although there is no indication of the social status of these youths, some may have been drawn from neighbouring gentry households.[21] Among the Leicestershire gentry, John Bellers was a page in Henry V's household in France at a time when he cannot have been much older than seven years.[22] William Villers was also a royal page at the court of Edward IV in 1479 and 1480, when he was probably in his early to mid-teens.[23] Edward Trussell, too, spent some time in a noble household, that of lord Hastings, but in his case his father, William Trussell, had died, and Hastings owned the boy's wardship and marriage.[24]

Although these examples confirm that some Leicestershire children spent part of their formative years in the households of others, they cannot be taken to imply that the practice of fostering was as widespread as the author of the *Italian Relation* suggests. The gentry could, alternatively, send their sons to one of the county's five schools at Leicester, Melton Mowbray, Loughborough, Castle Donington or Burrough-on-the-Hill.[25] By 1508, the school at Burrough which was run by the rector, Richard Alkborough, had ten scholars, some of whom were drawn from the neighbouring gentry families of Assheby, Skeffington and Villers.[26] Assheby lived sufficiently close to Burrough to have been a day-boy but Alkborough most probably provided board and lodgings as well as tuition.

While there is little direct evidence of childhood experiences in Leicestershire, we are slightly better served for adolescent experiences. Many gentry adolescents and young men from the county progressed to higher education. Thomas Danet of Bromkins-

[20] *Italian Relation*, p. 24.   [21] *Alice de Bryene*, p. 124.
[22] Wedgwood, *Biographies*, p. 63.
[23] E101/412/10, fo. 36; E101/412/11, fo. 35.
[24] PROB11/7/10/76v–9. Hastings arranged for Edward's wardship and marriage to be sold with the first option to John Donne at £40 below the market value. Donne was Hastings' brother-in-law.
[25] N. Orme, *English Schools in the Middle Ages*, London, 1973, pp. 307, 311, 323.
[26] *Ibid.*, p. 220.

thorpe attended Merton College at Oxford, from where he graduated as Bachelor in 1455. By 1471, he had become Doctor of Theology and this high academic attainment led him into royal service. In 1475, he was involved in negotiations at Namur between Edward IV and Charles the Bold, duke of Burgundy, and by the following year he had been appointed as king's almoner.[27] Another Leicestershire youth, William Villers, who was uncle or cousin of the king's page of the same name, also went to Oxford. He graduated as Bachelor in 1453, later becoming rector at Brooksby where his family held the advowson.[28] Both Danet and Villers were younger sons and it is clear that their attendance at university was intended to equip them for careers in religion.[29]

The favoured option for older sons and heirs, on the other hand, was the Inns of Court. Some seventeen Leicestershire gentry attended Lincoln's Inn during the fifteenth century, while one, Richard Neele, was a member of Gray's Inn.[30] A further sixteen gentry had legal knowledge, from which we may infer that they had some formal legal training.[31] No doubt, many Leicestershire fathers would have agreed with the sentiments underlying Agnes Paston's reinforcement of her husband's injunction to their son, Edmund, 'to lerne the lawe, for . . . ho so ever schuld dwelle at Paston, schulde have nede to conne defende hym self'.[32] Not only was knowledge of the law necessary to the gentry for the defence of their own property but legal practice was also a lucrative source of income.[33] Whether pursued at university or one of the Inns of Court, education was valued, therefore, not merely, or in some cases, one suspects, not even, for its inherent worth but for the career paths and

---

[27] A. B. Emden, *A Biographical Register of the University of Oxford to* A.D. *1500*, 3 vols., Oxford, 1957–9, I, p. 540.

[28] *Ibid.*, III, p. 1949; C138/12/22 MS 2.

[29] It appears that Oxford rather than Cambridge was the preferred destination for Leicestershire scholars. I have not discovered the names of any Leicestershire gentry in the register for Cambridge (A. B. Emden, *A Biographical Register of the University of Cambridge to 1500*, Cambridge, 1963), though this may be a product of a failure of evidence rather than a reflection of realities.

[30] *Lincoln's Inn, Admissions; Lincoln's Inn, Black Books; Readings and Moots*, p. xxxii; *The Middle Temple Bench Book*, ed. J. B. Williamson, 2nd edn, London, 1937, p. 1.

[31] Some may even have served apprenticeships in the central courts (M. J. Bennett, 'Provincial gentlefolk and legal education in the reign of Edward II', *B.I.H.R.*, 57, 1984, pp. 203–7).

[32] *Paston Letters 1422–1509*, II, p. 72.   [33] See above, pp. 74–5.

economic opportunities it provided. As with so many other aspects of their lives, the gentry's attitude towards formal education was essentially practical and utilitarian.

Of course, reading can also be for recreation and pleasure. Admittedly, Thomas Keble's library reflected his professional concerns and included a wide range of law books but he also owned copies of Mandeville's *Travels*, Boccaccio's *Decameron* and two separate editions of *The Consolation of Philosophy* by Boethius.[34] The *Travels* and both editions of Boethius were printed but the *Decameron*, to judge by its description and price, was a manuscript edition. It was bound in black satin, richly decorated with gilded silver clasps and was worth £2-13-4. Keble also read histories. He bequeathed his son, Walter, all his chronicles, except for a treasured, manuscript volume of Froissart's *Chronicles* which he left to lady Hungerford.[35] The estimated worth of this library, excluding the bequest to lady Hungerford, was £21-14-4, or about one fifth of the value of all Keble's household goods, furnishings and hangings.[36] Keble was obviously prepared to spend liberally to satisfy his broad intellectual tastes. Mention has already been made, too, that children were exhorted to read English poetry, but there is no reason to assume that the enjoyment of vernacular verse was confined to the young. Two surviving copies of Chaucer's *Troilus and Criseyde*, for instance, contain elements of Leicestershire dialect, a fact which suggests that they were probably written by a native of the area for a native audience.[37]

Surprisingly, an inventory made after the death of Ralph Shirley III, fails to mention any books whatsoever.[38] That John Rudding, the compiler of the inventory, should have overlooked these valuable possessions had they existed, seems improbable. Nor are books often mentioned in Leicestershire wills and the exceptions, apart from Thomas Keble's will, refer only to devotional works such as mass books and primers.[39] As the cost of manuscript volumes was measured in pounds and the cost of even printed works was rarely below a shilling, it is doubtful

---

[34] *Common Lawyers*, p. 445 n. 24, 446.

[35] PROB11/12/3/22v–3. The volume was kept in the chamber over the parlour and valued at £2-13-4 (*Common Lawyers*, p. 436).

[36] *Common Lawyers*, pp. 447, 432–9.

[37] A. McIntosh et al., *A Linguistic Atlas of Late Medieval English*, 4 vols., Aberdeen, 1986, I, p. 210.　　[38] L.R.O. 26D53/1949.

[39] PROB11/11/23/182v–3v; L.R.O. 5D33/180.

that testators subsumed their collections under the general terms, 'goods and chattles', or 'stuff of household' in their wills. That so few specific references were made to books, suggests that reading was not a favoured recreation among the majority of the gentry.[40]

For most of these men, their pleasures were at once more simple and more strenuous. Hunting was a gentlemanly pursuit which not only provided an outlet for their energies but also enriched their tables with a variety of game. One particular mark of social distinction was the possession of a deer park which entailed the removal of land from cultivation or pasturage, the building of deer leaps and fences and the employment of labour to maintain them, all of which involved considerable expense. Ownership of a deer park was therefore a sign of status reserved mainly to the wealthier gentry. The Shirleys, for instance, had a park or frith at Staunton Harold where they hunted red and tallow deer.[41] Besides providing venison for the Shirley's own household, their deer park was an important source of grace and favour and patronage which was dispensed to valued friends and relatives. In 1444, Ralph Shirley II distributed sixteen deer among his relatives, friends and acquaintances.[42] Ralph III granted his mother, Eleanor, the right to hunt for two does every winter and two bucks in summer for life. If she were averse to the exertion which hunting involved, she could, alternatively, appoint a 'sufficient deputy' to take the kill on her behalf.[43] Presumably, 'sufficient' implied someone of gentle status. The same Ralph later bequeathed the keepership of his park to his nephew and namesake.[44]

However, few gentry possessed, or, indeed, could have afforded the luxury of, a deer park. But William Turpyn was content to substitute illusion for reality by keeping two tame deer at Wigston.[45] Obviously, these animals did not provide Turpyn with the thrill of the hunt but he no doubt derived as much visual satisfaction from the deceit as did men of the nineteenth century from their newly built 'medieval' castles. In order to satisfy their pretensions, the more wealthy and

---

[40] The Pastons, on the other hand, were, like the Kebles, avid readers (Bennett, *The Pastons and their England*, pp. 110–13).

[41] L.R.O. 26D53/293. Fallow deer may have been intended.

[42] *Ibid.*   [43] L.R.O. 26D53/83.

[44] PROB11/19/1/8v.   [45] L.R.O. 5D33/86, fo. 87.

upwardly mobile gentry could also create hunting-parks where none had existed before. In these cases, a royal licence was required and this usually entailed additional expense. Nevertheless, in 1448, Thomas Palmer was granted a licence to empark 300 acres at Holt without payment of any fine or fees.[46] Moreover, the grant included rights of free warren in all Palmer's demesne lands and woods in Holt, Prestgrave, Drayton, Bringhurst, Easton, Keythorpe, Tugby, Goadby, Medbourne, Lubenham, Leire and Frolesworth.

Free warren, in fact, provided the gentry with a more common object of the hunt than deer, giving them exclusive rights to all the smaller game on their own lands. These rights were fiercely, if vainly, defended against poachers. In 1468, Sir Thomas Berkeley accused William Purley of entering his free warren at Wymondham and stealing twenty hares, two hundred rabbits, twelve pheasants and twenty partridges.[47] Richard Neele's free warren at Prestwold was also prey to poachers, and William Villers of Brooksby discovered that his neighbours, John Trussell of Rearsby and John Sandy of Gaddesby, yeomen, had regularly stolen his pheasants over a ten-year period from 1441 to 1451.[48]

The gentry were just as adept at poaching as their social inferiors were and the free warren of absentee landlords provided them with their favourite targets. Alan Moton helped himself to a hundred rabbits and partridges and twenty hares and pheasants from lord Grey of Ruthin's free warren at Barwell, while John Langham, Baldwin Bugge, Thomas and Richard Hotoft and Thomas Appleby all hunted illegally in queen Katherine's chase of Leicester.[49] Accusations of poaching sometimes indicate that the hunters used bows and arrows, though Thomas Farnham's possession of a greyhound reveals that dogs were also employed.[50] But whether the gentry hunted in their own or poached from their neighbours' free warrens, the numbers and variety of game-birds and animals available to them point to the potential richness of their diet.

It is clear from the kitchen utensils at Staunton Harold and Humberstone that roast meats played an important part in gentry

[46] *C.Ch.R.*, 1427–1516, VI, p. 100.   [47] *Village Notes*, IV, p. 316.
[48] *T.L.A.S.*, 18, 1934–5, p. 43; L.R.O. 5D33/177.
[49] *Village Notes*, I, p. 145; ibid., III, p. 69; ibid., VI, p. 17.
[50] *Quorndon Records*, p. 144.,

diets. Staunton Harold's kitchen contained five spits, one of which was suitable for roasting large carcasses while another two were specifically designed for poultry.[51] The kitchen at Humberstone was even better equipped, with no fewer than ten spits ('broches') of various sizes.[52] Alice de Bryene's household accounts reveal that she regularly dined on pork, mutton, lamb, pigeons and beef, most of which would have been roasted.[53] Having access to the coast, she also served fresh fish, molluscs and crustaceans but the Leicestershire gentry probably relied more heavily on smoked and salted fish or fresh-water fish from their own brooks and streams. The de Bryene household was also occasionally served rabbits and partridges but the fact that game was a comparatively rare adjunct to her diet suggests that Alice did not own rights of free warren on her lands, though there was no shortage of rabbits on her *caput* of Acton and on the nearby manor of Bures.[54]

Rich as the gentry's diet undoubtedly was, it cannot be considered as particularly healthy. In addition to meat, they consumed vast quantities of bread and ale. Bread was baked daily for the de Bryene household, with production levels regularly above fifty, and rarely below thirty, white loaves each day. In one year from 1418 to 1419, 124 quarters of barley were devoted to brewing and, as the common yield from 2 quarters of barley was 112 gallons of ale, the total household consumption can not have been far short of 7,000 gallons for that year. The drinking of ale witnessed a marked increase during the warmer summer months. In August, 1413, when the harvest was being gathered, the added demand by Alice's boon workers raised production of ale to over 1,000 gallons for the month. By way of contrast, the only reference to vegetables in her accounts is to green peas, used for making pottage, and the alliums, onions and garlic. Surprisingly, fresh fruit receives no mention whatsoever, though Alice did buy imported dried fruits, figs, dates, raisins and currants.

The gentry's demand for imported luxuries extended, to a lesser degree, to household furnishings. Ralph Shirley III owned six pieces of Flemish carpet and Thomas Keble had cushions

---

[51] L.R.O. 26D53/1949.   [52] *Common Lawyers*, p. 438.
[53] For this and the following, see *Alice de Bryene*, pp. 1–5 and *passim*. The page references are too numerous to cite individually.
[54] *Ibid.*, p. 134.

covered with Bruges silk.[55] Both men also owned wall hangings, tapestries and bed coverings which bore intricate designs and were sufficiently expensive to suggest that they may have originated in the Low Countries. In the great chamber beneath the hall at Staunton Harold a counterpoint decorated with leaves and flowers and lined with wild beasts was worth £1-13-4, while a similar item in the great sealed chamber was valued at £2. Six tapestry hangings at Humberstone were priced at £4-10-0 and a counterpoint at £5.

Despite the presence of these luxury furnishings at Staunton Harold and Humberstone, the general impression one forms of the interior of gentry houses is that the emphasis was not entirely on display. At Humberstone, the 'sore worn' red say in the hall, the 'brokyn carpet' in the chamber over the buttery, the 'olde brokyn' feather bed in the clerk's chamber and the 'soreworne' tapestry counterpoint in the parlour were mirrored by similar signs of wear and tear at Staunton Harold. In the inner parlour there, a hanging of red say was 'old [and] stayned'. Four pieces of red say in the wardrobe chamber were 'well worn', and the tapestry in the great chamber beneath the hall was 'old and sore worn'. 'Old', 'stained', 'worn' and 'torn' were adjectives used, either singly or in a variety of permutations, to describe numerous other items. Nevertheless, the value of soft furnishings, whatever their state of decay, greatly surpassed the value of furniture at both Staunton Harold and Humberstone. The price of chairs, tables and cupboards was often measured in pence and rarely rose above a few shillings. Beds, however, especially the great feather beds with fabric canopies, could fetch between £1 and £2, a fact which helps to explain why they were often bequeathed in wills.[56]

What the gentry saved on furniture, they spent lavishly on plate. The author of the *Italian Relation* believed that most Englishmen of rank owned at least £100 worth of silver plate and, on this occasion, his views appear vindicated, at least as far as the upper gentry were concerned.[57] Ralph Shirley III owned two dozen assorted silver, silver-and-gilt and gilt goblets, pots,

---

[55] L.R.O. 26D53/1949; *Common Lawyers*, p. 435. It should be stressed that the use of carpets here does not denote floor coverings but rather rectangles of fabric used to drape items of furniture.

[56] See, for example, PROB11/1/15/118–19; PROB11/16/11/81–1v; L.R.O. 5D33/180.

[57] *Italian Relation*, p. 29.

bowls and basins, eighteen spoons and a gold chain worth a total of £197-10-6.[58] Thomas Keble's even more extensive collection of plate was valued at £255-17-10.[59] In addition to their monetary worth, many items of plate had sentimental value, too. John Hotoft had given his wife a silver and gilt rose-cup as a morning-gift after their marriage and he remembered to ensure that she retained possession of it following his death.[60] Thomas Pulteney's part-gilt basin and ewer were family heirlooms which he bequeathed to his son with instructions that they be passed on within the family.[61] John Turville's silver basin and ewer were similarly directed from heir to heir 'while the world endureth'.[62] The cost of such large pieces helps to explain why they were so highly treasured. Ralph Shirley III owned a pair of basins and ewers worth £11-1-8 and £16-4-4 respectively, while Thomas Keble's two sets were priced at £30-10-0 for the pair.[63]

To judge from their descriptions, the value of some silver items lay as much in the artistry of their design as in the weight of precious metal used. Gerard Danet of Bromkinsthorpe, for instance, owned an embossed ('pounsed') silver and gilt vessel and a gilt cup with a raised bottom displaying a greyhound's head, a motif derived from Danet's coat of arms.[64] The cover on Thomas Keble's gold salt was decorated with fine, gold oak-leaves.[65] Valued at £5, this salt was considered a suitable gift for lady Hungerford.[66] Walter Oudeby, Keble's 'cousin', owned a silver and gilt great-cup patterned with enamel shepherds.[67] But although the gentry took delight in particular items of precious metal, they also regarded silver and gold as an investment which could later be sold to raise capital. John Hotoft ordered that some of his silver be sold to raise money for his funeral expenses and Gerard Danet proposed the sale of a gold or silver chain to provide marriage portions for his daughters, Elizabeth and Mary.[68]

The gentry who could not afford gold or silver plate, found a satisfactory substitute in pewter. According to the author of the

---

[58] L.R.O. 26D53/1949. [59] *Common Lawyers*, pp. 442–3.
[60] PROB11/1/15/118. [61] PROB11/15/24/193v.
[62] PROB11/15/15/119v.
[63] L.R.O. 26D53/1949; *Common Lawyers*, p. 443.
[64] L.R.O. 5D33/180. [65] *Common Lawyers*, p. 443.
[66] PROB11/12/3/23. [67] PROB11/11/29/223.
[68] PROB11/1/15/118; L.R.O. 5D33/180.

Italian Relation, the English used tin to 'make vessels as brilliant as if they were of fine silver; and these are held in great estimation'.[69] Ralph Shirley's pewter was valued at £2-13-4, while Thomas Keble's pewter was worth £3-3-0.[70] Everard Dygby II, who does not appear to have owned any silver-ware at all, bequeathed his pewter to his son, John, and daughters, Alice and Ellen.[71] Dygby also owned a number of brass pots, and similar brass-ware was to be found in the Shirley and Keble households.

A further object of lavish expenditure for the gentry was clothing. On this point, contemporary foreign writers and native legislators and commentators alike were agreed, though whereas foreigners approved of English standards of dress, English governments and moralists roundly censured the vanity and wastage involved in the ownership of extravagant raiment.[72] Thomas Keble owned eighteen gowns ranging in colour from scarlet, crimson, violet and murrey to blue, green and brown.[73] Two of these, a night gown of grey wool (musterdevillers) and a brown tawny gown, were decorated with black lambs' wool and another was furred with fox. Keble's black velvet jacket worth £1-6-8 was edged with martens' fur. Ralph Shirley owned a black velvet jacket, too, valued at £2.[74] His wardrobe was valued at £9-10-0 while that of Thomas Keble was worth £14-19-0.[75]

As in the case of beds, clothes were sufficiently expensive to be passed from one generation to the next. Thomas Keble retained his three wives' wardrobes after they died and then bequeathed them to a variety of nieces and female cousins and friends after his own death.[76] Elizabeth Sotehill similarly bequeathed a gown to her kinswoman, Catherine, and John Kendale left two silk belts with silver buckles to his kinswomen, and a violet gown and hood to his nephew or cousin and namesake.[77] When a suitable beneficiary could not be found to receive gifts of apparel,

---

[69] *Italian Relation*, p. 11. [70] L.R.O. 26D53/1949; *Common Lawyers*, p. 438.
[71] PROB11/16/11/81–IV.
[72] *Italian Relation*, p. 22; J. Scattergood, 'Fashion and morality in the late middle ages', in *England in the Fifteenth Century. Proceedings of the 1986 Harlaxton Symposium*, ed. D. Williams, Woodbridge, 1987, pp. 255–72; *E.H.D., 1327–1485*, nos. 681, 692.
[73] *Common Lawyers*, pp. 443–4. [74] L.R.O. 26D53/1949.
[75] The latter sum omits the value of clothes belonging to Keble's dead wives. These garments were estimated to be worth £8-18-4.
[76] PROB11/12/3/23. [77] PROB11/15/19/151v; L.R.O. 5D33/180.

garments could still be unstitched to provide cloth for other purposes. Thomas Keble adopted this strategy, arranging for his doublets and other clothes of velvet and silk to be made into vestments 'and disposid for my soule'.[78] The pious intent of this bequest was no doubt designed to expunge the sin of pride which attended his possession of such grand attire in the first place.

Extravagance in clothing, however, was not merely frivolous pandering to the gentry's propensity to sin. Clothes may not have made the man but they did indicate what he was made of, a lesson which, for some inexplicable reason, escaped the attention of Henry VI's minders in April 1471. On that occasion, they paraded their witless king through London, dressed in 'a long blue gown of velvet as though he had no more to change with'.[79] The citizens, noticing the king's poverty, failed to rally to his cause. Clothes affirmed in a very public way that their owner could, in the words of William Harrison, 'bear the port, charge and countenance of a gentleman'.[80] Any comparison, therefore, between the richness of gentry attire and the shabby comfort of their private apartments once again highlights that distinction between the public *persona* and the private person.[81] Social status counted for little were it not publicly proclaimed to, and recognized by, the rest of society. Clothing, like the façades of gentry houses, was intended to impress. The insides of houses and their furnishings, which were not open to public gaze, could be, and were, much more prosaic.

A distinction between the public and private sides of gentry religion is equally marked, though it must be admitted in this case that evidence of their personal spirituality is difficult both to find and interpret. According to the *Italian Relation*, the English attended mass daily and recited the Lord's Prayer and the office of Our Lady 'in a low voice, after the manner of churchmen; ... nor do they omit any form incumbent upon good Christians'.[82] In paying due regard to the forms of their religion, the gentry provide no exception to this generalization. Many gentry households contained their own chapels where daily

---

[78] PROB11/12/3/23.
[79] Ross, *Edward IV*, p. 166, citing *The Great Chronicle of London*, p. 215.
[80] Quoted by Mingay, *The Gentry*, p. 2.
[81] See above, p. 141.   [82] *Italian Relation*, p. 23.

masses could be heard without too much interruption to more profane routines.[83] Dispensations were sought from the papacy, and granted, for them to hear masses before day-break and to have portable altars; and numerous gentry owned mass books and primers which could act as guides for their owners' devotions.[84]

Nevertheless, respect for the superficial forms of religion does not necessarily indicate a deep-rooted spirituality. Regular attendance at mass may have merely provided a welcome respite from worldly concerns, an interlude of repose or, alternatively, it may have been a tiresome duty, performed out of habit. It is very difficult, if not impossible, to know what the laity thought about during their religious observances. Even the possession of an occasional pious or liturgical book is no guarantee that it was ever opened and read, especially if it had been received as part of a bequest, which may reveal its value to the benefactor rather than to the beneficiary. But although the fifteenth-century gentry are, for most of their lives, silent about spiritual matters, they are much more forthcoming in their last wills and testaments.

Of course, the historian needs to approach wills with some caution. First, they were invariably drawn up by clerks or notaries whose ample experience in performing this task led them to use set forms and phrases which may not have reflected the testator's own sentiments. For example, the bequest of one's soul to God, His mother and all the company of heaven or to some similar variation of the heavenly host, appears with such regularity that it was clearly a convention. Second, the imminent prospect of death may have concentrated the testator's mind on God and religion in a way that does not truly indicate the strength of his former conviction. However, despite the use of conventional forms and despite probable changes in the depth of piety over a lifetime, wills still remain one of the most important sources for the social historian. It may be argued, indeed, that as testators contemplated death, their own earthly mortality and the future welfare of their immortal souls, they were more likely to reveal not only their

---

[83] For example, at Humberstone: *Common Lawyers*, pp. 444–5; at Holt: *T.L.A.S.*, 13, 1922–4, pp. 234, 240.
[84] *Papal Registers, 1427–47*, VIII, pp. 38, 362; *ibid.*, 1431–47, IX, pp. 231, 242 and *passim*; PROB11/12/3/23; PROB11/11/23/183v.

heart-felt attitudes towards religion but also their innermost selves as individuals.[85]

The greatest certainty in the mind of a gentleman was that God kept an accurate tally of all sins committed on earth.[86] Ultimately, if these debits on the Almighty's account-roll were not otherwise atoned for, one's soul would be subject to the cleansing but painful flames of Purgatory. To ease the soul's passage through Purgatory, the gentry spared no effort to square the account by ordering masses and prayers and by making pious bequests both to the Church and to the poor. Henry Sotehill exhorted his wife to keep his obit annually during her lifetime with a requiem mass at the parish church of Stockerston.[87] John Hotoft wished for a thousand masses to be sung on the day of his funeral and he arranged for further masses during the seven years after his death, leaving £46-13-4 for this express purpose.[88] Ralph Shirley III also requested a thousand masses at his funeral as did Thomas Keble.[89] Keble went on to leave 7 marks per year for twelve years, a total of £56, to find a priest at Humberstone to say daily *placebo* and *dirige* and mass for the repose of his own soul and the souls of his wives, his cousin, Richard Hotoft, his parents and of his dead son, Edward Keble.

Some gentry even began planning their obits long before they drafted their wills. Almost ten years before he drew up his will, Ralph Woodford conveyed to the Augustinian abbey at Owston for eighty years, 2s. in annual rent from a messuage and croft in Twyford in return for an annual requiem mass with *placebo* and *dirige* for the souls of Ralph and Elizabeth, his wife.[90] Thomas Hasilrigge similarly leased lands at Noseley to the wardens and chaplains there for twenty-four years in return for two red roses and masses for the souls of himself, his son, William, and their wives.[91]

In addition, testators made bequests to individuals and religious institutions on the understanding that the beneficiaries pray for the repose of their benefactor's soul. Henry Sotehill bequeathed 20s.

[85] See J. P. Cooper's introduction to McFarlane, *The Nobility of Later Medieval England*, p. xxxvii.
[86] See, for example, Ecclesiastes, 12:14.
[87] PROB11/14/31/244.   [88] PROB11/1/15/118.
[89] L.R.O. 26D53/1948; PROB11/12/3/22v.
[90] *C.A.D.*, III, D840.   [91] L.R.O. DG21/28.

to the Grey Friars in London to pray for his and his father's souls
during the life of Henry's wife, Joan.[92] Thomas Keble left 5
marks to Leicester Abbey, 5 marks to the college at the New-
arke, also in Leicester, 20s. to the bead-house there, 13s 4d. to
each of Leicester's three houses of friars belonging to the Domi-
nicans, the Austins and the Franciscans, 20s. to the White Friars
in London, £2 to the convent at Clerkenwell, £2 to the prioress
and convent of Langley and various sums of money, livestock
and household goods to named relatives and friends, including a
gold salt and a book to lady Hungerford, to be remembered in
their prayers.[93]

Some gentry bequests were towards the fabric of churches.
William Bradgate left 4 marks to his parish church and half a
mark to the churches of Ashby Magna and Bruntingthorpe,
though he donated merely 6d. to the more distant Lincoln
Cathedral.[94] Thomas Burton left money, usually half a mark but
sometimes as much as a mark, to thirteen parish churches in
Leicestershire.[95] John Woodford's donation of 10 marks to the
parish church at Wyfordby was specifically *ad fabrica campanilia*.[96]
John's great-grandson, Ralph, left no money to his parish church
of St Mary at Ashby Folville but on the off-chance that his
previous benefactions had escaped notice, he drew attention in his
will to the fact that he had earlier paid more than 5 marks towards
the making of the chancel and another £2 towards the making of
the church's steeple.[97] These sums were considered sufficient for
Ashby Folville. Besides, numerous other churches and religious
foundations had claims on Ralph's benevolence, including his
private chapel in the parish church at Sproxton, to which he
donated 20s. towards the making of a new table dedicated to St
John the Baptist.

Most donations to churches and religious houses involved small
sums of money and there was a marked reticence on the part of
benefactors permanently to alienate parcels of their finite landed
resources. Ralph Shirley III, however, who clearly, and probably
justifiably, had much on his conscience,[98] was uncharacteristically liberal in his bequests to the church. Originally, his lands in
Wiltshire, Gloucestershire and Bristol were intended to endow
Geronden Abbey for ninety-nine years to find a priest to sing for

[92] PROB11/14/31/244. [93] PROB11/12/3/22v–3. [94] L.R.O. 5D33/180.
[95] *Ibid.* [96] B. L. Cotton Claudius, A XIII, fo. 62.
[97] PROB11/11/23/183–4. [98] See above, pp. 143, 147.

his soul and those of his parents, his wives and his father- and mother-in-law, Thomas and Elizabeth Warner.[99] It was planned that the abbey would also administer alms for the poor. But Ralph soon changed his mind about the arrangement and a line was scored through this section of his will.[100] Nevertheless, he went on to order that £10 of the £10-6-8 issuing annually from the same lands should go towards finding an 'honest priest' to pray at Loughborough and to maintain a free school there for the term of ninety-nine years, with the reversion to Ralph's right heirs. He bequeathed the remaining 6s. 8d. to his servant, John Loutt, for life, with reversions to Geronden Abbey and then to Ralph's right heirs. At fifteen years' purchase, the lands in question could have fetched over £150 but it is worth noting that Ralph never intended that the family should permanently lose control of such valuable possessions. Instead, he struck a balance between the needs of his soul and the future economic welfare of his family.

In other circumstances, Ralph Shirley III's conscience may have led him to found a chantry, but his bequest to the chantry priest of St Michael's church at Melbourne in Derbyshire to found a free school implies that the Shirleys already possessed a chantry there. In fact, very few new chantries appear to have been established in Leicestershire in the fifteenth century. The exceptions were those of Bartholomew Brokesby, John Boyville and Thomas Keble. In 1450, Bartholomew Brokesby's executors were licensed to found a chantry with two chaplains in the parish church of Saxelby.[101] John Boyville was granted a licence in 1465 to alienate land in mortmain worth £10 yearly for the establishment of a perpetual almshouse, though he died before his intention was realized.[102] Nevertheless, his attorney, Henry Sotehill, and his other executors were granted another licence three years later, allowing them to alienate £12 worth of land to found not only Boyville's almshouse but also a perpetual chantry dedicated to the Virgin Mary and housed in St Peter's church at Stockerston.[103]

---

[99] L.R.O. 26D53/1948.

[100] The will is also printed in *Stemmata Shirleiana*, pp. 410–16, but this edition fails to reflect the author's changes of heart found in the original.

[101] L.A.O. Epis. Reg. XIX [Lumley], fo. 14.

[102] *C.P.R.*, 1461–7, p. 486.   [103] *Ibid.*, 1467–77, p. 113.

It seems that Richard Hotoft wished to endow a perpetual priest to say divine service before the altar in Humberstone parish church rather than, as his brother, Thomas, maintained, to order a chantry to be built there.[104] At least, this was the interpretation made of Richard's intent by his cousin, Thomas Keble. Keble was probably correct, for the Hotofts already had a chantry at Stretton.[105] This chapel notwithstanding, Keble did eventually arrange for another at Humberstone, for he requested that a house be built there for the chantry priest out of the return from lands he had bought at Stretton and elsewhere.[106]

The permanent alienation of land worth about £150 made the founding of new chantries in the fifteenth century unattractive to all but the wealthiest gentry. Bartholomew Brokesby's and Thomas Keble's lucrative careers in the law and in noble service ensured that they at least could afford the expense. Other superior families, such as the Shirleys, had little need for new foundations. They simply made bequests to pre-existing establishments. For most of the gentry, however, their own families had first call on their benevolence. The attitude of Robert Moton was probably typical of these men. He arranged for a chantry to be founded only if his heirs died without lawful issue.[107]

The gentry clearly had faith in the efficacy of prayers and masses to ease their souls through Purgatory. They also had hope of ultimate repose in heaven, for not a single Leicestershire will reveals any anxiety about the torments of hell. But the gentry also realized and, indeed, had it on high authority, that faith and hope were as nothing without charity.[108] While 'charity' to St Paul obviously means more than doling out gifts to the poor,[109] Christ Himself had proclaimed to a young man that whoever gave to the poor 'shalt have treasure in heaven'.[110] This was a message not lost on the gentry.

John Boyville's almshouse was intended to provide shelter for three poor people.[111] Thomas Keble also ordered the building of an almshouse attached to his chantry at Humberstone.[112] Ralph

---

[104] C1/42/90–2. [105] C1/42/89. [106] PROB11/12/3/22v–3v.
[107] PROB11/11/25/201. [108] 1 Corinthians, 13:1–13, esp. v. 13.
[109] *Ibid.*, v. 3. [110] St Matthew, 19:21. [111] *C.P.R.*, 1467–77, p. 113.
[112] PROB11/12/3/22v–3v.

Woodford allowed for the donation of a more modest 13s. 4d. to the poor, though he extended additional benevolence to his poor tenants who were forgiven a quarter year's rent.[113] Ralph Shirley III's original grant to Geronden Abbey had stipulated that the house find lodgings for four poor men and one woman but, later in his will, where the bequest to Geronden was reduced, the poor, as they usually do, lost out.[114] But their loss was somebody else's gain; Ralph directed his largesse into founding two schools instead. Nor was Shirley alone in offering his charity to education. Thomas Keble left 20 marks towards funding scholars at Oxford and Cambridge to study arts and divinity.[115]

Apart from doles to the poor and donations to education, the gentry also made bequests to public works. John Kendale, originally of Twycross in Leicestershire, had moved to London to become a pewterer and left 40s. yearly to repair the highway at Hampstead where he had relatives and where he himself may have lived.[116] Geoffrey Sherard left a similar sum to mend the bridge and highway around the village of Stapleford.[117] The bridge between Gerard Danet's house and the Augustinian friary in Leicester must have been greatly dilapidated for Danet bequeathed a considerable £10 towards its mending.[118]

Despite these charitable bequests, it is by no means certain that they were made in the spirit intended by St Paul. For instance, there appears to be a hint of family self-interest in Gerard Danet's mending of a bridge between his house and Leicester or in Geoffrey Sherard's paving of the roads around Stapleford where he held a manor. There is much more than a hint of personal self-interest attached to gifts to the poor. It soon becomes apparent, in fact, that solicitude for the sufferings of the poor was not the gentry's prime motivation. Thomas Keble may have felt some concern for, and responsibility towards, his father's servants, Joan Nichol and Emmitt Lyez, who both had grown old and poor, but the relief he ordered for them was in return for their prayers for his soul and the souls of his friends and relatives.[119] Ralph Shirley III also expected that the recipients of alms at Geronden would

[113] PROB11/11/23/183–3v.   [114] L.R.O. 26D53/1948.
[115] PROB11/12/3/23.   [116] PROB11/5/24/185v.
[117] PROB11/9/23/176v–7.   [118] L.R.O. 5D33/180.
[119] PROB11/12/3/22v.

pray for his soul.[120] Given that the poor were especially beloved of God, the reasoning behind the gentry's bequests was that prayers from this quarter would be listened to more attentively and receive greater favour.[121]

Although true (or Pauline) charity was not directed towards the poor, the gentry were not totally devoid of this virtue. In ordering masses and prayers for the souls of relatives and friends, they displayed a genuine concern for the welfare of others within their own social circle. The most usual beneficiaries of this concern were departed wives, parents and dead children but the gentry often extended their charity to a wider group than this. Thomas Keble ordered masses for his cousins and prayers for the soul of his good lord, William Hastings.[122] Ralph Woodford similarly ordered prayers for a cousin, John Bellers, for all his ancestors in general and for his great-grandparents in particular.[123] Ralph Shirley III's bequest for masses for the souls of his parents-in-law, Elizabeth and Thomas Warner, suggests that they had no son of their own who could shoulder responsibility for the ease of their souls.[124] Henry Sotehill's charity was even more expansive. He called on the Grey Friars in London to pray for all Christian souls.[125]

Leicestershire wills leave a strong impression that the gentry's religion satisfied important psychological needs. They were familiar with the Church's doctrine on Purgatory and they relied completely on the clergy's rôle as mediator between man and God. They found comfort in the familiar. There is never any sign of those inner doubts and torments which later racked Luther and which were to rend western Christendom asunder. Nor is there ever any suggestion of anti-clericalism or any hint that the Church was not providing value for money. Admittedly, Ralph Shirley III required his executors to ensure that the chantry priest at Melbourne 'be an honest priest and of good virtuous disposition and living'. He further expected his executors to find 'an honest priest' to sing and pray at Loughborough.[126] But we should not be tempted to read too much into these requests. Ralph was

[120] L.R.O. 26D53/1948.
[121] B. L. Manning, *The People's Faith in the Time of Wycliff*, 2nd edn, Hassocks, 1975, p. 148.
[122] PROB11/12/3/22V–3v.   [123] PROB11/11/23/183v.
[124] L.R.O. 26D53/1948. See J. T. Rosenthal, *The Purchase of Paradise. Gift Giving and the Aristocracy, 1307–1485*, London, 1972, p. 16.
[125] PROB11/14/31/244.   [126] L.R.O. 26D53/1948.

merely displaying a similar discrimination towards the clergy to that shown by John Dounton who, over 100 years earlier, had demanded 'a fit chaplain' to say masses for his soul in Withcote parish church.[127] Like any purchaser of goods and services, these men expected nothing short of the best that money could buy. That they continued to disburse sums of money to the Church, either as outright gifts or in return for masses and prayers, indicates their satisfaction with its ministrations. To borrow Dr Carpenter's phrase, their religion was 'utterly conventional'.[128]

Wills provide one further indicator of the perceived effectiveness of the Church's ministrations. Although testators never lost sight of the treasury of grace amassed by their own pious bequests, the anticipated intercession of the clergy on their behalf left them free to turn their gaze from their prospects in the next world to what was left of this. Ralph Shirley III prefaced his will by saying that he was dreading the profile of death, but to most of the gentry, including Ralph himself, of as much, if not greater, concern than the spectre of death was the spectacle of their departing. Nowhere was the gentry's preoccupation with their status in this world so marked as it was at their funerals when they were on the point of leaving it.

Those gentry who contemplated and ordered their own funerals embarked upon the task with opulent vision and an eye for detail, combining in their arrangements the drama of the liturgy with the public spectacle and theatricality of a medieval mystery play. The backdrop was provided by the local parish church or a church attached to one of Leicestershire's monastic houses. Some testators, such as John Shirley, were content to be buried 'where hit shall please God'.[129] In his case, it pleased God that his final

---

[127] L.R.O. 5D33/180.

[128] C. Carpenter, 'The religion of the gentry of fifteenth-century England', in *England in the Fifteenth Century. Proceedings of the 1986 Harlaxton Symposium*, ed. D. Williams, Woodbridge, 1987, pp. 53–74, esp. p. 58. If the Leicestershire gentry were attracted to Lollardy, they managed to conceal the fact in their wills. Thomas Noveray, a minor gentleman from Ilston-on-the-Hill, and John Belgrave, whose activities were centred on the parish of St Martin in Leicester and who may have been related to the Belgraves of Belgrave, seem to have been the only Lollards with gentry connections (J. Crompton, 'Leicestershire Lollards', *T.L.A.H.S.*, 44, 1970, for 1968–9, pp. 25–6, 29–30, 31). The *Italian Relation*'s cryptic reference to 'various opinions concerning religion' (p. 23) may be nothing more than an indication of differing English and Italian observances. [129] L.R.O. 26D53/1947.

resting place be a chapel attached to the church of Geronden Abbey.[130] But all of the gentry who had specific plans in mind requested burial within the churches rather than outside in the churchyard. For Ralph Woodford, the chosen spot was before the image of Our lady in the church at Ashby Folville, towards the making of which, it may be recalled, he had paid 5 marks.[131] Gerard Danet, who had taken up residence in London, offered his executors the choice of the middle of the church of Blackfriars, 'if possible', or in the parish church of St Faith before the high altar.[132] Richard Perwych wished to be buried in the Lady Chapel of Lubenham parish church, while Robert Moton said he wanted to be interred in Peckleton church.[133] Like most of the gentry, he probably assumed that his body would lie beside those of his ancestors.

Paradoxically, the leading rôle in the ensuing drama was reserved for the deceased. By necessity, his was a passive contribution but lighting was used to focus attention on him. Ralph Shirley III requested 'torches and other lights brennying about my corps'.[134] Gerard Danet specified the number of torches at his funeral, thirteen and four great tapers.[135] In addition, Danet wished twelve escutcheons of arms to be arranged around his body. Thomas Pulteney ordered twenty-four torches, each emblazoned with his arms.[136]

The size of, and the parts played by, the remainder of the cast were determined by the amount of money the deceased had previously arranged to disburse. To ensure the presence at his funeral of as many clergy as possible, Thomas Pulteney bequeathed the payment of 8d. to every priest and 2d. to every clerk.[137] Ralph Woodford was similarly discriminating towards the orders of clergy in his bequests. He left 4d. to be paid to every priest who attended his funeral, 2d to every surpliced clerk and 1d. to clerks 'without surplice'.[138] While the prayers and masses offered by the clergy during the funeral assisted the deceased's soul in Purgatory, in our extended metaphor of funerals as theatrical productions they also provided the background score for the occasion.

[130] L.R.O. 26D53/1948.
[131] PROB11/11/23/182v–3v.
[132] L.R.O. 5D33/180.
[133] PROB11/14/30/233; PROB11/11/25/201.
[134] L.R.O. 26D53/1948.
[135] L.R.O. 5D33/180.
[136] PROB11/15/24/193v.
[137] *Ibid.*
[138] PROB11/11/23/182v–3v.

No large-scale spectacle would be complete without its cast of extras, and gentry funerals were no exception to the rule. The core of this group was probably drawn from the household staff and tenants. Elizabeth Sotehill willed her staff to 'bring me to the ground' and Ralph Woodford ensured the presence of his servants at his funeral by offering extra wages if they were there to pray for him.[139] Their ranks, however, were swelled by the poor who were attracted by the traditional doles made to them on these occasions. John Hotoft ordered the sale of some of his silver 'in all possible haste' to raise £20 to be given to the poor at his funeral.[140] Both Thomas Keble and Ralph Shirley III left £20 for distribution among the poor on the day of their burials.[141] At times, some of these recipients of charity were expected to play a more active rôle in the drama. Ralph Woodford achieved a suitably sombre tone by having five poor men dress in black gowns with hoods and hold five torches above his hearse. For this they received 4d. each.[142] Twenty-four poor men at Thomas Pulteney's interment were to receive gowns bearing Pulteney's insignia, the leopard's head, on the front and back.[143]

The gentry were clearly prepared to expend large sums of money on their burials. According to John Rudding, Ralph Shirley III's funeral expenses amounted to £120-16-1.[144] The cost to Thomas Keble's estate of gifts to the poor at his funeral, gifts to the Church and bequests for masses and prayers came to about £100.[145] This sum does not include bequests of goods for pious purposes or bequests to lay-folk for their prayers. It almost certainly underestimates the cost of the funeral, for Keble's will makes no mention of a coffin or a funeral-feast.[146]

Some gentry requested tangible memorials to be erected after the funeral, and they set aside money to pay for these. Thomas Pulteney left £2 to the monastery at Combe towards glazing a window in the cloister. Thomas Keble requested a tomb to be erected over his and his wives' grave at Humberstone church. If this tomb was built, it has not survived, though the incised slab

[139] PROB11/15/19/151v; PROB11/11/23/182v–3v.   [140] PROB11/1/15/118.
[141] L.R.O. 26D53/1948; PROB11/12/3/22v–3.   [142] PROB11/11/23/183–3v.
[143] PROB11/15/24/193v.   [144] L.R.O. 26D53/1949.
[145] PROB11/12/3/22v–3v.
[146] Thomas Pulteney ordered his executors to provide a dinner on the day of his funeral.

from the tomb of Keble's cousin, Richard Hotoft, has escaped destruction.[147] John Turville bequeathed 10 marks for building an alabaster or marble tomb over his grave in All Saints' church at Thurlaston and this memorial to John and his wife still remains there today.[148]

On the other hand, John Shirley, with a dozen children and a widow to provide for, had little to spare for prayers and masses for his soul's ease, for gifts to the Church, for imaginatively lavish obsequies or for expensive memorials. Instead, he requested his 'due mortuarye' without prescription and entrusted his soul to God's mercy before going on to make provision for his large family.[149] It was left to John's son, Ralph III, to resolve the dilemma posed by the conflicting interests of family, immortal soul and proclamations of status. The fact that at the time of his own death, Ralph had still not paid his father's bequests to his brothers, suggests that at their expense he may have provided John with the masses and prayers his soul deserved and the funeral his status demanded.[150] Whatever tensions and disputes may have arisen in the family as a result of Ralph's action, these were private matters which he and his kin would have learned to live with. Largesse, on the other hand, was publicly dispensed. If the Shirley's were to maintain face in their county, that public generosity could not be scrimped on.

Extravagant expenditure on funerals made them very different occasions from the relative simplicity of baptisms. No doubt this difference was dictated by practical considerations. Baptisms were hastily organized, whereas funerals could be contemplated and planned. But funerals also stand in stark contrast to that careful husbanding of economic resources we have already witnessed the gentry exercising in relation to their estates.[151] This contrast naturally raises the question, why? Of all those gentry upon whose obsequies we have focussed attention, only one, Thomas Keble, might be termed a *parvenu* and, even in his case, the epithet is a little strained. Few, if any, of these men needed to announce, paradoxically at their funerals, that they had 'arrived' among the upper strata of county society. By the richness and variety of their attire, they had, after all, been announcing this fact

[147] Pevsner, *The Buildings of England: Leicestershire and Rutland*, p. 272.
[148] PROB11/15/15/119v; Pevsner, *The Buildings of England: Leicestershire and Rutland*, p. 409.   [149] L.R.O. 26D53/1947.   [150] L.R.O. 26D53/1948.
[151] See chapter 3 above.

throughout their lives. Nevertheless, their funerals do reveal a perceived need to reaffirm the position they already held, a need dictated by what Thomas Keble referred to as 'the unstablenesse of the world'.[152] Theirs was a competitive society which, like our own, extended small mercy to those incapable of meeting its challenges.

[152] PROB11/12/3/22v.

CONCLUSION

When John Leland's perambulations in the 1530s and 1540s brought him to Leicestershire, one of the first villages he visited was Stonton Wyville.[1] In the fifteenth century, the manor had belonged to the Wyvyll family, but in Leland's day it was held by Mr Brudenell. As Leland travelled deeper into the county he alluded to some of the old, familiar fifteenth-century families. Skeffingtons were still to be found at Skeffington and Hasilrigges continued to reside at Noseley. The Belgraves of Belgrave, whose income had been £13 per year in 1436, were doing sufficiently well for Leland to remark favourably on their income of £50 per year.[2] But there were also other changes besides that at Stonton Wyville. At Peckleton, where Motons had lived since the twelfth century, there were now Vincents.[3] New names emerge, too, from among the shire's parliamentary representatives in the first half of the sixteenth century, Sacheverell, Manners and Cave.[4]

There is nothing particularly startling in these changes or in the way they had occurred. Margaret, widow of William Wyvyll, had been forced to sell the reversion of the manor of Stonton Wyville to Robert Brudenell, whom she later married, in order to raise money to execute her first husband's will.[5] The Motons had died out in the male line with the death of Edward Moton in 1511 and their manors devolved to the descendants of those granddaughters whom Sir Robert Moton had tried to disinherit back in the 1440s.[6] Sir Ambrose Cave, originally from Northamptonshire, arrived in Leicestershire by purchasing land, just as Thomas Palmer had done over a century earlier. The only difference between their two cases is that Cave's purchase, the

---

[1] *The Itinerary of John Leland*, I, pp. 13–21.   [2] See appendix 1.
[3] *T.L.A.S.*, 17, 1931–3, p. 94.
[4] Bindoff, *The House of Commons*, I, p. 128.
[5] *Pedigrees*, p. 110.   [6] See above, p. 148.

manor of Rothley, had belonged to the Knights of the Hospital of St John before the order was dissolved in 1540.[7] Such variations to the composition of the gentry were not new. They had been occurring throughout the fifteenth century and for numberless generations before. Nevertheless, they do serve to highlight Thomas Keble's observation about 'the unstablenesse of the world'.[8]

This instability is a theme which many historians writing about the fifteenth century have chosen to develop. Margaret Aston confidently asserts that those who lived at the end of the fourteenth and beginning of the fifteenth centuries 'were conscious of living in a period of disaster'.[9] J. Huizinga's magisterial study of forms of art and thought is Spenglerian in its gloominess.[10] His potent images of decline, decadence, death and decay mark the fifteenth century as the dull denouement of the middle ages. In England, it seems, the picture is no less achromatic. There, the emissaries of gloom and doom stress the economic depression, a disastrous and protracted war in France, the decline of kingship, the increasing lawlessness and 'political gangsterdom' of an overmighty nobility and the resulting drift to civil war.[11]

While images of decline and decay have for long dominated the historiography of fifteenth-century England, our study of the Leicestershire gentry reveals a more promising side to late medieval life. Although the Leicestershire gentry were not immune from the economic problems of the day, they overcame and survived these difficulties better than most.[12] Their landed resources were less extensive than those of the Church or the nobility but this fact supplies part of the reason for their success, for it enabled them to take a closer interest in, and acquire a more intimate knowledge of, their estates. Management of these estates was careful, though never conservative. In fact, the gentry were sufficiently flexible to alter their management techniques in the face of changing econ-

---

[7] Bindoff, *The House of Commons*, I, p. 595; *T.L.A.S.*, 12, 1921–2, pp. 36, 48.

[8] PROB11/12/3/22v.

[9] M. Aston, *The Fifteenth Century: The Prospect of Europe*, London, 1968, p. 10.

[10] J. Huizinga, *The Waning of the Middle Ages*, trans. F. Hopman, Harmondsworth, 1972.

[11] Postan, *Medieval Economy and Society*, p. 174; A. R. Myers, *England in the Late Middle Ages*, 8th edn, Harmondsworth, 1974, pp. 59–62; M. M. Postan, 'Some social consequences of the Hundred Years' War', *Econ. Hist. Rev.*, 12, 1942, pp. 1–12, esp. p. 3; S. B. Chrimes, *Lancastrians, Yorkists and Henry VII*, 2nd edn, London, 1966, *passim*, esp. p. 178; M. M. Postan, 'Revisions in economic history. The fifteenth century', *Econ. Hist Rev.*, 9, 1939, p. 166; Storey, *The End of the House of Lancaster*, pp. ixx, 5 and *passim*.

[12] See above, pp. 56–72.

omic circumstances. With the rising cost of labour, they converted, tentatively at first, to pasture. A drop in the price of arable land led them to exploit other resources such as woods and streams.

Many of the gentry also augmented their incomes by service in royal and noble households both in peace and war.[13] The most outstanding advance, socially and politically as well as economically, made by a Leicestershire gentry family, the Hastingses, was a product of royal service. But this case is exceptional and, usually, more assured and quite substantial rewards fell to those who, like Thomas Keble, carved out careers in the legal profession. Opportunism and flexibility were the hallmarks which made the gentry one of the economic success stories of the fifteenth century. Though some families, such as the Shirleys, experienced economic hardship, this was the product of long-lived dowagers and an abundance of offspring who placed a strain on finite resources, rather than any lack of entrepreneurial skill.[14] When families failed, it was for biological, rather than economic, reasons.[15]

Although most of the gentry made only modest economic gains by associating with the nobility, it should not be assumed that their prime motivation in the association was therefore political advancement. William Hastings may have provided a dazzling example of how service to the nobility could return handsome dividends but there were others who paid dearly for an over-zealous attachment to a disgraced political cause.[16] The more successful, such as Thomas Palmer and Thomas Erdyngton, flourished because they were equally flexible in their political affiliations as they were in the management of their estates. But in the intoxicating atmosphere of national politics, the key to survival for the majority was a wisely considered neutrality.

Within the bounds of their own county, however, the Leicestershire gentry were undisputed leaders rather than followers. Decades of responsibility for the government of their shire had strengthened their idea of community, an idea which also found expression in their more important social interactions.[17] Their social and political affiliations were neither merely parochial nor

[13] See above, pp. 72–74.   [14] See above, p. 153.
[15] See, for example, Palmer.
[16] For example, Sir William Fielding, Everard Dygby I, Thomas Everyngham.
[17] See above, chapters 4 and 5.

merely regional or national. Indeed, they were never *merely* anything. Even widely connected gentry such as Leonard and William Hastings, Thomas Everyngham and Thomas Erdyngton associated with a narrow group of friends and neighbours in their everyday transactions. In other English counties, the most important political unit was the noble affinity.[18] But in Leicestershire, which was not dominated by any regional magnate or magnates, the county itself provided political cohesion. This shire community stood at the hub of a series of interlocking social and political circles, some of which were parochial and narrow, some of which extended beyond the county border into neighbouring shires and some of which could be regarded as national in scope. In this, Leicestershire's experience seems to have differed from that of Warwickshire or Devon but more regional studies will need to be undertaken before the apparent conflict of views is resolved.[19] Undoubtedly, though, K. B. McFarlane's suspicion that gentry MPs had a greater independence of the lords than hitherto believed is not only vindicated but seems to have a wider application beyond the knights of the shire.[20]

The gentry's independence extended also to relationships within their own families.[21] Attempts to portray these men as subject to the demands of the wider kin and the lineage fail to withstand scrutiny. Disputes with relatives tended to centre on conflicting claims to property which suggest that self-interest rather than family interest was the main determinant of attitudes to kin. Nor should we neglect the simple determinant of personal taste. As Thomas Keble's family relationships show, some relations were liked and some were not and, I suspect, many were treated indifferently. The strongest ties were reserved for the gentry's immediate family, wives, children and parents, though here, too, there was room for a range of family feeling. Unfortunately, the attitudes and concerns of wives or, indeed, of gentry women in general, are not so well documented. Women usually reveal themselves in letters and although the Paston letters amply expose them as forceful characters in their own right, no such collection of correspondence survives for Leicestershire. Never-

---

[18] Carpenter, 'Political society in Warwickshire', pp. 94–8; Cherry, 'The Courtenay earls of Devon', pp. 71, 76ff.   [19] *Ibid.*

[20] McFarlane, 'Parliament and "bastard feudalism" ', in *England in the Fifteenth Century*, pp. 12, 20–1.   [21] See above, chapter 6.

theless, the regular involvement of women in land transactions as feoffees, or as executors and supervisors of wills, indicates that their rôle was not passive.

No more was passivity the stamp and mark of their husbands. The world they inhabited may have been unstable but they were sufficiently resourceful to meet the economic and political challenges of their day. Words which compellingly spring to mind to describe them are 'self-assured' and 'confident'. Of course, these epithets may well be a measure of the gentry's success at masking inner uncertainties behind a public face.[22] But I doubt that this was the case. Even at the approach of death, the gentry were confident of their place in the next world. They could hardly have been less so about their position in this.

K. B. McFarlane warned us against underrating the capacity of these men.[23] However, studies which focus on the nobility tend to do just that, presenting the gentry as pawns in a larger political game played by their social superiors.[24] But on the smaller chessboard provided by a single county, and specifically a county such as Leicestershire which was not controlled by magnates, the gentry themselves were the major pieces. Lord Hastings recognized as much when he retained the king's knight, Sir William Trussell II, and the astute lawyer, Thomas Keble. For this reason, the gentry deserve our consideration, not as appendages to the nobility in their retinues, but in their own right and on their own terms.

[22] See above, pp. 141, 197–8.
[23] McFarlane, 'Parliament and "bastard feudalism" ', p. 12.
[24] More recently, Richmond has detected a similar trend even among studies which focus on the gentry themselves (C. Richmond, 'After McFarlane', *History*, 68, 1983, pp. 57–60).

Appendix I

The Leicestershire gentry, income and office holding, 1422–1485

	Income	Sheriff	MP	JP	Escheator	Commission of array	Coroner	Tax collector
KNIGHTS								
BEAUMONT	£100		★	★				
BERKELEY	£90	★	★	★		★		
ERDYNGTON	£170	★	★					
FERRERS	£100	★						
FIELDING	£58	★	★	★		★		
HARCOURT	[£80][1]	★	★	★		★		
HASTINGS		★						
MERNYON (MARMYON)	£40							
MOTON	£66+£26[2]	★	★	★	★	★		
NEELE			★	★		★		
NEVILLE of Holt	£120			★				
SHIRLEY	£100+£92					★		
TRUSSELL of Elmesthorpe	£100	★	★					
WOODFORD	£40+£26	★		★				
DISTRAINEES								
ASSHEBY of Lowesby	£30+£10	★	★	★	★	★		
ASTLEY	£22		★	★				
BELLERS	[£13]		★	★				
BOYVILLE	£100		★	★		★		

	Income	Sheriff	MP	JP	Escheator	Commission of array	Coroner	Tax collector
BROKESBY	£230		★	★		★		
DYGBY	£40		★					
HASILRIGGE	£5 + freehold³							★
HOTOFT	£24		★	★	★	★		
MALORY of Walton	£20							
PALMER	£46		★	★	★	★		
PULTENEY	£33 + £13			★	★	★		
STAUNTON of Sutton-on-Soar		★	★			★		
WYVYLL	£30							
ESQUIRES	£20							
ACTON	£9						★	★
ADYNGTON (ALYNGTON?)	£20							
APPLEBY								
BAUDE								
BELGRAVE of Belgrave	£13							★
BRABESSON	£26							★
BUGGE	£39⁴		★	★				
BURGH	£26		★		★	★		
CHARNELS	£5 + freehold							
CHESILDEN	£31							
COTON of Thurcaston	£11							
COTON of Rearsby	£10				★			

Appendix I (cont.)

	Income	Sheriff	MP	JP	Escheator	Commission of array	Coroner	Tax collector
DANET of Gaddesby	£26				*		*	*
DANET of Bromkinsthorpe	£22							
DANSEY	£26							
DANVERS								
DERBY	£11							
ENTWYSELL		*						
EVERYNGHAM	£17	*	*	*		*		
FARNHAM of Netherhall	£5 + freehold		*	*		*		
FOULESHURST	£6	*	*					
GERMAN								
GRYMMESBY	£40			*				
HETON	£126⁵			*	*			
KEBLE	£20			*		*		
KYNSMAN	£26							*
LAGO	£20							*
LANGHAM of Gopsall								
LANGTON	£20							
MARSHALL	£12 + £5							
MAYLE (MAYELL)	£20							
MERBURY								
NEVILLE of Rearsby	£6				*			
PAYN	£26							*

	Income	Sheriff	MP	JP	Escheator	Commission of array	Coroner	Tax collector
PERWYCH				★				
SHERARD	£53	★		★		★		
SKEFFINGTON of Skeffington	£26							
SOTEHILL				★		★		
STAUNTON of Donington			★	★				
TEMPLE						★		★
TURPYN				★	★			
TURVILLE								
VILLERS	£7 + £6	★		★	★	★		
WALSH	£13		★	★		★		★
WALSHALE								
WHATTON	£6 + £13				★			
GENTLEMEN								
BELGRAVE of North Kilworth								
BLABY	£6							★
BLACKFORDBY	£5						★	
DRAPER of Hose								★
FARNHAM of Overhall	£6							
GERVEYS								★
HERDEWYN of Leicester	£8							★
LANGHAM of Kilby	£6							★

Appendix 1 (cont.)

	Income	Sheriff	MP	JP	Escheator	Commission of array	Coroner	Tax collector
NOVERAY	£6							*
POUTRELL	£6							
PURLEY	£5							
SAMPSON	£5							
SUTTON	£5							
WONER	£5							
SUB GENTRY								
ADERSTON								*
ARDERN								*
ASSHEBY of Lubbesthorp	£5 + freehold							*
ATTEWELL of Foxton							*	
ATTEWELL of Drayton								*
BAILLY								*
BARESBY of Thorpe Satchville								*
BARESBY of Catthorpe								*
BARNEVILE	£6							
BASSET								*
BLYTHE								*
BONETON								*
BOSON								*
BOYDELL								*
BRADGATE	£5							*

	Income	Sheriff	MP	JP	Escheator	Commission of array	Coroner	Tax collector
BROKESBY of Oadby								*
BURTON	£6							*
CHAPMAN								*
COK								*
CONWAY								*
COOTE								*
CURTEYS								*
DEWY								*
DRAPER of Fenny Drayton								*
DUNHAM	£6							*
DYSON								*
EGGE								*
ERYSTON								*
ESSYNG								*
FANCHERE								*
FERMOUR								*
FRANK								*
FREMAN of Witherley								*
FREMAN of Lutterworth								*
GISSING								*
GOLDSMITH	£5							*
GROTE								*
GRYSTON								*

Appendix 1 (cont.)

	Income	Sheriff	MP	JP	Escheator	Commission of array	Coroner	Tax collector
HALYDAY								★
HARDEWYN of Bredon	£5							★
HICHEBONE								★
HUNT of Burbage								★
HUNT of Barkeston								★
HUNTON								★
HYLLEY								★
ILYFF								★
INGOLD								★
JOYE								★
KENDALE	£5						★	
LATHUM								★
MALLESTON								★
MALORY of Croxton	£6							★
MALORY of Sadington	£5							★
MAUNSELL								★
MAYHEW								★
MERCER								★
NOBLE	£5							★
OTHEHALL							★	
PAGE of Ilston								★
PAGE of Glen								★

	Income	Sheriff	MP	JP	Escheator	Commission of array	Coroner	Tax collector
PAKEMAN								*
PALMER of Frolesworth								*
PARKER of Donington								*
PORTER								*
PRAT								*
PYKE								*
QUENBY	£6							*
ROTE								*
ROWS								*
SEYMPERE								*
SHEPEY								*
SMYTH								*
SOMERVILE								*
STANFORD								*
SYDE								*
SYMMES								*
TAYLOR								*
TRUSSELL of Sharneford								*
TRUSSELL OF Muston								*
TURNAR								*
WARDE								*
WARMYNGTON								*
WEBSTER								*

Appendix 1 (*cont.*)

	Income	Sheriff	MP	JP	Escheator	Commission of array	Coroner	Tax collector
WESTON								★
WRYGHT								★
WYMONDHAM								★

Notes

1 Incomes in square brackets are based on inquisitions *post mortem*.

2 Where two amounts are shown this indicates the income of two members of the one family such as mother or father and son.

3 Those seised of freehold worth £5 and more per annum but who failed to appear before the tax commissioners (E179/240/269).

4 This is based on Elizabeth Bugge's income of £13 and assumes that her dower right amounted to one third of the family income.

5 In all calculations, Keble's income has been taken as £26. The 1436 tax return separately records £100 as income derived from Keble's position as feoffee of James Ormond (Butler).

Most incomes have been drawn from the tax return for Leicestershire though, where necessary, the returns for neighbouring counties have also been consulted.

Appendix 2

Genealogical table (a)

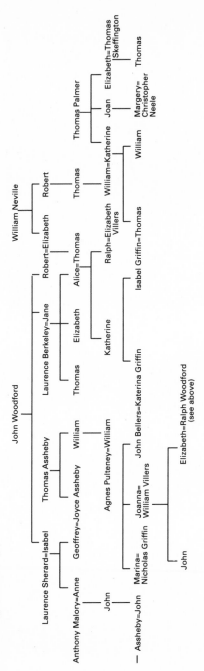

Genealogical table (b)

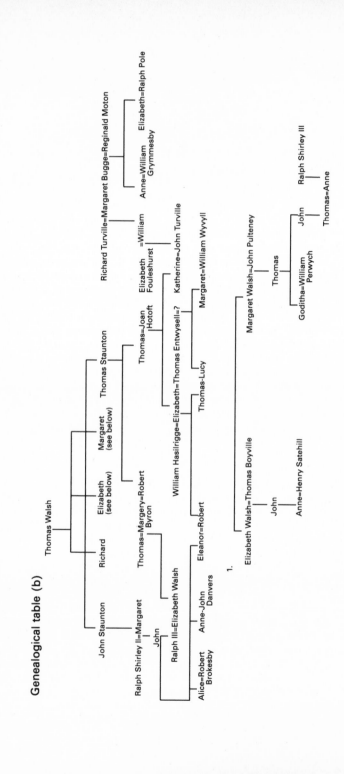

Appendix 3

BIOGRAPHICAL NOTES ON LEICESTERSHIRE'S LEADING GENTRY FAMILIES (KNIGHTS, DISTRAINEES AND ESQUIRES)

ACTON

Richard Acton was elected coroner sometime before 24 November 1430. On that date, and again on 3 August 1433, the king ordered his removal from office on the grounds that he was insufficiently qualified (*C.C.R.*, 1429–35, pp. 75, 216). On both occasions he was referred to as 'of Merston', i.e. Potters Marston. Despite his alleged 'insufficiency', Richard was assessed for the tax of 1436 on an income of £9 per annum and, as witness to a deed of gift in 1437, he is referred to as 'esquire' (E179/192/59; L.R.O. 44'88/187). The king's orders for his removal from office notwithstanding, Acton was still performing coronial duties in 1442 (KB9/241/84). In the same year, he was appointed to deliver the gaol of Leicester (*C.P.R.*, 1441–6, p. 79). The small manor of Potters Marston was held of the Benedictine priory of St Mary in Coventry which was in the habit of leasing out the manor house and demesne to farmers (*T.L.A.S.*, 14, 1921–2, pp. 169–71). Given the overlord's links with Coventry, it is probable that Richard Acton of Potters Marston was either the son of Richard Acton, alderman of Coventry in 1423, or, perhaps, the same man (*Coventry Leet Book*, p. 44).

ADYNGTON (ALYNGTON)

In 1412, Thomas Adyngton, esquire, was reported as holding lands worth £4 per annum in Northamptonshire and 'much' in Leicestershire (*Feudal Aids*, VI, p. 498). He was taxed in Leicestershire in 1436 on an income of £20 (E179/192/59). Between 1429 and 1435 he regularly appeared among those who attended the shire court to elect knights of the shire, though he himself never held office in the county (C219/14/1 pt 2 MS 102; C219/14/3 pt 2 MS 96; C219/14/5 pt 2 MS 102).

APPLEBY

In the fourteenth century, the Applebys were among Leicestershire's foremost families. They held the manor of Appleby Magna and had an interest in the manor of Appleby Parva as well as lands in Stretton-en-le-Frith. Beyond Leicestershire, their estate extended into Derbyshire, Staffordshire and North-amptonshire (*T.L.A.S.*, 11, 1919–20, pp. 429–42). Sir Edmund Appleby senior may have been a member of John of Gaunt's household. His son, Sir Edmund junior, represented Leicestershire in the parliament of 1379. In the fifteenth century, however, the family declined in status. John Appleby, esquire, who

Appendix 3

failed to appear before the Leicestershire tax commissioners in 1436 (E179/240/269), never attained knighthood. His grandsons and heirs, Edmund and Richard, were referred to merely as gentlemen. Edmund succeeded his grandfather in or before 1469 while still a minor. Disputes over property rights with the Longfords in 1447 and with the Vernons in 1476 were probably symptoms rather than causes of Appleby decline.

ASSHEBY

Sometime before 1388, Thomas Assheby I married Joan Burdet, daughter of John and heir of Richard Burdet (Rock. C. F3/10, unfoliated; *Pedigrees*, pp. 47–8). By means of this marriage, the Asshebys acquired the Burdet's manor of Lowesby. They also held the manor of Lubbesthorpe and lands in Newton, Cosby, Long Whatton and Baggrave as well as a manor in Derbyshire (C140/23/14 MS 2; *Pedigrees*, p. 48). Thomas I was probably a lawyer for he not only served regularly on commissions of the peace but he was also a member of the *quorum* (*C.P.R.*, 1422–9, p. 565; *ibid.*, 1429–36, p. 619; C66/414 MS 20v). He was dead by 1436 when his widow, Joan, and son, Thomas II, were assessed for the subsidy on incomes of £10 and £30 respectively (E179/192/59). In 1458, Thomas II was distrained for failing to assume knighthood (E159/234 MS 7). Unlike his father, Thomas II was never appointed as JP. In 1440, however, he was pricked as sheriff for Leicestershire and Warwickshire (Lists and Indexes, IX, p. 145). He died on 20 April 1467 leaving a son, William I, aged twenty-four, and a daughter, Joyce, who married Geoffrey Sherard (*q.v.*) (C140/23/14 MS 2; Nichols, III, p. 208). William Assheby I maintained his father and grandfather's record of service in local administration; in 1462, during his father's lifetime, he was appointed escheator and, from 1474 to 1485, he was regularly commissioned to serve as JP (*List of Escheators*, p. 171; *C.P.R.*, 1467–77, p. 619; *ibid.*, 1476–85, p. 564). He must have had some legal expertise, for, like his grandfather before him, William was a member of the *quorum* (C66/542 MS 29v). He also served on the commission of array appointed in Leicestershire in May 1484 (*C.P.R.*, 1476–85, p. 400). William I married Agnes, daughter of Richard Illingworth, the Nottinghamshire lawyer and chief baron of the exchequer (*Pedigrees*, p. 48; Foss, *Biographia Juridica*, p. 366). Agnes bore two children who survived to adulthood, William II and Catherine. William I died on 14 January 1500 (*C.I.P.M.*, 15 Hen. VII, no. 334).

ASTLEY

Thomas Astley, esquire, of Nailstone was the husband of Joan Gresley, Henry VI's nurse. In 1436, his declared income was £22 per annum (E179/192/59). In November of the same year, he was elected knight of the shire for Leicestershire (*Return*, p. 330). According to *V.C.H. Staffs.*, xx, p. 164, this Thomas acquired the manor of Patshull in 1451 in right of his mother, Isabel Harcourt. However, Thomas Astley died sometime between May and July 1437; on 20 May 1437, a commission was issued to Astley to remit £79-8-3¼ to the borough of Leicester from the fifteenth and tenth (*C.F.R.*, 1430–7, p. 351); on 12 July 1437, a grant of

Biographical notes

£40 annually from the issues of Warwickshire and Leicestershire was made to Joan, 'late the wife of Thomas Asteley, esquire' (*C.P.R.*, 1436–41, p. 204). The Thomas Astley who inherited Patshull in Staffordshire in 1451 must therefore have been Thomas's and Joan's son, Thomas II. Thomas II was distrained in Staffordshire in 1466 for failing to assume knighthood (E159/242). Following the death of Thomas I, the family's interests appear to have shifted to Staffordshire.

BAUDE

The Baude family had landed interests in Essex as well as Leicestershire. The quarter knight's fee they held in Lubenham was known as 'Bawdesmanor' (*Feudal Aids*, III, p. 123; *Pedigrees*, p. 51). Their interest in Leicestershire came to an end in 1442 when Thomas Baude, esquire, sold his manor at Lubenham to Thomas Palmer (*q.v.*) (*C.C.R.*, 1441–7, p. 117).

BEAUMONT

Thomas Beaumont, knight, was second son of John, fourth lord Beaumont (G.E.C., II, p. 61). His marriage in 1426 to Philippa, daughter and heir of Thomas Maureward, brought him the manors of Overton Quartermarsh (Coleorton), Goadby Marwood, Congerstone, Osgathorpe and Cotes. His estate also extended into Dorset and Northamptonshire (C145/319/46–7; C140/2/18; E149/209/8; E153/1880 MS 3; Nichols, III, p. 742; *Pedigrees*, p. 28). In 1436, these lands produced an annual income of £100 (E179/192/59). Sir Thomas received commissions to serve as a justice of the peace in 1424, 1426, 1431, 1432 and 1436 (*C.P.R.*, 1422–9, p. 565; *ibid.*, 1429–36, p. 619; *ibid.*, 1436–41, p. 584). However, he was never a member of the *quorum* and his name fails to appear among the sheriffs' accounts of payments made to active JPs (C66/414–40; E101/590/34). It seems that he found military service a more congenial pursuit than local administration; in 1425 and 1436, he fought in France where he was a member of the household and retinue of the duke of Bedford (*Warrants for Issues, 1399–1485*, p. 24; B. L. Harl. 6166, fo. 69v; *D.K.R.*, 48th report, p. 265). Sir Thomas Beaumont died in 1457 and was succeeded by his son, John. John was killed fighting for Henry VI at Towton in 1461 after which battle his lands were forfeited and granted to Richard Hastings (*Rot. Parl.*, V, p. 477; *C.P.R.*, 1461–7, p. 187). John's cousin, Sir Henry Beaumont, king's squire, was knight of the shire in Leicestershire in 1446 (Wedgwood, *Biographies*, p. 57).

BELGRAVE

The Belgrave family held lands in Leicester, Thurmaston, Birstall, Countesthorpe, Houghton and Whatton but their *caput* at Belgrave was not referred to as a manor until 1512 (*V.C.H. Leics.*, IV, p. 421; *C.I.P.M.*, 4 Hen. VII, no. 419; *T.L.A.S.*, 16, 1929–31, pp. 51–61). In 1436, William Belgrave was taxed on his declared income of £13 per annum (E179/192/59). His father, also called William, was either receiver or deputy receiver of the honor of Leicester in 1414 (Somerville, I, p. 566). One of these Williams was bailiff of the honor in 1430

Appendix 3

(E372/275 MS 32v). The William Belgrave of Belgrave who was commissioned to collect the fifteenth and tenth in 1434 was almost certainly the son who was taxed in 1436 (*C.F.R.*, 1430–7, p. 191). In 1436, in a plea of damage against a neighbour, William II is referred to as 'esquire', whereas his son, John, was accorded gentlemanly status (L.R.O. 5D33/172; *C.I.P.M.*, 4 Hen. VII, no. 419). John's son, Richard, who was twenty-eight years old when his father died in 1488, succumbed to ill-health before September 1508. He left a son, William, and three daughters, Anne, Brigett and Katherine, for whom he provided £6-13-4 to be set aside annually 'towards their marriage and preferment' (PROB11/16/17/127r).

BELLERS

John Bellers I married Elizabeth Sutton, daughter and heir of Anthony Sutton or Howby. Bellers died *c.* 1421, a year or so before his father-in-law, whereupon his widow remarried (C139/1/6 MS 2). When Elizabeth died in 1427, the Howby inheritance of a third part of the manor of Medbourne passed to her son, John Bellers II (C139/32/1 MS 2). From his father, John II inherited the manors of Eye Kettleby and Sysonby, valued at £10 per annum, and lands at Sutton, Somerby and Dalby Parva (*V.C.H. Leics.*, v, p. 232; *Village Notes*, IV, pp. 114, 183; *T.L.A.S.*, 13, 1923–4, pp. 93ff; C140/52/27; E149/232/11). John II's total landed income must have exceeded £40 per year for in 1466 he was distrained for failing to become a knight (E159/242). He was first commissioned as JP in May 1444 and thereafter received regular appointments to the bench (*C.P.R.*, 1441–6, p. 473; *ibid.*, 1446–52, p. 590; *ibid.*, 1452–61, p. 669). Despite these repeated commissions, Bellers was never a member of the *quorum*; the only evidence of his having actually sat on the bench appears in March 1450 when the sheriff paid him for twelve days service (C66/407–535; E101/590/34 MS 10). Nevertheless, he does appear to have had some legal expertise; from 1429, he was paid 13s. 4d. annually for providing Thomas Palmer (*q.v.*) with 'good council' (L.R.O. DE 221/4/1/42). It may be added that this date places in doubt Wedgwood's claim that Bellers was born *c.* 1415 (Wedgwood, *Biographies*, p. 63; Wedgwood, *Register*, p. 159). During the 1440s and 50s, John II also served on various *ad hoc* commissions (*C.P.R.*, 1446–52, pp. 140, 412; *ibid.*, 1452–61, p. 409; *C.F.R.*, 1445–52, p. 171). He was first elected knight of the shire for Leicestershire in April 1432 and he was returned again in 1435, 1450 and 1470 (*Return*, pp. 321, 327; Wedgwood, *Register*, p. 653). His election to the readeption parliament in 1470 indicates his attachment to the Lancastrian cause. A further sign of this attachment is the fact that Bellers was omitted from the commissions of the peace throughout the 1460s, was appointed to the bench again in 1470 and was subsequently removed from office when Edward IV returned to power (*C.P.R.*, 1467–77, p. 619). In fact, the only office Bellers held under the Yorkist regime was in 1462 when he received a commission to assess the subsidy in Leicestershire (*C.F.R.*, 1461–71, p. 99). His association with the house of Lancaster had been long-standing; as a boy, he was page to Henry V in France and in 1443 he went to France again in the retinue of the duke of Somerset (Wedgwood, *Biographies*, p. 63; *D.K.R.*, 48th report, p. 357); by 1451, he had progressed to become an esquire of the king's chamber (E101/410/6, fo. 40v). He died *sine prole* in January 1477, leaving two sisters, Elena Dekyn and Marina Green, and a nephew, John Villers (*q.v.*), as his coheirs (C140/52/27).

BERKELEY

Sir Laurence Berkeley's estate straddled the border between Leicestershire and Rutland. In Leicestershire, he held the manors of Wymondham and Coston (E179/240/269; *Feudal Aids*, III, p. 118; Nichols, II, pp. 143, 413; *V.C.H. Rut.*, II, p. 160). Sir Laurence's declared annual income in 1436 was £90 (E179/192/59). He was elected to parliament as knight of the shire for Leicestershire in December 1421 and again in January 1432 (*Return*, pp. 300, 319). He served on various *ad hoc* commissions before being pricked as sheriff for Warwickshire and Leicestershire in 1439 (*C.P.R.*, 1416–22. p. 444; *ibid.*, 1429–36, pp. 520, 529; *C.F.R.*, 1430–7, p. 260; Lists and Indexes, IX, p. 145). Sometime before 1420, he married Jane Woodford, daughter of John and sister of Sir Robert Woodford (*q.v.*). Links between the two families were further strengthened when one of his daughters, Alice, married her first cousin, Thomas Woodford (Wedgwood, *Biographies*, p. 68; *Pedigrees*, p. 3). Another daughter, Elizabeth, married Sir William Hussey, serjeant-at-law and, from 1481, chief justice of the king's bench (*D.N.B.*, X, p. 323). Sir Laurence Berkeley was killed in France in 1458 (Wedgwood, *Biographies*, p. 68). His son and heir, Thomas, was a lawyer (*Lincoln's Inn, Admissions*, p. 10; *Lincoln's Inn, Black Books*, I, pp. 19, 23). Thomas Berkeley, esquire, was pricked as sheriff for Warwickshire and Leicestershire in 1454 (Lists and Indexes, IX, p. 145). Between 1442 and 1485, he was regularly commissioned as justice of the peace (*C.P.R.*, 1441–6, p. 473; *ibid.*, 1446–52, p. 590; *ibid.*, 1452–61, p. 669; *ibid.*, 1467–77, p. 619; *ibid.*, 1476–85, p. 563). Although Thomas sat on the bench of justices, despite his legal training, he does not appear to have been a member of the *quorum* (E101/590/34 MSS 11, 12; C66/451–557). In the early years of Yorkist government, there may have been doubts about Berkeley's loyalty for he was omitted from commissions of the peace between 1461 and 1470. Perhaps the source of these doubts, if, indeed, they existed, can be traced to 1459 when Thomas was included on the commission of array appointed to suppress the duke of York's rebellion (*C.P.R.*, 1452–61, p. 560). Whatever the reason, Thomas's retirement from local government office was only temporary. In 1470, he was appointed JP in Rutland and he became that county's sheriff in 1471. It appears that he was also knighted about this time, though Wedgwood erroneously claims that this honour was bestowed sometime between 1463 and 1469 (*C.P.R.*, 1467–77, p. 626; Lists and Indexes, IX, p. 113; Wedgwood, *Biographies*, p. 68). Sir Thomas represented Leicestershire in the parliament which first met in 1472 and he was elected by the shire again in 1483 (Wedgwood, *Register*, p. 653). He married twice, first to Emma, daughter of William Brokesby, who bore him a son, Morris, and second to Sybil Systerwold, daughter of John and widow of Sir William Lacon (B.L. Harl. 265, fo. 2*). Thomas Berkeley died in 1490.

Appendix 3

There appears to have been a number of interrelated Boyville families with estates in south-east Leicestershire and south-west Rutland. An inquisition *post mortem* held after the death of Richard Boyville of Tur Langton in 1465, refers to him as the son and heir of William Boyville, brother of Thomas (C140/17/23 MS 2). The inquisition also reveals Richard's feoffees in 1442 as including Thomas, John and Hugh Boyville. In 1436, three members of the family, John, Hugh and William, appeared before the Leicestershire tax assessors to declare their annual incomes of £100, £20 and £10 respectively (E179/192/59). William, brother of Thomas and father of Richard, was possibly an uncle of John Boyville whose father was also called Thomas (Nichols, II, p. 916, wrongly collated between pp. 812–20; *Pedigrees*, p. 102). To complicate matters, there may have been two Thomas Boyvilles, one of Stockerston (father of John), and one of Tur Langton (brother of William) (see C1/69/183). The identity of Hugh Boyville is also a mystery. He is variously described as 'of Stockerston' and 'of Ridlington', both manors belonging to the main branch of the family. (More strictly, the Boyvilles held the manor of Ayston in Rutland but Ayston was a hamlet of Ridlington. (*V.C.H. Rut.*, II, p. 59)). There is a suggestion that Hugh may have been John's younger brother (Wedgwood, *Biographies*, p. 99). The identity of John Boyville, MP for Leicestershire in 1453, is also disputed (*Return*, p. 348). According to Wedgwood, he was born in 1410, the son of another John Boyville, MP (Wedgwood, *Biographies*, p. 98). Farnham, on the other hand, refers to only one John, son of Thomas (*Pedigrees*, p. 102). This John was born *c*. 1394 (*C.P.R.*, 1401–5, p. 499). While it is biologically possible for John I to have sired a son by 1410, there is no evidence of his having done so. We must assume, therefore, that the John Boyville who was MP in 1453 was the same John who was born *c*. 1394. In addition to two manors in Rutland, John Boyville held the manors of Cranoe, Stockerston, Slawston and Lubenham in Leicestershire (*V.C.H. Rut.*, II, p. 59; *V.C.H. Leics.*, v, pp. 82, 223, 298, 304; *Village Notes*, v, p. 118; L.R.O. 5D33/172). He was elected knight of the shire for the county of Leicester in 1423, 1426, 1427, 1435 and 1453 and for Rutlandshire in 1429 (*Return*, pp. 306, 311, 313, 316, 327, 348). The king appointed him sheriff of Rutland in 1432 and 1446 (Lists and Indexes, IX, pp. 112, 113). In addition, John served on various *ad hoc* commissions in both Rutland and Leicestershire (*C.P.R.*, 1429–36, pp. 137, 520; *ibid.*, 1436–41, p. 249; *ibid.*, 1441–6, p. 61; *ibid.*, 1461–7, pp. 313, 566, 570). In 1466, the year before his death, he was fined, not for the first time, for failing to assume knighthood (E159/242; E159/234). His first wife, Elizabeth, widow of Sir Robert Langford, bore him three daughters, his coheirs, Elizabeth, Anne and Margaret. His estate was divided in 1468 among Edmund Cokayn, Elizabeth's son, and Edmund's aunts, Anne Sotehill and Margaret Restwold (*Village Notes*, v, p. 118; *Pedigrees*, p. 102; L.R.O. 5D33/172).

Biographical notes

BRABESSON

Nicholas Brabesson of Eastwell, esquire, was appointed to collect the subsidy on knights fees in 1428 (*Feudal Aids*, III, p. 106; *C.F.R.*, 1422–30, p. 220). His income in 1436 was £26 per annum (E179/192/59). He was one of the electors who returned Everard Dygby (*q.v.*) and Bartholomew Brokesby (*q.v.*) to parliament in 1429 (C219/14/1 pt 2 MS 102). Nicholas died before January 1466 (*C.F.R.*, 1461–71, p. 146). The John Brabesson who was commissioned to collect two fifteenths and tenths in 1468 was probably Nicholas's heir (*ibid.*, 1461–71, p. 232). In 1486, after the death of Roger Brabesson, the family's manor and lands in and around Eastwell were divided between his daughters and coheirs, Joan and Margaret (*Pedigrees*, pp. 80–1).

BROKESBY

Bartholomew Brokesby, esquire, played an active rôle in Leicestershire affairs throughout the first half of the fifteenth century. The shire electors first returned him to parliament in 1409 and he was elected again in 1422, 1425, 1427, 1429 and 1432 (*Return*, pp. 274, 303, 308, 313, 316, 321). On two occasions, in 1411 and 1419, he was appointed sheriff in the county (Lists and Indexes, IX, p. 145). Following his first election to parliament, he was regularly commissioned to serve as JP (*C.P.R.*, 1408–13, p. 481; *ibid.*, 1413–16, p. 420; *ibid.*, 1416–22, p. 454; *ibid.*, 1422–9, p. 565; *ibid.*, 1429–36, p. 619; *ibid.*, 1436–41, p. 584; *ibid.*, 1441–6, p. 473; *ibid.*, 1446–52, p. 590). As a member of the *quorum*, Brokesby attended the sittings of the bench with unsurpassed routine (C66/414 MS 20v; E101/590/34 MSS 2–4, 6–9). He served, too, on numerous *ad hoc* commissions, mainly in Leicestershire but also in Sussex, Kent and Shropshire (*C.P.R.*, 1408–13, p. 478; *ibid.*, 1413–16, p. 178; *ibid.*, 1416–22, pp. 207, 212, 251, 416; *ibid.*, 1422–29, pp. 121, 276, 277, 354; *ibid.*, 1429–36, pp. 50, 126, 523, 529; *ibid.*, 1436–41, pp. 268, 369, 537; *ibid.*, 1441–6, pp. 62, 155, 430; *ibid.*, 1446–52, p. 140). In 1415 he followed Henry V on the king's expedition to France (*D.K.R.*, 44th report, p. 568). The Brokesby estate consisted of two manors, Frisby and Dalby Parva, and extensive lands in the hundreds of East Goscote and Framland as well as holdings in Suffolk (*C.C.R.*, 1461–8, p. 190; C141/5/13 MS 2; Bodl. Lib. Wood Empt. 7, *passim*). In 1436, Bartholomew's income from lands and annuities was £230, making him one of the wealthiest members of the Leicestershire gentry (E179/192/59). Of this £230, £130 undoubtedly derived from annuities; Brokesby was executor of the will of Thomas Arundel, Archbishop of Canterbury, feoffee and executor of Arundel's niece, Joan, lady Abergavenny, who made him a beneficiary under her will, and feoffee of Joan's son-in-law, James Butler, earl of Ormond (C67/38 MS 27; *C.P.R.*, 1416–22, pp. 305, 306; *ibid.*, 1422–9, p. 486; Dugdale, II, p. 1032; *C.P.R.*, 1429–36, p. 506; *ibid.*, 1436–41, p. 435). He was later feoffee of Ormond's son and heir (*C.P.R.*, 1429–36, p. 27; H.M.C., *Hastings*, I, pp. 1, 2). Given his economic resources, it is hardly surprising that his failure to assume knighthood attracted a fine in 1439 (E372/284). Brokesby died on 15 August 1448 and was succeeded by his octogenarian brother, Edmund (C139/136/43 MS 2). Beyond this date, it is difficult to reconstruct the Brokesby family.

Edmund cannot have survived for long but, in the absence of an inquisition *post mortem*, we are unable to say when he died or, more important, who was his heir. In 1453, Sir Leonard Hastings arranged for his daughter, Joan, to marry a John Brokesby, son of Bartholomew (H.M.C., *Hastings*, I, pp. 300–1). This Bartholomew must have been a nephew or great-nephew of Bartholomew I. As Bartholomew II was not party to the agreement with Hastings, he must have been dead by 1453. He was possibly the same Bartholomew Brokesby of Frisby whose executors wished to found a chantry in Saxulby church in 1450 (L.A.O. Epis. Reg. XIX [Lumley], fo. 14), though it is more commonly assumed that this was a bequest of Bartholomew I (Roskell, *The Commons in the Parliament of 1422*, p. 157). That Bartholomew II had a brother, William, is suggested by Wedgwood (*Biographies*, p. 114) and by the fact that in an enfeoffment of 1472, John Brokesby's heirs are given as first, his issue, then his illegitimate half-brother, William, and finally, Henry Brokesby, nephew of Bartholomew (II?) (*Village Notes*, II, p. 262). John himself later had a son, unimaginatively named Bartholomew, and a daughter (C141/5/13 MS 2; PROB11/7/10/77v). The pedigree provided by Nichols (Nichols, III, p. 406) fails to resolve these problems of identification.

BUGGE

Baldwin Bugge, esquire, held the manors of Wigston Magna, Thurlaston, Normanton Turville, Stoke Golding and Croft (E149/158/12; Nichols, IV, pp. 715, 995, 1001; *T.L.A.S.*, 14, 1925–6, pp. 211–12). The £13 which his widow, Elizabeth, declared as her income in 1436 was probably her dower right of one third of the family income (E179/192/59). Like many others caught up in the chauvinistic fervour of 1415, Baldwin indented to serve in Guienne (E101/69/5 MS 442). He first entered parliament in 1425 and was returned again the following year (*Return*, pp. 308, 311). In 1428 he was appointed escheator and in 1431 he was commissioned as tax assessor (*List of Escheators*, p. 170; *C.P.R.*, 1429–36, p. 137). Baldwin Bugge died in August 1435 and was succeeded by his sister, Margaret, who married in turn Richard Turville (*q.v.*), Reginald Moton (*q.v.*) and Thomas Everyngham (*q.v.*) (*Pedigrees*, p. 6).

BURGH

Following the death of Henry Burgh, esquire, in March 1495, an inquisition *post mortem* revealed that he held the manor of Burrough-on-the-Hill and lands at Knossington, Horninghold, Barsby, Branston, Frolesworth, Leicester, Thorpe Satchville and Halyok (*C.I.P.M.*, 10 Hen. VII, no., 1081). Henry's father, John, was possibly the same John Burgh who represented Leicestershire in the parliaments of 1421 and 1433 (*Pedigrees*, pp. 19–20; *Return*, pp. 297, 324), who was nominated to the commission of the peace in 1416, 1422, 1431 and 1432, and who served as escheator of Warwickshire and Leicestershire in 1422 (*C.P.R.*, 1416–22, p. 454; *ibid.*, 1429–36, p. 619; *ibid.*, 1436–41, p. 503; *C.F.R.*, 1422–30, p. 13). John Burgh was not only a member of the *quorum* of justices in 1431 and 1432 but he also received payment for sitting on the bench (C66/429 MS 28v;

C66/431 MS 26v; E101/590/34 MSS 2–6). He may have been the same John Burgh who served in France in 1439 (E404/56/316), but the contemporary presence of a number of John Burghs makes it difficult to be certain on this point (see *C.P.R.*, 1429–36, pp. 136, 623, for reference to a John Burgh of Rutland and *C.P.R.*, 1441–6, p. 477, for John Burgh of Shropshire; the Leicestershire MP and the Rutland JP and commissioner may have been the same man). John Burgh was taxed in Leicestershire in 1436 on an income of £26 per annum (E179/192/59).

CHARNELS

John Charnels of Snarestone in Leicestershire, esquire, inherited the manor of Bramcote in Warwickshire in 1429 from his mother, Margaret, daughter and heir of Sir Thomas Grendon (Dugdale, II, p. 1122). John's son, William, later conveyed his rights at Bramcote to Thomas Burdet (*Pedigrees*, p. 97). John Charnels failed to appear before the Leicestershire tax commissioners in 1436 (E179/240/269). He was one of the electors who returned Bartholomew Brokesby and Baldwin Bugge to the parliament of 1425 (C219/13/3 pt 2 MS 98). However, he does not seem to have played an active rôle in county administration.

CHESILDEN

The Chesildens acquired the manor of Allexton before 1428 through the marriage of Robert Chesilden to Anne or Amice Burgh, daughter and heir of William Burgh (*T.L.A.S.*, 11, 1919–20, p. 419; *Village Notes*, I, pp. 14–15; E149/141/20; *C.C.R.*, 1422–9, pp. 376–7). Robert was dead by 1436, when his widow was taxed on her income of £31 (E179/192/59). When Anne died on 7 March 1445, her son, John I, was also dead, and she was succeeded by her grandson, John II (C139/118/14 MS 6; E149/179/12 MS 2; Farnham erroneously dates Anne's death to Sunday, 11 March 1442, see *T.L.A.S.* 11, 1919–20, p. 420). John Chesilden II lived on his estate at Uppingham in Rutland while his younger brother, William, lived at Allexton (C1/19/473). The Chesildens' association with Leicestershire ended in or before 1451 when John II sold his interest in Allexton (*C.C.R.*, 1447–54, pp. 265–6; *T.L.A.S.*, 11, 1919–20, pp. 421, 426). After a period of attendance at Lincoln's Inn, he represented Rutland in the parliaments of 1453 and 1468 (*Lincoln's Inn, Admissions*, p. 11; *Lincoln's Inn, Black Books*, I, p. 21; Wedgwood, *Register*, p. 356).

COTON

John Coton, esquire, originally from Ridware in Staffordshire, acquired the manors of Thurcaston and Keyham in Leicestershire early in the fifteenth century through marriage to Isabel, daughter and heir of William Fauconer (*Pedigrees*, p. 123). In 1434, he was among the Staffordshire gentry who swore an oath not to maintain peace-breakers, but two years later, he was taxed in Leicestershire on an annual income of £11 (*C.P.R.*, 1429–36, p. 400; E179/192/

59). He died 24 June 1478 and was succeeded by his kinsman, Richard Coton (C140/66/34 MS 2).

COTON

An inquisition *post mortem* held after the death of Thomas Coton of Rearsby, esquire, in October 1505, revealed that he held 'Cotons Maner' at Rearsby, worth £20-2-6, lands at Humberstone worth £6-8-6, lands at Leicester and Thurmaston worth £4-19-0 and other minor parcels of land at Assheby Parva, Queniborough, Sileby and Rotherby (*C.I.P.M.*, 21 Hen. VII, no. 159). The Cotons had obtained their interest in Rearsby in 1436 through the marriage of William Coton to Mary, daughter and coheir of John Folville (*Pedigrees*, p. 79). In 1436, William was assessed on his annual income of £10 (E179/192/59). He was appointed escheator for Warwickshire and Leicestershire in 1453 (*List of Escheators*, p. 171). The two Coton families do not appear to have been related.

DANET (OF GADDESBY)

There is no evidence to support Nichol's claim that the Danets were 'long seated at Gaddesby' in the hundred of E. Goscote (Nichols, III, p. 969). The family appears to have acquired a manor there early in the fifteenth century by the marriage of John Danet, esquire, to Thomasine, daughter and heir of William Wheteley (*T.L.A.S.*, 13, 1923–4, p. 263). Danet also held land in Cossington of John German (*q.v.*) (L.R.O. 44'28/107). In 1422, John Danet was serving as under-sheriff and coroner (JUST3/31/11 MS 3; JUST3/31/12 MS 5). Two years later, when the sheriff was ordered to elect a new coroner, Danet was still holding both offices (*C.C.R.*, 1422–9, p. 165). He occupied the coronership again in 1444 (*C.P.R.*, 1441–6, p. 319; KB9/247/44). He was also appointed escheator in November 1438 and tax collector in 1445 (*List of Escheators*, p. 170; *C.F.R.*, 1437–45, p. 329). Both John and Thomasine were dead by 1460 or 1463 when their daughters and coheirs, Elizabeth and Eleanor, wives of John Sandy and Richard Chamber respectively, petitioned the chancellor, George Neville, to act in their defence against their father's feoffees (C1/28/494). The Danet's only son, Bartholomew, had already died *vita patris sine prole*.

DANET (OF BROMKINSTHORPE)

Richard Danet of Bromkinsthorpe, esquire, was possibly related to John Danet (*q.v.*) (Nichols, III, pp. 235, 969). In addition to their manor at Bromkinsthorpe, this branch of the family held land in Ratby and North Kilworth, an estate valued in 1494 at £13-6-8 per annum (*C.I.P.M.*, 9 Hen VII, no. 1069). In 1463, however, Richard Danet had been assessed for the subsidy on an annual income of £22 (E179/192/59). Richard married twice, first to Matilda or Maud Knightley, and second to Mabel Pykewell, daughter of John Pykewell, described in 1431 as a wool-merchant of Leicester, and John's wife, Margaret, who was taxed as a widow in 1436 (L.R.O. 5D33/174, fo. 256; *Village Notes*, VI, p. 242; *Calendar of Plea and Memoranda Rolls . . . of the City of London . . . A.D. 1413–1437*,

p. 249; E179/192/59; cf. Nichols, III, p. 235, where he mistakenly claims that Matilda Knightley was Danet's second wife and Mabel the first). Matilda bore Richard a son, Robert I, and Mabel produced three further sons, John, Thomas and Robert II. Following Richard Danet's death sometime before 1451, Mabel became the second wife of Thomas De la Hey whose daughter and sole heir, Joan, married Mabel's eldest son, John (*Village Notes*, VI, p. 242). The Thomas Danet of Bromkinsthorpe who graduated as bachelor of arts from Merton College, Oxford, in 1455 and who rose to become Doctor of Theology (1471), prebend and then dean of St George's chapel at Windsor (1472, 1481), negotiator on Edward IV's behalf with the duke of Burgundy (August 1475) and king's almoner (1476) was probably John's younger brother. (Emden, *A Biographical Register of the University of Oxford*, I, p. 540; *C.P.R.*, 1467–77, pp. 359, 604; *ibid.*, 1476–85, p. 285). Of John's five children, Gerard, the eldest, found a lucrative career through the law. His admission to Lincoln's Inn in 1483 led eventually to the stewardship of Chelmesmore in Warwickshire during the reign of Henry VII, and service in the household of Henry VIII (*Lincoln's Inn, Admissions*, p. 23; *Materials for a History of Henry VII*, ed. W. Campbell, Rerum Britannicorum Medii Aevi Scriptores, Rolls Series, 2 vols., London, 1873–7, I, p. 454; *Letters and Papers, Foreign and Domestic, Henry VIII*, 2nd edn, 21 vols., London, 1864–1920, Kraus repr., New York, 1965, I, p. 15). Shortly before he was to accompany Henry VIII to the 'Field of Cloth of Gold' in May 1520, Gerard Danet died, a wealthy enough man to bequeath £100 and £80 towards the marriage of his daughters, Elizabeth and Mary (*Letters and Papers, Henry VIII*, III, pp. 241, 243; L.R.O. 5D33/180).

DANSEY

John Dansey senior was a retainer of Joan Beauchamp, lady Abergavenny, who, in her will of 1434, bequeathed him £20 (Dugdale, II, p. 1032). After Joan Beauchamp's death, Dansey became a feoffee of her son-in-law, James Butler, earl of Ormond (*C.P.R.*, 1429–36, p. 506; H.M.C., *Hastings*, I, pp. 1–2). Dansey and his son, John junior, were closely associated with another member of the Beauchamp–Ormond affinity, Bartholomew Brokesby (*q.v.*); the two families held adjoining lands in Gaddesby, both Danseys regularly acted as Brokesby's feoffees and they were sufficiently trusted for the latter to include them among the executors of his will (Bodl., Lib. Wood Empt. 7, fos. 138, 164r–5 (mispaginated as 183r–4); H.M.C., *Hastings*, I, p. 300; *Village Notes*, II, p. 261). Much of John senior's declared annual income of £26 in 1436 must have derived from annuities, for when John junior's inquisition *post mortem* was taken in 1494, the net value of his lands at Somerby and Little Dalby was only £7-16-0 (E179/192/59; *C.I.P.M.*, 14 Hen. VII, no. 133).

DANVERS

Early in the fifteenth century, John Danvers 'the younger' of Shakerston married Margaret, daughter and coheir of John Walcote of Swithland and of his wife, Elizabeth, daughter and heir of Sir John Waleys of Swithland (*Pedigrees*, pp. 85,

114). Despite the increase in landed resources acquired through this marriage, John and his fifteenth-century descendants (his son, John II, the elder; grandson, Thomas; and great-grandson, John III) failed to become involved in county administration. Nor were they ever included among the named electors who attended the county court in Leicester (C219/13–17). However, John II, esquire, was occasionally approached by neighbours to act as witness and feoffee. In 1458, he witnessed Thomas Erdyngton's (*q.v.*) enfeoffment concerning lands at Charley (L.R.O. 5D33/108/87). Sometime before 1475, Thomas Farnham (*q.v.*) enfeoffed Danvers with lands in Quorndon, Loughborough, Barrow and Mountsorell and further entrusted him with the execution of his will (*Quorndon Records*, pp. 155–6). John Danvers III married Anne, daughter of John Shirley (*q.v.*). As Anne is not mentioned in her father's will we may assume that the marriage took place before John Shirley's death in 1485 and not in 1527, as claimed by E. P. Shirley (L.R.O. 26D53/1947; *Stemmata Shirleiana*, pp. 39, 56; *Pedigrees*, p. 116).

DERBY

The inquisition held after the death of William Derby, esquire, in 1498, revealed that he died seised of eleven messuages and 360 acres of land in Gaddesby of which nine messuages and 300 acres were worth £8. He also held lands at Barsby, South Croxton, Foxton and Great Bowden worth £6-19-4 (*C.I.P.M.*, 14 Hen. VII, no. 132). William was probably the son of Thomas Derby whose income in 1436 was £11 per annum and who paid 6s. 8d. as his share of the £40 raised in Coventry in 1461 to send forty men with the earl of Warwick against Henry VI (E179/1921/59; *Coventry Leet Book*, p. 317). Thomas Derby's lands in Gaddesby abutted those of Bartholomew Brokesby (*q.v.*) for whom he regularly acted as witness to land transactions (Bodl. Lib. Wood Empt. 7, fos. 103v–4, 138, 164v–5, 178).

DYGBY

The Dygby family held the manors of Tilton and Kibworth Beauchamp and lands at Donington-le-Heath, Ravenstone, Billesdon, Halstead and Whatborough in Leicestershire (E149/209/7; C140/1/7 MS 2; E153/1880 MS 12). In addition, they were seised of the manor of Stoke Dry in Rutland and of other lands in Derbyshire, Lincolnshire, Warwickshire and Huntingdonshire where, in 1434, Everard Dygby I took the oath not to maintain peace-breakers (*V.C.H. Rut.*, II, p. 233, *D.K.R.*, 48th report, p. 360; *C.P.R.*, 1429–36, p. 375). In 1436, Everard's declared annual income was £40 and, not surprisingly, he was later fined £2-13-4 for failing to assume knighthood (E179/192/59; E159/234). He married twice, first to Elizabeth, daughter of Roger Hunt, and then to Agnes, daughter and eventual heiress of John Clerk of Whissendine, Co. Rutland (*Pedigrees*, p. 131; Nichols, III, p. 436; *V.C.H. Rut.*, II, pp. 171, 174, 223, 258). Agnes appears to have borne him six sons and at least one daughter (L.R.O. 5D33/179, fo. 109; PROB11/16/11/81v; see Villers). Everard I was elected knight of the shire for Leicestershire in 1429, but thereafter his interest focussed more on Rutland where he was elected MP in 1447, twice in 1449, 1450 and 1459 (*Return*, pp. 316, 336, 339, 342, 345, 353). In 1459 he was also pricked as sheriff for the county (Lists and Indexes, IX, p. 113). Between 1446 and 1459 he was regularly appointed to Rutland's bench of JPs, no doubt as a result of his legal expertise, and to *ad hoc* commissions in the same county, including the commission of array to resist the duke of York's rebellion of 1459 (*C.P.R.*, 1441–6, p. 477; *ibid.*, 1446–52, p. 593; *ibid.*, 1452–61, p. 675; *Lincoln's Inn, Black Books*, I, p. 21; *C.P.R.*, 1446–52, pp. 140, 319; *ibid.*, 1452–61, p. 557). In 1449, Dygby had been one of York's feoffees for his manor of Hambleton in Rutland (*C.P.R.*, 1446–52, p. 218), but his political sympathies lay with the Lancastrians. He was a member of the duke of Somerset's retinue in France in 1443–4, and later, in 1461, he fought for Henry VI at Towton where he was killed (*D.K.R.*, 48th report, pp. 357, 358, 360; *Rot. Parl.*, V, p. 477; *C.P.R.*, 1461–7, p. 153). Most of Dygby's forfeited lands were granted to Walter Devereux, lord Ferrers, though Alice Russel, 'for her true heart to the king and his father', received an annual grant of £10 from the confiscated estate (*C.P.R.*, 1461–7, pp. 153, 177). However, Everard's heir, Everard II, must have been granted possession of his patrimony soon after Edward IV's return to power in 1471. In March 1472, he was appointed to a commission of array in Rutland, and the following year he received his first commission to sit on the county's bench of JPs (*C.P.R.*, 1467–77, pp. 350, 627). Before 1469, when he was under nineteen years old, Everard II married Jacquetta, daughter of Sir John Ellis. The marriage produced two sons and four daughters (PROB11/16/11/81–1v). Everard II died in 1509 and was buried in Tilton church (Pevsner, *The Buildings of England: Leicestershire and Rutland*, p. 411).

ENTWYSELL

In 1478, Thomas Entwysell I, esquire, of Dalby-on-the-Wolds, one of lord Hastings' indentured retainers since 1474 and sheriff of Leicestershire in 1482–3, was granted custody of all the manors and lands formerly belonging to the late William Hasilrigge (*q.v.*) (*C.P.R.*, 1476–85, p. 106; Lists and Indexes, IX, p. 146). Entwysell had earlier married as his second wife, Elizabeth, daughter and coheir of Thomas Staunton and widow of William Hasilrigge (*Pedigrees*, p. 56). The grant of 1478 further gave Entwysell the custody and marriage of Hasilrigge's son and heir, Thomas, who was promptly wedded to Lucy, one of Thomas I's daughters by his first marriage to Edith Bracebridge. The other two children of this marriage, Margaret and Thomas II, were also disposed of in a double marriage, Margaret to William Wyvyll (*q.v.*) of Stonton Wyville and Thomas II to Wyvyll's niece and heir, Katherine Warde (*Pedigrees*, p. 110). Thomas Entwysell I was dead by 1507, and his son, Thomas II, died *sine prole*, thereby ending this family's brief association with Leicestershire (*T.L.A.S.*, 12, 1921–2, pp. 230–2).

Appendix 3

ERDYNGTON

Sir Thomas Erdyngton held the manors of Barrow-on-Soar, Braunstone, Knossington and Houghton in Leicestershire and manors in Warwickshire and Dorset (*Feudal Aids*, III, pp. 121, 122; C139/69/23; *Quorndon Records*, p. 140; Dugdale, II, p. 673). With a declared annual income of £170, he was one of Leicestershire's wealthiest knights (E179/192/59). About 1415, he married, while still under age, Joyce, granddaughter and coheir of Hugh, lord Burnell, and widow of Sir Adam Peshale (H.M.C., *Hastings*, I, p. 282; G.E.C., V, p. 90; *ibid.*, II, p. 435; L.R.O. 5D33/176, fo. 63). The marriage was barren of children, a fact which, in 1444, when Joyce was past child-bearing age, prompted Erdyngton to sell the reversion of his estate to viscount Beaumont for 1,000 marks (*C.P.R.*, 1441–6, pp. 279–80; H.M.C., *Hastings*, I, pp. 72–3; L.R.O. 5D33/108/98). Erdyngton was first pricked as sheriff of Warwickshire and Leicestershire in 1434 when aged about thirty-two years, and was sheriff there again in 1445 (Lists and Indexes, IX, p. 145; Wedgwood, *Biographies*, p. 302; C139/69/23 MS 3). He was returned knight of the shire for Leicestershire in the parliament which met in 1446 but he had already been MP for Warwickshire in 1440 (Wedgwood, *Register*, p. 61; Wedgwood, *Biographies*, p. 302). He was serving Henry VI as king's knight by 1443 but was sufficiently flexible in his political affiliations later to serve Edward IV in the same capacity (*C.P.R.*, 1441–6, p. 205; *ibid.*, 1461–7, pp. 136, 362). Thomas Erdyngton died *sine prole* in 1467 (*T.L.A.S.*, 15, 1927–8, p. 153).

EVERYNGHAM

Thomas Everyngham, esquire, acquired an interest in the manors of Thurlaston (Newhall), Normanton, Stoke Golding, Wigston Magna and Croft by his marriage, after 1445, to Margaret, sister and heir of Baldwin Bugge (*q.v.*). Margaret had formerly been the wife of John Turville (*q.v.*) and, after Turville's death, of Reginald Moton (*q.v.*) (C140/49/21 MS 4; C1/22/114a–d; Wedgwood, *Biographies*, p. 307). Everyngham was pricked as sheriff for Warwickshire and Leicestershire in 1446 (Lists and Indexes, IX, p. 145). He was returned as knight of the shire for Leicestershire to the first parliament of 1449 and again to the parliament of 1453 (*Return*, pp. 339, 348). During the 1450s, he was appointed to the bench of JPs and to various *ad hoc* commissions in the county, including the commission of array issued to resist the duke of York's rebellion in 1459 (*C.P.R.*, 1452–61, pp. 669, 53, 219, 402, 560). Earlier in his career, Everyngham had been a soldier. He seems to have been present at the battle of Agincourt, and he was in France again during the summer of 1422 (Nicolas, *History of the Battle of Agincourt*, p. 355; D.K.R., 44th report, p. 637). In 1426, for service in France and Ireland, he was granted the office of constable of Dublin castle. When this grant was renewed in November 1427, Everyngham was referred to as 'king's esquire' and given permission to discharge his duties by deputy (*C.P.R.*, 1422–9, pp. 383, 394). In 1443, he was further rewarded with the lieutenancy of Harfleur (*C.P.R.*, 1441–6, p. 203). War service and royal service as king's esquire led to close association with Lancastrian lords. Thomas was feoffee for James Butler, son and heir of the earl of Ormond, and for John, duke of Somerset (H.M.C., *Hastings*, I, pp. I, 346; *C.P.R.*, 1441–6, p. 349). Furthermore, John viscount Beaumont used his influence with his son-in-law, lord Lovell, in an attempt to have his 'wilbeloved Thomas Everyngham' awarded the stewardship of Bagworth (*Paston Letters, 1422–1509*, III, p. 143, no. 381). As late as May 1460, Henry VI recalled Thomas's good service to his father and himself in the French wars and, more recently, his efforts against the Yorkist rebels. For these labours Henry granted him the stewardship of Cottingham in Yorkshire (*C.P.R.*, 1452–61, p. 580). Everyngham was probably killed in 1461, fighting for the king's cause at Towton (*Rot. Parl.*, V, p. 477).

FARNHAM

Thomas Farnham of Netherhall, esquire, was the younger son of John Farnham of Quorndon (*Quorndon Records*, p. 19). Thomas clearly possessed legal expertise; in a dispute with his nephew, Robert, of the senior branch of the family, Robert claimed that his uncle was 'a clerk and a writer, a maker of deeds and a great courtholder' (*ibid.*, p. 146). This legal career was apparently lucrative; in 1436 Thomas was taxed on his annual income of £17 whereas Robert of the senior branch admitted to an income of only £6 per annum (E179/192/59). Surprisingly, although Farnham was regularly appointed to the bench of JPs between 1439 and 1457, despite his legal knowledge he does not appear to have been a member of the *quorum* (*C.P.R.*, 1436–41, p. 585; *ibid.*, 1441–6, p. 473; *ibid.*, 1446–52, p. 590; *ibid.*, 1452–61, p. 669; C66/445–84). Nevertheless, he was regularly appointed to *ad hoc* commissions in Leicestershire, including four commissions of gaol delivery and the commission of array of 1459 (*C.P.R.*, 1452–61, p. 560). He married twice, but only his first wife, Maud Hercy of Nottinghamshire, produced any children, a son, John (*Pedigrees*, p. 70; *Quorndon Records*, pp. 19, 154). John was also attracted to the law, being admitted to Lincoln's Inn in 1457 (*Lincoln's Inn, Admissions*, p. 13). However, his career did not flourish. As a result of mounting debt, he began selling parts of his patrimony soon after his father's death in 1462, despite Thomas Farnham's earlier attempts to prevent such action by entailing the estate (L.R.O. 5D33/174, fo. 163 no. 9; *Quorndon Records*, pp. 154–6). John's death in or around 1507 marked the end of an undistinguished life.

FERRERS

Thomas Ferrers I, esquire, was second son and heir male of William, lord Ferrers of Groby (G.E.C., V, p. 357). By his marriage in 1419 to Elizabeth, sister and coheir of Baldwin Freville, he acquired Tamworth Castle in Staffordshire. On the death of his father in 1445, Thomas inherited six manors including the manor of Flecknoe in Warwickshire. Hithe in Oxfordshire and Woodham Ferrers in Essex but, apart from parcels of land worth £20 per year in the hundreds of Sparkenhoe, Gartree and Guthlaxton, most of the family's Leicestershire estate devolved to Thomas's niece, Elizabeth Grey (C139/174/34; *C.C.R.*, 1454–61, p. 324; G.E.C., V, p. 357 n. a). Nevertheless, Thomas was well provided for; even before his father's death his declared annual income was £100 (E179/192/59). Thomas I's elder son and heir, Thomas II, married Anne, daughter of Sir Leonard Hastings (*q.v.*) in 1448. The parents were obviously keen on the match for Hastings provided Anne with a marriage portion of £300 while Thomas I transferred to the couple land valued at 40 marks yearly with the promise of an additional grant valued at 20 marks (H.M.C., *Hastings*, I, p. 300). On two occasions, Thomas II was pricked as sheriff for Warwickshire and Leicestershire, first, in 1460 when he was referred to as esquire, and again in 1468 by which time he had been knighted (Lists and Indexes, IX, p. 145). According to Wedgwood, he died in 1498 (*Biographies*, p. 318).

FIELDING

Sir William Fielding was son of John Fielding and his second wife, Margaret Purefoy (Wedgwood, *Biographies*, p. 314; Dugdale, I, p. 87). In addition to the family *caput* at Lutterworth and lands at Stormsworth in Leicestershire, William held the manor of Newnham Paddox in Warwickshire, purchased by his father in 1433, and he acquired the manor of Martinsthorpe in Rutland by marriage to Agnes, daughter and heir of John de Seyton (Nichols, IV, pp. 251, 294, 368; *V.C.H. Warws.*, VI, p. 175; *V.C.H. Rut.*, II, p. 85). William was first appointed to the Leicestershire bench of JPs in 1448, and continued to serve in this capacity throughout the 1450s (*C.P.R.*, 1446–52, p. 590; *ibid.*, 1452–61, p. 669). As a lawyer, he was a member of the bench's *quorum* on each occasion (Wedgwood, *Biographies*, p. 314; C66/465–86). In October 1449, he was elected knight of the shire for Leicestershire and was elected again to the parliament held at Coventry in 1459 to attaint the Yorkist lords (*Return*, pp. 342, 353). The same year, he was also appointed to the commission of array to resist the duke of York's rebellion (*C.P.R.*, 1452–61, p. 560). Fielding's political sympathies were strongly Lancastrian. His omission from Edward IV's pardon in March 1461 suggests that he had fought at Wakefield (*C.C.R.*, 1461–8, p. 55). Although a pardon was eventually granted in 1462, Fielding continued to be regarded with suspicion; he was dropped from the commission of the peace and his sole contribution to county government during the 1460s was as a tax assessor in 1463 (Wedgwood, *Biographies*, p. 314; *C.F.R.*, 1461–71, p. 99). At the readeption, the Yorkist government's misgivings were vindicated. Fielding's continuing loyalty to the Lancastrian cause was rewarded by his immediate appointment to the shrievalty in Cambridgeshire and to the bench in Leicestershire, where he may also have been returned as MP to the readeption parliament (Lists and Indexes, IX, p. 13; *C.P.R.*, 1467–77, p. 619; Wedgwood, *Register*, p. 386). He was killed fighting for queen Margaret at the battle of Tewkesbury in 1471 (*Paston Letters 1422–1509*, V, p. 104). Although the family had a declared annual income of £58 in 1436, William accepted distraint rather than assume the dignity of knighthood (E179/192/59; E159/234 MS 7). He was eventually knighted, however, probably on the field of battle at Tewkesbury, for after his death he is referred to as *Sir* William Fielding (Warkworth, *Chronicle*, p. 18; *C.C.R.*, 1476–85, p. 70). Sir William's son and heir, Everard, was not so closely associated with Henry VI's regime. He was appointed to most commissions of the peace between 1477 and 1485 and, like his father before him, was a member of the *quorum* (*C.P.R.*, 1476–85, p. 564; C66/542 MS 29d). In 1481, he was pricked as sheriff for Leicestershire and Warwickshire, serving, too, on various *ad hoc* commissions, including the commission of array of 1484 (Lists and Indexes, IX, p. 146; *C.P.R.*, 1476–85, pp. 354, 396, 400). His will of 1515 makes reference to his wife, Phyllis, and four sons (PROB11/17/5/30r).

FOULESHURST

Thomas Fouleshurst, esquire, of Crewe in Cheshire, arrived in Leicestershire through his marriage to Joan, daughter and heir of Baldwin Fitzpiers of Glenfield (*Village Notes*, II, p. 315). He was returned as a knight of the shire for Leicestershire in 1423 and again in 1431 (*Return*, pp. 306, 319). In 1431 he was also appointed to the commission to raise a loan in the county (*C.P.R.*, 1429–36, p. 126). His last recorded appointment was as sheriff in 1433 (Lists and Indexes, IX, p. 145). Thomas failed to appear before the tax commissioners in Leicestershire in 1436, though he may have been taxed in Chester for which a tax return does not survive (E179/240/269; Gray, 'Incomes from land in England in 1436', p. 622 ns. 1, 2). There is no evidence to connect him with the Richard Fouleshurst who was assessed in Leicestershire in 1436 on his income of £5 (E179/192/59). The last reference to Thomas is in January 1439 when he tried to recover a dept of 200 marks from John Brewster of Warwick (*C.P.R.*, 1436–41, p. 105). Elizabeth Fouleshurst who married William Turville (*q.v.*) was probably Thomas's daughter (*Pedigrees*, p. 6).

GERMAN

John German, esquire, held a quarter knights fee at Cossington and lands at Thorp Langton and Leicester (*Feudal Aids*, III, p. 120; L.R.O. 44'28/107, 109a; Nichols, III, p. 221). In 1436 he was taxed on an income of £6 (E179/192/59). Before 1412, he married Joan, daughter of Geoffrey Poutrell, gentleman, of Ratcliffe. Joan bore three daughters, Margaret, Isabel and Elizabeth (L.R.O. 44'28/53, 107, 115). Isabel and Elizabeth married Alexander Blythe and Ralph Botiller respectively but it appears that Margaret remained unmarried. John German was still alive in 1462 when he leased tenements in Leicester to John Drele and John Gillot for ten years at 10s. per year (L.R.O. 44'28/53). By 1477, however, his daughter Margaret had possession of the estate (L.R.O. 44'28/115). German failed to play a major rôle in Leicestershire administration though he did act as a juror in the sheriff's court in 1446 (E199/45/13 MS 7).

GRYMMESBY

William Grymmesby, esquire, was a member of Henry VI's household in the 1450s, first as a page, then as yeoman of the stole, king's serjeant, treasurer of the chamber and esquire of the body (E404/69/20; *P.P.C.*, VI, p. 225; *C.P.R.*, 1452–61, pp. 352, 360, 432, 541–2). Although he was variously described as of Grimsby in Lincolnshire and of London, his links with Leicestershire were forged through marriage to Anne, daughter and coheir of Reginald Moton (*q.v.*) (*Rot. Parl.*, v, p. 477; *Pedigrees*, pp. 62–3). In Lincolnshire, he served as escheator and represented the county as knight of the shire in 1449 and again at the parliament held in Coventry in 1459 (*C.P.R.*, 1452–61, p. 328; *Return*, pp. 339, 353). In January 1460, his services in repressing the Yorkist rebellion were rewarded by Henry VI's grant of the keepership of the fishery and swans at Thornmere in Yorkshire, and the following month the king granted him for life a further £10 annually from the Lincolnshire estate forfeited by Sir Henry Ratford (*C.P.R.*, 1452–61, pp. 541–2, 591). Grymmesby's good fortune, however, was short-lived. His presence at Wakefield and Towton with queen Margaret ensured his exclusion from Edward IV's pardon and, in April 1461, orders were issued for his arrest (*Rot. Parl.*, v, p. 477; *C.P.R.*, 1461–7, p. 28). He fled to the continent where he spent the next eight years as a Lancastrian exile (Griffiths, *The Reign of King Henry VI*, p. 889). One may be tempted to interpret this self-imposed exile as a measure of Grymmesby's loyalty to the former king, but no doubt his decision to flee was as much dictated by an understandable desire for self-preservation. During his absence, some of his forfeited lands in Lincolnshire were divided between two members of Edward IV's household, but other lands, probably her dower rights, were granted to William's wife, Anne (*C.P.R.*, 1461–7, pp. 224, 336–7). By March 1469, Grymmesby had made his peace with the new regime, receiving a pardon under the privy seal (*C.P.R.*, 1467–77, p. 152). At the readeption, he was appointed to two commissions, including a commission of oyer and terminer in Leicestershire but, despite the circumstance that his earlier pardon had not extended to the recovery of his lands, his rôle in support of his former allies was otherwise undistinguished (*C.P.R.*, 1467–77, pp. 246, 248, 359). This fact probably accounts for his return to favour. In 1472 he was elected as a burgess for the borough of Grimsby and he was included on all commissions of the peace in Leicestershire issued between 1475 and 1482 (*Return*, p. 361; *C.P.R.*, 1467–77, p. 619; *ibid.*, 1476–85, p. 563). No doubt, too, Grymmesby's rehabilitation was aided by his close association with William lord Hastings for whom he was acting as feoffee by May 1475 (*C.P.R.*, 1467–77, p. 517; H.M.C., *Hastings*, I, p. 3). William Grymmesby died after 1482 and was succeeded by his son, Henry, who died *sine prole* before 1515, whereupon his sister, Anne Vincent, inherited her brother's estate (*T.L.A.S.*, 17, 1931–7, p. 133; *Pedigrees*, p. 63).

HARCOURT

Sir Robert Harcourt was son and heir of Sir Thomas Harcourt of Stanton Harcourt in Oxfordshire and Ellenhall in Staffordshire. In Leicestershire, he held the manors of Market Bosworth, Stretton and Gilmorton and lands worth a total of £28-7-10 per annum (C138/48/64 MSS 2, 6, 8). Sir Thomas's inquisition *post mortem*, held in September 1420 when his son was only ten years old, further reveals that the entire estate was valued at just under £80 yearly. Sir Robert was pricked as sheriff of Leicestershire in 1444 but thereafter his interests turned more to Oxfordshire and Berkshire where he was regularly appointed as JP between 1446 and 1470, served as sheriff in 1455 and was elected as knight of the shire (Oxford) in 1447, 1450 and 1460 (Lists and Indexes, IX, pp. 145, 108; *C.P.R.*,

1441–6, p. 476; *ibid.*, 1446–52, pp. 586, 593; *ibid.*, 1452–61, pp. 660, 675; *ibid.*, 1461–7, pp. 559, 570; *ibid.*, 1467–77, p. 625; *Return*, pp. 336, 345, 355). He was a member of Margaret of Anjou's household in 1446 and had earlier been one of the queen's creditors to the value of £15-18-6 (B.L. Addl. MSS, fos. 13d, 5). Harcourt was a steward at the University of Oxford in 1466, but four years later he was killed in a skirmish (Emden, *A Biographical Register of the University of Oxford*, II, p. 868). In 1474 his son, John, was involved in a dispute with his mother or step-mother, Margaret Byron, over her dower rights (Wedgwood, *Biographies*, pp. 419–21; *C.P.R.*, *1467–77*, p. 423; *Village Notes*, VI, p. 172).

HASILRIGGE

Thomas Hasilrigge I, esquire, of Fawdon in Northumberland, acquired the manors of Noseley, Humberstone, Newton Harcourt and Gilmorton by his marriage to Isabel, daughter and coheir of Roger Heron and of Margaret Hastings, half sister to Sir Richard and Sir Leonard Hastings (*q.v.*) (*Pedigrees*, p. 56). Although Margaret Hastings died in 1406, her manors were settled on her second husband, John Blaket, for life, with the result that the Hasilrigges did not take possession until 1434 (*T.L.A.S.*, 12, 1921–2, p. 228; L.R.O. DG21/27). In 1436, Thomas failed to appear before the Leicestershire tax commissioners but in 1439 he was fined £3-6-8 for failing to assume knighthood, so his income must have greatly exceeded £40 per annum (E372/284 MS 28). His son, Thomas II, was married before 1437 to Elizabeth, daughter of Sir Robert Broket. In 1458, Thomas II demised on his son and heir, William, and William's wife, Elizabeth Staunton, the manor of Humberstone (L.R.O. 5D33/177, fo. 38). Seven years later, the two men leased land at Nosely to the warden and chaplains of the chantry there for twenty-four years in return for two red roses and masses for the souls of Thomas and William and their wives (L.R.O. DG21/28). When Thomas II died in 1467, William was aged thirty and more, but he survived his father by only seven years (L.R.O. 5D33/177, fos. 38–9). His widow proceeded to marry as his second wife Thomas Entwysell I (*q.v.*) who was granted the custody and marriage of William's heir, Thomas III, during the latter's minority (*Pedigrees*, p. 56; *C.P.R.*, *1475–85*, p. 106). Thomas III was married to Entwysell's daughter and ultimate coheir, Lucy. His younger brother, Robert, was married to Eleanor, daughter of John Shirley (*q.v.*) who brought him a marriage portion of £66-13-4 (*Stemmata Shirleiana*, pp. 39, 55; PROB11/19/1/ 8v). Robert eventually became steward and then constable of Castle Donington in 1517 and 1526 respectively (Somerville, I, pp. 573–4) but throughout the fifteenth century, the Hasilrigges eschewed public office of any kind. In 1449, 1450 and 1455, Thomas II did, however, attend the shire court to elect the county's representatives to parliament, and the Edmund Hasilrigge of Noseley who was an elector in 1467 was probably Thomas II's younger brother (C219/ 15/7 pt 2 MS 102; C219/16/1 pt 2 MS 105; C219/16/3 pt 2 MS 69; C219/17/1 pt 2 MS 112). Despite this apparent lack of concern with county administration, Thomas Hasilrigge II was sometimes called upon by his fellows to witness their deeds and charters (H.M.C., *Hastings*, I, p. 296; L.R.O. DE221/4/3/60).

Appendix 3

The Hastingses were originally from Yorkshire where they held the manors of Slingsby and Allerton (*V.C.H. Yorks (N.R.)*, I, p. 559; *ibid.*, II, p. 422). Although a Ralph Hastings inherited Kirby Muxloe in Leicestershire in 1365 from his maternal uncle, Sir Robert Herle, it was Ralph's second and third sons, Sir Richard and Sir Leonard, who gradually made the latter county the family's main field of interest (Bell, *The Huntingdon Peerage*, p. 11; H.M.C., *Hastings*, I, pp. 21–2). Sir Richard Hastings divided his energies between Yorkshire and Leicestershire. In 1422 he was appointed steward of Knaresborough for the duchy of Lancaster and, also in Yorkshire, he was sheriff twice, in 1426 and 1434, was returned as MP in 1425 and 1429 and was regularly commissioned to sit on the bench of JPs in the North Riding (Somerville, I, p. 524; Lists and Indexes, IX, p. 162; *Return*, pp. 309, 317; *C.P.R.*, 1422–9, p. 572; *ibid.*, 1429–36, p. 628). In Leicestershire he was also sheriff (1415, 1423, 1427, 1433) and JP from 1424 to 1431 (Lists and Indexes, IX, p. 145; *C.P.R.*, 1422–9,. p. 565; *ibid.*, 1429–36, p. 619). Not only was Sir Richard active in the administration of two shires but in 1416 he indented to serve Henry V in France. Three years later, he received £42-9-4¼ in war wages (Dunham, 'Lord Hastings' indentured retainers 1461–1483', pp. 136–7). In 1421, he indented to go to France again with ten mounted men-at-arms and thirty mounted archers (E101/70/6 MS 725). The name of Sir Richard's first wife is unknown but in 1427 he received a papal dispensation to marry as his second wife Elizabeth, daughter of Henry lord Beaumont and widow of William lord Deincourt, when he was aged about forty-four and she was under twenty-two years old (*Papal Registers*, VII, p. 529; G.E.C., IV, p. 126; *ibid.*, II, p. 61; H.M.C., *Hastings*, I, p. 295). He died in 1436 *sine prole* and was succeeded by his brother, Sir Leonard (C139/83/58 MS 5). Sir Leonard Hastings apparently moved the family *caput* to Kirby Muxloe but, in addition to this manor, he also held the manors of Newton Harcourt, Wistow, Kilby, Braunstone and Fleckney in Leicestershire and manors in Warwickshire and Northamptonshire (C139/162/22 MS 5; H.M.C., *Hastings*, I, pp. 136, 149). Like his brother before him, Sir Leonard played an active rôle in local administration. He was appointed JP in Leicestershire from 1448 until his death in 1455, was sheriff there in 1453, was elected to parliament in June 1455 and served on *ad hoc* commissions (*C.P.R.*, 1446–52, pp. 590, 412, 298; *ibid.*, 1452–61, p. 669; Lists and Indexes, IX, p. 145; *Return*, p. 351). Like Sir Richard, he was also a soldier, serving in the retinue of the earl of March at Agincourt and in France again in 1441 (Nicolas, *History of the Battle of Agincourt*, p. 336; D.K.R., 48th report, p. 346). Sir Leonard married Alice, daughter of lord Camoys, who bore him four sons, William, Richard, Ralph and Thomas, and three daughters, Elizabeth, Anne and Joan (G.E.C., II, pp. 506–8). Elizabeth married John Donne who, like her father, was a servant of the duke of York and who became an esquire of the body to Edward IV (PROB11/7/10/77v–8; *C.P.R.*, 1461–7, pp. 430–1). Anne married Thomas Ferrers II (*q.v.*), while her remaining sister, Joan, married John Brokesby (*q.v.*) (H.M.C., *Hastings*, I, pp. 300, 301; *Village Notes*, III, p. 141). A month after the death of his father in October 1455, William Hastings, esquire, was pricked as sheriff for Leicestershire at the age of twenty-four (Lists and

Indexes, IX, p. 145). He replaced his father on the commission of the peace in 1457 but, as Yorkist influence declined over the winter of 1458–9 and the spring and summer of 1459, Hastings was dropped from the commission (*C.P.R.*, 1452–61, p. 669; Ross, *Edward IV*, pp. 19–21). If he was at the 'Rout of Ludford Bridge' with the Yorkist lords in October 1459, his rôle must have been relatively inconspicuous for he was not attainted by the Coventry parliament but was instead fined £100 and pardoned his misdemeanours (*Rot. Parl.*, v, pp. 349, 368; *C.P.R.*, 1452–61, pp. 552, 577). He may have been with the earl of March at the battle of Mortimer's Cross the following year and was certainly at the battle of Towton where he was knighted (*Paston Letters*, I, p. 197). Under Edward IV, he received immediate preferment. He was a trusted councillor; he was created chamberlain of the household; on 8 May 1461, he became receiver general of the duchy of Cornwall and, soon after, constable and steward of Rockingham Castle and master of the London mint (Lander, 'Council, administration and councillors, 1461 to 1485', p. 168; *C.P.R.*, 1461–7, pp. 9, 13, 26, 130). In June of the same year he was summoned to parliament as baron Hastings (*C.C.R.*, 1461–8, p. 61).

HETON

William Heton, esquire, of Oakham in Rutland and of Hose in Leicestershire was escheator in Nottinghamshire and Derbyshire in 1439, MP for, and sheriff in, Rutland in 1442 and 1452 respectively and JP in Leicestershire between 1424 and 1457 (Wedgwood, *Biographies*, p. 441). He was feoffee for William lord Roos of Hamelak in 1408 and an executor of Roos's will (*C.P.R.*, 1408–13, p. 25; *Early Lincoln Wills*, p. 137). This association with the Roos family continued over the next few decades. In 1421, Heton was appointed steward of the Roos estate following the death of John, and during the minority of Thomas, lord Roos (*C.P.R.*, 1416–22, p. 341). He was still steward and receiver for the estate in 1430, and later the same year he was acting as feoffee for Thomas (E372/275 MS 52v; *C.P.R.*, 1429–36, p. 62). When Margaret, lady Roos, widow of William, died in 1438, her inquisition *post mortem* reveals that Heton was her feoffee, too (C139/104/39). The duke of York also used his services as a feoffee in 1449 for his manor of Hambleton in Rutland (*C.P.R.*, 1446–52, p. 218). The William Heton who was steward in Nottinghamshire for Humphrey, duke of Buckingham from January 1440 to at least michaelmas 1441 was probably the same man (Rawcliffe, *The Staffords, Earls of Stafford and Dukes of Buckingham*, pp. 204–5). Heton was a lawyer who attended Lincoln's Inn in 1428 and who was a member of the *quorum* of JPs at his first appointment to the bench in 1424 (*Lincoln's Inn, Admissions*, p. 5; C66/414 MS 20v). However, his service to the nobility probably prevented his appointment to the *quorum* on subsequent commissions. In 1436 he was taxed on an income of £40, most of which probably derived from fees (E179/192/59). William appears to have had a son, John, but it is not clear whether or not this John was the same man who temporarily held the manor of Knaptoft between 1456 and 1465 by marriage to Isabel, widow of Thomas Kynsman (*q.v.*) (C67/42 MS 40; C1/26/345). The

Appendix 3

identity of the John Heton who was appointed escheator in Leicester in 1455 is not clear (*List of Escheators*, p. 171).

HOTOFT

Richard Hotoft the elder, esquire, held the manors of Humberstone and Thurmaston in Leicestershire (*V.C.H. Leics.*, IV, p. 439; *Pedigrees*, pp. 37–8). He was elected knight of the shire for the county in 1414 and again in 1421 (*Return*, pp. 284, 297). In the intervening years he was appointed to the bench of JPs, and later, in 1427, he was serving as escheator (*C.P.R.*, 1413–16, p. 420; *ibid.*, 1416–22, p. 545; *List of Escheators*, p. 170). In 1422 he was a tax collector in the county, a task usually reserved for the sub-gentry, but in 1431 he had progressed to become a tax assessor (*C.F.R.*, 1422–30, p. 5; *C.P.R.*, 1429–36, p. 137). He died c. 1434 and was succeeded by his son, Richard the younger (*Pedigrees*, p. 38). Richard II's declared income in 1436 was £24 per annum but his estate soon increased when his kinsman, John Hotoft, bequeathed him lands in Stretton (PROB11/1/15/118–19). Both he and his younger brother, Thomas, were lawyers, an occupation which usually brought considerable financial reward (C66/457 MS 25v; *Lincoln's Inn, Admissions*, p. 18). Certainly by 1458, Richard was sufficiently wealthy to attract a fine for failing to assume knighthood (E159/234 MS 7). For almost three decades Richard II played an active rôle in county administration. He was appointed escheator in 1434 and was elected to parliament on seven occasions between 1436 and 1455, including once for Warwickshire and twice for the borough of Warwick (*Return*, pp. 330, 336, 340, 342, 349, 351; Wedgwood, *Register*, p. 16). He was appointed to most commissions of the peace in Leicestershire between 1436 and 1460 and was placed on numerous *ad hoc* commissions, as tax assessor (1450, 1463) to raise loans (1440, 1449), of enquiry (1439, 1440, 1457), gaol delivery (1447, 1457), arrest (1461) and array (1459). To a lesser degree, his services were used in Warwickshire where he was JP (1460) and commissioner of arrest (1441) and enquiry (1461). His last official appointment was as JP for Rutland in 1464 (*C.P.R.*, 1461–7, p. 570). The Hotoft family had close associations with the house of Lancaster. Richard II's kinsman, John, who had bequeathed him lands in Stretton in 1437, had been controller of the prince of Wales' household in 1411 and later became keeper of the wardrobe for Henry VI (*Handbook of British Chronology*, 3rd edn., p. 81). Richard II's brother, Thomas, was also employed in the royal household from about 1437 and throughout the 1440s and 50s (E101/408/24, fo. 43v; E101/409/9, fo. 35v; E101/410/6, fo. 39v). No doubt these contacts with the court assisted Richard's career. In 1441 he was made feodary of the duchy of Lancaster's honor of Leicester and bailiff of Leicester borough (Somerville, I, pp. 569, 570). In 1440 he was retained by the duke of Buckingham with a fee of £2 per year, and two years later, when he was admitted to the ducal council, he was awarded an additional £5 annually (Rawcliffe, *The Staffords, Earls of Stafford and Dukes of Buckingham*, pp. 220, 234). He also acted as feoffee for Henry lord Grey of Codnor (L.R.O., 5D33/177, fo. 32). Although Richard appears to have had a daughter, Joan, she must have predeceased her father because, at his death, his heir was his brother, Thomas (for reference to

Joan, see PROB11/1/15/119). There followed a dispute between Thomas Hotoft and Thomas Keble (*q.v.*), his kinsman, over the terms of Richard's will, especially regarding the disposition of the lands at Stretton (C1/40/290; C1/42/ 90–2). These lands, however, eventually came into the possession of Keble (*C.I.P.M.*, 17 Hen. VII, no. 497). The Hotoft manor of Humberstone was sold, also to Keble, sometime between 1475 and 1485 (*Pedigrees*, p. 38).

KEBLE

The Keble family acquired the manor of Rearsby before 1433 by the marriage of Walter Keble, esquire, to Agnes, daughter and coheir of John Folville (*Pedigrees*, p. 79). Walter was assessed for the 1436 tax on an income of £126, £100 of which derived from his services to James Butler, son and heir of the earl, of Ormond, for whom he acted as feoffee (E179/192/59; *C.P.R.*, 1429–36, p. 506; *ibid.*, 1436–41, p. 435). He was feoffee, too, for Joan lady Abergavenny and was later a beneficiary under, and executor of, her will (*C.P.R.*, 1416–22, p. 305; Dugdale, II, p. 1032). In 1436 he saw service in France in the retinue of Humphrey, duke of Gloucester (*D.K.R.*, 48th report, p. 308). Walter died *c.* 1463, leaving two sons, John and Thomas. The elder of these sons, John, inherited Rearsby and numerous parcels of land, valued when he died in 1485 at over £53 per annum (*C.I.P.M.* 2 Hen VII, no. 164). John was appointed to all commissions of the peace between 1483 and 1485 and to four *ad hoc* commissions during the same period, twice to assess a subsidy and twice on commissions of array (*C.P.R.*, 1476–85, pp. 564, 354, 396, 400, 489). The career of John's younger brother, Thomas, was even more successful. He was sworn to the council of the duchy of Lancaster in 1478 as an apprentice-at-law, and a few years later, in 1483, was promoted to the duchy post of attorney general (Somerville, I, pp. 406, 454; *Grants, etc. from the Crown during the Reign of Edward the Fifth*, p. 65). He received further preferment as justice of assize on the northern circuit (1494) and as king's serjeant (1495) (*Common Lawyers*, pp. 74–7; *Readings and Moots*, I, p. xlv). In Leicestershire, he served as JP on all commissions between 1474 and 1485, always as a member of the *quorum*, and on numerous *ad hoc* commissions (*C.P.R.*, 1467–77, p. 619; *ibid.*, 1476–85, p. 563 and *passim*; C66/533–57). He entered parliament in 1478 as burgess for Lostwithiel, but never represented Leicestershire (Wedgwood, *Biographies*, p. 508). His skills as a lawyer were widely recognized. In 1481 the borough of Coventry appointed him to act on its behalf in a lawsuit against the prior there, and was sufficiently impressed by his efforts on its behalf to offer him the town's next recordership, an offer Keble declined to accept (*Coventry Leet Book*, pp. 474, 524, 526–8). Within Leicestershire, Keble's services were no less in demand. He had a close association with the Hastings family, acting as feoffee for William lord Hastings on many occasions between 1475 and 1483 (*C.P.R.*, 1477–85, p. 517; H.M.C., *Hastings*, I, pp. 3, 37, 297). Lady Hastings was godmother of Keble's son, Walter, and her daughter-in-law, lady Hungerford, received bequests under the terms of Thomas's will (PROB11/12/3/22v–3). Thomas married three times, first to Marjory Palmer, second to Agnes Saltby and finally to Margaret Basset. Both Marjory and Agnes bore sons, Edward and Walter respectively, but only Walter survived his father (L.R.O. 5D33/180; PROB11/12/3/22v). Thomas died in 1500 seised of two manors at Humberstone and manors at Congerstone and Thrussington, both acquired by purchase in the late fifteenth century (*C.I.P.M.*, 17 Hen. VII, no. 497).

KYNSMAN

Thomas Kynsman I, esquire, acquired a knight's fee in Knaptoft through his marriage to Agnes, daughter and heir of John Paynell (*Feudal Aids*, III, p. 125; *Pedigrees*, pp. 44–5). In 1436 he was taxed on an income of £20 per year (E179/192/59). Agnes and Thomas had two children, Thomas II and Elizabeth. By 1456 Thomas II had died *sine prole*, whereupon his widow married John Heton (*q.v.*) who held the manor of Knaptoft until his wife's death in 1465 or 1466. The manor then passed to John Turpyn (*q.v.*) as husband to Thomas's sister and heir, Elizabeth (*Pedigrees*, pp. 44–5; C1/26/345). Thomas Kynsman senior occasionally appeared at the shire court to elect Leicestershire's representatives to parliament but otherwise, neither he nor his son played an active rôle in the administration of the county (C219/13/4; C219/14/2 pt 2 MS 96; C219/14/3 pt 2 MS 96).

LAGO

William Lago of Lubenham was taxed on an income of £26 in 1436 (E179/192/59). In September 1432 he had been commissioned to collect the fifteenth and tenth granted in the previous parliament (*C.F.R.*, 1430–7, p. 107). On two occasions, he is recorded as having attended the shire court to elect the county's MPs, first in 1425 and again in 1449 (C219/14/5 pt 2 MS 102; C219/15/7 pt 2 MS 102). Serving as a juror in 1453, he is referred to as 'esquire' (L.R.O. 5D33/172).

LANGHAM

Robert Langham, esquire, of Gopsall, was one of the electors who returned Robert Moton and Bartholomew Brokesby to parliament in 1422 (C219/13/1). In addition to Gopsall, he held lands in the neighbouring villages of Twycross, Orton-on-the-Hill and Congerstone in the west of the county and at Lowesby in the east (*Village Notes*, III, p. 300). In 1444 he bound himself in an obligation of 110 marks to Robert Moton as surety to deliver to Moton the manor of Basset House (*T.L.A.S.*, 17, 1931–3, pp. 125–6). He married Margaret Charnels, and their son, John, who was still a minor in 1444, later married Joan, daughter of Thomas Appleby (*Pedigrees*, p. 29). Robert Langham died in or before 1453 when his widow and son were named in a plea for debt as the executors of his will (*Pedigrees*, p. 30).

LANGTON

In 1428 a John Langton held a moiety of a knight's fee at West Langton in the hundred of Gartree (*Feudal Aids*, III, p. 124). Eight years later, a Thomas Langton, probably John's son, was taxed on his income of £20 per year (E179/192/59). It is possible that Thomas may have had some association with John Bellers, for on each occasion that Bellers was elected to parliament, 1432, 1435 and 1450, Langton was present among the electors at the shire court (C219/14/3 pt 2 MS 96; C219/14/5 pt 2 MS 102; C219/16/1 pt 2 MS 105). The John Langton who was feodary of the honor of Leicester in 1461 was probably not a member of this family (Somerville, I, p. 569).

MALORY

William Malory of the manor of Walton-on-the-Wolds acquired the manor of South Croxton before 1391 by marriage to Elizabeth, daughter and heir of John Ashby (*Pedigrees*, p. 137). In 1436, John Malory I, their son, was taxed on his income of £20 (E179/192/59). A William Malory, probably John's younger brother, was also assessed on his income of £6. Significantly, at the death of John's grandson in 1489, his inquisition *post mortem* reveals that only the manor of Walton was worth £20 and that the entire estate was valued at over £32 (*C.I.P.M.*, 15 Hen. VII, no. 296). Inquisitions *post mortem* provide notoriously low evaluations so it comes as no surprise that in 1466 John I was fined for failing to assume knighthood (E159/242). His income, therefore, must have exceeded £40 per annum. Between 1429 and 1467 he regularly appeared at the shire court to elect Leicestershire's MPs but he himself appears to have eschewed service in the county (C219/14–17). John I's son, Anthony, was married in 1439 to Anne, daughter of Lawrence Sherard (*q.v.*) (Nichols, II, p. 333; *ibid.*, III, p. 497). Anthony died *vita patris*. When his father died in 1469, therefore, the succession passed to John I's grandson, John II, aged twenty-six (C140/31/17). By this date, John II was already married to Cecily, daughter of John Cotton of Staffordshire (Nichols, III, p. 501). Like his grandfather before him, John II attended the county court for elections but otherwise played no part in shire administration (C219/17/3 pt 3 MS 137). When he died in 1489, his son, John III, aged thirty-two, succeeded him (*Pedigrees*, p. 138). John III's marriage to a daughter of William Assheby produced five daughters among whom the family estate was eventually divided.

MARMYON (MERNYON)

Sir Mauncer Marmyon came from Lincolnshire where, in 1434, he took the oath not to maintain peace-breakers (*C.P.R.*, 1429–36, p. 382). He acquired a temporary interest in Leicestershire by marriage to Elizabeth, daughter and heir of John Wolf of Frolesworth, and widow of Robert Walshale (*q.v.*) (*C.F.R.*, 1445–52, p. 118). The marriage took place between 1431, the year Walshale died, and 1435, when Marmyon attended the shire court at Leicester (*T.L.A.S.*, 12, 1921–2, opp. p. 192; C219/14/5 pt 2 MS 102). The following year he was taxed in Leicestershire on his income of £40 (E179/192/59). Marmyon was elected MP for Lincolnshire in 1447 and, in 1448, he was pricked as sheriff of the county (*Return*, p. 336; Lists and Indexes, IX, p. 79). When Elizabeth Marmyon died in 1449, her manor of Frolesworth devolved to her son by her first marriage, William Walshale (*q.v.*) (E149/186/22). Marmyon appears to have held land in

Galby in his own right but this land had been leased in 1423 and, after the death of Elizabeth, his interest in Leicestershire came to an end (*Village Notes*, II, p. 275; *Pedigrees*, p. 93).

MARSHALL

A number of Marshall or Marchall families appear in Leicestershire in the early fifteenth century and it is not clear what, if any, relationship there was between them. There was a John Marchall of Kilby who witnessed Thomas Asteley's charter of demise of the manor of Newton Harcourt in 1439 (*C.C.R.*, 1435–41, p. 345). In 1455, this same John exchanged land at Kilby with Richard Langham (H.M.C., *Hastings*, I, p. 100). There was also a John Marshall of Upton in the west of the county who married Katherine, one of the coheirs of the manor of Countesthorpe (*Pedigrees*, p. 24). He was an elector at the shire court in 1426 and 1429 (C219/13/4; C219/14/1 pt 2 MS 102). On the latter occasion there were, in fact, two John Marshalls present, though the origin of the second is not stated in the return. In 1372, another John Marshall had been married to Agnes, daughter and coheir of Sir John Waleys of Swithland (*Pedigrees*, pp. 114, 116). According to Farnham, nothing more is heard of Agnes or her husband after 1380 when they recovered seisin and damages at Swithland against the other coheir (*Pedigrees*, p. 114). Nevertheless, in 1436 an Agnes Marshall was taxed on an income of £5 (E179/192/59). On the same occasion, a John Marshall was assessed on his income of £12, but it is not stated if this John was of Swithland, Kilby or Upton. The existence of yet another John Marshall of Bottesford in the hundred of Framland in the north-east of the county, who attended Merton college in 1446 and who later became rector of Redmile, only serves to confuse matters further (Emden, *A Biographical Register of the University of Oxford*, II, p. 1228).

MAYLE (MAYELL)

John Mayle held land at Kirby Muxloe. In 1423, in a covenant between Sir John Blaket and Sir Richard Hastings, he helped to decide the terms of the settlement (H.M.C., *Hastings*, I, p. 294). From the covenant, it seems that Mayle was one of Sir Richard's servants for he had a grant of £2 annually for life from Hastings' manor of Braunstone. Two years earlier, he acted as attorney for Hugh Kent, so it would appear that he had some legal expertise (H.M.C., *Hastings*, I, p. 18). In 1427 and 1429, he was among those who returned Bartholomew Brokesby to parliament (C219/13/5 pt 2 MS 102; C219/14/1 pt 2 MS 102). Mayle was assessed in 1436 on an income of £20 per annum (E179/192/59). He served on three commissions of gaol delivery in 1441 and 1442 (*C.P.R.*, 1436–41, pp. 538, 573; *ibid.*, 1441–6, p. 79).

MERBURY

John Merbury of Hereford, esquire, acquired the manors of Cotesbach, Newbold Verdon, Braunstone and Hemington in Leicestershire through marriage to Agnes, daughter and heir of Thomas Crophill (*Pedigrees*, p. 31). Agnes had been married twice before, to Walter Devereux by whom she had a son, also called Walter, and to John del Par of Westmorland (*C.P.R.*, 1429–36, pp. 144–5). John Merbury had also been married to Alice Oldcastle who may have been the mother of his daughter and heir, Elizabeth (*Pedigrees*, p. 31; *C.P.R.*, 1401–5, p. 116). The marriage between John and Agnes was solemnized between 1415 and 1417 (*C.P.R.*, 1413–16, p. 321; *ibid.*, 1416–22, p. 88). John was a king's esquire to Henry IV, Henry V and Henry VI (*C.P.R.*, 1399–1401, pp. 187, 344; *ibid.*, 1413–16, pp. 42, 321; *ibid.*, 1422–9, p. 91). He served regularly as JP in Herefordshire between 1404 and 1437 and on numerous *ad hoc* commissions. He was pricked as sheriff in the same county in 1405, 1414, 1419, 1422, 1426, 1430 and 1434 (Lists and Indexes, IX, p. 60). In 1419, 1421 (twice), 1425 and 1427, he was elected knight of the shire for Hereford (*Return*, pp. 292, 297, 299, 308, 313). Before 1419 he had been chamberlain of south Wales and, two years later, he was appointed, during pleasure, as chief justice there (*C.P.R.*, 1416–22, pp. 253, 368). The latter appointment was renewed soon after the accession of Henry VI (*C.P.R.*, 1422–9, p. 3). Also in Wales, Merbury was steward and constable of duchy of Lancaster lands in Brecon in 1415, and steward of Kidwelly from 1417 (Somerville, I, p. 639). Agnes Merbury died in 1436 and her husband died two years later (C139/75/32 MS 12; C139/87/43 MS 16). By this time, Agnes's grandson by her first marriage, Walter Devereux, had married John's daughter and heir, Elizabeth. Agnes's estate and her third husband's interest in it therefore passed to the Devereux family.

MOTON

The Motons, a knightly family, had been settled on their manor of Peckleton since the twelfth century (*T.L.A.S.*, 17, 1931–3, pp. 94–5). In addition to their *caput* at Peckleton, they held the manors of Sapcote and Stony Stanton and lands at Sutton and Countesthorp in Leicestershire, but in the fifteenth century their estate also extended into Staffordshire, Lincolnshire and Oxfordshire (*C.C.R.*, 1435–41, p. 475; *ibid.*, 1447–54, p. 24; C139/118/17 MS 2; *V.C.H. Oxon.*, VIII, p. 151; C1/13/163). Sir Robert Moton I, aged seventeen years at the death of his father in 1391, married twice, first to Margery Malory, daughter of Sir Anketin Malory of Warwickshire, who bore him a son and daughter, Reginald and Margery, and second to Elizabeth, daughter of Edward Mulso and widow in turn of Reginald Lathbury and Baldwin Bugge (*q.v.*) (*Early Lincoln Wills*, p. 110; *Pedigrees*, opp. p. 62; Nichols, IV, p. 870; *Visitation*, p. 59). This second marriage was the source of family conflict in the 1440s and 50s between Sir Robert and his son Reginald's family, for it produced a second son, William, for whom Robert wished to make provision at the expense of Reginald's daughters and heirs (C1/22/114a–d). Farnham pours scorn on the suggestion, originally made by Nichols, that Sir Robert was attempting to disinherit his granddaughters. However, the record is quite explicit on the matter of Sir Robert's schemes (*T.L.A.S.*, 17, 1931–3, p. 127; Nichols, IV, p. 869; C1/22/114c). Reginald had married his step-mother's sister-in-law, Margaret Bugge, sister and heir of Baldwin and widow of Richard Turville (*q.v.*). At his death, *vita patris*, in 1445, Reginald's daughters and heirs, Anne and Elizabeth, were aged nine and seven respectively (C139/118/

17 MS 2). Anne later married William Grymmesby (*q.v.*), and Elizabeth married Ralph Pole of Derbyshire (*Pedigrees*, opp. p. 62; *Plumpton Correspondence*, p. 163). Despite Sir Robert I's best efforts on behalf of his second son, the Moton inheritance eventually devolved on Anne and Elizabeth's grandsons, George Vincent and German Pole, when William's grandson, Edward, son of Robert II son of William, died *sine prole* in 1511 (*T.L.A.S.*, 17, 1931–3, p. 110; *Pedigrees*, opp. p. 62). Sir Robert Moton was elected with Bartholomew Brokesby as knight of the shire for Leicestershire in 1422 (*Return*, p. 302). Although he made regular appearances at the shire court as an elector, his administrative service was otherwise undistinguished (C219/13–16). He sat on two commissions of array in 1436 and had been on a commission of oyer and terminer thirty years earlier, in 1406, but he was about seventy-six years old before he was pricked as sheriff in 1451 (*C.P.R.*, 1405–8, p. 230; *ibid.*, 1429–36, pp. 520, 523; *Lists and Indexes*, IX, p. 145). In a suit brought before the chancellor, a John Archer claimed that Robert Moton had examined certain deeds which the latter had declared to be 'good, true and lawfully made' (C1/14/24). It appears, therefore, that Moton had some legal expertise, though not necessarily formal training in the profession. Nevertheless, despite his presumed knowledge of the law, he never sat on the bench as JP. At least in his youth, he was more attracted to martial pursuits. In early June, 1402, he was at sea with Henry IV's admiral, Richard lord Grey of Codnor (*C.P.R.*, 1401–4, p. 175; *Handbook of British Chronology*, 3rd edn, p. 140), and he was with Grey again as a member of his retinue in France in 1415 (Roskell, *The Commons in the Parliament of 1422*, p. 205). Moton had links with other lords, too; with William lord Lovel, for whom he witnessed a charter in 1430; with James Butler, son of the earl of Ormond, for whom he was also a witness in 1449; and with John viscount Beaumont and John Stafford, bishop of Bath and Wells, each of whom acted as Moton's feoffee in 1441 (*C.C.R.*, 1429–35, p. 58; H.M.C., *Hastings*, I, p. 2; *C.C.R.*, 1435–41, pp. 475, 478). Both he and his son, Reginald, associated with Bartholomew Brokesby as witness and feoffee respectively (Bodl. Lib. Wood Empt. 7, fos. 65–5v, 103v–4, 178 (185)). It was probably through this association with Brokesby that Reginald became known to Joan Beauchamp, lady Abergavenny, who bequeathed him 100 marks in her will and a further 100 marks towards the marriage of Reginald's elder daughter (Dugdale, II, p. 1032). Sir Robert Moton died before 1457 and was succeeded at Peckleton by his son, William (*Pedigrees*, opp. p. 62). William played a much more active rôle than his father in Leicestershire affairs. He received regular commissions of the peace between 1469 and 1482 (*C.P.R.*, 1467–77, p. 619; *ibid.*, 1476–85, p. 563); in 1467 he served as escheator (*List of Escheators*, p. 171); he was appointed to three *ad hoc* commissions in 1471, 1472 and 1473, including a commission of array (*C.P.R.*, 1467–77, pp. 287, 350, 405); he was pricked as sheriff in 1471 and, in 1478, he was elected to parliament (*Lists and Indexes*, IX, p. 146; *Return*, p. 364). In May 1480, he was appointed receiver of the honor of Leicester for life (Somerville, I, p. 566). William Moton had close links with lord Hastings. Before April 1475, he had been feoffee for Hastings' manors in the shires of Lincoln, Leicester, York, Northampton and Sussex (H.M.C., *Hastings*, I, p. 296). The following month, on the eve of Hastings' departure for France, Moton was again enfeoffed with manors in these and other counties, and he

continued to act as Hastings' feoffee until his death in 1482 (*C.P.R.*, 1467–77, p. 517; H.M.C., *Hastings*, I, p. 3; *C.F.R.*, 1471–85, p. 234).

NEELE

Sir Richard Neele's association with the law can be traced back to at least 1442 when he was a member of the *quorum* on Leicestershire's bench of JPs and when he gave his second reading (C66/451 MS 29v; *Readings and Moots*, I, p. xxxii). A member of Gray's Inn, he was appointed serjeant-at-law in November 1463 and king's serjeant the following year (*Middle Temple Bench Book*, p. 1; *C.C.R.*, 1461–8, p. 173; *C.P.R.*, 1461–7, p. 387). According to conventional wisdom, Henry VI made him a justice of the king's bench in October 1470 but, on the return of Edward IV, he was transferred in May 1471 to the court of common pleas where he remained until his death in 1486 (Foss, *Biographia Juridica*, p. 474; *D.N.B.*, XIV, p. 167; *T.L.A.S.*, 17, 1931–3, p. 5; *C.P.R.*, 1467–77, pp. 227, 229). However, Neele was a justice of the king's bench before the readeption on 18 April 1469, when he was granted 110 marks annually to maintain his estate (*C.P.R.*, 1467–77, p. 176). In December 1441 he was elected to the parliament which assembled at Westminster the following month (C219/15/2 pt 2 MS 97). It should be noted here that on this point and on much else besides, the entries for Neele in *D.N.B.* and Wedgwood are unreliable. Both claim that the MP was father of the judge, though there is no evidence that this was the case (see *D.N.B.*, XIV, p. 167; Wedgwood, *Biographies*, p. 625; Wedgwood, *Register*, pp. 31, 348, 653; see *Register*, p. 744 n. 1, where Wedgwood's editors later correct his error). In 1442 he also received his first commission of the peace, and thereafter he regularly served as JP in numerous counties, including Leicestershire, until 1485 (*C.P.R.*, 1441–6, p. 473). During the same period, he was appointed to a great number of *ad hoc* commissions including gaol delivery, enquiry, oyer and terminer and as tax assessor. Neele acquired his *caput*, the manor of Prestwold, before 1448 by marriage to Isabel, daughter and coheir of William Ryddyngs (*Pedigrees*, p. 67; cf. *D.N.B.*, XIV, p. 167, where it is claimed he married Isabella Butler of Warrington in Lancashire). This marriage produced two sons, Christopher and Richard (*Pedigrees*, pp. 36, 67; C1/56/236). Sometime after 1476, he took as his second wife, Agnes, daughter and heir of John de Seyton of Rutland and widow of William Fielding (*q.v.*). Christopher Neele added the manor of Keythorp to the family's estate by marriage to another heiress, Margery Rokes, granddaughter and coheir of both Thomas Palmer (*q.v.*) and his second wife, Elizabeth Bishopsden (*Pedigrees*, p. 36; *T.L.A.S.*, 17, 1931–3, p. 49). Nichols claims that Sir Richard Neele also purchased the manor of Tugby but it appears that this manor was not bought until the sixteenth century (Nichols, III, p. 481; *T.L.A.S.*, 17, 1931–3, pp. 49–50).

NEVILLE (OF HOLT)

William Neville was granted the manor of Lubenham in 1450, soon after his marriage to Katherine, daughter and coheir of Thomas Palmer (*q.v.*) and of his second wife, Elizabeth Bishopsden (L.R.O. DE220/58–60). Following Palmer's death in 1475, he further acquired Trussel's manor and Holt's manor, both at Holt, and the manors of Prestgrave and Drayton (*V.C.H. Leics.*, V, p. 222; *C.I.P.M.*, 13 Hen. VII, no. 20; L.R.O. 5D33/174, fo. 263). William was son of Thomas Neville of Rolleston, the wealthy Nottinghamshire esquire whose income in 1436 was £120 per annum (L.R.O. DE220/59; E179/240/266). At Thomas Neville's death in 1482, William was forty-six years old which means he was fifteen years when he married (L.R.O. 5D33/177, fo. 51). At the inquisition taken in 1476 after her father's death, Katherine's age is given as thirty years and more, but she was probably at least nine years old in 1450 because her son was over forty in 1498 (C140/55/9 MS 2; L.R.O. 5D33/177, fo. 51). Katherine died before 1485, about which time William took as his second wife, Jane Fraunceys, daughter and coheir of John Fraunceys of Derbyshire (*Pedigrees*, p. 36; *T.L.A.S.*, 13, 1923–4, p. 217). William Neville died in 1497 and was succeeded by Thomas, his elder son by his first wife (*C.I.P.M.*, 13 Hen VII, no. 20). Thomas had married, in 1472, when he was about fifteen years, Isabel, daughter of Nicholas Griffin of Northamptonshire. Griffin provided a marriage portion of £233-6-8, payable over three years, while William settled on the couple lands worth £10 with the promise of additional lands worth £16-13-4 after the death of his own father (L.R.O. De220/90-1). The marriage produced nine children, including, in addition to Thomas's heir, William, five other sons for whom Thomas provided lands he had purchased in Great Easton and Medbourne (*C.I.P.M.*, 19 Hen. VII, no. 691). A few days before his death in April 1503, Thomas bequeathed £10 towards the marriage of each of his three daughters (PROB11/13/27/229). He was first appointed to the bench of JPs in Leicestershire in May 1485, but it is not certain whether the Thomas Neville, JP in Nottinghamshire in 1478 and 1479, was the same man (*C.P.R.*, 1477–85, pp. 564, 568). G. F. Farnham refers to Thomas as a knight, though on what authority is not stated (*Quorndon Records*, p. 20).

NEVILLE (OF REARSBY)

The Thomas Neville, esquire, whose income in 1436 was £6 per annum was probably the same Thomas of Rearsby who was commissioned two years earlier to collect the fifteenth and tenth (E179/192/59; *C.F.R.*, 1430–7, p. 191). In June 1402, on the basis of information provided by Sir Thomas Rempston, orders had been issued for Neville's arrest (*C.P.R.*, 1401–5, p. 125). As Rempston had been commissioned the previous month to arrest those attempting to subvert the new regime, it is probable that Neville was involved in such subversive activity (*C.P.R.*, 1401–5, pp. 127, 129). In later life, however, his sins amounted to the conventional tardy repayment of debts. Before 1451 Thomas Neville, esquire, had owed 5 marks to Margaret Pykewell (*Village Notes*, VI, p. 242). In 1454, when he is described as of Rearsby, gentleman, and of Newark in Nottinghamshire, he owed £40 to William Villers (*q.v.*) of Brooksby (L.R.O. 5D33/172).

PALMER

Thomas Palmer, esquire, was first elected as knight of the shire for Leicestershire in 1433, and he was returned to parliament on six further occasions between 1439 and 1467, including once for the county of Rutland in 1450 (*Return*, pp. 324, M3, 333, 339, 345, 358; Wedgwood, *Biographies*, p. 658). He was twice appointed as escheator, in 1430 and again in 1439 (*List of Escheators*, p. 170). Between 1432 and 1475 he received regular commissions of the peace, mainly in Leicestershire but also in Northamptonshire (1424–32) and Rutland (1434–58). During his career, he was appointed to close to thirty *ad hoc* commissions in the same counties and to a commission of gaol delivery in Warwickshire in 1428 (*C.P.R.*, 1422–9, p. 499). Four of these *ad hoc* commissions were commissions of array in Leicestershire in 1436, 1457, 1459 and 1470. The Palmer family, originally of Carlton in Northamptonshire, first moved to Leicestershire in 1416 when Thomas's father, William, purchased Trussel's manor at Holt (*T.L.A.S.*, 13, 1923–4, p. 215). Thomas added to the estate in 1427 when he bought the second manor at Holt, Holt's manor, and the nearby manors of Prestgrave and Drayton (L.R.O. 5D33/174, fo. 255). In 1442, he bought the manor of Lubenham from Thomas Baude (*q.v.*) (*C.C.R.*, 1441–7, p. 117; L.R.O. 5D33/174, fo. 260), but he later alienated this manor to his daughter, Katherine, and her husband, William Neville (*q.v.*) (L.R.O. DE220/58). Although Thomas Palmer's declared income in 1436 was £46, he escaped paying a fine for failing to assume knighthood until 1466 (E179/192/59; E159/242). His ability to purchase entire manors suggests, however, even greater wealth, no doubt acquired through his knowledge of the law. In his commissions of the peace he was regularly of the *quorum* (C66/431–535); he may have been the 'Palmer' who was admitted to Lincoln's Inn before 1456 or who attended the Middle Temple (*Lincoln's Inn, Admissions*, p. 13; *Register of Admissions to the Honourable Society of the Middle Temple*, I, ed. H. A. C. Sturgess, London, 1949, p. 3); he was not only feoffee to William lord Zouche but also provided 'good counsel', for which he was awarded the stewardship of Zouche's manor of Thorpe Arnold (L.R.O. 5D33/177, fo. 82). The fact that by 1444 Palmer was feoffee to Nicholas Assheton and Walter Moyle, both serjeants-at-law at that time, further reveals his close association with the legal profession (*C.P.R.*, 1441–6, p. 268). Thomas was also associated with Richard duke of York. In 1449 he was one of the feoffee's for York's manor of Hambleton in Rutland (*C.P.R.*, 1446–52, p. 218). Clearly, however, Palmer's labours on the duke's behalf went far beyond acting as his feoffee because in April 1462, Edward IV granted him £16 annually for ten years from lord Roos's forfeited manor of Freeby for 'good service to the king's father and the king and his losses to the amount of £340' (*C.P.R.*, 1461–7, p. 182). On this occasion, and again in 1466 when the grant was renewed, Palmer was referred to as 'king's servant' (*C.P.R.*, 1461–7, p. 532). In 1463, he received further preferment as receiver of the honor of Leicester (Somerville, I, p. 566). Not surprisingly, his affiliations with the house of York brought him into contact with William Hastings for whom he acted as feoffee between 1460 and 1475 and who, it appears, was one of the executors of Palmer's will (H.M.C., *Hastings*, I, pp. 295, 296, 101). Thomas Palmer married twice. By his first wife, Margaret, he had two daughters, Elizabeth and Margaret. His second wife was Elizabeth, daughter and coheir of Sir William Bishopsden, through whom Palmer acquired the manors of Thornton and Lyndon in Warwickshire (*V.C.H. Warws.*, v, p. 80; *ibid.*, IV, p. 223). This second marriage was solemnized before 1429 and produced two more daughters, Joan and Katherine (L.R.O. DE221/4/1/96; *Pedigrees*, pp. 36, 93). When Thomas died in 1475, his heirs were his daughters Elizabeth, wife of William Greneham and former wife of Thomas Skeffington (*q.v.*), Margaret Burgh, Katherine, wife of William Neville (*q.v.*), and Margaret or Margery, wife of Christopher Neele (*q.v.*) and daughter of Palmer's fourth daughter, Joan Rokes (C140/55/9 MS 2; *Pedigrees*, p. 93).

PAYN

Little is known of the Thomas Payn who paid tax in 1436 on his income of £36 (E179/192/59). He was escheator for Leicestershire and Warwickshire in 1432, and for the same and following year he attended the shire court for the elections (*List of Escheators*, p. 170; C219/14/3 pt 2, MS 94; C219/14/4 pt 2 MS 88). In pardons granted to his debtors, he is referred to as 'esquire' (*C.P.R.*, 1436–41, pp. 6, 459).

PERWYCH

In the early fifteenth century, William Perwych and his son, John, were apparently delinquents in southern Leicestershire. In February and May of 1413 they were accused of threatening the residents of Market Harborough and Great Bowden with violence and murder, and in June of the same year, William and a band of adherents assaulted James Bellers while he was returning home from parliament, leaving him for dead (*C.P.R.*, 1408–13, p. 478; *ibid.*, 1413–16, pp. 36, 114). In 1427, John was one of the electors who returned Bartholomew Brokesby (*q.v.*) and Sir John Boyville (*q.v.*) to parliament (C219/13/5 pt 2 MS 102). Boyville was Perwych's overlord in a manor at Lubenham. John died before 1455 when his son and heir, Richard, escaped from John Boyville's custody to marry without permission (*Pedigrees*, p. 51). In his will, drawn up in February 1503 and proved in 1505, Richard refers to himself as the elder, suggesting that he had a son of the same name. A Richard Perwych did, in fact, administer the will, though another son, Edmund, was appointed executor (PROB11/14/30/233). Richard's heir was William who in 1480 had married Goditha, daughter of Thomas Pulteney (*q.v.*) (*Pedigrees*, p. 49). The only office held by any member of the family between 1422 and 1485 was that of JP to which Richard was appointed during the readeption (*C.P.R.*, 1467–77, p. 619).

PULTENEY

John Pulteney, esquire, of the manors of Pulteney and Misterton, was taxed in 1436 on an income of £33 (E179/192/59). On the same occasion, a Goditha Pulteney was assessed on her income of £13. She was clearly the widow of Thomas Pulteney who in 1428 held a moiety of a knight's fee in Pulteney and

Misterton, but the relationship between Thomas and John is uncertain (*Feudal Aids*, III, p. 124; *Pedigrees*, p. 52). It is probably fair to assume, however, that John was Thomas's nephew. John was escheator in Leicestershire in 1440–1, commissioner of gaol delivery the same year and JP in 1460 (*List of Escheators*, p. 170; *C.P.R.*, 1436–41, p. 538; *ibid.*, 1452–61, p. 669). In 1458 he was fined for failing to assume knighthood (E159/234). He married Margaret, daughter of Thomas Walsh (*q.v.*), by whom he had a son Thomas (*Pedigrees*, p. 54). He died in 1469 when Thomas was aged about twenty-eight years (E149/222/12 MS 2). Thomas was pricked as sheriff in November 1478, served as JP from 1482 to 1485 and was commissioner of array in 1484 (Lists and Indexes, IX, p. 146; *C.P.R.*, 1476–85, pp. 564, 400). A year earlier he had been appointed to assess the subsidy in Leicestershire (*C.P.R.*, 1476–85, p. 396). He was knighted in 1487 at the coronation of Elizabeth of York (Shaw, *The Knights of England*, I, p. 142). Thomas's son, John, died *vita patris* in 1493 (*C.I.P.M.*, 8 Hen. VII, no. 788). Thomas died in 1507 when his grandson, Thomas, aged twenty-seven years, was his heir (*C.I.P.M.*, 22 Hen. VII, no. 204).

SHERARD

Laurence Sherard, esquire, was son of Robert Sherard who indented to serve Henry V in France in 1415 (E101/69/5 MS 419). The family's *caput* was the manor of Stapleford in Leicestershire but Laurence also inherited the manor of Barrow in Cottesmore, Rutland, through his mother, Agnes Hauberk (*V.C.H. Rut.*, II, p. 123). He was pricked as sheriff of Rutland in 1437, but his first official appointment was in the previous year as commissioner of array for Leicestershire where he later became sheriff (1443–4) and JP (1444–50) (Lists and Indexes, IX, pp. 112, 145; *C.P.R.*, 1429–36, p. 520; *ibid.*, 1441–6, p. 473). Sometime before 1420, Laurence married Isabel or Elizabeth Woodford, daughter of John and sister of Sir Robert Woodford (*q.v.*) (Nichols, II, p. 333). Their daughter, Anne, married Anthony Malory (*q.v.*) in 1439 (Nichols, III, p. 497); their eldest son, Robert II, married Elizabeth Durant, daughter and heir of John Durant of Cottesmore in Rutland (L.R.O. DG40/481). This marriage must have taken place before 1445 when Robert was independently established at Cottesmore (*C.P.R.*, 1444–6, p. 346). Robert was still alive in 1452 when he was pricked as sheriff of Rutland (Lists and Indexes, IX, p. 113) but he probably died before 1457 to be succeeded by his brother, Geoffrey (*C.C.R.*, 1454–61, p. 208). Geoffrey was appointed sheriff of Rutland in 1467, 1479 and 1483 (Lists and Indexes, IX, p. 113); he was JP on all commissions of the peace in Leicestershire between 1474 and 1485 and he also served on numerous *ad hoc* commissions in the county including four commissions of array (*C.P.R.*, 1467–77, pp. 190, 350, 405, 619; *ibid.*, 1476–85, pp. 396, 400, 489, 563). By 1477 he was a servant of William Hastings, though in what capacity is unclear as his name never appears among Hastings' feoffees (L.R.O. DG40/282). This fact suggests that Sherard may have been a household servant rather than a legal advisor. He seems, however, to have had some legal expertise, for he was of the *quorum* of JPs in November 1475 and in July 1483 (C66/535 MS 26v; C66/552 MS 18v). The name 'Sherard' appears, too, among those attending Lincoln's Inn in 1489

(*Lincoln's Inn, Admissions*, p. 25). Geoffrey married Joyce, daughter of Thomas Assheby (*q.v.*) of Lowesby. He died in 1492 and was succeeded by his eldest son, Thomas, who by that date was already married to Margaret Hellewell and was the father of four sons, each of whom is mentioned in their grandfather's will (PROB11/9/23/176v–7; *V.C.H. Rut.*, II, p. 159).

SHIRLEY

When Hugh Shirley died in 1403 his estate included manors in Warwickshire, Suffolk, Derbyshire and Nottinghamshire (*Stemmata Shirleiana*, p. 37). Under the terms of the will of Hugh's maternal uncle, the third and last Ralph, lord Basset of Drayton, Hugh was to receive the Basset inheritance provided he assumed the name and arms of Basset (*Stemmata Shirleiana*, pp. 34, 376). As this bequest was made at the expense of lord Basset's true heirs, Thomas earl of Stafford and Alice Chaworth, Hugh and his son, Sir Ralph I, did not have immediate and peaceful seisin of the property in question (G.E.C., II, pp. 3–4, n.f.). On 8 August 1424, however, Basset's last surviving feoffee, John Brown, released to Sir Ralph I numerous manors including the manors of Ragdale, Dunton Basset, Willows and Ratcliffe-on-Wreake in Leicestershire (*C.A.D.*, V, A11388). Sir Ralph must have had *de facto* tenure of these manors before 1424 for he was appointed to Leicestershire's bench of JPs between 1415 and 1422, and served on two Leicestershire commissions, including a commission of array, in 1419 (*C.P.R.*, 1413–16, p. 420; *ibid.*, 1416–22, pp. 212, 251, 454). He was elected knight of the shire for the county in November 1420, a few days after being pricked as sheriff for Derbyshire and Nottinghamshire (*Return*, p. 295; Lists and Indexes, IX, p. 103). In the tradition of Ralph Basset, he went to France in 1415–16, though whether he found the experience as financially rewarding as his great-uncle had done must remain a mystery (L.R.O. 26D53/2545; E404/31/175; McFarlane, *The Nobility of Later Medieval England*, p. 31). Nevertheless, Sir Ralph Shirley expanded the estate he inherited by a judicious marriage to Joan, daughter and heir of Thomas Bassett, thereby adding the manor of Brailsford to the family holdings in Derbyshire (Dugdale, I, p. 622). Joan Bassett was dead before 1419, by which date Sir Ralph had taken Alice Cockayne as his second wife (*H.M.C. Rut.*, IV, p. 52). Alice died in 1466 (E149/219/9). The removal of the family's *caput* to Leicestershire was achieved through the marriage in 1423 of Sir Ralph's son and heir, Ralph II, to Margaret, daughter of John, and sister and heir of Thomas Staunton of Staunton Harold (L.R.O. 26D53/254; E149/127/12). At the time of their marriage, Ralph II was about fifteen years old while his wife was barely eighteen years. Margaret bore a son, John, who was born before 1426 but she must have died soon after this date. Ralph II's second wife, Elizabeth, daughter of Sir Thomas Blount, was dead by 1457, but she had borne him five daughters and a son (L.R.O. 72′30/1/37; L.R.O. 26D53/192–3; *Village Notes*, IV, pp. 296–7). By 1458, Ralph II was married for the third time, to Lucy Ashton, widow of Sir Bertram Entwistle (L.R.O. 26D53/195; *Stemmata Shirleiana*, p. 49). Ralph Shirley II was an esquire of the chamber during the 1440s (E101/409/9, fos. 36v–7; E101/409/11, fo. 38; E101/409/16, fo. 35), but his career seems to have been otherwise undistinguished. He died in 1466, a few months

after the death of his step-mother, Alice Cockayne (C140/19/18 MS 3). He was
succeeded by his son John who, of all the fifteenth-century Shirleys, managed to
make do with only one wife. John had married Eleanor Willoughby of
Nottinghamshire by 1456 and she presented him with a large family of twelve
children (L.R.O. 26D53/1947; *Stemmata Shirleiana*, p. 51). In his will, dated 26
March 1485, he made provision for eleven of these children (L.R.O. 26D53/
1947). John's son and heir, Ralph III, had already married around 1474, when he
was about fourteen years old, to Elizabeth, daughter and coheir of Thomas
Walsh (*q.v.*) (L.R.O. 26D53/543). Their only child, a daughter Anne, married
Sir Thomas Pulteney (*q.v.*) (L.R.O. 5D53/86, fo. 1). In 1496, Ralph III married
Anne Vernon of Derbyshire but by 1507 he had a third wife, Anne Warner
(L.R.O. 26D53/2552; *Stemmata Shirleiana*, p. 39). By his fourth and final wife,
Joan Sheffield, Ralph III eventually sired a son, Francis (Dugdale, II, p. 622).
Ralph III died in 1513 (L.R.O. 26D53/1948). The Shirley family was undoub-
tedly one of Leicestershire's most wealthy knightly families. Nevertheless, after
the death of Sir Ralph I in or around 1443, no member of the family assumed the
dignity of knighthood, preferring instead to accept distraint for failing to do so
(*Stemmata Shirleiana*, p. 43; E159/234). In 1436, Sir Ralph had been assessed in
Derbyshire on an income of £100 per year but his mother, Beatrice, wife of
Hugh had an income of £92 while another Ralph Shirley probably Sir Ralph's
son, was assessed on £40 (E179/240/266). Beatrice lived until 1440 while Ralph
II's step-mother almost outlived him (C139/101/65 MS 2; E149/219/9). John
Shirley had a step-mother and a large family to provide for, too. Shirley
resources, therefore, were thinly spread during the fifteenth century. In the
1470s, both John and Ralph III were members of lord Hastings' retinue
(Dunham, 'Lord Hastings' indentured retainers 1461–1483', pp. 119, 120), but
during the period considered for office bearing, neither man performed administrative service in the county. Ralph III did, however, become sheriff of
Leicestershire in 1493 (Lists and Indexes, IX, p. 146). There was, nevertheless, a
family tradition of activity on behalf of the duchy of Lancaster. Hugh Shirley
had been constable of Castle Donington from 1400 and master-forester at
Duffield in 1402 (Somerville, I, pp. 573, 556); Sir Ralph I was appointed master-
forester in the honor of Leicester for life in 1414 (Somerville, I, p. 568); Ralph III
was master-forester at Duffield in 1493, steward and then constable at Melbourne, steward of Appletree hundred and steward of Castle Donington
(Somerville, I, pp. 557, 558, 559, 573).

SKEFFINGTON

Two John Skeffingtons were taxed in Leicestershire in 1436 (E179/192/59). One
had an income of £26 and was almost certainly John Skeffington of the manor
of Skeffington in the hundred of East Goscote (*V.C.H. Leics.*, V, pp. 7, 215;
Pedigrees, pp. 92–3). The income of the other John Skeffington, of Arnesby, was
£5. He was probably the son of John of Skeffington. John I attended the shire
court to elect Baldwin Bugge (*q.v.*) and John Boyville (*q.v.*) in 1425 (C219/13/4).
John II married Margaret, daughter and heir of William Ouldbeif. Their son,
Thomas I, married Elizabeth, one of the daughters and coheirs of Thomas

Palmer (*q.v.*) by his first wife. Thomas I was one of the electors who returned John Bellers (*q.v.*) and Robert Staunton (*q.v.*) to parliament in 1450 (C219/16/1 pt 2 MS 105). He attended the shire court again in 1460 to elect his father-in-law, Thomas Palmer, and Robert Staunton to parliament (C219/17/1 pt 21 MS 112). Thomas I died before 1476 by which date his wife was remarried to William Greneham (C140/55/9 MS 2). His son, Thomas II, was father of Sir William Skeffington, Henry VIII's master of the ordnance and deputy in Ireland (*D.N.B.*, XVIII, p. 323). The Skeffingtons avoided local office in Leicestershire during the fifteenth century.

SOTEHILL

Henry Sotehill of Lincolnshire, esquire, acquired the manor of Stockerston in Gartree hundred in right of his wife Anne, daughter and coheir of John Boyville (*q.v.*) (*V.C.H. Leics.*, v, p. 304; *Pedigrees*, pp. 102–6; *Village Notes*, v, p. 118). Boyville died *c.* 1467 but it is possible that Sotehill had married Anne as early as 1451 when he bought land at Allexton from John Chesilden (*q.v.*) (*C.C.R.*, 1447–54, pp. 265–6). By 1450, he was a member of Sir John Fastolf's council, clearly as a legal advisor, and he continued in this rôle until Fastolf's death in 1459 (*Paston Letters*, II, pp. 38, 134; *ibid.*, I, p. 86). No doubt it was through his association with Fastolf that Henry forged links with the Yorkist party. He was feoffee for Richard earl of Warwick by 1453, and he served Richard duke of York in the same capacity (*C.P.R.*, 1452–61, p. 49; *ibid.*, 1476–85, pp. 279, 341). From 1456 to 1466, Sotehill was an apprentice-at-law in the duchy of Lancaster where, once again, his connections were with the earl of Warwick, first as the latter's under-steward at Pontefract in 1458–9 and, from 1460, as his deputy chief steward of the North Parts (Somerville, I, pp. 425, 454). In April 1461, he was appointed king's attorney general, a position he held until July 1471 (*C.P.R.*, 1461–7, p. 6). By July 1471, Henry's earlier affinity with Warwick was now viewed with suspicion, and the fact that he had been elected to the readeption parliament would have strengthened doubts about his loyalty (E404/71/6/39). Nevertheless, by 1472 he was returned to the bench of JPs for the West Riding where he had regularly been JP since 1454 (*C.P.R.*, 1467–77, p. 638, *ibid.*, 1452–61, p. 683; *ibid.*, 1461–7, p. 577). In November 1475 he was transferred from the Yorkshire commissions of the peace to those of Leicestershire and Rutland where he continued to act as JP until 1484 (*C.P.R.*, 1467–77, pp. 619, 627; *ibid.*, 1476–85, pp. 563, 570). In both counties he was also appointed to numerous *ad hoc* commissions including two commissions of array in Leicestershire in 1484 (*C.P.R.*, 1476–85, pp. 400, 489). By Anne Boyville, Henry fathered four sons and two daughters (PROB11/10/15/121). His eldest son and heir, John, was married, probably in 1475, to Elizabeth Plumpton, granddaughter and coheir of Sir William Plumpton. The arrangements for this marriage had been made in 1464 when Elizabeth was three years old, and the agreement between Henry Sotehill and Sir William Plumpton envisaged that the wedding would take place when Elizabeth turned fourteen years (*Plumpton Correspondence*, pp. lxxi, lxxxviii). John and Elizabeth produced six sons and two daughters before he died in 1493 and she in 1506 (PROB11/15/19/152). Their eldest son, Henry, married

Biographical notes

to Joan Empson, daughter of Henry VII's chancellor of the duchy of Lancaster and financial advisor, predeceased his mother (PROB11/14/31/244).

STAUNTON (OF SUTTON-ON-SOAR)

Thomas Staunton of Sutton-on-Soar was a cousin of the Margaret Staunton who married Ralph Shirley (*q.v.*) (*Pedigrees*, p. 101). He was taxed in Nottinghamshire in 1436 on an annual income of £30 but, as he was distrained in 1467 for failing to assume knighthood, his true income was evidently much higher (E179/240/266; E159/243). Thomas's father, also called Thomas, was a king's esquire who had served in Guienne in 1415 (*C.P.R.*, 1413–16, pp. 278, 388; E101/69/6 MS 471). Thomas the younger was also a king's esquire and marshal of the hall of the household by 1433 in which year he was appointed master-forester in Derbyshire (*C.P.R.*, 1429–36, p. 272). Although he relinquished this office in 1439 in favour of Robert Babthorp, other preferments were bestowed upon him (*C.P.R.*, 1436–41, p. 351); in 1439, as usher of the chamber, he was granted the constableship of Dryslwyn castle and the keepership of Glincothy forest, both in Wales (*C.P.R.*, 1436–41, p. 298); in 1442, he received confirmation of an earlier grant of £18 from the manor of Bolsover in Derbyshire (*C.P.R.*, 1441–6, p. 63). Thomas was also appointed to duchy of Lancaster offices in Derbyshire and Leicestershire. He was steward and receiver of Melbourne from 1437, though from 1444 the stewardship was held jointly with his son, John (Somerville, I, pp. 557, 558; Somerville accords this Thomas the constableship of Melbourne in 1418 as well, but on that occasion the office was probably in his father's hands). In 1444, Thomas and John were jointly appointed to the constableship of Castle Donington for life, and in 1449, Thomas alone was appointed to the receivership of the honor of Leicester (Somerville, I, pp. 573, 566). During the political turmoil of February and March 1450, Staunton was entrusted with keeping William de la Pole, duke of Suffolk, in the Tower, though he was relieved of this post on 19 March (*Rot. Parl.*, v, p. 177; *C.P.R.*, 1446–52, p. 311). In 1440 and 1448, he was pricked as sheriff for Nottingham and Derbyshire (Lists and Indexes, IX, p. 103). He and Richard Hotoft (*q.v.*), another duchy of Lancaster official, were returned by the Leicestershire electors to the parliament which assembled at Bury St Edmunds in 1447 to effect the downfall of Humphrey duke of Gloucester (*Return*, p. 336). Continuing service in the household, however, must have kept Thomas in London for long periods (E101/410). He was appointed to only two commissions during the 1450s, the first in 1453 to raise a loan in Nottingham, Derbyshire and Rutland, and the second in 1457 on the Leicestershire commission of array (*C.P.R.*, 1452–61, pp. 53, 402). Despite close links with Henry VI and with one of the king's staunchest supporters, John viscount Beaumont, for whom Staunton had been feoffee since 1437 (*C.P.R.*, 1436–41, p. 35), Thomas probably played a relatively minor rôle during the upheavals of 1460 and 1461. He and his son, John, received a pardon for past transgressions in February 1462 (C67/45 MS 39). John had even become a page of Edward IV's chamber by 1466 (E101/411/15; E101/412/2, fo. 35). Thomas had three daughters, Elizabeth, Margaret and Katherine, and two sons, John and Thomas, both of whom died *vita patris sine prole* (*Village Notes*, II, p. 370; *ibid.*, V, p. 77; *W.H.R.*, no. 265). Elizabeth married William Hasilrigge (*q.v.*) as her first husband and then Thomas Entwysell (*q.v.*) (*Pedigrees*, pp. 56–7). Katherine married John Turville (*q.v.*) while Margaret married John Wylys (*Pedigrees*, p. 101). Thomas Staunton died in 1483, his son John having died in 1476 (*C.F.R.*, 1471–85, pp. 253, 100).

STAUNTON (OF DONINGTON)

Robert Staunton of Castle Donington, esquire, was the brother of Thomas Staunton (*q.v.*) of Sutton-on-Soar. His first wife was Agnes Lathbury of Derbyshire but, according to Farnham, he married a second time to Margery, daughter and coheir of Richard Byron of Lancashire, widow of Thomas Walsh (*q.v.*) of Wanlip who, says Farnham, died in 1493 (*Stemmata Shirleiana*, p. 48; *Pedigrees*, p. 141). Robert Staunton, however, had possession of Wanlip long before 1493. In a pardon dated November 1468, he is referred to as 'Robert Staunton of Onelip, esquire, *alias* of Donington' (C67/46 MS 19). His pardon at the readeption also refers to him as of Wanlip and Castle Donington, though in this case he is accorded the status of gentleman (C67/44 MS 3). Thomas Walsh, in fact, died in 1463 and Robert had evidently married his widow by 1468 (*C.F.R.*, 1461–71, p. 94). According to E. P. Shirley, Elizabeth and Katherine Staunton were Robert's daughters but he has mistakenly attributed to Robert the offspring of Thomas Staunton (*q.v.*) (*Stemmata Shirleiana*, p. 48; see *Village Notes*, II, pp. 370–1; *ibid.*, V, p. 77; *W.H.R.*, no. 265). That Robert had a son, also called Robert, is evidenced by the fact that his pardon of 1470 and another of 1462 refers to him as Robert senior (C67/44 MS 3; C67/45 MS 44). The writ of *diem clausit extremum* issued after the death of Robert Staunton in 1471, almost certainly signifies the death of Robert senior's son (*C.F.R.*, 1471–85, p. 2). Robert senior was elected to parliament as burgess for Grimsby in 1447 and was returned again in 1450 and 1467 as knight of the shire for Leicestershire (*Return*, pp. 336, 345, 358). Between 1454 and 1482 he was regularly appointed to Leicestershire commissions of the peace and, until 1473, he also served on *ad hoc* commissions including commissions of array in 1457, 1459 and 1472 (*C.P.R.*, 1452–61, pp. 402, 560; *ibid.*, 1467–77, p. 350). He received, too, commissions of the peace in Derbyshire between 1443 and 1457. From 1453 to 1457 he was steward for the earl of Stafford in Nottingham and Leicestershire (Rawcliffe, *The Staffords, Earls of Stafford and Dukes of Buckingham*, p. 204). Sometime before 1475, he became a feoffee for lord Hastings (H.M.C., *Hastings*, I, p. 296). Before Hastings left England for France in 1475, he again enfeoffed Staunton with his estate (*C.P.R.*, 1467–77, p. 517). By 1480, Robert Staunton was Hastings' deputy steward at Castle Donington and he himself became steward there in 1485 (Somerville, I, pp. 572, 573). Robert appears to have had legal expertise; between 1454 and 1482 he was regularly appointed to the *quorum* of JPs and, sometime between 1467 and 1471 he, along with his brother, Thomas, acted as pleaders before chancery on behalf of Thomas Hotoft (C66/478–548; C1/40/290). He died, apparently without issue, before August 1489 (Somerville, I, p. 573; cf. Wedgwood, *Biographies*, p. 802, where it is suggested, on flimsy evidence, that Staunton died before January 1483).

Biographical notes

TEMPLE

In 1428, Robert Temple of Sibson was appointed to collect the subsidy on knights' fees (*Feudal Aids*, III, p. 106). He attended the shire elections in 1422 and 1429 which both returned Bartholomew Brokesby (C219/13/1; C219/14/1 pt 2 MS 102), but there is no discernible connection between the two men. Robert held parcels of land at Temple, Wellsborough, Sibson, Carleton, Sheepy Parva and Barton-in-the-Beans but none of these holdings is identifiable as a manor (*C.A.D.*, VI, C4306, C4574). Nicholas Temple, esquire, son of Thomas son of Robert, had seisin of the family lands by 1462 (*C.A.D.*, VI, C6328, C6437). He was escheator in Leicestershire in 1475–6 (*List of Escheators*, p. 171) and one of the electors who returned William Trussell (*q.v.*) and William Moton (*q.v.*) to the parliament which met in 1478 (C219/17/3 pt 3 MS 137).

TRUSSELL (OF ELMESTHORPE)

Sir William Trussell I was knight of the shire for Leicestershire in the parliament which assembled in December 1421 (*Return*, p. 300). Until the election of December 1441, his name often heads the lists of electors in the county court (C219/13–15). Despite these contributions to local affairs, Trussell's interests appear to have been military in nature. He fought at the battle of Agincourt in 1415, in the retinue of Humphrey duke of Gloucester, and his involvement in the war continued until at least 1430 when he went to France again in the retinue of Richard Beauchamp, earl of Warwick (Nicolas, *History of the Battle of Agincourt*, p. 333; *D.K.R.*, 44th report, p. 564; *D.K.R.*, 48th report, p. 269). Links with Gloucester continued, however. In 1436, Sir William witnessed a conveyance of the manor of Ashby de la Zouche to the duke (H.M.C., *Hastings*, I, p. 1). In 1446 and 1449, he was acting with Sir Leonard Hastings (*q.v.*) as a witness to grants of land in Leicestershire. These associations, first with Gloucester and then with Hastings, may have no political significance. Nevertheless, given the fact that Trussell received a pardon on 7 June 1450, immediately following the collapse of Cade's rebellion in which the fate of Gloucester, who died in mysterious circumstances in 1447, had more than historical interest to the commons in Kent, and in which the name of Hastings' employer, the duke of York, was invoked, one's suspicions about Trussell's political affiliations in 1450 are aroused (*C.P.R.*, 1446–52, pp. 355, 356; 'Stowe's Memoranda', in *Three Fifteenth-Century Chronicles*, pp. 95, 97; C. L. Kingsford, *English Historical Literature in the Fifteenth Century*, repr. New York, 1972, p. 360). Unfortunately, it has proved impossible to confirm or deny these suspicions, for Trussell disappears from the record throughout the remainder of the 1450s. He died in 1464 and was succeeded by his son, Sir Thomas, aged forty years and more (C140/9/16 MS 6; E149/214/10 MS 1). If Sir William Trussell's political sympathies may have lain with the Yorkists, those of his son tilted towards the opposite direction. In 1440 Sir Thomas indented to serve Humphrey Stafford, earl of Stafford and duke of Buckingham, for life with six armed men in return for an annuity of 10 marks from Oakham in Rutland (Rawcliffe, *The Staffords, Earls of Stafford and Dukes of Buckingham*, p. 235). Sir Thomas may have been with the duke at Ludford in 1459 or at Northampton in 1460. His presence at either of these affrays would certainly help to explain his inclusion among other Lancastrian supporters whose lands in Rutland and Northamptonshire were taken into the king's hands in May 1461 (*C.P.R.*, 1461–7, p. 35). However, he was sufficiently in favour by 1467 to receive a commission of the peace in Leicestershire, and in October 1469 and February 1470, Edward IV's teetering government appointed him to commissions of array in Warwickshire and Leicestershire respectively (*C.P.R.*, 1467–77, pp. 196, 199, 618). Sir Thomas was dead by November 1471 when his son, William II, was licensed to enter his estate (*C.P.R.*, 1467–77, p. 306). Sir William II was a trusted servant of Edward IV. He was knight of the body from 1472 to 1481, and in 1475 he indented to serve the king in France with six spears and sixty archers (Wedgwood, *Biographies*, p. 878; *C.P.R.*, 1467–77, p. 470; E101/71/6 MS 987). He was returned knight of the shire for Leicestershire in 1472 and 1478 when, on both occasions, his brother (?), Edward, appeared among the electors (*Return*, pp. 361, 364; C219/17/2 pt 2 MS 131; C219/17/3 pt 3 MS 137). In 1475 he was pricked as sheriff for the county (*Lists and Indexes*, IX, p. 146). Some months earlier, in March, Trussell became one of lord Hastings' indentured retainers (Dunham, 'Lord Hastings' indentured retainers 1461–1483', p. 141). When he died in 1481, in addition to his *caput* at Elmesthorpe in Leicestershire, Sir William II was seised of manors and lands in eight other counties, valued conservatively at about £200 per annum. (C140/78/83 MS 2–14). Back in 1436, his grandfather's declared income had been half that amount (E179/192/59). The custody of Sir William II's son, Edward, who was still a minor, was granted to lord Hastings (*C.P.R.*, 1476–85, pp. 275–6). Edward's death in June 1499 was followed six months later by that of his infant son, John (*C.I.P.M.*, 14 Hen. VII, no. 411; *ibid.*, 22 Hen. VII, no. 232).

TURPYN

John Turpyn, esquire, acquired the manor of Knaptoft by marriage before 1466 to Elizabeth, daughter and heir of Thomas Kynsman I (*Pedigrees*, pp. 44–5; Nichols, IV, p. 225; *Village Notes*, V, pp. 391–2). John was a lawyer, being admitted to Lincoln's Inn in 1460 and becoming marshal of the society in 1474 (*Lincoln's Inn, Admissions*, p. 14; *Lincoln's Inn, Black Books*, I, p. 62; *Readings and Moots*, I, pp. ix, x, xi). He was appointed to the Leicestershire bench of JPs in January 1483 and twice in May 1485, on each occasion as a member of the *quorum* (*C.P.R.*, 1476–85, p. 564; C66/549 MS 29v; C66/557 MS 23v). His son, William, married Mary, possibly a daughter of Thomas Neville (*q.v.*) of Holt. William was attending Lincoln's Inn by 1489 (*Lincoln's Inn, Admissions*, p. 25).

TURVILLE

The family of Turville acquired the manor of Aston Flamville by the marriage before 1399 of Richard Turville to Katherine, daughter and heir of Sir William Flamville (*Pedigrees*, pp. 4–5). Richard's son, also Richard, married Margaret Bugge, sister and heir of Baldwin (*q.v.*) (*Pedigrees*, p. 5; Nichols, II, p. 465). This Richard died about 1435 but the much married Margaret lived until 1474 (C140/

49/21 MS 4). At her death, her grandson, John Turville, inherited her manors of Normanton Turville, Thurlaston, Stoke Golding, Wigston Magna and Croft (C140/49/21 MS 4). John was the son of William Turville and his wife, Elizabeth, daughter of Thomas Fouleshurst (*q.v.*). John married Katherine, daughter and coheir of Thomas Staunton (*q.v.*) who bore him six children before his death in 1506 (*C.I.P.M.*, 22 Hen. VII, no. 199; PROB11/15/15/119v; *W.H.R.*, no. 765). Very occasionally, the name Turville appears among the lists of Leicestershire electors, including Richard Turville who helped to elect his brother-in-law, Baldwin Bugge, in 1426 (C219/13/4). However, between 1422 and 1485, no member of the family served in any office within the shire.

VILLERS

When John Villers I died in 1416, he held a messuage at Kirby Muxloe, called 'Pakeman's Place', and lands at Barton, Ravenstone, Wigston, Odston and Turlangton in addition to his *caput*, the manor of Brooksby (C138/12/22 MS 2). In the inquisition *post mortem*, his heir is given as his son, John II, aged twelve years and more. In 1429, in an inquisition *probatio aetatis*, jurors claimed that William Villers, son and heir of John Villers (I) was born on 1 September 1405 (C139/42/74 MS 2). William may have been a younger brother of John II who had apparently died between 1417 and 1429 (*C.P.R.*, 1416–22, pp. 28, 339). That William was the ultimate heir of John I becomes apparent in a pardon granted to him in July 1447 where he is referred to as William Villers of Brooksby, esquire, *alias* of Kirby (C67/39 MS 39). William was taxed in 1436 on his income of £6, but the identity of the John Villers whose income on the same return is recorded as £7 is unclear (E179/192/59). William was appointed to a commission of array in 1436 and to a commission of enquiry in 1450 (*C.P.R.*, 1429–36, p. 520; *ibid.*, 1446–52, p. 384). Until 1460, he regularly attended the shire court for elections (C219/13–17). At the election of 1429, however, an Alexander Villers is listed among the named electors (C219/14/1 pt 2 MS 102). Alexander may have been William's great-uncle (Nichols, III, pp. 197–8). William married Joanna, daughter of John Bellers I (*q.v.*) and sister and coheir of John Bellers II. Their son, John Villers III, acquired the manors of Eye Kettleby and Sysonby in 1477 as his share of his maternal uncle's estate (C140/52/27; C140/76/57 MS 2). In 1446, William had granted John III all his lands and tenements in Kirby but John sold the manor there to William Hastings in 1474 for 200 marks (H.M.C., *Hastings*, I, pp. 20–1, 19). The John Villers who died in 1506 was probably the son of John III (*C.I.P.M.*, 22 Hen. VII, no. 329; *Visitations*, p. 30). The identity of Geoffrey Villers who was appointed escheator in 1468 is not clear, but as a Geoffrey Villers had been lord of Brooksby in the fourteenth century, there is strong reason to suppose that the escheator was a member of the same family (*List of Escheators*, p. 171; H.M.C., *Hastings*, I, p. 83).

WALSH

Thomas Walsh, esquire, was sheriff of Warwick and Leicestershire in 1456–7 (Lists and Indexes, IX, p. 145). Between 1456 and 1460 he was regularly appointed to Leicestershire commissions of the peace, and in 1459 he was placed on the commission of array to resist the duke of York's rebellion (*C.P.R.*, 1452–61, pp. 669, 560). In 1459 or 1460, he was appointed, probably by queen Margaret for whom he was a squire, as receiver of the honor of Leicester (Somerville, I, p. 566; *T.L.A.H.S.*, 52, 1976–7, p. 42). His support for the Lancastrian cause, however, was sufficiently inconspicuous for him to receive a pardon in February 1462 (C67/45 MS 39). He died before October 1463 when a writ of *diem clausit extremum* was directed to the escheator in Warwickshire and Leicestershire (*C.F.R.*, 1461–71, p. 94). Thomas married Margery Byron in 1449 (*C.C.R.*, 1447–54, p. 108). His heirs were his daughters, Helen and Elizabeth, who married respectively Sir William Littleton and Sir Ralph Shirley (*q.v.*) (*V.C.H. Worcs.*, III, p. 120 n. 70; L.R.O. 26D53/543). Thomas's father was Richard Walsh who held the third part of a knight's fee at Wanlip in 1428 and who was taxed on his income of £13 in 1436 (*Feudal Aids*, III, p. 120; E179/192/59). He may have been one of the Walshes admitted to Lincoln's Inn before 1420 and in 1428 (*Lincoln's Inn, Admissions*, pp. 3, 5). Between 1426 and 1447, Richard regularly attended the shire court at election time (C219/13–15). Richard's elder brother, also Thomas, was a lunatic by 1422 when he was placed in the custody of his sister, Margaret, and her husband, Sir Thomas Gresley (*C.P.R.*, 1416–22, p. 409, *ibid.*, 1422–9, p. 4). He was later transferred to the care of his nephews, John and Hugh Boyville (*q.v.*) (*C.P.R.*, 1436–41, p. 424).

WALSHALE

In 1428, Robert Walshale I held the manor of Frolesworth by a quarter of a knight's fee in right of his wife, Elizabeth, daughter and heir of John Wolf (*Feudal Aids*, III, p. 124; *T.L.A.S.*, 12, 1921–2, pp. 190–4). He may have attended Lincoln's Inn before 1420 (*Lincoln's Inn, Admissions*, p. 3). When Robert died in 1421, his widow married Mauncer Marmyon who held Frolesworth until his wife's death in 1449, whereupon it passed to her son, William Walshale (*C.F.R.*, 1445–52, p. 118; E149/186/22). William first married Margaret, daughter of Sir Thomas Everyngham of Warwickshire, but by 1451 he was married to Joan Garton, daughter and heir of John Garton, through whom he laid claim to certain lands in Coventry (C1/16/518). In October 1451, however, the authorities in the town bought off his claim for £10 (*Coventry Leet Book*, p. 268). Joan was probably the mother of William's son and heir, Robert II, but before he died in 1462, William took a third wife, named Katherine (C67/45 MS 15; *C.F.R.*, 1461–71, p. 113; E159/242; L.R.O. 5D33/177, fo. 77). At Robert's death in 1511 the Walshale connection with Frolesworth came to an end (*T.L.A.S.*, 12, 1921–2, p. 195).

WHATTON

Thomas Whatton and John Whatton were taxed in 1436 on incomes of £13 and £6 respectively (E179/192/59). They may have been brothers. They held lands at Long Whatton and Mountsorell, though neither of these tenements is identifiable as a manor (*Village Notes*, IV, pp. 296–9; *Quorndon Records*, p. 132). In

1417, Thomas received a pardon for the death of his brother, George, at Long Whatton (*C.P.R.*, 1416–22, p. 101). He was first appointed to Leicestershire's bench of JPs in 1418 but he was not appointed again until 1436 (*C.P.R.*, 1416–22, p. 454; *C.P.R.*, 1436–41, p. 585). Between 1436 and 1445 he was regularly on the *quorum* on the bench (C66/440–59). His legal training had been at Lincoln's Inn before 1420 (*Lincoln's Inn, Admissions*, p. 3). Thomas's last appointment as JP was in 1448 (*C.P.R.*, 1446–52, p. 590). In 1439, 1441 and 1442 he served on five *ad hoc* commissions of enquiry and gaol delivery (*C.P.R.*, 1436–41, pp. 368, 369, 538, 573; *ibid.*, 1441–6, p. 79). From 1427, during the minority of John Beaumont, he was feoffee for John's lands (*C.F.R.*, 1422–30, p. 174). Perhaps this association with Beaumont had an influence on John Whatton's later career. He had been a commissioner to enquire into weights and measures in 1422 (*C.P.R.*, 1416–22, p. 423). Apart from an appearance at the shire court in 1429 to elect Bartholomew Brokesby and Everard Digby (*q.v.*), we hear nothing more of him until 1447 when he was an esquire of the chamber (C219/14/1 pt 2 MS 102; E101/410/9, fo. 43; E101/409/16, fo. 34v; E101/401/1, fo. 30v). On 1 November 1459, the Leicestershire electors returned him to the parliament which met at Coventry to attaint the Yorkist lords, and six days later he was appointed escheator (C219/16/5 MS 62; *List of Escheators*, p. 171). His son and heir, Robert, was granted a pardon in May 1462 (C67/45 MS 26). John died in 1460 (Wedgwood, *Biographies*, p. 939).

WOODFORD

By the beginning of the fifteenth century, the Woodfords had built up a large estate in the north-east of Leicestershire comprising seven manors acquired either by purchase or by marriage to heiresses (B.L. Cotton Claudius, A XIII). When John Woodford, former commissioner of array (1399) and JP in Leicestershire (1401) died in 1401, his son, Robert, was a minor (*C.P.R.*, 1399–1401, pp. 212, 560; *ibid.*, 1401–5, p. 102). In 1409, however, Sir Robert settled his affairs in England before departing for France (B.L. Cotton Claudius, A XIII, fo. 223). He may also have attended Lincoln's Inn before 1420 (*Lincoln's Inn, Admissions*, p. 3). He was taxed in 1436 on an income of £40, but his mother, Mabil, was still alive then and the income from her dower property was a further £26 (E179/192/59). Sir Robert was present at the county court for the elections of 1429 and 1433 but he himself was never elected to parliament or appointed to public office (C219/14/1 pt 2 MS 102; C219/14/4 pt 2 MS 88). His wife, Isabel, daughter of Sir William Neville of Rolleston, bore him seven children, but the eldest son, Thomas, died *vita patris*. When Sir Robert died in 1456, he was succeeded by his grandson, Ralph (C139/162/20 MS 2; *C.F.R.*, 1452–61, p. 160). Ralph was pricked as sheriff in November 1466 and he received two commissions of the peace in December 1470 (Lists and Indexes, IX, p. 145; *C.P.R.*, 1467–77, p. 619). However, his service to the readeption was pardoned in January 1472 (C67/48 MS 19). Ralph married Elizabeth Villers, daughter of William (*q.v.*). She bore him four sons and a daughter (PROB11/11/23/182v–3v). The eldest son and heir, William, died in his father's lifetime in 1487, leaving a daughter, Margaret as his heir (*C.I.P.M.*, 3 Hen. VII, no. 352).

WYVYLL

Robert Wyvyll, esquire, held a quarter knight's fee at Stonton Wyville of the duchy of Lancaster (*Feudal Aids*, III, p. 122). He served on two *ad hoc* commissions of enquiry and arrest in 1414 and 1422, but 1422 was the last time he or any member of his family held office in the fifteenth century (*C.P.R.*, 1416–22, p. 444; *ibid.*, 1413–16, p. 179). Until 1435, he regularly attended the shire court for elections (C219/13–14). In 1429, his son, William I, was also an elector (C219/14/1 pt 2 MS 102). William's last recorded appearance at elections was in November 1450 when he helped to return John Bellers and Robert Staunton to parliament (C219/16/1 pt 2 MS 105). Robert Wyvyll's income in 1436 was £20 per annum (E179/192/59). William I's son, William II, was the last of the Wyvylls at Stonton. He died in May 1494 when his heir was his cousin, Katherine Warde, aged eleven, daughter of William II's aunt Margaret (*C.I.P.M.*, 10 Hen. VII, no. 1049). However, Katherine did not receive the manor of Stonton Wyville. William II's widow, Margaret, daughter of Thomas Entwysell, sold the manor to Robert Brudenell, whom she took as her second husband, in order to raise money to perform her first husband's will (*Pedigrees*, p. 110).

BIBLIOGRAPHY

A   MANUSCRIPT SOURCES

Public Record Office

C1	Early Chancery Proceedings
C66	Patent Rolls
C67	Patent Rolls – Supplementary, Pardons
C138–41	Chancery, Inquisitions *post mortem*, Hen. V. – Rich. III
C143	Chancery, Inquisitions *ad quod damnum*
C145	Chancery, Miscellaneous Inquisitions
C219	Parliamentary Writs and Returns
E36	Exchequer, Treasury of the Receipt
E101	Exchequer, King's Remembrancer, Accounts Various
E149	Exchequer, King's Remembrancer, Inquisitions *post mortem*
E153	Exchequer, King's Remembrancer, Escheators' Files
E159	Exchequer, King's Remembrancer, Memoranda Rolls
E179	Exchequer, King's Remembrancer, Subsidy Rolls
E199	Exchequer, King's Remembrancer, Sheriffs' Accounts
E368	Exchequer, Lord Treasurer's Remembrancer, Memoranda Rolls
E372	Exchequer, Pipe Office, Pipe Rolls
E404	Exchequer, Warrants for Issues
JUST3	Justices Itinerant, Gaol Delivery Rolls
KB9	King's Bench, Ancient Indictments
PROB11	Prerogative Court of Canterbury Wills

Bodleian Library

Wood Empt. 7 Brooksby Cartulary

British Library

Additional Manuscripts (Addl. MSS)   23938 Compotus roll of Queen Margaret's expenses coming into England

Cotton Claudius, A XIII   Woodford Cartulary

Egerton Rolls   8770–5 Beauchamp accounts 3 Hen. IV–14 Hen. VI

Bibliography

Harley Manuscripts

265 *Registrum Chartarum*
Familiae de Berkeley
6166 The King's Book ... 17 Hen. VII

Leicester Museum

As all manuscripts stored here must now be ordered through, and consulted in, the Leicestershire Record Office, they appear under the following entry.

Leicestershire Record Office

5D33	Farnham Manuscripts
72'30	Charters and Deeds
44'28	Rothley Manuscripts
26D53	Ferrers Collection
DE220	Peake Manuscripts
DE221	Peake (Neville of Holt) Manuscripts
DG5	Winstanley Manuscripts
DG21	Hazlerigg Manuscripts
DG40	Gretton (Sherard) Manuscripts
10D34	Wyggeston Hospital

Lincolnshire Archives Office

Episcopal Registers	XII	[Buckingham]
	XIII	[Beaufort]
	XIV, XV	[Repingdon]
	XVI	[Flemyng]
	XIX	[Lumley]
	XX	[Chedworth]

Rockingham Castle

F3/10   Cartularium de Kirby Bellars

B   PUBLISHED SOURCES

The Account of the Great Household of Humphrey, First Duke of Buckingham for the Year 1452–3, ed. M. Harris, Camden Miscellany 28, 4th ser. 29, London, Royal Historical Society, 1984.

The Babees Book, ed. F. J. Furnivall, London, E.E.T.S. o.s. 32, 1868, Greenwood repr., New York, 1969.

A Book of Precedence etc., ed. F. J. Furnivall, London, E.E.T.S. e.s. 8, 1869, Kraus rept, New York, 1975.

The Book of the Knight of La Tour-Landry, ed. T. Wright, London, E.E.T.S. o.s. 33, 1906, Greenwood rev. edn, New York, 1969.

Bibliography

Calendar of Charter Rolls, VI, 5 Hen. VI–8 Hen. VIII, 1427–1516, London, H.M.S.O., 1927.

A Calendar of Charters and Other Documents Belonging to the Hospital of William Wyggeston at Leicester, ed. A. H. Thompson, Leicester, Backus, 1933.

Calendar of the Close Rolls Preserved in the Public Record Office, 1422–85, 9 vols., London, H.M.S.O., 1933–54.

Calendar of Entries in the Papal Registers Relating to Great Britain and Ireland, VI–XIII, London, H.M.S.O., 1904–55.

Calendar of the Fine Rolls Preserved in the Public Record Office, 1422–85, XV–XXI, London, H.M.S.O., 1935–61.

Calendar of Inquisitions Post Mortem Preserved in the Public Record Office, Henry VII, 3 vols., London, H.M.S.O., 1898–1955.

Calendar of the Patent Rolls Preserved in the Public Record Office, 1399–1485, 15 vols., London, H.M.S.O., 1900–11.

Calendar of Plea and Memoranda Rolls Preserved among the Archives of the Corporation of the City of London at the Guildhall, A.D. 1413–1437, ed. A. H. Thomas, Cambridge, Cambridge University Press, 1943.

Calendar of Plea and Memoranda Rolls Preserved among the Archives of the Corporation of the City of London at the Guildhall, A.D. 1437–1457, ed. P. E. Jones, Cambridge, Cambridge University Press, 1954.

Calendar of State Papers and Manuscripts Existing in the Archives and Collections of Milan, I, ed. A. B. Hinds, London, H.M.S.O., 1912.

Calendar of State Papers and Manuscripts Relating to English Affairs Existing in the Archives and Collections of Venice, I, 1202–1509, London, H.M.S.O., 1864, Kraus repr., Nendeln, Liechtenstein, 1970.

Calendars of Lincoln Wills, I, 1320–1600, ed. C. W. Foster, London, British Record Society, XXVIII, 1902, Kraus repr., New York, 1968.

Capgrave, John, *The Chronicle of England*, ed. F. C. Hingeston, Rerum Britannicorum Medii Aevi Scriptores, Rolls Series, 1, London, Longman, 1858.

Caxton's Book of Curtesye, ed. F. J. Furnivall, London, E.E.T.S. e.s. 3, 1868, Kraus repr., New York, 1975.

The Cely Letters 1472–1488, ed. A. Hanham, London, Oxford University Press, 1975.

Child-Marriages, Divorces and Ratifications etc. in the Diocese of Chester, A.D. 1561–6, ed. F. J. Furnivall, London, E.E.T.S. o.s. 108, 1897, Kraus repr., New York, 1978.

Chronicle of the Rebellion in Lincolnshire, 1470, ed. J. G. Nichols, Camden Miscellany 1, London, Camden Society, 1847.

The Coventry Leet Book, ed. M. D. Harris, London, E.E.T.S. o.s. 134, 135, 138, 146, 1907–8, Kraus repr., New York, 1971.

Defoe, D. *A Tour through England and Wales*, 2 vols., London, Everyman, 1928.

A Descriptive Catalogue of Ancient Deeds in the Public Record Office, 6 vols., London, H.M.S.O., 1890–1915.

Documents Illustrative of the Social and Economic History of the Danelaw, ed. F. M. Stenton, Records of the Social and Economic History of England and Wales, v, London, British Academy 1920.

The Domesday of Inclosures 1517–1518, ed. I. S. Leadam, 2 vols., London,

Bibliography

Historical Society of Great Britain, 1897, Kennikat repr., Port Washington, NY, 1971.

Early Lincoln Wills, ed. A. Gibbons, Lincoln, 1888.

Early Records of Furnival's Inn, ed. D. S. Bland, Newcastle-upon-Tyne, King's College, 1957.

Early Treatises on the Practice of the Justice of the Peace in the Fifteenth and Sixteenth Centuries, B. H. Putnam, Oxford Studies in Social and Legal History, VIII, Oxford, Oxford University Press, 1924.

Elyot, Sir Thomas, *The Gouernour*, introd. F. Watson, London, J. M. Dent, 1937.

An English Chronicle of the Reigns of Richard II, Henry IV, Henry V, and Henry VI. Written before the Year 1471, ed. J. S. Davies, Camden o.s. 64, London, Camden Society 1856, Johnson repr., New York, 1968.

English Historical Documents c. 500–1042, ed. D. Whitelock, 2nd edn, London, Eyre Methuen, 1979.

English Historical Documents 1427–1485, ed. A. R. Myers, London, Eyre and Spottiswoode, 1969.

Farnham, G., *Leicestershire Medieval Village Notes*, 6 vols., Leicester, W. Thornley and Son, 1929–33.

Medieval Pedigrees, Leicester, W. Thornley and Son, 1925.

Farrer, W., *Honors and Knights' Fees*, 3 vols., London, Spottiswoode, Ballantyre and Co., 1923–5.

Fletcher, W. G. D., *The Earliest Leicestershire Lay Subsidy Roll, 1327*, Lincoln, J. Williamson, [1891?].

Fortescue, Sir John, *De Laudibus Legum Anglie*, ed. S. B. Chrimes, Cambridge, Cambridge University Press, 1942, repr. 1949.

The Governance of England, ed. C. Plummer, London, Oxford University Press, 1885.

Grants, etc. from the Crown during the Reign of Edward the Fifth, ed. J. G. Nichols, Camden o.s. 60, London, Camden Society, 1854.

The Grey of Ruthin Valor, ed. R. I. Jack, Sydney, Sydney University Press, 1965.

The Historical Collections of a Citizen of London in the Fifteenth Century, ed. J. Gairdner, London, Camden n.s. 17, London, Camden Society 1876, Johnson repr., New York, 1965.

Historical Manuscripts Commission, *Report on the Manuscripts of . . . Reginald Rawdon Hastings . . .*, I, London, H.M.S.O., 1928.

Twelfth Report, Appendix, Part IV, *The Manuscripts of . . . the Duke of Rutland*, 4 vols., London, H.M.S.O., 1888–1905.

Fifty-Fifth Report on the Manuscripts in Various Collections, 8 vols., II, London, H.M.S.O., 1903.

Sixty-Ninth Report (Middleton), London, H.M.S.O., 1911.

Historie of the Arrivall of Edward IV in England and the Finall Recouerye of his Kingdomes from Henry VI A.D. 1471, ed. John Bruce, Camden o.s. 1, London, Camden Society, 1838.

The Household Book of Dame Alice de Bryene, ed. V. B. Redstone, Suffolk Institute of Archaeology and History, Bungay, Paradigm Press, 1984.

Bibliography

The Household of Edward IV. The Black Book and the Ordinance of 1478, ed. A. R. Myers, Manchester, Manchester University Press, 1959.

The Illustrated Journeys of Celia Fiennes 1685–c. 1712, ed. C. Morris, London, Macdonald and Co. Ltd, 1982.

Index of Ancient Petitions of the Chancery and the Exchequer, Lists and Indexes, I, revised edn, London, P.R.O., 1892, Kraus repr., New York, 1966.

Ingulph's Chronicle of the Abbey of Croyland with the Continuations by Peter of Blois and Anonymous Writers, trans. H. T. Riley, London, Bohn's Antiquarian Library, 1854.

Inquisitions and Assessments Relating to Feudal Aids . . . 1284–1431, 6 vols., London, H.M.S.O., 1899–1920, Kraus repr. Nendeln, Liechtenstein, 1973.

Issues of the Exchequer, ed. F. Devon, London, Record Commission, 1837.

The Itinerary of John Leland, ed. L. T. Smith, 4 vols., London, George Bell and Son, 1906, Centaur Press repr., London, 1964.

John of Gaunt's Register, 1371–1375, ed. S. Armitage Smith, 2 vols., Camden, 3rd ser. 20 and 21, London, Camden Society, 1911.

John of Gaunt's Register, 1379–1383, ed. E. C. Lodge and R. Somerville, 2 vols., Camden, 3rd ser. 56 and 57, London, Camden Society, 1937.

Langland, William, *The Vision of Piers Plowman*, ed. A. V. C. Schmidt, London, Dent, 1978.

Letters and Papers, Foreign and Domestic, Henry VIII, 2nd edn, 21 vols., London, H.M.S.O., 1864–1920, Kraus repr., New York, 1965.

Letters and Papers Illustrative of the Wars of the English in France during the Reign of Henry the Sixth, ed. J. Stevenson, Rerum Britannicorum Medii Aevi Scriptores, Rolls Series, 2 vols., London, Longman, 1861–4.

Letters of Queen Margaret of Anjou, ed. C. Monro, Camden o.s. 86, London, Camden Society, 1863, Johnson repr., London, 1968.

List and Index of Warrants for Issues, 1399–1485, P.R.O., Lists and Indexes, Supplementary series no. IX, vol. 2, London, H.M.S.O., New York, Kraus Reprint Corporation, 1964.

List of Escheators for England, A. C. Wood, compiler, typescript volume, Round Room, London, P.R.O. 1932.

List of Sheriffs for England and Wales, P.R.O., Lists and Indexes no., IX, London, H.M.S.O., 1898.

Materials for a History of Henry VII, ed. W. Campbell, Rerum Britannicorum Medii Aevi Scriptores, Rolls Series, 2 vols., London, Longman, 1873–7.

The Middle Temple Bench Book, ed. J. B. Williamson, 2nd edn, London, The Middle Temple, 1937.

The Paston Letters 1422–1509, ed. J. Gairdner, 6 vols., London, Chatto and Windus, 1904, Ams Press repr., New York, 1965.

Paston Letters and Papers of the Fifteenth Century, ed. N. Davis, parts I and II Oxford, Oxford University Press, 1971–6.

The Plumpton Correspondence, ed. T. Stapleton, Camden o.s., 4, London, Camden Society, 1839.

Proceedings and Ordinances of the Privy Council of England, ed. N. H. Nicolas, 7 vols., London, Record Commission, 1834–7.

Proceedings before the Justices of the Peace in the Fourteenth and Fifteenth Centuries,

Bibliography

Edward III to Richard III, ed. B. H. Putnam, London, Spottiswoode, Ballantyne and Co. Ltd, 1938.

Quorndon Records, ed. G. Farnham, London, Mitchell Hughes and Clarke, 1912.

Readings and Moots at the Inns of Court in the Fifteenth Century, I, ed. S. E. Thorne, London, Selden Society, LXXI, 1954 for 1952.

Records of the Borough of Leicester, ed. M. Bateson, revised by W. H. Stevenson and J. E. Stocks, 3 vols., London and Cambridge, 1899–1905.

The Records of the Honorable Society of Lincoln's Inn. Admissions, 1420–1790, London, Lincoln's Inn, 1896.

The Records of the Honorable Society of Lincoln's Inn. The Black Books, I, 1422–1586, London, Lincoln's Inn, 1897.

Register of Admissions to the Honourable Society of the Middle Temple, I, ed. H. A. C. Sturgess, London, Butterworth, 1949.

The Register of Thomas Langley Bishop of Durham 1406–1437, ed. R. L. Storey, 3 vols., London Surtees Society, CLXIV, CLXVI, CLXIX, 1956–9.

A Relation, or Rather a True Account, of the Island of England, ed. C. A. Sneyd, Camden o.s. 37, London, Camden Society, 1847.

Reports of the Deputy Keeper of the Public Records, 41st report (Calendar of the Norman Rolls, Hen. V), London, H..M.S.O., 1880.

42nd report (Calendar of the Norman Rolls, Hen. V), London, H.M.S.O., 1881.

44th report (Calendar of the French Rolls, 1–10 Hen. V), London, H.M.S.O., 1883.

48th report (Calendar of the French Rolls, Hen., VI), London, H.M.S.O., 1887.

Return of Every Member, Part I, Parliaments of England, 1213–1702, London, House of Commons, 1878.

Rotuli Parliamentorum; ut et Petitiones et Placita in Parliamento, II–VI, London, 1767–77.

Shirley, E. P., *Stemmata Shirleiana*, 2nd edn, London, Nichols and Sons, 1873.

A Small Household of the Fifteenth Century, ed. K. L. Wood-Legh, Manchester, Manchester University Press, 1956.

The Statutes of the Realm, 11 vols., London, Record Commission, 1810–28.

The Stonor Letters and Papers 1290–1483, ed. C. L. Kingsford, 2 vols., Camden 3rd ser., 29–30, London, Royal Historical Society, 1919.

Testamenta Vetusta, ed. N. H. Nicolas, 2 vols., London, 1826.

Thomson, S. D., 'Some Medbourne Deeds from the Peake (Neville of Holt) Manuscripts (Third Deposit)', unpublished University of London Diploma in Archives Administration, 1955.

Three Books of Polydore Vergil's English History, Comprising the Reigns of Henry VI, Edward IV and Richard III, ed. Sir Henry Ellis, Camden o.s. 29, London Camden Society, 1844.

Three Fifteenth-Century Chronicles, ed. J. Gairdner, Camden n.s. 28, London, Camden Society, 1880.

Transcripts of Charters Relating to the Gilbertine Houses of Sixle, Ormsby, Catley, Bullington, and Alvingham, ed. F. M. Stenton, Horncastle, Publications of the Lincoln Record Society, 18, 1922 for 1920.

Bibliography

Valor Ecclesiasticus, 6 vols., London, Record Commission, 1810–34.

Visitation of the County of Leicester in the Year 1619 Taken by William Camden, ed. J. Fetherston, London, Harleian Society, II, 1870.

Walter of Henley's Husbandry, ed. E. Lamond, London, Longman, Green and Co., 1890.

Warkworth, John, *A Chronicle of the First Thirteen Years of the Reign of King Edward the Fourth*, ed. J. O. Halliwell, Camden o.s. 10, London, Camden Society, 1839.

Worcestre, William, *Itineraries*, ed. J. H. Harvey, Oxford, Oxford University Press, 1969.

Wrottesley, G., *Pedigrees from the Plea Rolls*, London, Harrison and Sons, 1892.

C   SECONDARY SOURCES

Archer, R. E., 'Rich old ladies: the problem of late medieval dowagers', in *Property and Politics: Essays in Later Medieval English History*, ed. A. J. Pollard, Gloucester, Alan Sutton, 1984, pp. 15–31.

Armstrong, C. A. J., 'The inauguration ceremonies of the Yorkist kings and their title to the throne', *T.R.H.S.*, 4th ser., 30, 1948, pp. 51–73.

Ashley, M., *The English Civil War*, London, Thames and Hudson, 1974.

Astill, G. G., 'The medieval gentry: a study in Leicestershire society, 1350–1399', unpublished PhD thesis, University of Birmingham, 1977.

Aston, M., *The Fifteenth Century: The Prospect of Europe*, London, Thames and Hudson, 1968.

Avery, M. E., 'An evaluation of the effectiveness of the court of chancery under the Lancastrian kings', *The Law Quarterly Review*, 86, 1970, pp. 84–97.

'The history of the equitable jurisdiction of chancery before 1460', *B.I.H.R.*, 42, 1969, pp. 129–44.

Baker, A. H. R., 'Changes in the later middle ages', in *A New Historical Geography of England before 1600*, ed. H. C. Darby, Cambridge, Cambridge University Press, 1976, pp. 186–247.

Barton, J. L., 'The medieval use', *The Law Quarterly Review*, 81, 1965, pp. 562–77.

Basin, T., *Histoire de Charles VII*, II, 1445–50, ed. Charles Samaran, Paris, Les Classiques de l'histoire de France au moyen âge, 1944.

Bean, J. M. W. '"Bachelor" and retainer', *Medievalia et Humanistica*, n.s., 3, 1971, pp. 117–31.

The Decline of English Feudalism, 1215–1540, Manchester, Manchester University Press, 1968.

Bell, H. N., *The Huntingdon Peerage*, London, Baldwin, Cradock & Joy, 1820.

Bennett, H. S., *The Pastons and their England. Studies in an Age of Transition*, 2nd edn, Cambridge, Cambridge University Press, 1968.

Bennett, M. J., *Community, Class and Careerism: Cheshire and Lancashire Society in the Age of 'Sir Gawain and the Green Knight'*, Cambridge, Cambridge University Press, 1983.

'A county community: social cohesion amongst the Cheshire gentry, 1400–1425', *Northern History*, 8, 1973, pp. 24–44.

Bibliography

'Provincial gentlefolk and legal education in the reign of Edward II', *B.I.H.R.*, 57, 1984, pp. 203–7.

Beresford, M., *The Lost Villages of England*, London, Lutterworth, 1954.

Beresford, M., and Hurst, J. G., *Deserted Medieval Villages*, London, Lutterworth, 1971.

Beresford, M. W., and St Joseph, J. K. S., *Medieval England. An Aerial Survey*, Cambridge Air Surveys, II, Cambridge, Cambridge University Press, 1958.

Bindoff, S. T., *The House of Commons, 1509–1558*, 3 vols., London, History of Parliament Trust, 1982.

Britnell, R. H., 'Minor landlords in England and medieval agrarian capitalism', *Past and Present*, 89, 1980, pp. 3–22.

Brooke, C. N. L., 'Marriage and society in the central middle ages', in *Marriage and Society. Studies in the Social History of Marriage*, ed. R. B. Outhwaite, London, Europa Publications, 1981, pp. 17–34.

Butler, J., *Fifteen Sermons Preached at the Rolls Chapel and a Dissertation upon the Nature of Virtue*, ed. W. R. Matthews, London, G. Bell and Sons, 1967.

Cam, H., 'The legislators of medieval England', *Proc. Brit. Acad.*, 31, 1945, pp. 127–50.

Cam, H. M., *The Hundred and the Hundred Rolls. An Outline of Local Government in Medieval England*, London, Methuen, 1930.

Liberties and Communities in Medieval England, Cambridge, Cambridge University Press, 1944.

'Shire officials: coroners, constables and bailiffs', in *The English Government at Work 1327–1336*, III, ed. J. F. Willard *et al.*, Cambridge, Mass., The Medieval Academy of America, 1950, pp. 143–83.

Camden, W., *Britannia*, trans. Richard Gough, 2nd edn, 4 vols., London, John Stockdale, 1806, Georg Olms Verlag repr., Hildesheim and New York, 1974.

Cantor, L. M., 'The medieval parks of Leicestershire', *T.L.A.S.*, 46, 1970–1, pp. 9–24.

Carpenter, C., 'The Beauchamp affinity: a study of bastard feudalism at work', *E.H.R.*, 95, 1980, pp. 514–32.

'The religion of the gentry of fifteenth-century England', in *England in the Fifteenth Century. Proceedings of the 1986 Harlaxton Symposium*, ed. D. Williams, Woodbridge, Boydell Press, 1987, pp. 53–74.

Carpenter, M. C., 'Political society in Warwickshire c. 1401–72', unpublished PhD thesis, University of Cambridge, 1976.

The Catholic Encyclopedia, ed. C. G. Herbermann *et al.*, 16 vols., New York, Robert Appleton Co., 1907–17.

Cherry, M., 'The Courtenay earls of Devon: the formation and disintegration of a late medieval aristocratic affinity', *Southern History*, 1, 1979, pp. 71–97.

Chew, H. M., *The English Ecclesiastical Tenants-in-Chief and Knight Service*, London, Oxford University Press, 1932.

Chrimes, S. B., *Lancastrians, Yorkists and Henry VII*, 2nd edn, London, Macmillan, 1966.

Cokayne, G. E., *The Complete Peerage*, 2nd edn, 12 vols., rev. V. Gibbs, London, 1910–59.

Bibliography

Collingwood, R. G., *Roman Britain*, new edn, London, Oxford University Press, 1953.

Cooper, J. P., 'The counting of manors', *Econ. Hist. Rev.*, 2nd ser., 8, 1956, pp. 377–89.

Cornwall, J., 'The early Tudor gentry', *Econ. Hist. Rev.*, 2nd ser., 17, 1964–5, pp. 456–75.

'The people of Rutland in 1522', *T.L.A.H.S.*, 37, 1961–2, pp. 7–28.

Coss, P. R., *The Langley Family and its Cartulary. A Study in Late Medieval 'Gentry'*, Dugdale Occasional Papers, 22, Oxford, Dugdale Society, 1974.

Creasey, J., 'Industries of the countryside', in *Seasons of Change. Rural Life in Victorian and Edwardian England*, ed. S. Ward, London, Allen & Unwin, 1982, pp. 66–98.

Crompton, J., 'Leicestershire lollards', *T.L.A.H.S.*, 44, 1970 for 1968–9, pp. 11–44.

Curtis, J., *A Topographical History of the County of Leicester*, Ashby de la Zouch, 1831.

Darby, H. C., and Versey, G. R., *Domesday Gazeteer*, Cambridge, Cambridge University Press, 1975.

Denholm-Young, N., *The Country Gentry in the Fourteenth Century*, Oxford, Oxford University Press, 1969.

'Feudal society in the thirteenth century: the knights', *History*, n.s., 39, 1944, pp. 107–19.

History and Heraldry 1254–1310, London, Oxford University Press, 1965.

Dictionary of National Biography, ed. Sir L. Stephen and Sir S. Lee, 21 vols., London, Oxford University Press, 1937–8.

Dockray, K., 'Why did fifteenth-century English gentry marry?: the Pastons, Plumptons and Stonors revisited', in *Gentry and Lesser Nobility in Late Medieval Europe*, ed. M. Jones, Gloucester, Alan Sutton, 1986, pp. 61–80.

Driver, J. T., 'The knights of the shire for Worcestershire during the reigns of Richard II, Henry IV and Henry V', *Transactions of the Worcestershire Archaeological Society*, n.s., 40, 1963, pp. 42–64.

Du Boulay, F. R. H., *An Age of Ambition. English Society in the Late Middle Ages*, London, Nelson, 1970.

'Who were farming the English demesnes at the end of the middle ages', *Econ. Hist. Rev.*, 2nd ser., 18, 1965, pp. 443–55.

Dugdale, Sir William, *The Antiquities of Warwickshire*, 2 vols., London, 1730.

Monasticon Anglicanum, ed. J. Caley, H. Ellis and B. Bandinel, 6 vols., London, Longman, 1817–30.

Dunham, W. H., 'Lord Hastings' indentured retainers, 1461–1483', *Transactions of the Connecticut Academy of Arts and Sciences*, 39, 1955, pp. 1–175.

Dury, G. H., *The East Midlands and the Peak*, London, Nelson, 1963.

Dyer, C., 'A small landowner in the fifteenth century', *Midland History*, 1, 3, 1972, pp. 1–14.

Warwickshire Farming 1349–c. 1520. Preparations for Agricultural Revolution, Oxford, Oxford University Press, 1981.

Elton, G. R., 'The rolls of parliament, 1449–1547', *Historical Journal*, 22, 1, 1979, pp. 1–29.

Bibliography

Emden, A. B., *A Biographical Register of the University of Cambridge to 1500*, Cambridge, Cambridge University Press, 1963.

A Biographical Register of the University of Oxford to A.D. 1500, 3 vols., Oxford, Oxford University Press, 1957–9.

Everitt, A., *The Community of Kent and the Great Rebellion, 1640–60*, Leicester, Leicester University Press, 1966.

ed., *Suffolk and the Great Rebellion 1640–1660*, Ipswich, Suffolk Records Society, III, 1961.

Farnham, G. 'Ashby-de-la-Zouch, manorial notes', *T.L.A.S.*, 15, 1927–8, pp. 85–96.

'Frolesworth: the descent of the manor', *T.L.A.S.*, 12, 1921–2, pp. 189–95.

'Notes on the descent of the manor of Claybrook', *T.L.A.S.*, 12, 1921–2, pp. 201–11.

'Quenby, the manor and hall', *T.L.A.S.*, 16, 1929–31, pp. 16–42.

'Rothley: the descent of the manor', *T.L.A.S.*, 12, 1921–2, pp. 35–98.

Farnham, G. F. 'Belgrave', *T.L.A.S.*, 16, 1929–31, pp. 42–71.

'Charnwood Forest and its historians', *T.L.A.S.*, 15, 1927–8, pp. 2–32.

'The Charnwood manors', *T.L.A.S.*, 15, 1927–8, pp. 140–292.

'Gaddesby: notes on the manor', *T.L.A.S.*, 13, 1923–4, pp. 257–80.

'Hallaton: the descent of the manor', *T.L.A.S.*, 13, 1923–4, pp. 142–8.

'Market Bosworth: the Harcourt family', *T.L.A.S.*, 15, 1927–8, pp. 103–23.

'Notes on the manor of Ragdale', *T.L.A.S.*, 14, 1925–6, pp. 184–97.

'Prestwold and its hamlets in medieval times', *T.L.A.S.*, 18, 1934–5, pp. 3–84.

'Potters Marston: some notes on the manor', *T.L.A.S.*, 12, 1921–2, pp. 169–77.

'The Skeffingtons of Skeffington: appendix', *T.L.A.S.*, 15, 1927–8, pp. 104–28.

'Stoke Golding: manorial history', *T.L.A.S.*, 14, 1925–6, pp. 206–15.

Farnham, G. F., and Herbert, A., 'Fenny Drayton and the Purefey monuments', *T.L.A.S.*, 14, 1925–6, pp. 88–112.

Farnham, G. F., and Skillington, S. H., 'The manor of Peckleton', *T.L.A.S.*, 17, 1931–3, pp. 94–144.

Farnham, G. F. and Thompson, A. H. 'The castle and the manor of Castle Donington', *T.L.A.S.*, 14, 1925–6, pp. 32–77.

'The manor and advowson of Medbourne 1086–1550', *T.L.A.S.*, 13, 1923–4, pp. 92–132.

'The manor, house and chapel of Holt', *T.L.A.S.*, 13, 1923–4, pp. 200–45.

'The manor of Noseley', *T.L.A.S.*, 12, 1921–2, pp. 214–71.

'The manors of Allexton, Appleby and Ashby Folville', *T.L.A.S.*, 11, 1919–20, pp. 406–75.

Ferguson, A. B., *The Indian Summer of English Chivalry*, Durham, NC, Duke University Press, 1960.

Ffoulkes, C., *Armour and Weapons*, Wakefield, EP Publishing Ltd, 1973.

Ffoulkes, C. J., 'European arms and armour', in *Social Life in Early England*, ed. G. Barraclough, London, Routledge and Kegan Paul, 1960, pp. 124–38.

Flandrin, J.-L., *Families in Former Times*, trans. R. Southern, Cambridge, Cambridge University Press, 1979.

Bibliography

Fleming, P. W., 'Charity, faith and the gentry of Kent 1422–1529', in *Property and Politics: Essays in Later Medieval English History*, ed. A. J. Pollard, Gloucester, Alan Sutton, 1984, pp. 36–58.

Fletcher, A., *A County Community in Peace and War: Sussex 1600–1660*, London, Longman, 1975.

Foss, E., *Biographia Juridica. A Biographical Dictionary of the Judges of England 1066–1870*, London, 1870.

Fox, L., *The Administration of the Honor of Leicester in the Fourteenth Century*, Leicester, Edgar Backus, 1940.

Gibson, S. T., 'The escheatries 1327–41', *E.H.R.*, 36, 1921, pp. 218–25.

Gillespie, J. L., 'Richard II's Cheshire archers', *Transactions of the Historic Society of Lancashire and Cheshire*, 125, 1974, pp. 1–39.

Girouard, M., *Life in the English Country House. A Social and Architectural History*, New Haven, Yale University Press, 1978.

Goody, F., Thirsk, J., and Thompson, E. P., eds., *Family and Inheritance: Rural Society in Western Europe 1200–1800*, Cambridge, Cambridge University Press, 1976.

Gray, H. L., 'Incomes from land in England in 1436', *E.H.R.*, 49, 1934, pp. 607–39.

Griffiths, R. A., *The Reign of King Henry VI*, London, Ernest Benn, 1981.

Hamilton, B., *Religion in the Medieval West*, London, Edward Arnold, 1986.

Handbook of British Chronology, ed. Sir F. M. Powicke and E. B. Fryde, 2nd edn, London, Royal Historical Society, 1961, 3rd edn 1986.

Handbook of Dates for Students of English History, ed. C. R. Cheney, London, Royal Historical Society, 1978.

Harding, A., *The Law Courts of Medieval England*, London, Allen and Unwin, 1973.

'The origins and early history of the keeper of the peace', *T.R.H.S.*, 5th ser., 10, 1960, pp. 85–109.

Harvey, B., 'The leasing of the abbot of Westminster's demesnes in the later middle ages', *Econ. Hist. Rev.*, 2nd ser., 22, 1969, pp. 17–27.

Harvey, S., 'The knight and the knight's fee in England', *Past and Present*, 49, 1970, pp. 3–43.

Haskell, A. S., 'The Paston women on marriage in fifteenth-century England', *Viator*, 4, 1973, pp. 459–71.

Hastings, M., *The Court of Common Pleas in Fifteenth Century England*, Ithaca, NY, Cornell University Press, 1947.

Haverfield, F., *The Roman Occupation of Britain*, London, Oxford University Press, 1924.

Herlihy, D., and Klapisch-Zuber, C., *Tuscans and their Families. A Study of the Florentine Catasto of 1427*, New Haven, Yale University Press, 1978.

Hexter, J. H., 'Storm over the gentry', *Encounter*, 10, 5, 1958, pp. 22–34. *Reappraisals in History*, London, Longmans, 1961.

Hicks, M. A., *False, Fleeting, Purjur'd Clarence. George, Duke of Clarence 1449–78*, Gloucester, Alan Sutton, 1980.

Highfield, J. R. L., and Jeff, R., eds., *The Crown and Local Communities in England and France in the Fifteenth Century*, Gloucester, Alan Sutton, 1981.

Bibliography

Hilton, R. H., *The Economic Development of Some Leicestershire Estates in the 14th and 15th Centuries*, London, Oxford University Press, 1947.

The English Peasantry in the Later Middle Ages, Oxford, Oxford University Press, 1975.

'Medieval agrarian history', in *V.C.H. Leicestershire*, II, pp. 145–98.

A Medieval Society. The West Midlands at the End of the Thirteenth Century, London, Weidenfeld & Nicolson, 1967.

ed., *Peasants, Knights and Heretics*, Cambridge, Cambridge University Press, 1981.

Holdsworth, Sir William, *A History of English Law*, 5th edn, 12 vols., London, Methuen, 1942.

Holly, D., 'Leicestershire', in *The Domesday Geography of Midland England*, ed. H. C. Darby and I. B. Terret, 2nd edn, Cambridge, Cambridge University Press, 1971, pp. 313–58.

Holmes, G. A., *The Estates of the Higher Nobility in Fourteenth-Century England*, Cambridge, Cambridge University Press, 1957.

Hoskins, W. G., *The Age of Plunder*, London, Macmillan, 1957.

Essays in Leicestershire History, Liverpool, Liverpool University Press, 1950.

Leicestershire. An Illustrated Essay on the History of the Landscape, London, Hodder and Stoughton, 1957.

The Midland Peasant, London, Macmillan, 1957.

Provincial England. Essays in Social and Economic History, London, Macmillan, 1965.

Houlbrooke, R. A., *The English Family 1450–1700*, London, Longman, 1984.

Howell, C., *Land, Family and Inheritance in Transition. Kibworth Harcourt 1280–1700*, Cambridge, Cambridge University Press, 1983.

Huizinga, J., *The Waning of the Middle Ages*, trans. F. Hopman, Harmondsworth, Penguin, 1972.

Hunnisett, R. F., *The Medieval Coroner*, Cambridge, Cambridge University Press, 1961.

'The reliability of inquisitions as historical evidence', in *The Study of Medieval Records. Essays in Honour of Kathleen Major*, ed. D. A. Bullough and R. L. Storey, Oxford, Oxford University Press, 1971, pp. 206–35.

Ingram, M., 'Spousals litigation in the English ecclesiastical courts c. 1350–c. 1640', in *Marriage and Society. Studies in the Social History of Marriage*, ed. R. B. Outhwaite, London, Europa Publications, 1981, pp. 35–61.

Ives, E. W., 'The common lawyers in pre-Reformation England', *T.R.H.S.*, 5th ser., 18, 1968, pp. 145–73.

The Common Lawyers of Pre-Reformation England: Thomas Kebell, A Case Study, Cambridge, Cambridge University Press, 1983.

Jacob, E. F., *The Fifteenth Century, 1399–1485*, Oxford, Oxford University Press, 1961, repr. 1976.

James, M., *Family, Lineage, and Civil Society*, London, Oxford University Press, 1974.

Jewell, H. M., *English Local Administration in the Middle Ages*, Newton Abbot, David and Charles, 1972.

Johnson, C., 'The collectors of lay taxes', in *The English Government at Work*

1327–1336, II, ed. W. A. Morris and J. R. Strayer, Cambridge, Mass., The Medieval Academy of America, 1947, pp. 201–26.

Jolliffe, J. E. A., *The Constitutional History of Medieval England*, 4th edn, London, Adam and Charles Black, 1961.

Keen, M. H., *England in the Later Middle Ages*, London, Methuen, 1973.

Kendall, P. M., *The Yorkist Age*, London, Allen and Unwin, 1962.

King, H. W., 'Ancient wills', *Transactions of the Essex Archaeological Society*, I, 146, 1878, pp. 142–52.

Kingsford, C. L., *English Historical Literature in the Fifteenth Century*, Franklin repr., New York, 1972.

Knowles, D. and Hadcock, R. N., *Medieval Religious Houses: England and Wales*, London, Longman, 1971.

Krause, J., 'The medieval household: large or small?', *Econ. Hist. Rev.*, 2nd ser., 9, 1957, pp. 420–32.

Lander, J. R., *Conflict and Stability in Fifteenth-Century England*, 3rd edn, London, Hutchinson, 1977.

'Council, administration and councillors, 1461–1485', *B.I.H.R.*, xxxii, 1959, pp. 138–80.

'Henry VI and the duke of York's second protectorate, 1455 to 1456', *B.J.R.L.*, 43, 1960–1, pp. 46–69.

Lapsley, G., 'Buzones', *E.H.R.*, 48, 1932, pp. 177–93, 545–67.

Laslett, P., *The World We Have Lost*, 2nd edn, London, Methuen, 1979.

Lloyd, T. H., *The Movement of Wool Prices in Medieval England*, Economic History Review Supplement 6, Cambridge, 1973.

Loyn, H. R., *Anglo-Saxon England and the Norman Conquest*, Harlow, Longman, 1981.

The Norman Conquest, 2nd edn, London, Hutchinson, 1967.

Macfarlane, A., *The Origins of English Individualism*, Oxford, Blackwell, 1978, repr. 1985.

McFarlane, K. B., 'Bastard feudalism', *B.I.H.R.*, 20, 1943–5, pp. 161–80.

England in the Fifteenth Century, ed. G. L. Harriss, London, Hambledon Press, 1981.

'England: the Lancastrian kings, 1399–1461', in *The Cambridge Medieval History*, III, ed. C. W. Previté-Orton and Z. N. Brooke, Cambridge, Cambridge University Press, 1959, pp. 363–417.

The Nobility of Later Medieval England, Oxford, Oxford University Press, 1973.

'Parliament and "bastard feudalism" ', *T.R.H.S.*, 4th ser., 26, 1944, pp. 53–79.

'The wars of the roses', *Proc. Brit. Acad.*, I, 1964, pp. 87–120.

McIntosh, A. *et al.*, *A Linguistic Atlas of Late Medieval English*, 4 vols., Aberdeen, Aberdeen University Press, 1986.

McKinley, R. A., 'The forests of Leicestershire', in *V.C.H. Leicestershire*, II, pp. 265–70.

'Medieval political history', in *V.C.H. Leicestershire*, II, pp. 74–101.

'The religious houses of Leicestershire', in *V.C.H. Leicestershire*, II, pp. 1–54.

McKisack, M., *The Fourteenth Century, 1307–1399*, Oxford, Oxford University Press, 1959.

Bibliography

Maddicott, J. R., 'The county community and the making of public opinion in fourteenth-century England', *T.R.H.S.*, 5th ser., 28, 1978, pp. 27–43.

'Magna Carta and the local community 1215–1259', *Past and Present*, 102, 1984, pp. 25–65.

Mann, Sir James, 'Arms and armour', in *The Bayeux Tapestry*, ed. Sir Frank Stenton, London, Phaidon Press, 1957, pp. 56–69.

European Arms and Armour, 2 vols., London, Wallace Collection Catalogues, 1962.

Manning, B. L., *The People's Faith in the Time of Wyclif*, 2nd edn, Hassocks, Harvester Press, 1975.

Margary, I. D., *Roman Roads in Britain*, 2 vols., London, Phoenix House Ltd, 1955.

Marsden, T. L., 'Manor House farm, Donington-le-Heath, Leicestershire, c. 1280', *Transactions of the Ancient Monument Society*, n.s., 10, 1962, pp. 33–43.

Medcalf, S., ed., *The Later Middle Ages*, London, Methuen, 1981.

Mills, M. H., 'The medieval shire house', in *Studies Presented to Sir Hilary Jenkinson*, ed. J. C. Davies, London, Oxford University Press, 1957, pp. 254–71.

Milsom, S. F. C., *Historical Foundations of the Common Law*, London, Butterworths, 1969.

Mingay, G. E., *The Gentry. The Rise and Fall of a Ruling Class*, London, Longman, 1976.

Mitterauer, M., and Sieder, R., *The European Family. Patriarchy to Partnership from the Middle Ages to the Present*, trans. K. Oosterven and M. Hörzinger, Oxford, Blackwell, 1982.

Moir, E., *The Justices of the Peace*, Harmondsworth, Penguin, 1969.

More, Sir Thomas, *Utopia*, Harmondsworth, Penguin, 1965.

Morgan, D. A. L., 'The king's affinity in the polity of Yorkist England', *T.R.H.S.*, 5th ser., 23, 1973, pp. 1–25.

Morris, J. E., *The Welsh Wars of Edward I*, Oxford, Oxford University Press, 1901, repr. 1968.

Morris, W. A., *The Medieval English Sheriff to 1300*, Manchester, Manchester University Press, 1927.

'The office of sheriff in the early Norman period', *E.H.R.*, 33, 1918, pp. 145–75.

'The sheriff', in *The English Government at Work 1327–1336*, II, ed. W. A. Morris and J. R. Strayer, Cambridge, Mass., The Medieval Academy of America, 1947, pp. 41–108.

Myers, A. R., *England in the Late Middle Ages*, 8th edn, Harmondsworth, Penguin, 1974.

'The household of queen Margaret of Anjou, 1452–3', *B.J.R.L.*, 40, 1957–8, pp. 79–113.

Neale, J. E., *The Elizabethan House of Commons*, revised edn, Harmondsworth, Penguin, 1963.

Newton Dunn, T. W., 'The Dwn family', *Transactions of the Cymmrodorion Society*, 1946–7, pp. 273–5.

Bibliography

Nichols, F. M., 'On feudal and obligatory knighthood', *Archaeologia*, 39, 1863, pp. 189–244.

Nichols, J., *The History and Antiquities of the County of Leicester*, 4 vols. in 8, London, 1795–1815, S. R. Publications repr., Wakefield, 1971.

Nicolas, Sir Nicholas Harris, *History of the Battle of Agincourt*, 2nd edn, London, 1832.

Ordnance Survey Maps, 1:50,000, 129, 130, 140, 141.

Orme, N., *English Schools in the Middle Ages*, London, Methuen, 1973.

Osborne, B., *Justices of the Peace 1361–1848*, Shaftesbury, Sedgehill Press, 1960.

Otway-Ruthven, J., *The King's Secretary and the Signet-Office in the XV Century*, Cambridge, Cambridge University Press, 1939.

Outhwaite, R. B., ed., *Marriage and Society. Studies in the Social History of Marriage*, London, Europa Publications, 1981.

Owen, C., *The Leicestershire and South Derbyshire Coalfield, 1200–1900*, Ashbourne, Moorland Publishing, 1984.

Ozment, S., *When Fathers Ruled. Family Life in Reformation Europe*, Cambridge Mass., Harvard University Press, 1983.

Painter, S., 'The family and the feudal system in twelfth-century England', *Speculum*, 35, 1, 1960, pp. 1–16.

   Studies in the History of the English Feudal Barony, Baltimore, The Johns Hopkins Press, 1943.

Payling, S. J., 'The widening franchise – parliamentary elections in Lancastrian Nottinghamshire', in *England in the Fifteenth Century. Proceedings of the 1986 Harlaxton Symposium*, ed. D. Williams, Woodbridge, Boydell Press, 1987, pp. 167–86.

Pelham, R. A., 'Fourteenth-century England', in *An Historical Geography of England before A.D. 1800*, ed. H. C. Darby, Cambridge, Cambridge University Press, 1936, pp. 230–65.

Petit-Dutaillis, Ch., *The Feudal Monarchy in France and England*, London, Routledge and Kegan Paul, 1936.

Pevsner, N., *The Buildings of England: Leicestershire and Rutland*, 2nd edn, Harmondsworth, Penguin, 1984.

Plucknett, T. F. T., *A Concise History of the Common Law*, 4th edn, London, Butterworth, 1948.

Pollard, A. J., *John Talbot and the War in France, 1427–1453*, London, Royal Historical Society, 1983.

   'The Richmondshire community of gentry during the Wars of the Roses', in *Patronage, Pedigree and Power in Later Medieval England*, ed. C. Ross, Gloucester, Alan Sutton, 1979, pp. 37–59.

   ed., *Property and Politics: Essays in Later Medieval English History*, Gloucester, Alan Sutton, 1984.

Pollock, Sir F., and Maitland, F. W., *The History of English Law before the Time of Edward I*, 2nd edn, 2 vols., Cambridge, Cambridge University Press, 1923.

Poole, A. L., *From Domesday Book to Magna Carta 1087–1216*, Oxford, Oxford University Press, 1951.

   Obligations of Society in the XII and XIII Centuries, Oxford, Oxford University Press, 1946.

Bibliography

Postan, M. M., 'Medieval agrarian society in its prime: England', *The Cambridge Economic History of Europe*, I, 2nd edn, Cambridge, Cambridge University Press, 1966, pp. 548–632.

The Medieval Economy and Society, London, Weidenfeld and Nicolson, 1972.

'Revisions in economic history. The fifteenth century', *Econ. Hist. Rev.*, 9, 1939, pp. 160–7.

'Some social consequences of the Hundred Years' War', *Econ. Hist. Rev.*, 12, 1942, pp. 1–12.

Power, E., *The Wool Trade in English Medieval History*, London, Oxford University Press, 1941.

Powicke, F. M., *King Henry III and the Lord Edward. The Community of the Realm in the Thirteenth Century*, 2 vols., London, Oxford University Press, 1947.

Powicke, M., *Military Obligations in Medieval England*, London, Oxford University Press, 1962.

Powicke, Sir M., *The Thirteenth Century, 1216–1307*, 2nd edn, Oxford, Oxford University Press, 1962.

Pugh, R. B., 'The king's government in the middle ages', *V.C.H. Wiltshire*, v, pp. 1–43.

Pugh, T. B., 'The magnates, knights and gentry', in *Fifteenth Century England 1399–1509*, ed. S. B. Chrimes *et al.*, Manchester, Manchester University Press, 1972, pp. 86–128.

Pugh, T. B., and Ross, C. D., 'The English baronage and the income tax of 1436', *B.I.H.R.*, 26, 1953, pp. 1–28.

Putnam, B. H., 'Shire officials: keepers of the peace and justices of the peace', in *The English Government at Work 1327–1336*, III, ed. J. F. Willard *et al.*, Cambridge, Mass., The Medieval Academy of America, 1950, pp. 185–217.

'The transformation of the keepers of the peace into the justices of the peace, 1327–1380', *T.R.H.S.*, 4th ser., 12, 1929, pp. 19–48.

Rawcliffe, C., *The Staffords, Earls of Stafford and Dukes of Buckingham*, Cambridge, Cambridge University Press, 1978.

Reeves, A. C., 'Some of Humphrey Stafford's military indentures', *Nottingham Medieval Studies*, 16, 1972, pp. 80–91.

Richardson, R. C., *The Debate on the English Revolution*, London, Methuen, 1977.

Richardson, H. G., 'The Commons and medieval politics', *T.R.H.S.*, 4th ser., 28, 1946, pp. 21–45.

Richmond, C., 'After McFarlane', *History*, 68, 1983, pp. 46–60.

John Hopton: A Fifteenth Century Suffolk Gentleman, Cambridge, Cambridge University Press, 1981.

Robertson, C. A., 'Local government and the king's "affinity" in fifteenth-century Leicestershire and Warwickshire', *T.L.A.H.S.*, 52, 1976–7, pp. 37–45.

Rosenthal, J. T., *Nobles and the Noble Life 1295–1500*, London, Allen and Unwin, 1976.

The Purchase of Paradise. Gift Giving and the Aristocracy, 1307–1485, London, Routledge and Kegan Paul, 1972.

Bibliography

Roskell, J. S., *The Commons in the Parliament of 1422*, Manchester, Manchester University Press, 1954.

The Commons and their Speakers in English Parliaments 1376–1523, Manchester, Manchester University Press, 1965.

The Knights of the Shire for the County Palatine of Lancaster (1377–1460), Manchester, Manchester University Press, 1937.

Ross, C., *Edward IV*, London, Eyre Methuen, 1974.

Richard III, London, Eyre Methuen, 1981.

ed., *Patronage, Pedigree and Power in Later Medieval England*, Gloucester, Alan Sutton, 1979.

Rowney, I., 'The Hastings affinity in Staffordshire and the honour of Tutbury', *B.I.H.R.*, 57, 1984, pp. 35–45.

Rowney, I. D., 'The Staffordshire political community 1440–1500', unpublished PhD thesis, University of Keele, 1981.

Russell, J. C., *British Medieval Population*, Albuquerque, University of New Mexico Press, 1948.

Saul, N., *Knights and Esquires: The Gloucestershire Gentry in the Fourteenth Century*, Oxford, Oxford University Press, 1981.

Savine, A., *English Monasteries on the Eve of the Dissolution*, ed. P. Vinogradoff, Oxford Studies in Social and Legal History, I, Oxford, Oxford University Press, 1909.

Sawyer, P., *The Age of the Vikings*, 2nd edn, London, Edward Arnold, 1971.

Sayles, G. O., *The Medieval Foundations of England*, 2nd edn, London, Methuen, 1966.

Scattergood, J., 'Fashion and morality in the late middle ages', in *England in the Fifteenth Century. Proceedings of the 1986 Harlaxton Symposium*, ed. D. Williams, Woodbridge, Boydell Press, 1987, pp. 255–72.

Schofield, R. S., 'The geographical distribution of wealth in England, 1334–1649', *Econ. Hist. Rev.*, 2nd ser., 18, 1965, pp. 483–510.

Scofield, C. L., *The Life and Reign of Edward the Fourth*, 2 vols., London, Frank Cass, 1923, new impression 1967.

Shaw, W. A., *The Knights of England*, 2 vols., London, Heraldry Today, 1971.

Sheehan, M. M., 'Choice of marriage partners in the middle ages', *Studies in Medieval and Renaissance History*, I, o.s., 11, 1978, pp. 3–33.

Sillem, R., 'Commissions of the peace, 1380–1485', *B.I.H.R.*, 10, 1932–3, pp. 81–104.

Sitwell, G. R., 'The English gentleman', *The Ancestor*, 1, 1902, pp. 58–103.

Smith, R. B., *Land and Politics in the England of Henry VIII. The West Riding of Yorkshire: 1530–46*, Oxford, Oxford University Press, 1970.

Somerville, R., *History of the Duchy of Lancaster*, I, 1265–1603, London, Chancellor and Council of the Duchy of Lancaster, 1953.

Starkey, D., 'The age of the household: politics, society and the arts c. 1350–c. 1550', in *The Later Middle Ages*, ed. S. Medcalf, London, Methuen, 1981, pp. 225–90.

Stenton, Sir F., *The First Century of English Feudalism 1066–1166*, 2nd edn, London, Oxford University Press, 1961.

Bibliography

Stenton, F. M., *Anglo-Saxon England*, 3rd edn, London, Oxford University Press, 1971.

'The changing feudalism of the middle ages', *History*, n.s., 19, 1934–5, pp. 289–301.

'The Danes in England', *Proc. Brit. Acad.*, 13, 1927, pp. 203–46.

'Introduction to the Leicestershire Domesday', in *V.C.H. Leicestershire*, I, pp. 277–305.

'Leicestershire survey', in *V.C.H. Leicestershire*, I, pp. 339–54.

Stevenson, E. R., 'The escheator', in *The English Government at Work 1327–1336*, II, ed. W. A. Morris and J. R. Strayer, Cambridge, Mass., The Medieval Academy of America, 1947, pp. 109–67.

Stone, L., 'The anatomy of the Elizabethan aristocracy', *Econ. Hist. Rev.*, 18, 1948, pp. 1–53.

The Crisis of the Aristocracy 1558–1641, abridged edn, Oxford, Oxford University Press, 1967.

'The English aristocracy – a restatement', *Econ. Hist. Rev.*, 2nd ser., 4, 1952, pp. 302–21.

The Family, Sex and Marriage in England 1500–1800, abridged edn, Harmondsworth, Penguin, 1979.

'Social mobility in England, 1500–1700', *Past and Present*, 33, 1966, pp. 16–55.

Storey, R. L., *The End of the House of Lancaster*, London, Barrie & Rockliff, 1966.

'Gentleman-bureaucrats', in *Profession, Vocation and Culture in Later Medieval England: Essays Dedicated to the Memory of A. R. Myers*, ed. C. H. Clough, Liverpool, Liverpool University Press, 1982, pp. 90–129.

'Lincolnshire and the Wars of the Roses', *Nottingham Medieval Studies*, 15, 1970, pp. 64–83.

Strayer, J. R., 'Introduction', in *The English Government at Work 1327–1336*, II, ed. W. A. Morris and J. R. Strayer, Cambridge, Mass., The Medieval Academy of America, 1947, pp. 3–40.

Stubbs, W., *The Constitutional History of England*, 5th edn, 3 vols., Oxford, Oxford University Press, 1903.

Tawney, R. H., *The Agrarian Problem in the Sixteenth Century*, London, Longmans, 1912.

'The rise of the gentry, 1558–1640', *Econ. Hist. Rev.*, 11, 1941, pp. 1–38.

'The rise of the gentry: a postscript', *Econ. Hist. Rev.*, 2nd ser., 7, 1954, pp. 91–7.

Taylor, C., *Village and Farmstead. A History of Rural Settlement in England*, London, George Philip, 1984.

Taylor, M. M., 'The justices of assize', in *The English Government at Work 1327–1336*, III, eds. J. F. Willard *et al.*, Cambridge, Mass., The Medieval Academy of America, 1950, pp. 219–57.

Tout, T. F., *The Place of the Reign of Edward II in English History*, 2nd edn, revised H. Johnstone, Manchester, Manchester University Press, 1936.

Treharne, R. F., 'The knights in the period of reform and rebellion, 1258–1267: a critical phase in the rise of a new class', *B.I.H.R.*, 21, 1946–8, pp. 1–12.

Bibliography

Trevor-Roper, H. R., 'The Elizabethan aristocracy: an anatomy anatomized', *Econ. Hist. Rev.*, 2nd ser., 3, 1951, pp. 279–98.

The Gentry 1540–1640, Economic History Review Supplement 1, London, 1953.

Trow-Smith, R., *A History of British Livestock Husbandry to 1700*, London, Routledge and Kegan Paul, 1957.

Vale, M. G. A., *Piety, Charity and Literacy among the Yorkshire Gentry, 1370–1480*, Borthwick Papers no. 50, York, St Anthony's Press, 1976.

The Victoria History of the County of Essex.

The Victoria History of the County of Hertfordshire.

The Victoria History of the County of Leicestershire.

The Victoria History of the County of Northamptonshire.

The Victoria History of the County of Oxfordshire.

The Victoria History of the County of Rutland.

The Victoria History of the County of Staffordshire.

The Victoria History of the County of Warwickshire.

The Victoria History of the County of Wiltshire.

The Victoria History of the County of Worcestershire.

The Victoria History of the County of Yorkshire (North Riding).

Virgoe, R., 'The Cambridgeshire election of 1439', *B.I.H.R.*, 46, 1973, pp. 95–101.

'The crown, magnates and local government in fifteenth-century East Anglia', in *The Crown and Local Communities in England and France in the Fifteenth Century*, ed., J. R. L. Highfield and R. Jeffs, Gloucester, Alan Sutton, 1981, pp. 72–87.

'An election dispute of 1483', *B.I.H.R.*, 60, 1987, pp. 24–44.

'The parliamentary subsidy of 1450', *B.I.H.R.*, 55, 1982, pp. 125–37.

'Three Suffolk parliamentary elections of the mid-fifteenth century', *B.I.H.R.*, 39, 1966, pp. 185–96.

Wagner, A. R., *English Genealogy*, London, Oxford University Press, 1960.

Heralds and Heraldry in the Middle Ages, 2nd edn, London, Oxford University Press, 1956.

Wainwright, F. T., 'Æthelflæd lady of the Mercians', in *The Anglo-Saxons*, ed. P. Clemoes, London, Bowes and Bowes, 1959, pp. 53–69.

Warner, M., *Alone of All Her Sex. The Myth and the Cult of the Virgin Mary*, London, Weidenfeld and Nicolson, 1976.

Wedgwood, J. C., *History of Parliament: Biographies of the Members of the Commons House 1439–1509*, London, H.M.S.O., 1936.

History of Parliament: Register of the Ministers and of the Members of both Houses 1439–1509, London, H.M.S.O., 1938.

White, A. B., *Self-Government at the King's Command*, Minneapolis, University of Minnesota Press, 1933.

Wilkinson, B., *Constitutional History of England in the Fifteenth Century (1399–1485)*, London, Longman, 1964.

Willard, J. R., et al., eds., *The English Government at Work 1327–1336*, 3 vols., Cambridge, Mass., The Medieval Academy of America, 1940–50.

Bibliography

Williams, D., ed., *England in the Fifteenth Century. Proceedings of the 1986 Harlaxton Symposium*, Woodbridge, Boydell Press, 1987.

Wolffe, B., *Henry VI*, London, Eyre Methuen, 1981.

Wood, M., *The English Medieval House*, London, Phoenix House, 1965.

Wright, S. M., *The Derbyshire Gentry in the Fifteenth Century*, Chesterfield, Derbyshire Record Society, VIII, 1983.

Yarwood, D., *The Architecture of Britain*, London, Batsford, 1976.

INDEX

Note: Whereas the spelling of place names has been modernized both here and in the text, personal names are presented in their most common fifteenth-century form. Additional information about individuals and families is contained in appendices 1 and 3 which, being arranged alphabetically, are therefore not indexed.

Index

Index

knights of the shire, 36, 77, 110, 111, 112, 116, 121–9
Knipton, 70
Kynsman, Elizabeth, 156n94

Lacy, William, 162
Lancashire, 4
Lancaster, duchy of, 15–18, 27, 64, 99–101, 125, 130
Langham (of Gopsall), John, 181
Langham (of Gopsall), Joyce, 159
Langham (of Kilby), Richard, 71n126
Langley, convent at, 189
Langton, 99
Lapsley, G., 132
Launde, prior of, 71
Launde Priory, 14
lawyers, 30, 85, 89, 92; professional, 74–5, 96, 97, 98, 100, 129
leather industry, 66
Leesthorpe, 91
Leicester, borough of, 3, 92–3, 177; building material in, 11, 140; burgesses of, 101, 111, 124, 126; coroners of, 108, 114; markets in, 66, 68; mayors of, 100, 101, 114n40
Leicester, honor of, 4, 15–18, 99–100, 101
Leicester Forest, 11, 17, 60, 61, 67
Leicestershire: gentry establishment in, 77–9, 92–3, 134; population and wealth of, 12–13; schools in, 177, 190; shire court in, 77, 121, 125; topography of, 8–12, 45
Leire, 181
Leland, John, 11, 199
Lex, John, 105–6
lime, see quarries, lime
Lincoln, bishop of, 130
Lincoln Cathedral, 189
Lincolnshire, 37, 39
Lincoln's Inn, 178
Little Dalby, 83, 84
Littleton, Thomas, 130n130
Littleton, William, 81, 161
Littleton, William, son of William, 143
Lloyd, T. H., 64
Longford, lady Elizabeth, 174
Long Whatton, 39, 49, 60, 62, 88n56, 154
Lostwithiel, 124n98
Loughborough, 60, 193; building material in, 11, 140; manor of, 9n15, 53; school at, 177, 190
Loutt, John, 190
Lovel, Anne, 165

Lovel, family of, 9n15, 27
Lovel, Francis, lord, 18
Lovel, John, lord, 18, 23, 120n79
Lovel, Sir Thomas, 20
Lovel, William, lord, 18, 23, 165
Lovel, Sir William, 23
Lowesby, 65
Lubenham, 66, 70, 195; manor of, 52, 82–3, 87, 97, 137, 181
Ludford Bridge, Rout of, 26, 98
Lutterworth, 21–2, 54
Lyez, Emmitt, 192
Lyez, Nichol, 192

McFarlane, K. B., 1–2, 3, 6, 72, 202, 203
Maddicott, J. R., 78
Maitland, F. W., 78
Malory, Anketin, 157–8
Malory, Margery, daughter of Anketin, 148, 157
Malory (of Walton), Anthony, 91
Malory (of Walton), family of, 42n74, 49
Malory (of Walton), John, 91
malt, 55, 67
Mann, Sir James, 31
Manners, family of, 199
Manston, William, 34n31
Margaret of Anjou, queen, 4, 99, 126
Market Harborough, 66
Markham, John, 130n130
marriage, 41, 68–9, 87, 155–73; between children, 142, 144, 146, 170–1
Marshall (Marchall), John, 71n126
Maxstoke (Warws.), 96
meadows, 9, 11, 65, 71
meat, 57, 181–2
Medbourne, 69, 87, 97, 181
Melbourne (Derb.), 100, 190, 193
Melton Mowbray, 70, 149, 177
Merbury, John, 46, 102
merchants, 30, 39
Middleton (Warws.), 144
mills, 53, 62, 81, 86
minstrels, 136
Misterton, 65, 67, 156
Montague, Thomas, earl of Salisbury, 94
Morley, lord, see Lovel, Sir William
Mortimer's Cross, battle of, 26
Moton, Alan, brother of Sir Robert I, 81, 157, 181
Moton, Anne, daughter of Reginald, 103n131, 148
Moton, Edward, son of Robert II, 145–6, 199

285

Cambridge studies in medieval life and thought
Fourth series

★*Also published as a paperback*

Titles in the series